All You Can Eat!

spicy cooking

All You Can Eat!

spicy

cooking

Over 600 fiery recipes to tantalize your taste buds!

Monica Bhide & Margaret Kaeter

Published by Adams Media, an F+W Publications Company
57 Littlefield Street, Avon, MA 02322 U.S.A.
www.adamsmedia.com

ISBN: 1-59337-742-8
Printed in the United States of America

J I H G F E D C B A

Previously published as the Everything® Mexican Cookbook
and the Everything® Indian Cookbook.

Contents

Introduction

▶ When you experience the craving that only spicy food can satisfy, you may find yourself facing the difficult decision—Indian or Mexican? Chickpea curry or chicken achiote? Thanks to *All You Can Eat: Spicy Cooking*, you have both types of cuisine at your fingertips!

The first part of this book offers the very best of Indian cuisine. From soups and snacks to entrees and desserts, all you need to know to prepare an Indian feast is right here. Whether you're in the mood for the spiciest dishes you can think of (Sizzling Tandoori Chicken, perhaps), or want to cool it down with a glass of Rose-Flavored Yogurt Drink, these easy-to-follow recipes will make preparing an authentic Indian meal easy, regardless of how much heat you care to include in your dishes.

The second part of *All You Can Eat: Spicy Cooking* celebrates one of the most exciting types of cuisine in the world. Mexican cooking combines hot peppers with mangos, and puts cayenne pepper in your chocolate—in other words, Mexican food breaks all the rules. The recipes featured in this book provide the opportunity for you to experience the variety and unique tastes—but most importantly the spice—that Mexican cooking has to offer.

Prepare your palate for the heat of Indian and Mexican cuisine, and enjoy *All You Can Eat: Spicy Cooking*.

Introduction to the Spice of India

▶ India's cuisine has been influenced greatly by the multitude of invaders throughout the country's history; the Mughals, Turks, Europeans, and Portuguese all left their mark. By adding their own cooking styles and ingredients, they provided a rich diversity, resulting in a unique cuisine. What holds this diverse cuisine together are the aromatic and flavorful spices. The art of Indian cooking is in blending the spices so that they are in perfect harmony in each dish.

Indian cooking categorizes foods into six tastes—sweet, sour, salty, spicy, bitter, and astringent. A well-balanced Indian meal contains all six tastes. This is accomplished, in part, by accompanying the dishes with a wide variety of condiments.

Chapter 1

Basics of Indian Cooking

Before you get started, there are a few things you need to know about the techniques and ingredients used in Indian recipes. This chapter covers the basics of what you should know to get started cooking delicious Indian meals.

Essential Techniques

It is important to understand a few simple cooking techniques before you begin your journey into the world of Indian cooking. These techniques can be used individually in recipes, but more often they are used in unison. By understanding the principles behind each technique, you can ensure the success of your recipes.

Dum (Steaming)

This refers to cooking the food in its own steam. You will notice that many recipes direct you to cover the cooking pot with a lid and reduce the heat to complete the cooking process. This is the modern-day version of dum—it helps the dish retain its aroma and helps the flavors seep in. In olden days, the lid of a cooking pot was sealed to the pot using wheat flour dough, thus ensuring that the steam would not escape. This pot was then placed on hot charcoals, and the dish was allowed to cook.

Tadka or Baghar (Tempering)

Tempering is the process of seasoning a dish with hot oil seasoned with spices. This can be done at the beginning of the recipe or at the end, depending upon the dish. It involves heating the oil until it is almost smoking, reducing the heat, and then adding the spices. The spices begin to sizzle and change color, indicating that they are cooked; then either more ingredients are added to it or the tempered oil is poured over a completed dish.

There are a couple of things to keep in mind with this process. When you add spices to hot oil, they will sizzle and splatter, so be prepared to remove the skillet from the heat immediately or have the additional ingredients on hand so you can add them quickly. Do not add any water to this seasoning; this will cause it to lose its flavor and potency. Also note that when you are adding spices to the heated oil, you should add them one at a time. Begin with the whole spices, then add the herbs, and then the powdered spices.

Bhunao (Sautéing)

This is the mostly commonly used cooking technique in Indian cooking. This technique requires sautéing ingredients over medium to high heat while constantly stirring. In the recipes where sautéing is required, you can add a bit of water to the ingredients to keep them from sticking to the pan. This technique allows the ingredients to release their true flavors. To ensure that the ingredients are fully cooked, continue to sauté until the fat begins to separate from the spice mixture or the masala that is being cooked.

Tandoori Cooking (Grilling)

Traditionally, roasting in the Indian kitchen was done in clay ovens called *tandoors*. All the recipes in this book have been modified to suit your grill or oven. Just remember: If a recipe calls for a dish to be marinated prior to grilling, make sure to follow the recipe's directions as to how long it should be marinated to ensure that the marinade is able to exude its flavors. Discard any remaining marinade per the recipe directions.

Talina (Deep-Frying)

Another key cooking technique used in Indian food is deep-frying. Traditionally, a deep vessel, similar to the Chinese wok, is used to heat the oil. You can use a deep fryer if you wish. Although some people like to reuse oil used for deep-frying, it is best to use fresh oil each time you deep-fry. The key to deep-frying is to let the oil return to frying temperature between fried batches. Also, do not use large quantities of oil to deep-fry—the quantity should be just enough to immerse the ingredients, usually about 1 or 2 inches of oil is enough.

> Safety is important when you are deep-frying, so please take appropriate precautions when using hot oil. Make sure the deep fryer or wok is not easily accessible to children.

Essential Ingredients

It's important to become familiar with the common ingredients, their usage, and their necessity in the cuisine. Once you have mastered these basic ingredients, you can begin to improvise on the recipes.

Basic Spices and Spice Mixes

Spices are used in Indian cooking to provide a myriad of flavors. They can be used whole, ground, toasted, rarely raw, individually, or as mixes. Chapter 2 introduces you to some basic spice mixtures. I would advise you to prepare these as needed (not in advance) to ensure that you get the best flavor each time.

Many Indian grocery stores now sell some of these spice mixes premade. These can be a real time saver if you are in a pinch. If you buy premade mixes, be sure to check the manufactured dates on the packages. Spices are covered in more detail later in this chapter.

Ginger-Garlic Paste

A mixture of minced ginger and garlic, this paste is used in many recipes in this book. I have provided a recipe for you to prepare this at home. Again, if you are in a pinch you can buy premade ginger-garlic paste at your local Indian grocer. This paste keeps for months if refrigerated. Ginger-garlic paste cooks quickly and can burn, so watch it carefully when you cook with it.

Oils

Traditionally, Indian cooking uses ghee, or clarified butter, as a cooking medium. Most of the recipes in this book have been prepared using any light vegetable oil of your choice. Ghee is used in some dishes to provide a unique nutty flavor to the dish. In some eastern Indian states, mustard oil is used as a cooking medium. This oil is very pungent and should be heated to a smoking point before using (to reduce its bitterness).

Olive oil is not used in traditional Indian cooking because it causes the spices to lose their individual flavors. Also, many Indian dishes require cooking at a very high heat, and olive oil tends to burn easily.

Souring Agents

Indian dishes have a balance of many flavors—hot, sour, sweet, salty, spicy—all in one recipe. Common souring agents are tamarind, lemon or lime juice, vinegar, tomatoes, and even yogurt. Tamarind and lemon juice can generally be substituted for each other in the recipes here, except in the recipe for Tamarind Chutney (see page 226). When a dried (as opposed to wet) souring agent is needed, *amchur* or dried mango powder is often used.

Tenderizers

Traditional Indian cooking uses raw papaya and yogurt as meat tenderizers. I have used plain yogurt in the recipes in this book.

There really is no such term as *curry* in the Indian language and no spice mix called "curry powder." Each region has its own special mixes and spices that are blended together to form "curries," or sauces.

Thickening Agents

You will notice the use of yogurt, chickpea flour, onions, and nut pastes in a number of recipes. These are traditionally used as thickening agents. They add a lot of body to sauces in Indian dishes.

Cooking with Spices

Using spices in Indian cooking is a 3,000-year-old tradition. Ancient Indian texts focused primarily on three characteristics of spices—their medicinal properties, their ability to act as food preservatives, and their ability to season food. Ayurveda, the ancient Indian art of healing, teaches that food plays an essential part in one's health and sense of well-being. For food specifically, it says that you should have sweet, tangy, salty, and hot all in the same meal or at least in the day; this helps balance out your sense of taste. Spices provide all of these flavors.

Combining Spices

Spices also add depth and complexity to food. They can be added individually or in "mixes." Use the spice mix recipes provided in this book or create your own. There really is no one right spice mixture—if it tastes good to you, it is the right mix! Many Indian grocery stores sell premade spice mixes that can be a real time saver if you are in a bind.

The secret to making perfect Indian dishes is in the spices. Understanding the flavors that they provide, at what point in the cooking process to add them, and in what order to add them is at the heart of Indian cuisine. Most spices need to be cooked before they are eaten to help release their flavors. There are a few that can be used raw, but raw green cardamom or cloves, for instance, are often used as a garnish.

Guidelines for Preparing Spices

If you are using oil or ghee (clarified butter) to cook your spices, ensure that the oil is hot before you add the spice. Hot oil has the ability to retain the flavor of the spice. If your oil is too cold, the spice will not release its flavor. Ghee is often used in India, as it has the ability to be heated to very high temperatures. It also retains spice flavors a lot better than oils.

If you need to roast spices, first make sure that you use a totally dry skillet—no oil or water. Second, ensure that the skillet is hot before you add the spices. Spices cook very quickly and can easily burn, so you must constantly stir and be ready to remove them from the heat as soon as they brown and you can smell their fragrance.

Be careful when making substitutions. Coriander powder, for instance, cannot be substituted for fresh coriander, or cilantro, and saffron cannot be substituted for turmeric. If you are unsure about a spice, check

Appendix A for more information. You can use ground spices for whole spices in some cases, but just remember that whole spices have a much stronger flavor. Taste to adjust seasoning as necessary, being careful not to overspice.

As you begin to gain an understanding of spices, their flavors and characteristics, and begin to cook some of the recipes in this book, I have one piece of advice: Follow the recommended steps and spice quantities the first time. As you gain more experience with the spices and are able to determine how to balance the amount of spices to add to a dish, you can improvise as you like.

Finally, make sure that you have all the spices ready to go before you start cooking. In many recipes the spices need to be added in quick succession and you will not have time to go looking for them in the middle of the cooking process. Remember, spices tend to burn easily, so having them at the ready will make the process easier. If your spices do burn, toss them away and begin again. There is nothing worse than the taste of burned spices!

Basic Indian Spice Pantry

Every Indian spice pantry needs to have the bare essentials to start cooking Indian meals. Make sure your shelves are always stocked with the following spices:

- Salt
- Red chili (whole and powder)
- Turmeric
- Coriander (whole and powder)
- Cumin seeds
- Mustard seeds
- Bay leaves
- Cinnamon
- Cloves
- Black peppercorns
- Asafetida
- Green and black cardamom
- Carom seeds (also called *ajowan* or *ajwain*)
- Mango powder
- Tamarind pulp
- Dried fenugreek leaves

Grinding and Storage Guidelines

Make sure that your spices are fresh—this is the golden rule of Indian cooking. Replace your spices at least once a year. How should you test freshness? Use your nose. If you open a package of spices and cannot smell the aroma, the spices have lost their potency and should not be used. Even for the mixed masala or spice mixtures, you will notice a difference in smell (and flavor!) if you prepare them fresh when you need them.

For grinding spices you can use a couple of different tools. You can use a mortar and pestle or a coffee grinder. (If you are using a coffee grinder, buy one to use just for the spices, since it will take on the smell of the spices.)

The best place to store the spices is in a cupboard or a drawer away from direct sunlight. If you can, use glass or clear plastic jars—this way you can see how much spice you have left. Also never use a wet spoon to remove spices from a jar. This will keep them fresh longer.

If you live in a very hot area, you can store your spices in the refrigerator to keep them fresh longer. Just make sure that you are using airtight jars.

What You'll Need

Indian cooking does not really require any specialized utensils. For most of the recipes, you can use your standard cooking pots and pans, measuring cups, and wooden spoons. Following is a list of the commonly used equipment for the recipes in this book:

- **A deep pan:** A dutch oven or a deep sauté pan can be used. To make the cooking process easier, use nonstick pans. In India a traditional cooking vessel like this is called a *karahi* and is similar to a wok.
- **Food processor:** This is a real time saver in the kitchen, perfect for mincing, chopping, and grating.
- **Blender:** Wonderful for making chutneys, drinks, and soups.
- **Sieve:** A sieve is perfect for draining whey and straining.

- **Spice grinder/coffee mill/mortar and pestle:** Use any one of these to grind dry spices.
- **Slotted spoon:** A metal spoon that is perforated is perfect for deep-frying.
- **Deep fryer/deep pan:** Either one can be used for deep-frying, with appropriate safety precautions.
- **Griddle:** A nonstick griddle is perfect for making Indian breads.

CHAPTER 2
Basic Recipes (Mool Vidhi)

Warm Spice Mix
(Garam Masala Powder)

Yields 2 tablespoons
Prep Time: None
Cook Time: 10 minutes

You can vary this recipe a bit—experiment with various spices until you find the combination that works for you.

8 cloves
4 teaspoons cumin seeds
3 green cardamom pods (whole)
2 black cardamom pods (whole)

1 (2-inch) cinnamon stick
2 teaspoons coriander seeds
1 teaspoon black peppercorns
1 bay leaf
Pinch of grated nutmeg (optional)

1. Heat a small skillet on medium. Add all the spices except the nutmeg, and dry roast the spices, stirring constantly. After about 5 minutes, the spices will darken and begin to release a unique aroma.
2. Remove the skillet from the heat, then add the nutmeg. Transfer the spice mix to a bowl and allow to cool for about 5 minutes.
3. Using a spice grinder, grind the spices to a fine powder. Store in an airtight jar. The spice mixture will keep for up to 3 months.

Indian Cheese
(Paneer)

Yields approx. 1 cup
Prep Time: None
Cook Time: 15–20 minutes, 2 hours to set

An extraordinary source of protein, paneer is one of the most versatile Indian ingredients. It keeps for about 1 week, refrigerated.

2 lemons, juiced

8 cups whole milk

1. Bring the milk to a boil in a large pan over medium heat. Line a sieve with several layers of cheesecloth. Set aside the sieve in a clean, dry sink.
2. Once the milk has reached the boiling point, remove the pan from the heat. Add the lemon juice slowly. The milk will begin to form a curd cheese. Using a wooden spoon, stir the mixture until all the milk has curdled, about 1 to 2 minutes. You will see the curd cheese, which is white, separating from the whey, a cloudy-looking liquid.
3. Pour the mixture into the cheesecloth-lined sieve to drain off the whey. When the cheese has cooled (about 20 minutes), fold the corners of the cheesecloth and squeeze to remove any remaining whey. To make the *paneer* firm, put it between 2 large plates and place something heavy (such as a large pot of water) on top to weigh it down. Once it has set for about 2 hours, remove the cloth.

Ginger-Garlic Paste
(Adrak Lasan Ka Paste)

2 serrano green chilies (optional)
½ cup fresh gingerroot, peeled
½ cup garlic cloves, peeled
1 tablespoon cold water

1. Remove the stems from the green chilies.
2. Place all the ingredients in a food processor and purée to form a smooth paste. Add no more than 1 tablespoon of water to help form a smooth consistency.
3. Store the paste in an airtight jar in the refrigerator. The paste will keep for up to 2 weeks in the refrigerator.

Yields 1 cup
Prep Time: 5 minutes
Cook Time: None

To freeze convenient portions of this paste, scoop 1-tablespoon portions into ice trays, freeze, and transfer to a container or plastic bag.

Tandoori Spice Mix
(Tandoori Masala)

½ teaspoon carom seeds
1 tablespoon Warm Spice Mix (see recipe on page 14)
½ teaspoon ginger powder
¼ teaspoon black salt
½ teaspoon dried fenugreek leaves
¼ teaspoon dried mango powder

1. Place the carom seeds in a resealable plastic bag and pound with a rolling pin.
2. Combine all the ingredients in a bowl and mix thoroughly. Transfer to an airtight jar and store.

Yields 4 tablespoons
Prep Time: 2 minutes
Cook Time: None

This recipe is quintessential in North India. You can also try adding red chili to it.

Chaat Spice Mix
(Chaat Masala)

Yields 3 tablespoons
Prep Time: None
Cook Time: 5 minutes

This zesty spice mix is sprinkled over dishes once they have been cooked, adding a very tangy flavor.

1 tablespoon cumin seeds
1½ teaspoons dried mint
   leaves
¼ teaspoon black peppercorns
¼ teaspoon carom seeds

Pinch of asafetida
1 teaspoon ginger powder
1 teaspoon dried mango
   powder
1 teaspoon black salt

1. Heat a small skillet on medium heat; dry roast the cumin seeds, mint leaves, black peppercorns, and carom seeds for about 2 minutes, until fragrant. Remove from heat and mix in the asafetida, ginger powder, dried mango powder, and black salt.
2. Grind all the ingredients using a mortar and pestle or a spice grinder.
3. Store in an airtight jar for up to 3 months. Sprinkle over salads or cooked dishes.

Hung Yogurt
(Dahi)

Yields 1½ cups
Prep Time: None
Cook Time: 2 hours
to drain

Yogurt has a wonderful creamy texture that holds during the cooking process, and it provides a cooling effect during spicy meals.

2 cups plain yogurt

1. Line a sieve with several layers of cheesecloth. Place the yogurt in the sieve and suspend over a bowl.
2. Let any liquid drain into the bowl, then discard the liquid. Tie the ends of the cheesecloth to form a pouch. Weigh it down using a few cans in a plastic bag as weight. Let it sit for about 2 hours to allow any remaining liquid to drain out.
3. Remove the cheesecloth. Transfer the yogurt to a container. Cover and refrigerate for up to 2 weeks.

Clarified Butter
(Ghee)

½ pound unsalted butter

1. Heat a heavy pan over low heat. Add the butter, allowing it to melt. Once the butter has melted, increase the heat, bringing the butter to a boil. The fat will start to separate and the butter will begin to foam.
2. Reduce the heat and simmer for about 15 minutes. Watch carefully, as it may burn. The milk solids will start to settle at the bottom, and the liquid butter will float to the surface. When the liquid butter becomes amber in color, remove from heat. Allow the liquid to cool to room temperature.
3. Strain the amber liquid into a jar; discard the remaining sediment.
4. Cover the jar and store, refrigerated, for up to 6 months.

Yields about ½ cup
Prep Time: None
Cook Time: 25 minutes

This butter lends a nutty taste to Indian cooking. Use sparingly, as it is high in fat.

Whole-Milk Fudge
(Khoya)

4 cups whole milk

1. In a heavy-bottomed pan, bring the milk to a boil, stirring constantly. As the quantity of milk starts to reduce, scrape any dried milk off the sides of the pan. Continue to cook until it reduces to the consistency of mashed potatoes.
2. Remove from heat and let cool. Transfer to a heat-resistant container. Store covered in the refrigerator for up to a week.

Yields about ⅓ cup
Prep Time: None
Cook Time: 30–40 minutes

To save time, you can also buy powdered Khoya at your local Indian grocer.

Fried Onions
(Barista)

Yields 1 cup
Prep Time: 5 minutes
Cook Time: 15 minutes, plus 10 minutes to cool

These caramelized onions are often used as a garnish.

4 cups vegetable oil
1 pound red onions, peeled
   and thinly sliced

1. In a deep pan, heat the oil until it is almost smoking. Reduce the heat to medium, and wait about 30 seconds.
2. Add the onions a few at a time and deep-fry until they are golden brown and crispy. Transfer the onions onto a paper towel to absorb the extra oil. Continue until all the onions have been fried.
3. When the onions have cooled off for about 10 minutes, roughly pound them with a rolling pin. Store in a jar for up to 2 months.

Roasted Saffron
(Kesar)

Yields ¼ teaspoon
Prep Time: None
Cook Time: 1 minute

Never fry saffron, as it will lose its taste. Saffron is generally added at the end of the cooking process for flavor and as a garnish.

¼ teaspoon saffron threads
2 tablespoons whole milk

1. Warm the milk over low heat until it is warm to the touch (but not hot).
2. In a dry skillet, dry roast the saffron threads over low heat until fragrant, less than 1 minute. Remove from heat.
3. Put the milk in a small bowl and add the saffron threads. Use immediately.

☀ Caution!
Don't try to substitute another spice for saffron. The aroma and flavor of this sophisticated spice cannot be duplicated.

CHAPTER 3
Starters and Snacks (Shurat)

Cucumber Cup Coolers
(Kheere Ki Katori)

Serves 4–6
Prep Time: 15 minutes
Cook Time: 10 minutes

These edible cups stuffed with a creamy garlic yogurt are so easy to make. Amaze your friends with this delight.

2 medium seedless cucumbers, peeled
½ teaspoon cumin seeds
½ cup yogurt, whipped
1 clove garlic, peeled

1 serrano green chili, seeded
1 teaspoon fresh lemon juice
Table salt, to taste
2 sprigs fresh cilantro, stemmed

1. *To make the cucumber cups:* Cut the cucumber crosswise into 1-inch pieces. Use a melon baller to scoop out the insides. Leave a ¼-inch border on the sides and the bottom. Set the cups upside down on a plate lined with paper towels to drain. Refrigerate.
2. Heat a skillet over medium heat. Add the cumin seeds and dry roast them until fragrant, about 1 to 2 minutes. Stir constantly to prevent the seeds from burning. Let them cool and then roughly pound them.
3. Using a hand blender or a mixing spoon, blend together the cumin seeds, yogurt, garlic, green chili, fresh lemon juice, and salt. Transfer the yogurt mixture to a mixing bowl.
4. Finely chop the cilantro. Add it to the yogurt mixture.
5. When you are ready to serve, place all the cucumber cups on a serving platter. Spoon the yogurt mix into each cup. These can be made ahead and refrigerated until ready to serve.

�֎ Cumin Seeds

Easily the most popular spice in Indian cooking, cumin seeds are known for their digestive powers. Cumin is never used raw. It is always either dry roasted or added to hot oil before other ingredients are added.

Spiced Crunchy Okra
(Chatpati Bhindi)

1½ pounds okra, rinsed and
   dried
1 teaspoon red chili powder
½ teaspoon Warm Spice Mix
   (see recipe on page 14)
1 teaspoon dry mango powder

3½ tablespoons chickpea flour
2 cups vegetable oil
1 teaspoon Chaat Spice Mix
   (see recipe on page 16)
Table salt, to taste

> **Serves 4**
> **Prep Time:** 10 minutes
> **Cook Time:** 15 minutes
>
> For a spectacular presentation, create a "nest" using the okra and nestle grilled shrimp or Chicken Tikka (page 26) in it.

1. Remove the stems from the okra. Cut each piece lengthwise into 4 pieces. Lay out the pieces in a large, flat dish; set aside.
2. In a small mixing bowl, mix together the red chili powder, spice mix, and dry mango powder. Sprinkle this mixture over the okra. Toss well to ensure that all the pieces are covered with the spice powder.
3. Sprinkle the chickpea flour over the okra. Toss again to ensure that each piece is lightly and evenly covered.
4. In a deep pan, add the vegetable oil to about 1 inch deep. Heat the oil over high heat until smoking, about 370°. Reduce the heat to medium-high. Add some of the okra and deep-fry until well browned, about 4 minutes. Remove with a slotted spoon and place on a paper towel to drain. Continue until all of the okra is fried. Let the oil return to its smoking point between batches.
5. Sprinkle the spice mix on the okra. Toss well and season with salt. Serve immediately.

☼ Buying Okra

Okra is commonly known in India as "ladies finger." When you buy okra, check for freshness by trying to snap the end. If it snaps, the okra is fresh. If it just bends, it is old. Before you cut up okra for any recipe, make sure that it is completely dry. The gummy liquid that appears when you cut it will disappear once the okra is cooked.

Fenugreek-Flavored Meatballs
(Methi Ke Kofte)

Serves 4
Prep Time: 10 minutes
Cook Time: 10 minutes

Serve these bite-sized meatballs with Mint-Cilantro Chutney (see page 226).

½ pound ground lean lamb
1 small onion, minced
1 tablespoon dried fenugreek leaves
¼ teaspoon Ginger-Garlic Paste (see recipe on page 15)

2 teaspoons Warm Spice Mix (see recipe page 14)
2 teaspoons fresh lemon juice
Table salt, to taste
2 tablespoons vegetable oil
Red onion rings, for garnish

1. Preheat oven to 500°, or turn on the broiler.
2. In a mixing bowl, combine all of the ingredients *except* the oil and red onion rings. Mix well, using your hands.
3. Divide the mixture into 8 equal parts and roll into balls. Using a pastry brush, brush the meatballs with the oil. Place all the meatballs on a baking sheet in a single layer.
4. Place the baking sheet under a hot broiler or in the oven and cook for 8 to 10 minutes, turning frequently until the meatballs are well browned on all sides and the meat is completely cooked through.
5. Garnish with red onion rings and serve hot.

❋ Dried Fenugreek

Dried fenugreek leaves, or kasoori methi, add a wonderfully powerful aroma to dishes. These dried leaves are not interchangeable with fenugreek seeds. Fenugreek seeds, a powerful, bitter spice, are used in pickling and for some curries.

Indian Cheese Manchurian
(Paneer Manchurian)

1½ tablespoons rice flour or corn flour

1½ tablespoons all-purpose flour

¼ teaspoon white pepper powder

¼ teaspoon table salt

1 teaspoon Ginger-Garlic Paste (see recipe on page 15)

Water as needed, at room temperature

Vegetable oil for deep-frying

½ pound Indian Cheese (see recipe on page 14), diced

Serves 4
Prep Time: 5 minutes
Cook Time: 10 minutes

These appetizers are so flavorful in themselves that they do not need any dipping sauce.

1. Combine the corn flour, all-purpose flour, pepper, salt, and Ginger-Garlic Paste in a medium-sized bowl. Mix thoroughly and add just enough cold water to make a thin batter. (A few tablespoons of water should be enough, but add more if needed.)

2. In a deep pan, heat 1 to 2 inches of vegetable oil to 370° on a deep-fry thermometer. To test the temperature, you can add a drop of the batter; if it rises to the top immediately, your oil is ready to use.

3. Dip a few pieces of the Indian Cheese in the batter, turning to coat all sides; add to the hot oil. Deep-fry until golden brown in color (turning them in the oil to prevent them from sticking together).

4. Remove the cheese from the oil using a slotted spoon and drain on paper towels. Let the oil return to temperature and continue this process until all the Indian Cheese is fried. Serve hot.

❄ Deep-Frying Made Easy

When deep-frying, make sure that the ingredients are all cut the same size to ensure even cooking. Add small quantities of the ingredient to the oil. This maintains the oil's temperature. Try using fresh oil—it will improve your final product!

Sweet Potatoes with Tamarind
(Shakarkhandi Ki Chaat)

Serves 4
Prep Time: 10 minutes
Cook Time: None

Serve this with Fresh Lime Soda (page 43).

4 small sweet potatoes
1½ tablespoons Tamarind Chutney (see recipe on page 226)
¼ teaspoon black salt
1 tablespoon fresh lemon juice
½ teaspoon cumin seeds, roasted and roughly pounded

1. Peel the sweet potatoes and cut them into ½-inch cubes. Cook in salted water to cover for 5 to 8 minutes or until just fork-tender. Drain and let cool.
2. Put all the ingredients in a bowl and toss gently. Scoop the sweet potatoes in equal portions into 4 bowls. Stick a few toothpicks into the cubed sweet potatoes and serve.

Sweet and Spicy Fruits
(Phal Ki Chaat)

Serves 5
Prep Time: 5 minutes, plus 20 minutes to chill
Cook Time: None

This dish can also be a healthy low-fat lunch, but with a lot of flavor. Serve this with Fresh Lime Soda.

½ small apple, peeled and diced
Handful of seedless grapes
1 small banana, sliced
½ small pear, peeled and diced
½ small mango, peeled and diced
1-inch slice watermelon, peeled and diced
Juice of ½ lemon
1 tablespoon chopped cilantro (optional)
¼ teaspoon black salt
1 teaspoon Chaat Spice Mix (see recipe on page 14)

Mix together all the ingredients in a bowl. Toss to ensure that the fruits are evenly coated with the spices. Chill for about 20 minutes, then serve.

Indian Cheese Tikka
(Paneer Tikka)

1 cup plain yogurt
1 tablespoon vegetable oil
½ teaspoon turmeric powder
1 teaspoon Warm Spice Mix (see recipe on page 14)
¼ teaspoon cumin powder
1 teaspoon Ginger-Garlic Paste (see recipe on page 15)
Table salt, to taste

2 cups Indian Cheese (see recipe on page 14), cubed (about ¾ by ½ inch)
1 onion, quartered and layers separated
1 tablespoon vegetable oil
1 teaspoon Chaat Spice Mix (see recipe on page 16)

Serves 4
Prep Time: 10 minutes, plus 1 hour to marinate
Cook Time: 8 minutes

Try substituting tofu in place of the Indian Cheese (paneer) for a different flavor.

1. In a mixing bowl, combine the yogurt, vegetable oil, turmeric powder, spice mix, cumin powder, Ginger-Garlic Paste, and salt; mix well.
2. Add the Indian Cheese and onions to the marinade, cover, and refrigerate for about 1 hour.
3. Preheat the broiler. Thread the cheese and onions alternately onto skewers. Broil about 4 inches from the heat for 5 to 8 minutes or until done, turning and basting once with oil. When the onions start to char around the sides, the *Paneer Tikka* is ready.
4. Serve warm, sprinkled with Chaat Spice Mix and accompanied by Green Chili Chutney (see recipe on page 238).

✷ Secret Behind Wooden Skewers

If you like to use wooden skewers, soak them in water for about 30 minutes before use. This will prevent them from burning during grilling.

Chicken Tikka
(Murgh Ka Tikka)

Serves 4
Prep Time: 5 minutes,
plus 5–6 hours
to marinate
Cook Time: 15 minutes

Punjabi Onion Salad
(page 68) and Mint-
Cilantro Chutney
(page 226) nicely
complement this dish.

¾ cup Hung Yogurt (see recipe on page 16)
1 tablespoon Ginger-Garlic Paste (see recipe on page 15)
1 teaspoon fresh lemon juice
1 tablespoon vegetable oil
½ teaspoon, or to taste, red chili powder
Table salt, to taste

½ teaspoon Tandoori Spice Mix (see recipe on page 15)
¼ teaspoon Warm Spice Mix (page 14)
1 pound skinless, boneless chicken breasts, cubed
2 tablespoons melted butter, for basting
Lemon wedges, for garnish

1. To make the marinade, combine the Hung Yogurt, Ginger-Garlic Paste, lemon juice, oil, red chili powder, salt, and the spice mixes in a mixing bowl; mix well. Add the chicken cubes. Cover, and let marinate in the refrigerator for 5 to 6 hours or overnight.
2. Heat oven to 400°.
3. Thread the chicken onto skewers and baste with the melted butter. Place the chicken on a baking sheet and roast in the hot oven for about 5 minutes. Turn once and baste with any remaining butter. Roast for another 10 minutes or until golden brown and the juices run clear.
4. Serve hot, garnished with lemon wedges.

❋ Gingerroot

Ginger is a rhizome native to India and China. Its name comes from a Sanskrit word, which translates to "a body with horns." In addition to its many healing powers, it is said to be quite the aphrodisiac!

Chinese Indian Chili Chicken
(Mirchi Wala Murgh)

2 tablespoons Ginger-Garlic
  Paste (see recipe on
  page 15)
2½ tablespoons soya sauce
1 tablespoon vinegar
1 teaspoon red chili powder
½ teaspoon sugar
½ teaspoon table salt

2 fresh seranno green chilies,
  seeded and minced
1–2 drops red food coloring,
  optional
1 pound boneless, skinless
  chicken, cubed
2 tablespoons vegetable oil

> **Serves 4**
> **Prep Time:** 10 minutes,
> plus 3 hours to marinate
> **Cook Time:** 15 minutes
>
> This dish packs a
> punch, so make sure
> you have something
> cold and sweet
> nearby like Fresh Lime
> Soda (page 43).

1. To make the marinade, combine the Ginger-Garlic Paste, soya sauce, vinegar, red chili powder, sugar, salt, green chilies, and red food coloring (if desired) in a mixing bowl or sealable plastic bag. Add the chicken pieces and mix well. Cover and marinate in the refrigerator for about 3 hours.
2. Heat the oil in a large skillet on high. Add the marinated chicken pieces, shaking off any excess marinade. Discard any remaining marinade. Stir-fry for about 5 to 7 minutes, until the chicken is cooked through. You can add 1 or 2 tablespoons of water if the mixture starts to stick or dry out. Remove from heat. (Depending on the type of chicken you select, your cooking times might vary slightly.)
3. To serve, place equal portions of the chicken on 4 appetizer plates. Serve hot.

❋ Hot Oil Is a Must
The most common mistake that people make with this recipe is not heating the oil to a high enough temperature before adding the chicken. Hot oil retains the flavor of spices much better than cold oil.

Semolina Pancakes
(Rava Uthapam)

1 cup coarse semolina or plain cream of wheat
1 cup plain yogurt
Salt, to taste
Water at room temperature, as needed
¼ teaspoon baking powder
¼ teaspoon carom seeds

¼ small red onion, peeled and finely chopped
1 small red bell pepper, seeded and finely chopped
½ small tomato, seeded and finely chopped
2 tablespoons vegetable oil

1. Combine the semolina, yogurt, and salt in a medium-sized mixing bowl; mix well. Add ¼ to ½ cup water to reach the consistency of pancake batter, ensuring that you do not have any lumps in the batter.
2. Add the baking powder. Set aside for about 20 minutes.
3. In a separate bowl, create the topping. Mix the carom seeds, onions, bell peppers, and tomatoes.
4. Heat a griddle on medium-low. Add a few drops of oil.
5. Ladle about ¼ cup of batter into the center of the griddle. It should have the thickness of a regular pancake. As the batter starts to cook, bubbles will begin to appear on the surface.
6. Add a small amount of topping to the pancake, while it is still moist. Press down gently with the back of your ladle. Add a few drops of oil around the sides of the pancakes to keep it from sticking.
7. Flip the pancake over and cook the other side for about 2 minutes. Remove the pancake from heat and place on a serving platter. Continue this until all the batter is used up. Serve warm.

Mixed Vegetables with Bread Rolls
(Mumbai Ki Pav Bhajji)

1 cup cauliflower florets
¼ cup diced carrots
¼ cup diced green bell pepper
¼ cup chopped French beans
6 tablespoons butter
1 small red onion, peeled and
   chopped
2 small tomatoes, chopped
1 tablespoon Ginger-Garlic
   Paste (page 15)
2 serrano green chilies, chopped

1 teaspoon red chili powder
¼ teaspoon turmeric powder
½ teaspoon table salt
4 medium boiled potatoes,
   peeled
8 square bread buns,
   cut horizontally
Minced cilantro, for garnish

> **Serves 4**
> **Prep Time:** 10 minutes
> **Cook Time:** 30 minutes
>
> If you like, you can add 1 tablespoon of commercially available pav bhajji masala. It provides a distinct aroma.

1. In a small amount of salted water, cook the cauliflower, carrots, bell peppers, and French beans together until soft. Drain, discard the water, and set the vegetables aside.
2. In a large skillet, melt 4 tablespoons of the butter over medium heat. Add the onions and sauté until transparent. Add the tomatoes and cook until the tomatoes soften, about 3 to 5 minutes. Add the Ginger-Garlic Paste and the green chilies. Use a potato masher or the back of a spatula to mash the mixture. Continue cooking until you see the oil separating from the sides of the tomatoes.
3. Add the red chili powder, turmeric powder, and salt; sauté for 1 minute. Add all the cooked vegetables and the potatoes. Continue to cook, stirring, for another 3 to 4 minutes. If the mixture starts to dry out, add 1 tablespoon of water. Remove from heat and transfer to a serving bowl.
4. Return the unrinsed skillet to the stove. Turn the heat to low. Butter the buns with the remaining butter. Place the buns buttered sides down on the skillet. Toast both sides until slightly crispy and golden brown. Remove from heat.
5. Serve the buns alongside the *bhajji*. Garnish the *bhajji* with cilantro.

Tapioca Delight
(Sabudana Vada)

Serves 4
Prep Time: 15 minutes,
plus 3 hours to soak
Cook Time: 15 minutes

Serve this alongside
the tangy Tamarind
Chutney (page 226).

1 cup tapioca
2 medium potatoes
2 serrano green chilies, minced
2 sprigs cilantro, stemmed and
   minced
Table salt, to taste

¼ cup roughly ground unsalted
   peanuts
1 tablespoon fresh lemon juice
Vegetable oil for deep-frying

1. Cover the tapioca with water and soak for about 3 hours. Leave some room in the bowl for expansion as the tapioca soaks up the water. After 3 hours, drain off any remaining water.
2. While the tapioca is soaking, peel and cut the potatoes into ½-inch cubes and boil in salted water to cover for 5 to 8 minutes or until just fork-tender. Drain and mash.
3. Put the drained tapioca in a mixing bowl and add all the other ingredients *except* the oil. Mix thoroughly with your hands.
4. Lightly oil your hands and form about ¼ cup of the mixture into a ball, then flatten it into a small patty. Continue lightly oiling your hands and making patties until you have used up all the mixture.
5. Fill a deep pan with 1 inch of oil and heat on medium. Add 1 patty at a time and cook until golden brown on each side, about 2 minutes per side. Remove the patties from the oil and drain on a paper towel. Serve hot.

❈ Too Hot?

If you find the green chilies are too hot for your taste, remove the seeds before you cook with them. You'll get the flavor, without the heat. One word of caution though, wear gloves when you deseed the chilies.

Flour Savories
(Marwari Sawali)

*2 cups white all-purpose flour
    (maida)
3 tablespoons Clarified Butter
    (see recipe on page 17)
¾ teaspoon carom seeds*

*½ teaspoon black pepper
Pinch of baking soda
Table salt, to taste
Oil for deep-frying*

> **Yields 20 pieces**
> **Prep Time:** 30 minutes
> **Cook Time:** 15 minutes
>
> Try serving these delightful chips alongside Raw Mango Chutney (page 237).

1. In a large, flat bowl, mix together the flour, butter, carom seeds, black pepper, baking soda, and salt. Add just enough water to knead into a stiff dough. (To use a food processor, place the flour, butter, carom seeds, black pepper, baking soda, and salt into the bowl fitted with the steel blade. Pulse a few times to mix the ingredients and then process briefly until the mix looks like coarse cornmeal. Gradually add water through the feed tube until the mixture just begins to stick together. Turn out onto a very lightly floured surface and knead a few times until the mixture forms a dough.) Let the dough rest, covered, for 30 minutes.
2. Divide the dough in half, and roll each portion into a log about 5 inches long. Slice each log into 10 pieces. Roll out each portion into a small disk a little thicker than a potato chip and about 4 inches in diameter. Prick each piece all over with a fork.
3. Heat the oil in a deep pan to 380° on a deep-frying thermometer. Fry 3 to 4 disks at a time (be careful not to overcrowd the pan). They are ready when they are light golden brown and a little puffy.
4. Remove the disks with a slotted spoon, and drain on a paper towel. Let the oil return to temperature. Continue until all the disks are fried. Serve alongside your favorite chutney.

Corn Fritters
(Maki Ke Pakore)

*1 cup corn kernels (fresh or
    frozen)*
*2 slices white bread, ripped
    into small pieces*
*½-inch piece ginger, peeled and
    grated*
1 serrano green chili, minced
Table salt, to taste

¼ teaspoon red chili powder
1 teaspoon minced cilantro
Juice of ½ lemon
2 tablespoons chickpea flour
Pinch of baking powder
*4 tablespoons water, at room
    temperature*
Vegetable oil for deep-frying

1. To make the batter, combine all the ingredients *except* the oil in a mixing bowl. Mix well, adding enough water to coat all vegetables.
2. In a deep pan, add the oil to about 1 inch depth. Heat the oil on high until smoking, then lower the heat to medium. Press a spoonful of the mixture between 2 spoons to get a nice compact fritter. Use 1 of the spoons to push the fritter into the oil. Add a few spoonfuls at a time, ensuring that the balls do not stick to one another. Be careful not to overcrowd the pan. Fry the fritter until golden brown, about 4 minutes.
3. Use a slotted spoon to remove the cooked fritters from the oil. Transfer to a paper towel to absorb the extra oil. Skim any loose bits from the oil and discard. Continue until you have used up all the mixture.
4. Serve immediately with your choice of chutney.

※ Bhutta, Makka, Maki, or Corn
Corn is very popular in India. The most popular way to eat corn is to grill it. Grill corn on the cob and sprinkle it with lemon juice and a little Chaat Spice Mix (page 16).

Pork Tikkas
(Pork Ke Tikke)

1 cup Hung Yogurt (see recipe on page 16)
1 small onion, peeled and minced
1 tablespoon Ginger-Garlic Paste (see recipe on page 15)
1 teaspoon Warm Spice Mix (see recipe on page 14)

¼ teaspoon red chili powder
¼ teaspoon turmeric powder
Table salt, to taste
1 pound lean boneless pork, cubed
1 tablespoon oil

> **Serves 4**
> **Prep Time:** Overnight to marinate
> **Cook Time:** 15 minutes
>
> Your guests will devour these succulent tikkas. Serve them along with chilled Saffron Lemonade (page 45).

1. In a bowl (or resealable plastic bag), mix together all the ingredients *except* the oil. Cover and refrigerate overnight.
2. Thread the pork onto skewers. (If you are using wooden skewers, soak them in water for 30 minutes so that they don't scorch or burn.) Discard any remaining marinade.
3. Cook on a hot grill to desired doneness (about 12 minutes for well done). Turn once during the cooking process and baste with oil. Serve hot.

❊ Hung Yogurt

Yogurt is used as a tenderizer in meat dishes and provides a perfect base for marinades. It is "hung" to drain out the whey and give it a creamier consistency.

Crunchy Bread Fritters
(Dabel Roti Ke Pakore)

Serves 4
Prep Time: 35 minutes
Cook Time: 25 minutes

A wonderful variation to this recipe is to make a chutney sandwich, dip the entire sandwich in the batter, and then deep-fry.

4 slices of white bread, crust removed
1 cup chickpea flour
Table salt, to taste
¼ teaspoon red chili powder

⅛ teaspoon carom seeds
1 teaspoon vegetable oil
Approximately ¾ cup warm water
Oil for deep-frying

1. Cut each slice of bread into 4 equal-sized pieces; set aside.
2. To make the batter, mix together the chickpea flour, salt, red chili powder, carom seeds, and the vegetable oil. Begin adding the warm water a little bit at a time. Beat well to ensure that there are no lumps. The batter needs to be thick. Let the batter rest for about 20 minutes.
3. Heat about 1 inch of the oil in a deep pan to 350° on a deep-fry thermometer. Dip each bread piece in the batter, let the excess batter drip off, and place the bread into the hot oil. Add a few pieces at a time. Reduce the heat to medium. Fry the fritters, turning them in the oil until they are golden brown on all sides.
4. Using a slotted spoon, remove the fritters from the oil and place on a double layer of paper towels to drain. Place in a warm (200°) oven. Let the oil return to temperature and continue until all the fritters are done. Serve hot.

※ Chutney Sandwiches

These could not be easier to make. Select your favorite chutney. Butter a slice of bread. On another slice of bread, slather on as much chutney as you desire. Cover with the buttered slice. Serve along with Spicy Papaya Salad (page 58).

Spiced Broccoli
(Chatpati Broccoli)

1 cup broccoli florets
1 tablespoon Ginger-Garlic Paste (see recipe on page 15)
1 tablespoon chickpea flour
¼ teaspoon dried mango powder

½ teaspoon coriander powder
¼ teaspoon, or to taste, red chili powder
Table salt, to taste
Vegetable oil for deep-frying

> **Serves 4**
> **Prep Time:** 15 minutes to marinate
> **Cook Time:** 20 minutes

> Broccoli is a relatively recent addition to the Indian cuisine. It is seasoned and deep-fried here for a crispy snack.

1. In a bowl, toss the broccoli florets with the Ginger-Garlic Paste and chickpea flour. Ensure that the florets are evenly coated. Let the florets marinate for 15 minutes.
2. In a small bowl, mix the dried mango powder, the coriander powder, red chili powder, and salt; set aside.
3. In a deep pan, heat about 1 inch of the oil to 350° on a deep-fry thermometer. Add a few pieces of broccoli at a time. Deep-fry until the florets are pale brown in color, about 3 minutes. Remove the broccoli with a slotted spoon and place on a paper towel to absorb the extra oil. Let the oil return to temperature. Continue until all the florets are fried.
4. Place all the florets on a serving platter and sprinkle with the prepared spice mixture. Serve immediately.

❈ Chickpea Flour—Not Just for Dinner
To this day, many Indian beauty books promise that chickpeas can help you achieve flawless skin. The secret is a facemask made of chickpea flour, turmeric powder, and water.

Puffed Rice Mix
(Bengali Jhal Muri)

Serves 4
Prep Time: 25 minutes
Cook Time: 10 minutes

Puffed rice loses its crispness once it is exposed to air. Store in an airtight container.

2 small potatoes
½ pound puffed rice
½ cup canned chickpeas, drained and rinsed
1 serrano green chili, seeded and chopped (optional)
¼ cucumber, peeled and chopped
1 small tomato, seeded and chopped

½ teaspoon cumin seeds, roasted and roughly pounded
¼ teaspoon Chaat Spice Mix (see recipe on page 16) (optional)
1 tablespoon mustard oil (optional)

1. Peel and cube the potatoes. Boil the potatoes in a large pot until they are tender. Drain off the water and let the potatoes cool to room temperature.
2. Mix together all the ingredients in a large bowl. Serve immediately.

Indian Cheese Cubes
(Khatti Paneer Chaat)

Serves 4
Prep Time: 5 minutes
Cook Time: None

A number of souring spices are added to the paneer (Indian Cheese) here, giving it a wonderful tangy taste.

8 ounces Indian Cheese (see recipe on page 14), cubed
2 tablespoons minced cilantro
½ teaspoon grated gingerroot
2 tablespoons fresh lemon juice

1 teaspoon dried mango powder
1 teaspoon dried pomegranate powder
½ teaspoon black salt

Mix together all the ingredients in a bowl. Serve immediately. This can also be refrigerated for a few hours before serving.

Potato Cutlets
(Aloo Ki Tikki)

4 small potatoes
2 serrano green chilies, minced
4 slices white bread
Table salt, to taste
¼ teaspoon black pepper
*   powder*

1 tablespoon minced cilantro
¼ cup crumbled Indian Cheese
*   (see recipe on page 14)*
6 tablespoons vegetable oil

> **Serves 4**
> **Prep Time:** 40 minutes
> **Cook Time:** 20 minutes
>
> Leave out the green chilies if you like your cutlets mild. Serve these with the Mint-Cilantro Chutney (page 226).

1. Boil the potatoes, then peel and mash them. Mix in the green chilies.
2. Soak the bread in water. Remove the bread and squeeze out all the water. Add the bread to the potato mixture and knead well. Add the salt, pepper, cilantro, and the Indian Cheese; mix well.
3. Divide the mixture into 8 equal portions. Rub a little bit of oil in the palms of your hands and flatten each portion into small disks.
4. Heat the oil in a skillet. Add the disks (or *tikkis*) 1 at a time. Fry for about 2 minutes on each side or until they turn golden brown. Remove the *tikkis* from the oil and place on a paper towel to drain off excess oil. Continue until all the *tikkis* are cooked. You can keep these warm in a warm oven. Serve hot.

❋ Easy Potatoes

A really easy way to "boil" potatoes is to microwave them! Simply prick the potato all over with a fork. Microwave for about 12 minutes, and your "boiled" potato is ready.

Onion Rings
(Pyaz Ke Pakore)

Serves 4
Prep Time: 25 minutes
Cook Time: 30 minutes

You can also make pakore with your choice of other vegetables like cauliflower, spinach, eggplant, or even green chilies.

1 cup chickpea flour
Table salt, to taste
¼ teaspoon red chili powder
¼ teaspoon cumin seeds, roasted and roughly pounded
Pinch of baking powder

1 teaspoon vegetable oil
Approximately ¾ cup warm water
2 medium-sized red onions, peeled and thinly sliced
Oil for deep-frying

1. To make the batter, mix together the chickpea flour, salt, red chili powder, cumin seeds, baking powder, and the vegetable oil. Add the warm water a little bit at a time. Beat well to ensure that there are no lumps.
2. Add the onions to the batter and make sure that they are well coated.
3. Heat about 1 inch of the oil in a deep pan to 350°. Add a few onion rings at a time to the hot oil. Reduce the heat to medium. Fry the onion rings, turning them in the oil until they are golden brown on all sides, about 2 to 3 minutes.
4. Using a slotted spoon, remove the onion rings from the oil and place them on a double layer of paper towels. Continue until all the onion rings are done. Serve hot. If you wish to serve them later, keep them warm in a 200° oven.

❋ Which Onion to Use

Indian onions are much stronger in taste than their American counterparts. I suggest using mild red onions. If you enjoy a stronger flavor, try white Vidalia onions, which are available in local grocery stores. If your onions are too bitter and you want to make them sweeter, soak them in cold water with a few tablespoons of salt for about 30 minutes. Drain, rinse well, and then use as desired.

Pomegranate Chaat
(Anardana Ki Chaat)

¼ *cup fresh raspberries*
¼ *cup seedless grapes*
1 *cup fresh pomegranate seeds*
¼ *cup fresh blueberries*
¼ *cup canned mandarin*
   oranges, drained

1 *tablespoon fresh lemon juice*
1 *tablespoon chopped cilantro*
1 *teaspoon Chaat Spice Mix*
   (see recipe on page 16)

Serves 4
Prep Time: 5 minutes,
plus 20 minutes to chill
Cook Time: None

Serve this with Fresh
Lime Soda (page 43)
or Fizzy Rose Drink
(page 42).

Rinse the fresh berries in cool water and drain. Mix together all the ingredients in a bowl. Toss to evenly coat the fruits with the spices. Chill for about 20 minutes, then serve.

Spicy Potato Snack
(Aloo Chaat)

4 *medium potatoes*
1 *cup sprouted mung beans*
   (bean sprouts)
2 *tablespoons Mint-Cilantro*
   Chutney (see recipe on
   page 226)

1 *tablespoon Tamarind Chutney*
   (see recipe on page 226)
¼ *teaspoon Chaat Spice Mix*
   (see recipe on page 16)
Table salt, to taste
1 *tablespoon chopped cilantro*

Serves 4
Prep Time: 5 minutes
Cook Time: 5 minutes

Try serving these
topped with sesame
seeds, bread crou-
tons, and minced
green chilies. For a
variation, pan-fry the
potatoes first.

1. Peel and dice the potatoes; boil in salted water, covered, for 5 minutes or until just fork-tender. Let cool.
2. Place all the remaining ingredients in a mixing bowl. Toss the potatoes in the mixture to coat the potatoes evenly with the spices. Serve immediately.

Curried Mixed Nuts
(Masala Nuts)

Yields 3 cups
Prep Time: None
Cook Time: 10 minutes

Try variations of this using your favorite nuts, and spice them to taste. Wooden chopsticks make great tools to stir the nuts.

1 teaspoon cumin seeds
1 teaspoon coriander seeds
1/4 teaspoon black peppercorns
2 cloves
1 dried red chili, roughly pounded

3 tablespoons vegetable oil
1/4 teaspoon ground ginger
3 cups raw mixed nuts
1 teaspoon table salt

1. Heat a small skillet on medium. Add the cumin seeds, coriander seeds, black peppercorns, cloves, and dried red chili. Toast the spices, stirring constantly, for about 3 to 5 minutes. They will darken and release a wonderful aroma. Remove from heat and transfer them to a bowl to cool. Using a spice grinder or a coffee grinder, grind the spices.
2. In a large skillet, heat the oil on low. Add the ground spice mixture, the ground ginger, and the nuts. Cook gently, stirring constantly for about 3 minutes. Cover and cook for an additional 5 minutes, shaking the pan occasionally.
3. Remove from heat, uncover, and sprinkle with salt. Cool to room temperature, then serve.

❋ Scorching Spices

Sometimes adding powdered spices to an already hot pan can scorch them. If this is a problem for you, try adding 1 tablespoon of water to the spices before you sauté them. The water will quickly evaporate and the spices will sauté without burning.

CHAPTER 4

Drinks, Teas, and Soups
(Sharbats, Chai, Aur Shorbas)

Rose-Flavored Yogurt Drink
(Gulabi Lassi)

Serves 4
Prep Time: 5 minutes
Cook Time: None

If you cannot find rose water, substitute your favorite syrup. Lassi has a short shelf life and is best served fresh.

3 cups Hung Yogurt (see recipe on page 16)
2 tablespoons sugar
1½ tablespoons rose water

½ cup water
5–6 ice cubes
Rose petals, for garnish

In a blender, combine the yogurt, sugar, rose water, water, and ice cubes; blend well. Add more water if you like a thinner consistency. Serve garnished with rose petals.

❋ Rose Water

Rose water is made, as the name suggests, from roses. Cotton balls doused in chilled rose water make wonderful facial cleansers.

Fizzy Rose Drink
(Gulabi Ka Sharbat)

Serves 4
Prep Time: 2 minutes
Cook Time: None

Rooh afza, a fragrant syrup used in desserts, milkshakes, and sherbets, is readily available in most Indian grocery stores or at *www.namaste.com.*

4 tablespoons rose syrup or rooh afza

4 cans lemon soda, chilled
1 sprig mint, stemmed

1. Put 1 tablespoon of rose syrup into a tall glass.
2. Pour in 1 can of lemon soda as slowly as you can. The rose syrup will stay at the bottom, and the lemon soda will form another layer on top. Repeat the same process for the remaining 3 glasses.
3. Garnish with mint and serve.

Fresh Lime Soda
(Nimbu Ka Sharbat)

2 tablespoons ginger juice
4 teaspoons sugar
¼ teaspoon black salt
1 tablespoon fresh lime juice

4 cans lime soda
Ice cubes
Thin lemon slices, for garnish

Add all the ingredients *except* the lemon slices to a blender; blend well. Serve immediately, garnished with thin lemon slices.

Serves 4
Prep Time: 5 minutes
Cook Time: None

This is one of the most popular drinks in India. To get ginger juice, place grated ginger in a garlic press and squeeze out the juice.

Mint-Ginger Cooler
(Jal Jeera)

1 tablespoon minced cilantro
1 tablespoon minced mint
2 teaspoons tamarind pulp
4 cups water
½ teaspoon black salt
1 teaspoon cumin seeds, roasted

1½ tablespoons sugar
1 teaspoon fresh lemon juice
¼ teaspoon ginger powder
Dried mint, for garnish

1. In a blender, blend the cilantro and mint with a bit of water to form a paste; transfer to a large jug.
2. Add the tamarind pulp, water, black salt, cumin seeds, sugar, lemon juice, and ginger; mix well. Chill and serve garnished with mint.

Serves 4
Prep Time: 10 minutes, plus time to chill
Cook Time: None

A digestive drink, Jal Jeera is often served with little chickpea fritters called boondi. Boondi look like small pearls and are available in most Indian stores.

Mango Yogurt Drink
(Aam Ki Lassi)

Serves 4
Prep Time: 5 minutes
Cook Time: None

You can use fresh ripe mangoes for this recipe—add a few teaspoons of sugar to the lassi if you do.

3 cups Hung Yogurt (see recipe on page 16)
1 cup canned mango pulp

½ cup water
5–6 ice cubes

Combine all the ingredients in a blender; blend well. Add more water if you like a thinner consistency. Serve immediately.

❊ More on Mangoes

Many varieties of mangoes have been cultivated in India for thousands of years. One very popular Indian favorite is the alphonso mango.

Nutty Milk
(Masala Doodh)

Serves 4
Prep Time: 5 minutes
Cook Time: 10 minutes

This refreshing drink can be served either hot or cold.

4 cups 2% milk
¼ teaspoon Roasted Saffron (see recipe on page 18)
4 tablespoons ground almonds
2 tablespoons ground unsalted pistachios

¼ teaspoon cardamom seeds, roughly pounded
4 teaspoons sugar

1. In a deep pan, bring the milk to a boil.
2. Add the saffron, almonds, pistachios, and cardamom. Lower the heat and simmer for 5 minutes.
3. Add the sugar and mix well. Remove from heat. Let cool and refrigerate if serving cold.

Cold Coffee
(Thandi Coffee)

4 cups 2% milk
4 tablespoons low-fat sweet-
    ened condensed milk
8 ice cubes

4 teaspoons instant coffee
    (such as Nescafé)
Powdered cinnamon, for garnish

Combine all the ingredients *except* the cinnamon in a blender; blend well. Serve immediately, garnished with powdered cinnamon.

> **Serves 4**
> **Prep Time:** 5 minutes
> **Cook Time:** None
>
> A simple, charming drink that is very refreshing.

Saffron Lemonade
(Kesari Shikanji)

4 cups cold water
Juice of 1 large lemon
4 tablespoons sugar
¼ teaspoon crushed saffron
    threads

Fresh mint and lemon slices,
    for garnish

In a blender, blend together all the ingredients *except* the garnishes until the sugar is dissolved. Serve garnished with mint leaves and lemon slices.

> **Serves 4**
> **Prep Time:** 5 minutes
> **Cook Time:** None
>
> Saffron seems to lend a certain sense of roy-alty to this refreshing cooler. You can also use orange juice instead of lemon juice.

❋ Juicing Lemons

Lemons that are at room temperature are easier to juice than cold ones. You can microwave lemons that have been in the refrigerator for a few seconds to make juicing easier.

Maharastrian Buttermilk
(Maharastrian Mattha)

Serves 4
Prep Time: 10 minutes
Cook Time: None

This is a spicier version of the North Indian lassi, or yogurt drink. It helps with digestion and is great served after a heavy meal.

2 cups plain yogurt
1 cup water
½ serrano green chili, seeded (optional)
1 tablespoon minced cilantro

¼ teaspoon cumin seeds, roasted
Table salt, to taste

Combine all the ingredients in a blender; blend well. Chill and serve.

Mixed Fruit Juice
(Ganga Jamuma Saraswati)

Serves 4
Prep Time: 5 minutes
Cook Time: Time to chill

Street vendors have been selling this drink in India for ages. Traditionally in India this juice is made with sweet limes and oranges.

2 cups sweetened tangerine juice
2 cups sweetened naval orange juice
¼ cup pineapple juice

2 tablespoons lemon juice
½ teaspoon black salt
Thin orange slices, for garnish

In a blender, blend together all the ingredients *except* the orange slices. Chill and serve garnished with orange slices.

❋ Selecting Pineapples

Trust your nose for this. Turn the pineapple upside down and smell the bottom. A ripe pineapple should smell sweet. Remember, pineapples do not ripen after they have been picked, so make your selection carefully.

Minty Yogurt Drink
(Pudine Ki Lassi)

½-inch piece ginger, grated
¼ teaspoon cumin seeds,
   roasted and roughly
   pounded
2 teaspoons minced fresh mint

¼ teaspoon black salt
2 teaspoons sugar
3 cups plain yogurt
1 cup water
6–8 ice cubes

Combine all the ingredients in a blender; blend well. Add more water if you like a thinner consistency. Serve immediately.

Serves 4
Prep Time: 10 minutes
Cook Time: None

If you use low-fat or nonfat yogurt, you might need less water than what's called for here.

Watermelon Cooler
(Kalingar Ka Sharbat)

3 cups chopped watermelon,
   seeded
8–12 ice cubes
¼ teaspoon black salt (optional)

1 tablespoon honey
¼ teaspoon fresh lemon juice
Fresh mint, for garnish

Combine all the ingredients *except* the garnish in a blender; blend well. If you like, you can strain the juice. Serve garnished with mint.

Serves 4
Prep Time: 5 minutes
Cook Time: None

In the summertime when watermelons are plentiful, serve this for breakfast. It makes a nice change from the standard orange juice.

Ginger Tea
(Adrak Ki Chai)

1½ cups water
1-inch piece fresh ginger, peeled and grated
1 (1-inch) cinnamon stick
3 cardamom pods, bruised
2 cloves
½ cup milk
1 tablespoon loose Indian tea leaves
Sugar, to taste

1. In a saucepan, heat the water. Add the ginger, cinnamon, cardamom, and cloves; bring to a boil.
2. Add the milk and continue to boil for 1 minute. Add the tea leaves and continue to boil for another 1 to 2 minutes.
3. Remove from heat and strain. Add sugar to taste and serve.

Grandma's Chai
(Dadi Ma Ki Masala Chai)

2 cardamom pods, bruised
1 clove
1½ cups water
½ cup milk
2 tea bags or 1 tablespoon loose tea
Sugar, to taste

Place the cardamom, clove, water, and milk in a pan over high heat; bring to a boil. Add the tea bags, cover, and turn off the heat. Let the tea steep for 2 minutes; then strain, add sugar to taste, and serve.

✳ Saffron Tea

If you are not a fan of caffeine, try this. Heat 1 cup of water. Add a pinch of saffron, a bruised cardamom, and tiny piece of cinnamon. Simmer for about 1 minute. Strain. Add honey for some sweetness, and serve.

Chilled Soup
(Thanda Shorba)

1 large cucumber, peeled and
   grated
1 small garlic clove, crushed
2 cups plain yogurt
2 cups water
Table salt, to taste

1 tablespoon vegetable oil
¼ teaspoon cumin seeds
1 teaspoon finely chopped
   fresh mint for garnish

Serves 6
Prep Time: 10 minutes,
plus 2½ hours to chill
Cook Time: 5 minutes

In the sweltering heat
of summer, this soup
has a wonderful
cooling effect.

1. Place the cucumber in a bowl and chill for about 30 minutes. Pour off the cucumber juice that collects in the bowl. Press down on the cucumber to get out as much juice as possible.
2. Combine the cucumber and garlic, then stir in the yogurt and water. Combine thoroughly. Add salt to taste. Set aside.
3. Heat the oil in a small skillet on medium. Add the cumin seeds and sauté for about 1 minute or until the seeds start to crackle and you can smell the aroma. Remove from heat.
4. Stir the cumin into the yogurt soup. Cover and refrigerate for 2 hours.
5. When ready to serve, pour equal portions into 6 shallow bowls and garnish with the mint.

※ Watermelon Skins

In the princely Indian state of Rajasthan, the watermelon skins are cooked to make a delightful side dish. After removing all the red flesh, you are left with the white flesh on the inside of the watermelon skin. Cut out this white flesh and set it aside. In a skillet, heat some oil, then add mustard seeds and cumin seeds. Add the white watermelon flesh, salt, and a pinch of garam masala. Cook for about 7 minutes or until tender. Serve hot.

Tangy Ginger Soup
(Adrak Ka Shorba)

Serves 4
Prep Time: 5 minutes
Cook Time: 30 minutes

You can omit the milk and add ½ cup of cream instead for a richer-tasting soup.

2-inch piece fresh gingerroot, peeled
2 tablespoons butter
1 teaspoon vegetable oil
1 teaspoon cumin seeds, roasted
¼ teaspoon turmeric powder
1 small tomato, chopped
2 dried red chilies, roughly pounded
1 serrano green chili, minced
2 cups milk
1 cup plain yogurt, whipped
Table salt, to taste
½ teaspoon dried mint

1. In a blender or with a hand grater, grind the ginger to a fine paste. If using a blender, you may add up to 1 tablespoon of water.
2. In a deep pan, heat the butter and the oil on medium. Add the ginger and sauté until well browned. Add the cumin and turmeric; sauté for about 20 seconds, then add the tomatoes. Cook for another 7 to 8 minutes or until the tomatoes are soft. Add the red and green chilies, then add the milk. Bring to a boil.
3. Reduce heat and add the yogurt. Simmer for about 20 minutes, stirring occasionally. Remove from heat. Add the salt. You can serve the soup as is or strained. Garnish with dried mint.

❈ Yellow Countertops?

Turmeric powder can stain your countertops. If you have yellow turmeric stains, use a cleaner with bleach—it usually gets rid of the stains. Baking soda or a few drops of lemon juice work well for this, too.

Mild Buttermilk Soup
(Chaas Ka Shorba)

1 tablespoon vegetable oil
6–8 curry leaves
¼ teaspoon black mustard
   seeds
1 dried red chili, roughly
   pounded

4 peppercorns, roughly pounded
¼ teaspoon cumin seeds,
   roughly pounded
2 garlic cloves, crushed
4 cups buttermilk
Table salt, to taste

Serves 4
Prep Time: 5 minutes
Cook Time: 20 minutes

Use curry leaves for this; curry powder is not a substitute. A lovely variation is to add 1 tablespoon of lightly roasted, thinly sliced coconut.

1. In a deep pan, heat the oil on medium. Add the curry leaves and mustard seeds. When the seeds pop, in quick succession add the red chili, peppercorns, cumin seeds, and garlic.
2. Reduce the heat to low. Add the buttermilk and mix well. Simmer on low heat for about 15 minutes. Add salt to taste. Serve immediately.

Goan Shrimp Soup
(Sopa De Camarao)

2 tablespoons butter
1 teaspoon vegetable oil
1 small onion, peeled and
   chopped
½ cup canned crushed
   tomatoes

½ teaspoon garlic paste
2 cups chicken stock
2 cups water
1 cup cooked medium-sized
   shrimp
Table salt, to taste

Serves 6
Prep Time: 15 minutes
Cook Time: 30 minutes

This simple soup can be cooked unattended for the most part. Serve this soup garnished with slit green chilies or even shredded cheese.

1. In a deep stockpot, heat the butter on medium. Add the vegetable oil. Add the onions and sauté for about 7 to 8 minutes, until soft. Add the tomatoes and garlic paste; sauté for another 2 to 4 minutes.
2. Add the chicken stock and water. Cook, covered, for about 15 minutes.
3. Add the cooked shrimp and salt. Simmer uncovered on low heat for about 5 minutes. Serve hot.

Special Goan Soup
(Sopa Grossa)

Serves 6
Prep Time: 15 minutes
Cook Time: 30 minutes

This traditional mild soup is made with Goan red rice; I use the more readily available basmati rice.

2 tablespoons butter
1 teaspoon vegetable oil
1 small onion, peeled and chopped
1 small tomato, chopped
2 small potatoes, peeled and chopped
1 cup cauliflower florets
$\frac{1}{2}$ cup green peas (fresh or frozen)
$\frac{1}{4}$ cup green beans (fresh or frozen)
4 cups chicken stock
2 tablespoons cooked rice
$\frac{1}{2}$ cup diced cooked chicken (your choice of cut)
Table salt, to taste

1. In a deep stockpot, heat the butter on medium. Add the vegetable oil. Add the onions and sauté for about 7 minutes, until soft. Add the tomatoes and sauté for another 7 minutes.
2. Add all the vegetables and the chicken stock. Cover, and cook until the vegetables are soft.
3. Add the rice, chicken, and salt. Simmer, uncovered, on low heat for about 10 minutes. Serve hot.

✵ Keeping Butter from Burning

When you are heating butter, always add a little bit of oil to the pan; this will keep the butter from burning. Before you add any spices, ensure that your oil is hot. Heated oil retains the flavors of spices.

Coconut and Tomato Soup
(Tamatar Ka Shorba)

4 large tomatoes, peeled
½ teaspoon cumin seeds,
   roasted
Table salt, to taste
1 cup water
1 (14-ounce) can light coconut
   milk

1 tablespoon vegetable oil
2 sprigs curry leaves, stemmed
½ teaspoon black mustard
   seeds
1 dried red chili, roughly
   pounded

> **Serves 4**
> **Prep Time:** 10 minutes
> **Cook Time:** 30 minutes
>
> Use vine grown tomatoes to get the divine red color that is characteristic of this soup.

1. Combine the tomatoes, cumin seeds, and salt in a blender; blend well.
2. In a deep stockpot, combine the blended tomatoes and the water. Heat on medium heat for about 20 minutes, stirring occasionally. Add the coconut milk and simmer for another 5 minutes.
3. While the soup is cooking, heat the oil in a skillet on medium. Add the curry leaves, mustard seeds, and the red chili. When the mustard seeds pop, remove the skillet from the heat and add the mixture to the soup; mix well.
4. Serve hot or cold, or poured over a mound of steaming rice.

❈ Peeling Tomatoes

Drop the tomatoes into a pot of boiling water for about 1 minute. Use a pair of tongs to transfer the tomatoes from the boiling water directly into a bowl of cold water. The skins will peel off easily. Your tomatoes are ready to use.

Spicy Kokum Drink
(Sol Kadhi)

Serves 4
Prep Time: 5 minutes, plus 1 hour to soak
Cook Time: 5 minutes, plus time to chill

You can find kokum, which is becoming increasingly popular in North America, at Indian grocers.

8 pieces kokum
1 cup hot water
2 cloves garlic, peeled and crushed
1½ (14-ounce) cans light coconut milk

Pinch of table salt
Pinch of sugar

1. Soak the *kokum* in the hot water for about 1 hour. Strain and reserve the pink liquid. Discard the *kokum*.
2. In a deep stockpot, combine the pink liquid with all the remaining ingredients; mix well. This beautiful pink soup should be served chilled in bowls that allow you to show off its color.

Spinach Soup
(Palak Ka Shorba)

Serves 4
Prep Time: 10 minutes
Cook Time: 45 minutes

This soup comes to you straight from my great-grandmother's kitchen. This nutritious soup can be prepared up to 2 days in advance.

1 tablespoon Clarified Butter (see recipe on page 17)
¼ teaspoon cumin seeds
1 small red onion, chopped
1½ teaspoons grated gingerroot
1 medium turnip, peeled and chopped

¼ teaspoon turmeric powder
¼ teaspoon red chili powder
Table salt, to taste
2 cups vegetable stock
1 pound frozen chopped spinach, thawed

1. In a stockpot, heat the Clarified Butter. Add the cumin seeds and stir-fry about 1 minute. Add the onion, ginger, and turnip; sauté for about 5 minutes on medium heat. Add the turmeric, red chili powder, and salt; sauté for about 1 more minute. Add the vegetable stock and cook, covered, on medium heat for about 20 minutes or until the turnips are soft.
2. Add the spinach and cook for another 5 to 8 minutes. Remove from heat and let cool.
3. Purée the spinach soup in a blender, then reheat it. Serve immediately.

CHAPTER 5
Salads (Salaads)

Sprouted Mung Bean Salad
(Moong Dal Ka Salaad)

Serves 4
Prep Time: 15 minutes, plus 20 minutes to chill
Cook Time: None

If you don't like eating raw beans, you can either sauté them lightly or boil them in lightly salted water for about 2 minutes.

1 clove garlic, crushed
½ English cucumber, finely diced
1 teaspoon grated fresh gingerroot
2 serrano green chilies, finely chopped (optional)
Table salt, to taste
2 teaspoons fresh lemon juice
¼ teaspoon sugar
1 cup sprouted mung beans (bean sprouts)
Finely chopped cilantro, for garnish

In a salad bowl, combine all the ingredients *except* the garnish. Chill for 20 minutes. Garnish with cilantro.

Indian-Style Coleslaw
(Kachumbars)

Serves 4
Prep Time: 10 minutes, plus 20 minutes to chill
Cook Time: None

Prepare this fresh; if left too long in the refrigerator, the cucumbers will release too much water.

1½ tablespoons fresh lemon juice
1½ tablespoons finely ground peanuts
¼ teaspoon red chili powder
Table salt, to taste
1 small red onion, peeled and diced
1 small tomato, diced
1 medium cucumber, peeled and diced
1 tablespoon finely chopped cilantro

In a bowl, combine the lemon juice, peanuts, red chili powder, and salt; mix well. Add the red onion, tomato, and cucumber; toss well. Chill for about 20 minutes. Serve chilled, topped with the cilantro.

Maharastrian Mung Salad
(Moong Dal Misal)

2 tablespoons vegetable oil
1 teaspoon Ginger-Garlic Paste
    (see recipe on page 15)
Pinch of asafetida (optional)
¼ teaspoon red chili powder
¼ teaspoon turmeric powder
2 small potatoes, peeled and
    diced
1 cup sprouted mung beans
    (bean sprouts)
3 cups water

Table salt, to taste
½ cup peeled and chopped
    red onion
¼ cup peeled and chopped
    tomato
1 tablespoon Dry Garlic
    Chutney (see recipe on
    page 228)
1 tablespoon fresh lemon juice
Fresh cilantro, for garnish

Serves 4
Prep Time: 10 minutes
Cook Time: 20 minutes

You can make this salad with different types of beans.

1. In a deep pan, heat the oil on medium. Add the Ginger-Garlic Paste, asafetida, red chili powder, and turmeric powder; sauté for about 30 seconds.
2. Add the potatoes and mung beans; sauté for 2 to 3 minutes. Add the water. Cover and cook over medium heat until the potatoes are soft, about 10 to 12 minutes. Remove from heat. (There may still be a little bit of water remaining—this is okay.) Add salt to taste.
3. Transfer the cooked mixture to a platter. Spread the onions and tomatoes on top. Sprinkle with the chutney and the lemon juice. Garnish with cilantro and serve at room temperature.

✳ Delicious Toppings

Many folks like to top their salads with bhel puri. Bhel puri is a crunchy snack commonly sold on the streets of India. It is comprised of puffed rice and tiny fried noodles made of chickpea flour and spices. This mix is readily available at your Indian grocers.

Spicy Papaya Salad
(Papete Ka Salaad)

Serves 4
Prep Time: 10 minutes, plus 30 minutes to chill
Cook Time: None

This salad looks magnificent as a centerpiece on the table during summertime. Use seasonal fruit of your choice to make variations.

2 tablespoons fresh lemon juice
½ teaspoon black salt
1 tablespoon finely chopped cilantro
½ teaspoon sugar
½ cup diced papaya
½ cup diced mango
½ cup diced kiwi
¼ cup chopped strawberries

In a bowl, combine the lemon juice, black salt, cilantro, and sugar; mix well. Add the papaya, mango, kiwi, and strawberries; gently toss. Chill for about 30 minutes, then serve.

Creamy Walnut Salad
(Akhrot Ka Raita)

Serves 4
Prep Time: 10 minutes, plus 20 minutes to chill
Cook Time: None

Raitas are made with fresh vegetables, cooked vegetables, or with spices or nuts. Serve this alongside Ground Meat–Stuffed Bread (page 210).

2 cups plain yogurt, whipped
1 teaspoon cumin seeds, toasted
¼ teaspoon red chili powder
½ teaspoon sugar
Table salt, to taste
¾ cup coarsely chopped walnuts

In a bowl, combine the yogurt, cumin seeds, red chili powder, sugar, and salt; mix well. Add the walnuts and mix well. (Add more walnuts if you prefer a nuttier taste.) Chill, covered, for about 20 minutes before serving.

Smoked Eggplant in Yogurt
(Baigan Ka Raita)

1 small eggplant
1 tablespoon vegetable oil
2 cups plain yogurt
1 small red onion, peeled and
    chopped
½-inch piece fresh gingerroot,
    grated
1 serrano green chili, seeded
    and minced

1 tablespoon minced cilantro
Table salt, to taste
½ teaspoon Warm Spice Mix
    (see recipe on page 14)
Ground red pepper (i.e.,
    cayenne pepper), for garnish

> **Serves 4**
> **Prep Time:** 10 minutes, plus 20 minutes to chill
> **Cook Time:** 50 minutes
>
> You can add some grated fresh coconut to this for a flavorful variation.

1. Heat the broiler. Brush the eggplant with vegetable oil. Place the eggplant under the broiler and cook until the eggplant is soft and the skin is charred—almost black. Remove from the broiler. Let cool, then peel off and discard the skin. Mash the eggplant into a smooth pulp. Set aside.
2. In a bowl, whip the yogurt. Add the onion, ginger, chili, cilantro, salt, and spice mix; mix well.
3. Add the eggplant pulp to the yogurt mixture and mix well. Chill, covered, for about 20 minutes. Serve garnished with the ground red pepper.

❋ Quick Eggplant Snack

This is a very common snack in eastern India. Thinly slice the eggplant. Season with salt and pepper. Add a pinch of turmeric powder. Set aside for about 15 minutes. Pan-fry in hot oil and serve immediately.

Fried Okra in Yogurt Sauce
(Bhindi Ka Raita)

Vegetable oil for deep-frying
½ pound okra, chopped
2 cups plain yogurt
1 tablespoon minced cilantro
½ teaspoon cumin powder
¼ teaspoon red chili powder
Table salt, to taste
1 tablespoon cumin seeds, toasted

1. Heat about 1 inch of oil in a deep pan to 350° on a deep-fry thermometer.
2. Add a few pieces of okra and deep-fry until crisp. Remove from the oil using a slotted spoon and transfer to a paper towel to drain. Continue until all the okra is fried. Set aside.
3. In a bowl, whip the yogurt. Add the cilantro, cumin powder, red chili powder, and salt; mix well.
4. Add the okra to the yogurt mixture. Sprinkle with cumin seeds, and serve.

✳ Toasting Cumin Seeds

To toast cumin seeds, heat a skillet on medium. Add the cumin seeds. Roast until the seeds release their aroma and begin to darken. Remove from heat and store in an airtight jar.

Potato and Yogurt Salad
(Aloo Ka Raita)

3 small potatoes
2 cups plain yogurt, whipped
½ cup cold water
1 teaspoon cumin seeds,
*   toasted and roughly pounded*

¼ teaspoon red chili powder
Table salt, to taste
Slit serrano green chilies, for
*   garnish*

> **Serves 4**
> **Prep Time:** 10 minutes,
> plus 20 minutes to chill
> **Cook Time:** 10 minutes
>
> This raita is so versatile it can be served alongside almost any dish. And it is easy to whip up even when you are rushed.

1. Peel and cut the potatoes into ½-inch dice; boil in salted water to cover for 5 to 8 minutes or until just fork-tender. Drain.
2. In a bowl, combine the yogurt, water, cumin seeds, red chili powder, and salt; mix well. (Omit the water if you prefer a thicker consistency.) Add the potatoes and mix gently.
3. Chill, covered, for 20 minutes. Serve garnished with slit green chilies.

Red Onion Salad
(Rani Pyaz)

1 cup frozen pearl onions,
*   thawed*
½ cup white vinegar
½ cup water
½ teaspoon ground black mus-
*   tard seeds*

1 serrano green chili, seeded
*   and chopped*
½ teaspoon table salt
A few drops red food coloring
*   (optional)*

> **Yields 1 cup**
> **Prep Time:** 10 minutes
> **Cook Time:** 20 minutes,
> plus 48 hours to set
>
> These onions have a short shelf life, so use them up quickly.

1. Boil the pearl onions in about 2 cups of water for about 5 to 7 minutes. Drain and set aside.
2. In a deep pan, bring the vinegar and water to a boil. Remove from heat and set aside.
3. In a bowl, combine the pearl onions, mustard seeds, green chili, salt, and food coloring; mix well. Pour the vinegar-water liquid over the onion mixture.
4. Cool and transfer to an airtight container. Refrigerate for 48 hours.

South Indian Cucumber Salad
(Kheera Pachadi)

Serves 4
Prep Time: 15 minutes,
plus at least
30 minutes to chill
Cook Time: 5 minutes

Do not add the
cucumbers until 30
minutes before you
are ready to serve, or
the salad will become
too watery.

2 cups plain yogurt, *whipped*
½ teaspoon table salt
1 serrano green chili, *minced*
2 teaspoons chopped cilantro
1 teaspoon sugar
1 large seedless cucumber
1 tablespoon unsweetened desiccated coconut
1 tablespoon vegetable oil

½ teaspoon black mustard
   seeds
4 fresh curry leaves
1 dried red chili, *roughly
   pounded*
Pinch of asafetida (optional)

1. In a bowl, combine the yogurt, salt, green chili, cilantro, and sugar;
   mix well. Refrigerate, covered, for at least 30 minutes.
2. Peel and cut the cucumber into ½-inch dice, then refrigerate.
3. About 30 minutes before serving, drain the cucumber and add it to
   the yogurt mixture along with the coconut. Set aside.
4. In a small skillet, heat the vegetable oil. When the oil is close to
   smoking (after about 1 minute), quickly add the mustard seeds, curry
   leaves, red chili, and asafetida. As soon as the mustard seeds start to
   sputter, remove from heat.
5. Pour over the cucumber-yogurt mix and serve immediately.

☀ Curry Leaves

*Curry powder has no relation to and is not a substitute for curry
leaves. If you buy the leaves in bulk, you can freeze them for use
at a later date.*

Chicken Tikka Salad
(Murgh Tikke Ka Salaad)

1 small head lettuce
8 cherry tomatoes
1 small seedless cucumber
1 small red onion, peeled
2 tablespoons fresh lemon juice

4 cups Chicken Tikka (see recipe on page 26)
1 tablespoon Chaat Spice Mix (see recipe on page 16)

Serves 4
Prep Time: 10 minutes
Cook Time: None

Generally, in India, salads are not the main dish, but are served on the side. This dish, however, can definitely be an entire meal.

1. Wash the lettuce thoroughly. Drain well. Tear the lettuce leaves into bite-sized pieces and place in a bowl; set aside.
2. Cut the tomatoes, cucumber, and red onion into ½-inch dice. Place in a bowl, add the lemon juice, and toss well.
3. Add the Chicken Tikka to the cucumber mixture; mix well. Divide the mixture into 4 equal portions.
4. Place a few lettuce leaves in 4 salad bowls. Add 1 portion of the Chicken Tikka mixture to each. Sprinkle each salad bowl with ¼ teaspoon of Chaat Spice Mix, and serve.

Red Radish Salad
(Mooli Ka Salaad)

10 small red radishes
1 small seedless cucumber
1 tablespoon finely chopped cilantro

2 tablespoons fresh lemon juice
1 garlic clove, peeled and crushed
Table salt, to taste

Serves 4
Prep Time: 20 minutes
Cook Time: None

Serve this with Lamb Curry with Turnips (page 117) and Simple Naan Bread (page 207).

1. Cut off the tops of the radishes and julienne the radishes as finely as you can. Peel the cucumber, cut it into small pieces, and julienne.
2. In a bowl, combine all the ingredients; toss to mix well. Serve immediately.

Sesame Potato Salad
(Til Aur Aloo Ka Salaad)

Serves 4
Prep Time: 10 minutes
Cook Time: 10 minutes

Serve this alongside Spinach Bread (page 211) or Carom-Flavored Fried Bread (page 220). The complex flavors harmonize.

4 medium potatoes
1 serrano green chili, minced
1 tablespoon sesame seeds, roasted
2 tablespoons fresh lemon juice
Table salt, to taste
A few tablespoons warm water

1 dried red chili, roughly pounded
½ teaspoon freshly ground black pepper
Finely chopped cilantro, for garnish

1. Peel and cut the potatoes into ½-inch dice; boil in salted water, covered, for 5 to 8 minutes or until just fork-tender. Drain.
2. In a large mixing bowl, combine the potatoes, green chili, sesame seeds, lemon juice, and salt; mix well. Add the warm water and toss well.
3. When you are ready to serve, sprinkle with the dried red chili, ground black pepper, and the chopped cilantro. Serve immediately.

Carrot and Tomato Salad
(Gajar Aur Tamatar Ka Salaad)

Serves 4
Prep Time: 10 minutes, plus time to chill
Cook Time: None

This mild salad can be prepared ahead of time and chilled until you are ready to serve. Serve this with Spicy Shrimp Rice (page 182).

2 ripe small tomatoes
2 small carrots, peeled
1 tablespoon minced fresh mint leaves
2 tablespoons fresh lemon juice

1 teaspoon cumin seeds, roasted and roughly pounded
1 teaspoon sugar
Table salt, to taste
A few dates, finely chopped (optional)

1. Cut the tomatoes and carrots into ½-inch dice and place them in a bowl; set aside.
2. In a separate bowl, combine the mint leaves, lemon juice, cumin seeds, sugar, and salt; mix well.
3. Pour the mint-lemon mixture on the tomatoes and the carrots; toss well. Cover, and chill in the refrigerator. Serve topped with a few dates, if desired.

South Indian Mango Salad
(Amba Pachadi)

2 cups plain yogurt, whipped

½ teaspoon table salt

1 serrano green chili, minced

2 teaspoons finely chopped cilantro

1 teaspoon sugar

2 small green mangoes, peeled and diced

2 tablespoons unsweetened desiccated coconut

¼ cup mung beans, cooked (optional)

1 tablespoon vegetable oil

½ teaspoon black mustard seeds

4 fresh curry leaves

1 dried red chili, roughly pounded

Pinch of asafetida (optional)

Serves 4
Prep Time: 20 minutes, plus at least 30 minutes to chill
Cook Time: 5 minutes

Try making this salad without the yogurt. You could also use grated mangoes rather than diced ones.

1. In a bowl, combine the yogurt, salt, green chili, cilantro, and sugar; mix well. Add the mangoes and coconut; mix well. If you are using mung beans, add them now. Refrigerate, covered, for at least 30 minutes.

2. In a small skillet, heat the vegetable oil. When the oil is close to smoking (after about 1 minute), quickly add the mustard seeds, curry leaves, red chili, and asafetida. As soon as the mustard seeds start to sputter, remove from heat; pour over the yogurt mixture. Serve immediately.

❊ Raw Mangoes

Watch any old Indian movie, and the minute the leading lady reaches for a green mango, the audience gasps, "She's pregnant!" In India, it is believed that because of its sour taste, pregnant women crave this crisp raw fruit. For an easy snack, slice the mango (with skin), sprinkle with Chaat Spice Mix (page 16) or black salt, and enjoy!

Minty Potato in Yogurt Sauce
(Aloo Pudine Ka Raita)

Serves 4
Prep Time: 10 minutes
Cook Time: 10 minutes, plus 20 minutes to chill

Serve this dish alongside White Chicken Rice (page 175). You can also make this salad with minced cooked spinach instead of the mint.

3 small potatoes
2 cups plain yogurt, whipped
1 teaspoon cumin seeds, roasted and roughly pounded
¼ teaspoon red chili powder
¼ teaspoon black salt
2 tablespoons chopped fresh mint leaves
Chopped fresh red chilies, for garnish

1. Peel and cut the potatoes into ½-inch dice; boil in salted water, covered, for 5 to 8 minutes or until just fork-tender. Drain.
2. In a bowl, combine the yogurt, cumin seeds, red chili powder, and salt; mix well. Add the potatoes and mint leaves, mixing gently.
3. Chill, covered, for 20 minutes. Garnish with red chilies and serve.

Maharastrian Cabbage Salad
(Bundh Gobi Ka Salaad)

Serves 4
Prep Time: 20 minutes, plus at least 1 hour to chill
Cook Time: None

Serve with Coconut and Tomato Soup (page 53) and Green Peas Stuffing (page 215).

2 cups finely shredded cabbage
¼ cup finely shredded red bell pepper
¼ cup shredded baby spinach
½ cup unsweetened desiccated coconut
¼ cup salted, roasted peanuts, roughly pounded
2 tablespoons fresh lemon juice
Table salt, to taste
Finely chopped cilantro, for garnish
Crushed black pepper, to taste, for garnish

In a bowl, combine the cabbage, red bell peppers, spinach leaves, coconut, peanuts, lemon juice, and salt; mix well. Cover and chill in the refrigerator for at least 1 hour. Sprinkle with cilantro and black pepper to garnish before serving.

Maharastrian Bread and Corn Salad
(Sanja)

2 slices white bread
2 tablespoons vegetable oil
½ teaspoon black mustard
 seeds
1-inch piece fresh gingerroot,
 peeled and chopped
1 small red onion, peeled and
 minced
1 serrano green chili, seeded
 and minced

Table salt, to taste
¼ teaspoon turmeric powder
1 dried red chili, roughly
 pounded
2 cups corn kernels, cooked
¼ cup unsweetened desiccated
 coconut
1 tablespoon fresh lemon juice
2 tablespoons minced cilantro

> **Serves 4**
> **Prep Time:** 15 minutes
> **Cook Time:** 5–10 minutes
>
> You can serve this dish for breakfast along-side Saffron Lemonade (page 45) or Maharastrian Buttermilk (page 46).

1. Cut the bread into small pieces; set aside.
2. In a medium skillet, heat the oil. Add the mustard seeds and ginger. When the mustard seeds crackle, add the onions, green chili, salt, turmeric powder, and red chili. Sauté until the onions are transparent, about 2 to 3 minutes.
3. Add the bread and the corn kernels to the skillet. Mix well, and cook for another 2 to 3 minutes.
4. Remove from heat and transfer to a serving platter. Sprinkle with coconut, lemon juice, and cilantro. Serve warm.

❈ Corn for Breakfast

Yes, you can have corn for breakfast. Heat a medium skillet, add some sweet corn (creamed), tiny cubes of bell pepper, a little bit of butter, grated cheese, and a few tablespoons of milk; mix well. Season with salt and pepper to taste. Serve atop lightly buttered bread of your choice.

Punjabi Onion Salad
(Punjabi Laccha)

Serves 4
Prep Time: 5 minutes
Cook Time: None

Add Chaat Spice Mix (page 16) to this dish instead of salt for a unique tangy flavor.

1 red onion, peeled
2 serrano green chilies, sliced
1 tablespoon fresh lemon juice

Table salt, to taste
½ teaspoon minced cilantro

Slice the onion into rings and arrange on a platter. Top with the green chilies, then sprinkle with lemon juice and salt. Garnish with cilantro and serve.

Coconut Milk Salad
(Nariel Ka Raita)

Serves 4
Prep Time: 10 minutes, plus 20 minutes to chill
Cook Time: None

The Indian name for this dish is misleading, since the term raita generally refers to a dish that has yogurt. This dish uses coconut milk instead.

1 small red onion, peeled
1 small tomato
1-inch piece fresh ginger, grated
1 serrano green chili, seeded and minced
2 tablespoons minced cilantro

2 tablespoons dried coconut flakes or fresh shredded coconut
4–6 tablespoons light coconut milk
Table salt, to taste

Chop the onion and the tomato and place in a large bowl. Add the ginger, green chili, cilantro, coconut, and salt; mix well. Pour the coconut milk onto the salad. Cover and refrigerate for at least 20 minutes. Serve cold.

Pineapple Salad
(Ananas Ka Raita)

2 cups plain yogurt, whipped
1 teaspoon red chili powder
1 teaspoon cumin seeds,
*   roasted and roughly pounded*
1 cup pineapple chunks (fresh,
*   or canned and drained)*

Table salt, to taste
1 tablespoon vegetable oil
½ teaspoon black mustard
*   seeds*
4 fresh curry leaves

1. In a bowl, combine the yogurt, red chili powder, and cumin seeds; mix well.
2. Add the pineapple chunks and salt to the yogurt mixture, and mix well. Set aside.
3. In a medium skillet, heat the oil. Add the mustard seeds and curry leaves. When the mustard seeds crackle, remove from heat and pour over the yogurt salad. Serve immediately.

Serves 4
Prep Time: 10 minutes
Cook Time: 5 minutes

This dish is very popular in South India. Serve this alongside Ginger-Flavored Lamb Chops (page 129) for a unique combination of flavors.

Grape Salad
(Angoor Ka Raita)

1 cup seedless green grapes
1 cup seedless black grapes
¼ cup red raspberries
¼ cup blackberries
2 tablespoons dried coconut
*   flakes or fresh shredded*
*   coconut*

1 teaspoon sugar
Table salt, to taste
¼ teaspoon black pepper
½ cup light coconut milk

1. In a large bowl, combine the grapes, berries, and coconut. Add the sugar, salt, and black pepper; mix well.
2. Pour the coconut milk onto the salad. Cover and chill for at least 1 hour. Serve cold.

Serves 4
Prep Time: 5 minutes, plus at least 1 hour to chill
Cook Time: None

Try using jaggery instead of regular sugar for a special sweet taste. Eat this as a side dish with Spicy Minced Lamb Kebabs (page 128).

Spiced Taro Salad
(Chatpata Arvi Ka Salaad)

Serves 4
Prep Time: 10 minutes
Cook Time: 20 minutes

You can spike up this mild salad with a pinch of red chili powder. If you cannot find taro, try yams or sweet potatoes.

2 taro roots (also called dasheen), peeled
2 potatoes, peeled
2 tablespoons fresh lemon juice
½ teaspoon black salt
2 tablespoons minced cilantro, plus extra for garnish

1. Place the taro roots and potatoes in a pot with enough water to cover; boil until just fork-tender. Drain and let cool.
2. Cut the taro and potatoes into cubes and place them in a large bowl. Add the lemon juice, black salt, and cilantro to the bowl and mix well.
3. Serve immediately, garnished with cilantro.

Shredded Carrot Salad
(Gajar Ka Salaad)

Serves 4
Prep Time: 10 minutes
Cook Time: 5 minutes

This brightly colored salad is a perfect side dish for Malabari Chili Fish (page 151).

2 cups shredded carrots
2 tablespoons roasted peanuts, roughly pounded
1 serrano green chili, minced
2 tablespoons fresh lemon juice
1 tablespoon vegetable oil
½ teaspoon black mustard seeds
Table salt, to taste

1. In a bowl, combine the carrots, peanuts, green chili, and lemon juice; mix well. Set aside.
2. In a small skillet, heat the oil. Add the mustard seeds. When the seeds begin to crackle, remove from heat and pour over the carrots.
3. Add salt to taste and mix well. Serve immediately.

CHAPTER 6
From the Vegetable Market (Subzi Mandi Se)

Baby Potatoes in a Creamy Sauce
(Dum Aloo)

Serves 4
Prep Time: 5 minutes
Cook Time: 55 minutes

Serve with Fried
Indian Bread (page
206) or Puffed Bread
(page 218).

12–14 small new potatoes,
   unpeeled
4 cups, plus 2 tablespoons
   vegetable oil
1 teaspoon cumin seeds
1 teaspoon grated gingerroot
1 medium-sized red onion, minced
½ teaspoon red chili powder
¼ teaspoon turmeric powder
¼ teaspoon Warm Spice Mix
   (see recipe on page 14)

½ teaspoon coriander powder
2 cloves
½ teaspoon fennel seeds or
   anise seeds
1 (1-inch) cinnamon stick
1 cup puréed tomatoes (fresh
   or canned)
1 cup plain yogurt, whipped
1 cup warm water
Salt, to taste

1. Thoroughly wash the potatoes and boil in water for 10 to 12 minutes, until fork-tender. Drain and let cool.
2. Heat the 4 cups of oil in a deep pan at 370° on a deep-fry thermometer. Prick the potatoes all over with a fork (this will allow the spices to seep in). Add a few potatoes to the oil and deep-fry until brown. Remove the potatoes with a slotted spoon and place on paper towels to drain off excess oil. Continue until all of the potatoes are fried, letting the oil return to 370° between batches. Set aside.
3. In a large skillet, heat the remaining 2 tablespoons of oil on high. Heat until just below the smoking point (about 45 seconds), then add the cumin seeds. When they begin to pop, add the ginger and onions; sauté until the onions are golden brown.
4. In quick succession, add the red chili powder, turmeric powder, spice mix, coriander powder, cloves, fennel seeds, and cinnamon stick. Stirring continuously, fry for about 30 seconds. Add the tomatoes and continue to stir for another 2 to 3 minutes. Add the yogurt and cook for another 5 minutes. Add the potatoes and fry for 1 more minute, stirring constantly. Add the water and return to a boil.
5. Reduce the heat, cover, and cook for about 20 minutes. Add salt to taste. Remove from heat and stir well. Serve hot.

Cheese and Spinach Curry
(Paalak Paneer)

2 tablespoons vegetable oil

1 medium-sized red onion, peeled and minced

2½ teaspoons Ginger-Garlic Paste (page 15)

¼ cup tomato purée (fresh or canned)

2 serrano green chilies, seeded and minced (optional)

¼ teaspoon turmeric powder

½ teaspoon Warm Spice Mix (page 14)

½ teaspoon cumin powder

½ teaspoon coriander powder

¼ teaspoon red chili powder

Table salt, to taste

1 (10-ounce) package chopped frozen spinach, thawed

½ cup water, at room temperature

1 cup Indian Cheese, fried (see below)

1 tablespoon heavy cream, for garnish

> **Serves 4**
> **Prep Time:** 10 minutes
> **Cook Time:** 45 minutes
>
> You can purée the spinach before you begin if you like your sauce really creamy. Serve this with hot Simple Naan Bread (page 207).

1. In a medium-sized pan, heat the vegetable oil on medium. Add the onion and fry, stirring continuously until the onions are golden brown in color, about 5 minutes.
2. Add the Ginger-Garlic Paste and sauté for 1 minute. Add the tomato purée and cook for 2 minutes.
3. Quickly add the green chilies, turmeric powder, spice mix, cumin powder, coriander powder, red chili powder, and salt; sauté for 30 seconds.
4. Add the spinach and fry for about 3 minutes, stirring constantly. Add the water and cook, uncovered, on low heat for about 20 minutes. If the mixture starts to dry out, add more water. Cook until the spinach is soft.
5. Add the Indian Cheese to the spinach mixture; sauté, uncovered, for 5 minutes. Garnish with the heavy cream and serve hot.

✻ Where Can I Find Fried Indian Cheese?

You can buy prefried Indian cheese (paneer) at your local Indian grocer. If you want to fry it at home, prepare the paneer as described on page 14. In a deep skillet, heat oil on medium. Pan-fry a few pieces of paneer until golden brown on all sides. Remove and place on a paper towel to absorb excess oil.

Punjabi Mustard Greens
(Sarson Da Saag)

Serves 4
Prep Time: 5 minutes
Cook Time: 45 minutes

This is a delicious dish from the Indian state of Punjab. Serve along with Indian Corn Flatbread (page 223).

1 pound frozen mustard leaves, thawed

¼ pound frozen spinach leaves, thawed

1 small turnip, peeled and diced

3 cups water (or more, as needed)

2 tablespoons Clarified Butter (see recipe on page 17)

1 teaspoon Ginger-Garlic Paste (see recipe on page 15)

2 tablespoons cornmeal

Table salt, to taste

Butter, cut into cubes, for garnish

1. In a deep pan, combine the mustard leaves, spinach leaves, and turnip. Add about 2 cups of the water and bring to a boil. Cook until the turnips become tender, about 12 minutes. Remove from heat and drain any water. Let the vegetables cool to room temperature.

2. Use a food processor to purée the vegetable mixture into a thick paste. Set aside.

3. In a large pan, heat the Clarified Butter, add the Ginger-Garlic Paste, and sauté for 30 seconds. Add the vegetable purée; sauté for 2 minutes. Add the cornmeal to the skillet and mix well. To ensure that the cornmeal does not form lumps, use the back of your cooking spoon to blend it in. Add salt to taste.

4. Add 1 cup of water to the skillet. Simmer for 25 minutes on low heat. Add more water if the vegetables start to become dry. Serve hot, garnished with a few butter cubes.

❋ Cornmeal Does Come from Corn

Cornmeal comes from maize, or corn, as the name suggests. This coarse yellow flour is used to provide texture to dishes. Don't mistake it for cornstarch, which is white and powdery and generally used as a thickening agent.

Potato Sticks
(Bengali Aloo Charchari)

4 medium potatoes, peeled
1 small red onion, peeled
2 tablespoons vegetable oil
¼ teaspoon turmeric powder

½ teaspoon red chili powder
Table salt, to taste
Approximately ¼ cup water,
* at room temperature*

> **Serves 4**
> **Prep Time:** 10 minutes
> **Cook Time:** 20 minutes
>
> Bengal, a state in eastern India where this dish originates, is often called Sonar Bangla (Golden Bengal) because of the fields of mustard that cover the countryside.

1. Cut the potatoes and the onions lengthwise, as you would for fries. Set aside.
2. In a medium-sized skillet, heat the vegetable oil on medium. Add the onions and sauté until transparent, about 3 to 4 minutes.
3. Add the potatoes to the skillet; sauté for another 3 to 5 minutes.
4. Add the turmeric, red chili powder, and salt to the skillet; sauté, stirring constantly, for 1 minute.
5. Add the water, cover, and cook until the potatoes are soft.

❋ Bengali Panch Phoron

Panch phoron, or five-spice mix, is a trademark of Bengali cuisine. Not to be confused with the Chinese five-spice powder, this mixture contains fennel, cumin, mustard, fenugreek, and wild fennel seeds (also called nigella seeds). Unlike some of the other spice mixes discussed in this book, this mix is stored unroasted. The seeds in the mixture are whole and not pounded.

Roasted Eggplant
(Baigan Ka Bhartha)

Serves 4
Prep Time: 10 minutes
Cook Time: 1 hour

To get an authentic smoked flavor, roast the eggplant over hot charcoal.

3 pounds eggplant (about 2 medium-sized eggplants)
4 tablespoons vegetable oil
1 small red onion, peeled and roughly chopped
1 teaspoon Ginger-Garlic Paste (see recipe on page 15)

¼ teaspoon red chili powder
1 teaspoon coriander powder
2 medium tomatoes, finely chopped
Table salt, to taste
Fresh chopped cilantro, for garnish (optional)

1. Preheat oven to 475°.
2. Brush the eggplant with 2 tablespoons of the vegetable oil. Place the eggplant on a foil-lined baking sheet and place it in the oven. Cook until the eggplant is soft and the skin is charred, about 40 minutes. Remove from the oven to cool.
3. Peel the eggplant and discard the skin. Mash the eggplant with a fork into a smooth pulp. Set aside.
4. In a large skillet, heat the remaining 2 tablespoons of vegetable oil over medium heat. Add the onions and sauté until transparent. Add the Ginger-Garlic Paste, red chili powder, and coriander powder; sauté for 30 seconds.
5. Add the tomatoes and sauté for about 5 minutes, stirring constantly. Use the back of your spatula to mash the tomatoes. When the mixture is ready, oil will start to separate from the mixture.
6. Add the eggplant and salt; mix well. Fry for about 7 to 10 minutes, stirring constantly. Remove from heat. Serve hot and garnish with cilantro (optional).

✸ Roasting Eggplants
You can use the burner on your gas stove to roast eggplant. Use tongs to hold the eggplant over the flame. Rotate constantly until all the sides are charred and the eggplant is roasted completely.

Mixed Vegetables
(Makki Ki Subzi)

2 tablespoons vegetable oil

½ teaspoon black mustard seeds

4–5 fresh curry leaves

1-inch piece ginger, peeled and julienned

2 cups cooked corn kernels or canned corn kernels, drained

1 red bell pepper, seeded and diced

1 green bell pepper, seeded and diced

1 yellow bell pepper, seeded and diced

1 dried red chili, crushed

Water, if needed

2 tablespoons unsweetened desiccated coconut

¼ teaspoon sugar

Table salt, to taste

> **Serves 4**
> **Prep Time:** 15 minutes
> **Cook Time:** 15 minutes
>
> The colors of the bell pepper make this dish very striking in appearance. Serve these with Spinach Bread (page 211) or Seasoned Bread (page 212).

1. In a large skillet, heat the vegetable oil on medium. Add the mustard seeds. When they begin to crackle, add the curry leaves and ginger. Sauté for a few seconds.
2. Add the corn, all the bell peppers, and the dried red chili. Sauté for several minutes until the bell peppers are tender. If the mixture starts to stick, add a few tablespoons of water at a time.
3. Add the coconut, sugar, and salt; sauté for 1 more minute. Serve hot.

❋ Chilies That Bite

If you bite into a green chili, don't reach for the water; it will not help soothe your mouth. Instead, use some sugar or plain yogurt to get instant relief from the heat.

Royal Mushrooms with Cashew Nut Sauce
(Nawabi Guchhi)

Serves 4
Prep Time: 10 minutes, plus 20 minutes to soak
Cook Time: 45 minutes

The Nawabs, the Muslim royals of ancient India, introduced nuts into Indian cuisine.

2 tablespoons unsalted cashew nuts
4 tablespoons vegetable oil
2 green cardamom pods
1 black cardamom pod
2 cloves
1 (1-inch) cinnamon stick
1 bay leaf
1 teaspoon minced garlic
½ teaspoon red chili powder
1 teaspoon coriander powder
1 small red onion, minced
Water, as needed
½ cup plain yogurt, whipped
½ cup whole milk
1 pound white button mushrooms, cleaned
Table salt, to taste

1. Soak the cashews in a cup of water for about 20 minutes. Drain and grind to a paste in a food processor. Set aside.
2. In a medium skillet, heat the vegetable oil on medium. Quickly add the green cardamom, black cardamom, cloves, cinnamon stick, bay leaf, and minced garlic; sauté for about 30 seconds.
3. Add the red chili powder, coriander powder, and minced onion; sauté for 2 minutes. If the spice mixture sticks to the pan, add a few tablespoons of water. Continue to sauté until the onions are golden brown, about 7 minutes. Add the cashew nut paste, and stir for 1 more minute.
4. Add the yogurt and milk; mix well. Simmer on low heat until the oil starts to separate from the spice mixture. If you prefer a thinner consistency, add water.
5. Add the mushrooms and salt, and cook for about 5 to 8 minutes or until the mushrooms are cooked completely. Serve hot.

☀ The Value of Fresh

One simple tip, worth its weight in gold, is to use fresh spices. If your spices do not have any aroma, they have lost their potency and should not be used. Fresh spices can completely alter the taste of a dish.

Dill and Potato
(Aloo Soa Ki Subzi)

2 tablespoons vegetable oil
½ teaspoon cumin seeds
2 green chilies, seeded and
   minced
3 medium potatoes, peeled
   and diced

½ cup frozen peas, thawed
¼ cup chopped fresh dill
¼ teaspoon turmeric powder
Table salt, to taste
Water, as needed

1. In a medium-sized skillet, heat the oil on medium. Add the cumin seeds. When they begin to crackle, add the green chilies; sauté for 10 seconds.
2. Add the potatoes and sauté for about 2 minutes. Add the peas, dill, turmeric, and salt; sauté for another 2 minutes.
3. Add a few tablespoons of water, cover, and cook on low heat until the potatoes and peas are cooked through, about 10 to 12 minutes. Serve hot.

Whole-Milk Fudge and Peas Curry
(Khoya Wale Matar)

2 tablespoons vegetable oil
1 (1-inch) cinnamon stick
2 cloves
1 teaspoon cumin seeds
½ teaspoon red chili powder
¼ teaspoon turmeric

1 teaspoon coriander powder
½ cup plain yogurt, whipped
2 cups frozen peas, thawed
½ cup Whole-Milk Fudge (see
   recipe on page 17)
Table salt, to taste

1. In a medium skillet, heat the oil on medium. Add the cinnamon stick, cloves, and cumin seeds. When the seeds begin to sizzle, add the red chili powder, turmeric powder, and coriander; stir for 10 seconds.
2. Add the yogurt and mix well. Sauté for about 5 minutes, or until the oil starts to separate from the spice mixture.
3. Add the peas, Whole-Milk Fudge, and salt. Simmer for about 10 minutes or until the peas are tender. Serve hot.

Chili Pepper Curry
(Mirchi Ka Salan)

Serves 4
Prep Time: 20 minutes
Cook Time: 30 minutes

This dish is not for the weak of stomach or heart. Serve this with Simple Basmati Rice (page 162) and a large pitcher of cold water!

8 large green chilies, (anaheim or cubanelle)
1 teaspoon tamarind pulp
1 teaspoon cumin seeds
2 teaspoons coriander seeds
1/4 teaspoon fenugreek seeds
1 teaspoon white poppy seeds
2 tablespoons sesame seeds
2 1/2 tablespoons unsweetened desiccated coconut

4 tablespoons vegetable oil
1 small red onion, minced
1 tablespoon Ginger-Garlic Paste (see recipe on page 15)
1/4 teaspoon red chili powder
1/4 teaspoon turmeric powder
Table salt, to taste
1 cup warm water

1. Remove the stems from the green chilies. Cut a slit down the side of each chili to remove the seeds, but don't separate the halves; discard the stems and seeds and set aside the chilies. Add the tamarind pulp to 2 tablespoons of warm water and set aside to soak.
2. In a small skillet, roast the cumin, coriander, fenugreek, poppy, and sesame seeds. As the spices start to darken and release their aroma (less than 1 minute), add the coconut and roast for another 15 seconds. Remove from heat and let cool. Grind to a powder using a pestle and mortar or spice grinder.
3. In a large skillet, heat the oil on medium. Add the green chilies. As soon as the chilies develop brown spots, use a slotted spoon to remove them from the skillet and set aside. In the same oil, sauté the minced onions and the Ginger-Garlic Paste until the onions are golden brown.
4. Add the red chili and turmeric powder, salt, and ground spices. Mix well and sauté for 2 minutes. Return the green chilies to the pan and add the water. Simmer, covered, for 5 to 8 minutes.
5. Strain the tamarind and discard the residue. Add the strained tamarind pulp and mix well. Cook for 1 more minute. Serve hot.

Fried Okra
(Bharwan Bhindi)

1½ pounds okra
1 tablespoon coriander powder
2 teaspoons turmeric powder
1½ teaspoons (or to taste) red chili powder
2 teaspoons Warm Spice Mix (see recipe on page 14)
2 teaspoons cumin powder
1 teaspoon dried mango powder

4 tablespoons vegetable oil
1 medium-sized red onion, peeled and chopped
1 tablespoon Ginger-Garlic Paste (see recipe on page 15)
2 serrano green chilies, slit lengthwise
Table salt, to taste
Water, as needed

Serves 4
Prep Time: 20 minutes
Cook Time: 20 minutes

Serve this with Red Radish Salad (page 63) and Simple Indian Bread (page 204).

1. Wash the okra and dry it well. Cut the stalk off each piece and make a lengthwise slit. Be careful not to cut all the way through.
2. In a bowl, combine the coriander powder, turmeric powder, red chili powder, spice mix, cumin powder, and dried mango powder. Mix well and set aside.
3. Using the pointed end of a knife or a tiny spoon, stuff a little bit of the dry spice mixture into each piece of okra.
4. In a large skillet, heat the oil on medium. Add the onions and the Ginger-Garlic Paste; sauté for about 3 minutes, until the onions are transparent. Add the okra and green chilies, and sauté for about 4 minutes. Add the salt and any remaining dry spice mixture. Reduce the heat to medium-low.
5. Add about 3 tablespoons of water, cover, and cook for about 10 minutes or until the okra is fork-tender. Serve hot.

Cabbage with Black Mustard Seeds
(Muttakos Poriyal)

Serves 4
Prep Time: 10 minutes
Cook Time: 15 minutes

Poriyals, or dried spiced vegetables, originated in southern India. Serve this with Lemon Rice (page 167).

2 tablespoons vegetable oil
1 teaspoon black mustard seeds
2 small dried red chilies, roughly pounded
8 fresh curry leaves

1 pound cabbage, finely shredded
Table salt, to taste
½ teaspoon turmeric powder
¼ teaspoon red chili powder
2 tablespoons coconut flakes

1. Heat the vegetable oil on medium. Add the mustard seeds, red chilies, and curry leaves. When the mustard seeds begin to crackle, add the cabbage.
2. Sauté the cabbage for 2 minutes. Add the salt, turmeric, and red chili powder; mix well and sauté for 1 more minute.
3. Cover, and cook on low heat until the cabbage is tender, about 8 minutes, stirring occasionally. If the cabbage is sticking to the pan, add a few tablespoons of water.
4. Add the coconut and cook for another 2 minutes over medium heat.

Dry-Spiced Carrot and Peas
(Gajar Mattar Ki Subzi)

Serves 4
Prep Time: 5 minutes
Cook Time: 20 minutes

The carrots and peas sautéed in cumin provide a healthy dish with a mild flavor.

2 tablespoons vegetable oil
1 teaspoon cumin seeds
2 medium carrots (fresh or frozen), peeled and diced
2 cups peas (fresh or frozen)

½ teaspoon red chili powder
¼ teaspoon turmeric powder
1 teaspoon coriander powder
Table salt, to taste
Water, as needed

1. In a medium-sized skillet, heat the vegetable oil over high heat. Add the cumin seeds. When the seeds begin to sizzle, add the carrots and peas; sauté for about 2 minutes.
2. Add the dry spices and salt, and mix well; sauté for about 2 minutes (if the dry spices begin to stick, add a few tablespoons of water).
3. Reduce the heat and add 2 to 3 tablespoons of water to the skillet. Cover and cook for about 15 minutes or until the carrots and peas are cooked. Serve hot.

Stir-Fried Cauliflower
(Gobi Ki Subzi)

1½ pounds cauliflower
3 tablespoons vegetable oil
1-inch piece fresh gingerroot,
    julienned
2 teaspoons coriander powder

½ teaspoon red chili powder
¼ teaspoon turmeric powder
Table salt, to taste
Water, as needed

Serves 4
Prep Time: 5 minutes
Cook Time:
15–20 minutes

If you have any left-over, use it in the recipe for Cauliflower Stuffing (page 214) to make some delicious stuffed bread.

1. Break the cauliflower into small florets. Set aside.
2. In a large skillet, heat the vegetable oil on high. Add the ginger and sauté for about 10 seconds. Add the cauliflower florets and sauté for about 3 to 4 minutes. Add the coriander, red chili, and turmeric powder; sauté for 1 minute.
3. Reduce the heat to low. Add the salt and 2 to 3 tablespoons of water. Cover and cook until the cauliflower is done, about 5 to 10 minutes. Serve hot.

Fenugreek-Flavored Potatoes
(Methi Aloo Ki Subzi)

4 medium potatoes
3 tablespoons vegetable oil
2 garlic cloves, crushed
2 tablespoons dried fenugreek
    leaves

¼ teaspoon turmeric powder
½ teaspoon red chili powder
1½ teaspoons coriander powder
Table salt, to taste
Water, as needed

Serves 4
Prep Time: 10 minutes
Cook Time:
15–20 minutes

If you want to use fresh fenugreek leaves in this dish, add about ¼ cup of the fresh leaves, minced.

1. Peel and dice the potatoes. Set aside.
2. In a large skillet, heat the vegetable oil on high. Add the garlic cloves and the potatoes; sauté for about 2 minutes.
3. Add the fenugreek leaves; turmeric, red chili, and coriander powder. Sauté for 1 minute, then add salt.
4. Reduce the heat and add 2 to 3 tablespoons of water. Cover and cook for about 8 to 10 minutes or until the potatoes are soft. Serve hot.

Potato Curry
(Assami Ril Do)

Serves 4
Prep Time: 10 minutes
Cook Time: 40 minutes

Serve this mouthwa-
tering curry with hot
Puffed Bread
(page 218).

10 small baby potatoes, peeled
3 tablespoons vegetable oil
2 teaspoons Ginger-Garlic Paste
  (see recipe on page 15)
1 dried red chili, roughly
  pounded

¼ teaspoon turmeric
1 small tomato, finely chopped
½ cup plain yogurt, whipped
½ cup water
Table salt, to taste

1. Boil the potatoes in water to cover until just fork-tender; drain. Lightly prick the potatoes with a fork. Set aside.
2. In a large skillet, heat the oil on high. Add the Ginger-Garlic Paste and sauté for about 10 seconds. Add the dried red chili and turmeric; mix well. Add the tomatoes and sauté for another 2 to 3 minutes.
3. Add the yogurt and cook for about 5 minutes. Add the potatoes. Sauté for 1 minute. Add the water and lower the heat. Cover, and cook for about 20 minutes. Add salt to taste. Serve hot.

✵ Avoid Staining Your Tupperware

Turmeric will turn things yellow—your Tupperware, for instance. To avoid staining any Tupperware in which you store turmeric-flavored dishes, spray the Tupperware with nonstick spray before using it.

Garlic Cauliflower
(Lehsuni Gobi Manchurian)

2 tablespoons corn flour

4 tablespoons all-purpose white
flour

¼ teaspoon white pepper
powder

¼ teaspoon table salt

1 tablespoon minced garlic

Vegetable oil for deep-frying,
plus 1 tablespoon

1 small head cauliflower,
broken into small florets

1 teaspoon finely minced garlic

2 teaspoons light soya sauce

1 teaspoon vinegar

2 tablespoons tomato ketchup

3 spring onions, finely chopped

1 tablespoon corn flour, dissolved in ¼ cup cold water

Water, as needed

> **Serves 4**
> **Prep Time:** 15 minutes
> **Cook Time:** 20 minutes
>
> Tomato ketchup is
> very popular in India
> and is often used in
> cooking. Serve this
> dish with steaming hot
> Vegetable Fried Rice
> (page 176).

1. In a mixing bowl, mix the 2 tablespoons corn flour, the white flour, pepper, salt, and 1 tablespoon minced garlic. Add enough water to make a thin batter.

2. In a deep pan, heat about 1 inch of vegetable oil to 370° on a deep-fry thermometer. Dip each piece of cauliflower in the batter and add to the hot oil, a few pieces at a time. Deep-fry until golden brown. Remove the cauliflower using a slotted spoon. Place the cauliflower on a paper towel to drain. Let the oil return to temperature and continue until all the cauliflower is fried. Set aside.

3. In a large skillet, heat the 1 tablespoon vegetable oil on medium. Add the finely minced garlic and sauté for 10 seconds. Quickly add the soya sauce, vinegar, tomato ketchup, and spring onions; cook for about 1 minute. Add water to desired consistency. Add more salt to taste, if desired. Simmer for about 5 minutes.

4. Add the corn flour dissolved in water and mix well. Add the cauliflower florets. Serve hot.

South Indian Rice and Vegetable Delight
(Bissi Bela Hulianna)

Serves 4
Prep Time: 15 minutes, plus 1 hour to soak
Cook Time: 60 minutes

Don't let the long list of ingredients worry you; you can buy the spice mix premade. I recommend the MTR's bissi bela hulianna.

½ cup pigeon peas (toor dal)
1½ cups basmati rice
½ cup cauliflower florets (fresh or frozen)
½ cup peas (fresh or frozen)
1 tablespoon vegetable oil
1 tablespoon chana dal or yellow split peas
¾ tablespoon split black gram, or black lentils (safeed urad dal)
1 (1-inch) cinnamon stick
2 cloves
2 teaspoons coriander seeds

½ teaspoon cumin seeds
½ teaspoon black mustard seeds
½ teaspoon fenugreek seeds
2 tablespoons unsweetened desiccated coconut
2 small tomatoes, finely chopped
1 tablespoon tamarind pulp, soaked in ¼ cup water for 10 minutes
½ teaspoon red chili powder
¼ teaspoon turmeric powder
Table salt, to taste

1. Rinse the *toor dal* 3 or 4 times; soak in 3 cups of water for 1 hour. Meanwhile, rinse the rice until the water runs clear; soak for 30 minutes in enough water to cover.

2. Bring the *toor dal* to a boil, using the soaking water, and cook for about 25 minutes. Drain and set aside. In a deep pan, combine the *toor dal*, the drained basmati rice, cauliflower, and peas. Add about 5 cups water and bring to a boil. Cover and simmer until the rice and vegetables are cooked through, about 15 to 20 minutes.

3. In a medium-sized skillet, heat the vegetable oil. Add the *chana dal*, *safeed urad dal*, cinnamon, cloves, coriander, cumin, mustard, and fenugreek seeds; sauté for about 1 minute or until the spices release their aroma. Remove from heat and let cool, about 6 minutes. Add the coconut. Using a spice grinder, grind this to a powder. Set aside.

4. When the rice is done cooking, add the tomatoes, tamarind pulp, red chili, and turmeric powder, and salt. Add the reserved spice mix. Stir well. Simmer until the tomatoes are soft, about 15 minutes. Add more water, if needed. (The consistency of the dish should be like thick porridge.) Serve hot.

Mixed Vegetables in Coconut Sauce
(Avial)

1 cup unsweetened desiccated coconut

1 tablespoon cumin seeds, toasted

2 serrano green chilies, seeded

½ pounds carrots, peeled

2 small potatoes, peeled

1 green banana or plantain, peeled (optional)

½ pound frozen cut green beans, thawed

½ cup plain yogurt, whipped

½ teaspoon turmeric powder

Table salt, to taste

1 tablespoon vegetable oil

1 teaspoon black mustard seeds

8 curry leaves

> **Serves 4**
> **Prep Time:** 15 minutes
> **Cook Time:** 10–15 minutes
>
> Use your choice of seasonal vegetables to make this dish. Serve with Simple Basmati Rice (page 162) and your choice of any hot pickle.

1. In a food processor, grind the coconut, cumin seeds, and green chilies along with a few tablespoons of water, to make a thick paste. Set aside.
2. Cut the carrots and potatoes into ¼-inch sticks. Peel and chop the banana. In a deep pan, combine the carrots, potatoes, banana, and green beans and enough water to just cover the vegetables. Cook over medium heat until the vegetables are soft, about 5 to 7 minutes. Drain off any remaining water.
3. Add the yogurt, the reserved coconut paste, turmeric, and salt to the vegetables. Simmer until the vegetables are completely cooked through, another 3 or 4 minutes. Remove from heat and set aside.
4. In a small skillet, heat the vegetable oil on medium. Add the mustard seeds and curry leaves. When the seeds begin to crackle, remove from heat and pour over the cooked vegetables. Serve hot.

※ Vegetable Drumsticks

The next time you are at your Indian grocer, ask for a can of vegetable drumsticks, and use it in this dish. Add this along with the other vegetables in Step 2. These delightful vegetables add something special to your dishes. Eat only the jellylike portion inside, discarding the outside skin.

Maharastrian Potatoes
(Batate Che Bhajji)

Serves 4
Prep Time: 5 minutes
Cook Time: 10 minutes

Serve these atop warm Simple Indian Bread (page 204) with Dry Garlic Chutney (page 228) on the side.

4 medium potatoes, peeled
½ teaspoon tamarind pulp, soaked in ¼ cup warm water for 10 minutes
2 tablespoons vegetable oil

½ teaspoon black mustard seeds
6–8 fresh curry leaves
¼ teaspoon turmeric powder
½ teaspoon red chili powder
Table salt, to taste

Dice the potatoes and boil in water for 5 to 8 minutes. Roughly mash the potatoes and set aside. Strain the tamarind pulp and discard the residue. Set aside. Heat the vegetable oil on medium. Add the mustard seeds; when they begin to crackle, add the curry leaves. Sauté for about 30 seconds. Add the mashed potatoes, tamarind pulp, turmeric powder, red chili powder, and salt; mix well. Sauté for about 3 minutes, adding a few tablespoons of water if the mixture starts sticking. Serve hot.

Bengali Potatoes
(Aloo Pooshto)

Serves 4
Prep Time: 10 minutes
Cook Time: 20 minutes

Use Indian white poppy seeds for this recipe. You must dry roast these, prior to cooking, to bring out their flavor.

4 medium potatoes, peeled
2 tablespoons white poppy seeds
3 tablespoons vegetable oil

½ teaspoon turmeric powder
½ teaspoon red chili powder
Table salt, to taste

Cut the potatoes into ½-inch dice. Set aside. Heat a small skillet on medium. Dry roast the poppy seeds until they start to change color, stirring constantly. Remove from heat and let the seeds cool. In a spice grinder, grind the seeds into a thick paste using a few tablespoons of water. Set aside. In a large skillet, heat the vegetable oil on medium. Add the potatoes, and sauté for 4 to 5 minutes. Add the poppy seed paste, turmeric powder, red chili powder, and salt; mix well. Sauté for another 2 to 3 minutes. Add about ½ cup water. Cover, and cook until the potatoes are tender, about 10 to 12 minutes. Serve hot.

Cauliflower Takatak
(Gobi Takatak)

*Vegetable oil for deep-frying,
   plus 2 tablespoons*
*1 small head cauliflower,
   broken into florets*
1 teaspoon cumin seeds
*1 small red onion, finely
   chopped*
1 tablespoon grated gingerroot

Table salt, to taste
¼ teaspoon red chili powder
*1 teaspoon dried fenugreek
   leaves*
½ cup plain yogurt, whipped
1 small tomato, finely chopped

Serves 4
Prep Time: 15 minutes
Cook Time: 30 minutes

Serve this dish immediately. Letting it sit for too long will make the cauliflower lose its crispiness.

1. Heat the oil in a deep pan or deep fryer to 375° on a deep-fry thermometer. Fry a few cauliflower florets at a time until golden brown. Remove from the oil with a slotted spoon and transfer to a paper towel to drain. Let oil return to temperature and continue until all the florets are fried. Set aside.
2. In a large skillet, heat the 2 tablespoons vegetable oil on medium. Add the cumin seeds. When they begin to sizzle, add the onions and ginger; sauté for 2 to 3 minutes, until the onions are transparent.
3. Add the salt, red chili powder, dried fenugreek leaves, and yogurt. Mix well and sauté for about 1 minute.
4. Add the tomatoes and fried cauliflower. Mix well and sauté for 1 to 2 minutes or until the cauliflower is heated through. Serve hot.

❈ Ginger Tips
To make ginger easier to grate, freeze it first. When buying ginger, choose young ginger that has not dried out.

Green Beans with Coconut
(Nariel Wale Hare Beans)

Serves 4
Prep Time: 10 minutes
Cook Time: 10–12 minutes

Serve this with the Malabari Coconut Rice (page 179).

2 tablespoons butter
1 teaspoon vegetable oil
½ teaspoon black mustard seeds
Pinch of asafetida
2 dried red chilies, roughly pounded
½ teaspoon turmeric powder

1 pound frozen cut green beans, thawed
Table salt, to taste
Water, as needed
2 tablespoons unsweetened desiccated coconut
2 tablespoons minced cilantro

1. In a large skillet, heat the butter and oil on medium. Add the mustard seeds and the asafetida. When the seeds begin to crackle, add the red chilies and the turmeric powder; then add the green beans and sauté for about 3 to 4 minutes.
2. Add salt to taste and about ½ cup of water. Cover and cook until the beans are almost cooked through, about 3 to 4 minutes.
3. Add the coconut and cilantro. Simmer for another 3 to 4 minutes. Serve hot.

❊ Snipping Herbs

Use kitchen shears to snip herbs like cilantro or mint; it is much easier than trying to cut them with a knife. Snip only as much as you need, since cut herbs do not store well.

CHAPTER 7
Chicken and Egg (Murgh Aur Ande)

Lollipop Chicken
(Lollipop Murgh)

2 tablespoons Ginger-Garlic Paste
  (see recipe on page 15)
4 tablespoons all-purpose flour
4 tablespoons corn flour
3 tablespoons soya sauce
1 teaspoon red chili powder
1 teaspoon sugar
½ tablespoon white vinegar
Water, as needed
8–10 small chicken drumsticks
  or chicken wings, skinned
1½ cups vegetable oil

1. In a large bowl, combine the Ginger-Garlic Paste, all-purpose flour, corn flour, soya sauce, red chili powder, sugar, and vinegar. Add enough water to make a thin, smooth consistency. Add the chicken and refrigerate for 3 to 4 hours.
2. In a deep pan, heat 5 to 6 tablespoons of vegetable oil. Add a few pieces of chicken to the oil, and pan-fry until crisp. If the oil begins to splatter, you can cover the pan with a splatter guard or a cover. Continue until all the pieces are cooked. Discard any remaining marinade.
3. Remove the chicken pieces and place on a paper towel to drain off any excess oil. Serve immediately.

❈ Light Spinach Salad

A spinach salad is the perfect side to many meat dishes in this book. Tear up some baby spinach leaves and place them in a bowl. Add 1 cup of green mango and a handful of pecans or walnuts. Add lemon juice and a pinch of Chaat Spice Mix (page 16). Mix well and serve.

Chicken with Pickling Spices
(Murgh Achari)

2 tablespoons mustard oil or
vegetable oil
½ teaspoon black mustard
seeds
½ teaspoon wild fennel seeds
(also called nigella seeds)
2 dried red chilies
¼ teaspoon fenugreek seeds
1 tablespoon Ginger-Garlic Paste
(see recipe on page 15)

8 skinless chicken thighs
½ teaspoon red chili powder
¼ teaspoon turmeric powder
Table salt, to taste
1 cup plain yogurt
1 cup water
Juice of ½ lemon

> **Serves 4–5**
> **Prep Time:** 10 minutes
> **Cook Time:**
> 30–35 minutes
>
> You can also substitute Indian Cheese (page 14), lamb, or potatoes for the chicken in this recipe—just adjust the cooking times accordingly.

1. In a large skillet, heat the oil until almost smoking. Reduce the heat to medium. Quickly add the mustard and nigella seeds, red chilies, and fenugreek seeds. Fry for about 30 seconds or until the seeds start to change color and release their aroma.
2. Add the Ginger-Garlic Paste and sauté for another 10 seconds. Add the chicken and sauté for about 2 minutes. Reduce heat to medium.
3. Add the red chili, and turmeric powder, and salt; sauté until the chicken is well browned on all sides.
4. Add the yogurt and mix well. Add about 1 cup of water. Reduce the heat to low, cover the skillet, and cook for 20 to 25 minutes or until the chicken is cooked and the fat begins to surface.
5. Add the lemon juice and cook for 1 more minute. Serve hot.

※ Cooking with Mustard Oil

Mustard oil is very pungent. When you are using it, make sure it's smoking hot first, then decrease the heat. It's now ready for use. Smoking the oil allows you to enjoy the taste without the pungency.

Ginger-Flavored Chicken Curry
(Murgh Adraki)

Serves 4–5
Prep Time: 10 minutes, plus 3–4 hours to marinate
Cook Time: 20–30 minutes

Use fresh tender ginger for this recipe. Serve with plain Simple Naan Bread (page 207).

2 tablespoons grated gingerroot
1 teaspoon coriander powder
1 teaspoon Warm Spice Mix (see recipe on page 14)
½ teaspoon red chili powder
¾ cup plain yogurt, whipped
4 tablespoons vegetable oil, divided

8 skinless chicken thighs
½ teaspoon cumin seeds
1 black cardamom pod
1 bay leaf
2 medium-sized fresh tomatoes, puréed
Table salt, to taste
Water, as needed

1. In a large bowl or resealable plastic bag, combine the ginger, coriander powder, spice mix, red chili powder, yogurt, and 2 tablespoons of the vegetable oil; mix well. Add the chicken and coat all pieces evenly with the marinade. Cover and refrigerate for 3 to 4 hours.
2. In a large skillet, heat the remaining 2 tablespoons of vegetable oil. Add the cumin seeds, cardamom, and bay leaf. When the seeds begin to sizzle, add the tomato purée.
3. Sauté over medium heat until the tomatoes are cooked and the oil begins to separate from the tomato mixture, about 3 to 4 minutes.
4. Add the chicken and the marinade to the tomato mixture, along with the salt. Mix well and cook for about 4 to 5 minutes. Add about ½ cup of water, cover, and cook for 20 minutes or until the chicken is completely cooked and the juices run clear, stirring occasionally. If you like a thinner gravy, add some more water. Remove the black cardamom pod and bay leaf before serving. Serve hot.

❈ Indian Cooking Oils
Indian cooking uses peanut, vegetable, mustard, sesame, and corn oil for cooking. There are two varieties of ghee that are used, vanaspathi (vegetable) and ghee (clarified butter). Indian cooking does not use any animal fat or lard as a cooking medium.

Sizzling Tandoori Chicken
(Murgh Tandoori)

¾ cup Hung Yogurt (see recipe on page 16)

1 tablespoon Ginger-Garlic Paste (see recipe on page 15)

1 tablespoon Tandoori Spice Mix (see recipe on page 15)

¼ teaspoon carom seeds

Table salt, to taste

2 tablespoons fresh lemon juice

A few drops of red food coloring (optional)

2 tablespoons vegetable oil

8 skinless bone-in chicken thighs

Melted butter for basting

Chaat Spice Mix, for garnish (see recipe on page 16)

Serves 4–5
Prep Time: 15 minutes, plus at least 8 hours to marinate
Cook Time: 25–35 minutes

Serve this with the Punjabi Onion Salad (page 68), Simple Naan Bread (page 207), and Creamy Black Gram Dahl (page 192).

1. In a large bowl, combine the yogurt, Ginger-Garlic Paste, Tandoori Spice Mix, carom seeds, salt, lemon juice, red food coloring, and vegetable oil. Add the chicken and mix well to coat the chicken evenly. Cover and refrigerate for at least 8 hours, overnight.
2. Preheat oven to 400°.
3. Place the chicken in a single layer in a roasting pan. Discard any remaining marinade. Roast for about 20 to 30 minutes or until the chicken is cooked and the juices run clear. Baste as needed with the melted butter. Brown under the broiler for 6 to 7 minutes, turning once.
4. Garnish with a sprinkling of Chaat Spice Mix and serve hot.

❊ Marinating Tip

When marinating chicken with bones, make small cuts in the chicken flesh. This allows the marinade to penetrate the chicken pieces. You can freeze the marinated chicken for use at a later date.

Butter Chicken
(Murgh Makhanwala)

Serves 4
Prep Time: 10 minutes
Cook Time: 20 minutes

The velvety butter sauce provides an excellent base for the Sizzling Tandoori Chicken. Serve with Simple Naan Bread (page 207) or with Simple Basmati Rice (page 162).

4 tablespoons butter
½ teaspoon vegetable oil
2 teaspoons Ginger-Garlic Paste (see recipe on page 15)
2 medium tomatoes, finely chopped
¼ cup tomato purée (canned or fresh)
½ teaspoon red chili powder
Table salt, to taste
1 teaspoon dried fenugreek leaves
1 recipe Sizzling Tandoori Chicken (page 95)
½ cup heavy cream

1. In a large skillet, heat the butter and oil on medium. Add the Ginger-Garlic Paste and sauté for about 30 seconds.
2. Add the tomatoes and the purée. Cook the tomatoes, stirring constantly. Use the back of a spatula to mash the tomatoes as they cook. Continue until the tomatoes are completely mashed and soft, about 10 minutes.
3. Add the red chili powder, salt, fenugreek leaves, and chicken and mix well. Simmer, covered, for about 10 minutes.
4. Add the cream and simmer for 1 minute. Serve hot.

❋ Naked Chicken

Indian marinades need skinless chicken to work their magic, so it's best to skin your poultry prior to use. Also, make deep incisions to help the marinade sink into the chicken for a much better tasting dish.

Chicken Curry
(Murgh Tariwala)

3 tablespoons vegetable oil
1 black cardamom pod
2 green cardamom pods, bruised
2 cloves
1 (1-inch) cinnamon stick
1 bay leaf
1 large red onion, finely
   chopped
1 tablespoon Ginger-Garlic Paste
   (see recipe on page 15)
2 medium tomatoes, finely
   chopped

½ teaspoon red chili powder
1 teaspoon Warm Spice Mix
   (see recipe on page 14),
   plus extra for garnish
¼ teaspoon turmeric powder
2 teaspoons coriander powder
Table salt, to taste
½ cup plain yogurt, whipped
2½ pounds skinless chicken
   pieces, cuts of your choice
Water, as needed
2 tablespoons minced cilantro

Serves 4–5
Prep Time: 15 minutes
Cook Time: 45 minutes

This is an easy-to-make, simple Chicken curry. Serve with Simple Basmati Rice (page 162) or Simple Indian Bread (page 204).

1. In a large skillet, heat the oil on medium. Add the cardamom, cloves, cinnamon stick, and bay leaf. When the spices begin to sizzle, add the onion and the Ginger-Garlic Paste. Sauté for about 5 to 7 minutes or until the onion is well browned.

2. Add the tomatoes and cook for about 8 minutes or until the tomatoes are soft and the oil begins to separate from the sides of the mixture.

3. Add the red chili powder, the spice mix, turmeric powder, coriander powder, and salt; cook for 1 minute. Add the yogurt and mix well. Cook, stirring constantly for 1 more minute.

4. Add the chicken and cook, stirring constantly for 5 to 7 minutes or until brown on all sides. Add 1 cup of water, cover, and simmer for 20 minutes or until the chicken is cooked through. Stir occasionally, and add more water if the sauce dries up or if you want a thinner gravy. Add the minced cilantro and cook for 1 minute. Serve hot, sprinkled with Warm Spice Mix.

Ginger Chicken Bites
(Adraki Murgh Tikka)

1 cup Hung Yogurt (see recipe
   on page 16)
2 tablespoons grated gingerroot
1 teaspoon fresh lemon juice
1 tablespoon vegetable oil
½ teaspoon (or to taste) red
   chili powder

Table salt, to taste
1½ pounds skinless, boneless
   chicken breast, cubed
2 tablespoons melted butter
Lemon wedges, for garnish

1. In a bowl or resealable plastic bag, combine the yogurt, grated ginger, lemon juice, oil, red chili powder, and salt; mix well. Add the chicken cubes. Marinate, covered and refrigerated, for 5 to 6 hours or, preferably, overnight.
2. Preheat oven to 425°.
3. Thread the chicken onto skewers and baste with the melted butter. Place the chicken on a foil-lined baking sheet and bake for about 7 minutes. Turn once and baste with any remaining butter. Bake for another 7 minutes or until golden brown and the juices run clear. Serve hot, garnished with lemon wedges.

✳ Tandoors

Tandoors are large clay ovens that are used to roast meats and bake breads. The meats cooked in a tandoor tend to stay moist on the inside and dry on the outside. Tandoors use charcoal for heating. They provide a characteristic taste to the food that is almost impossible to duplicate in a conventional home oven. Small, portable home-use tandoors are now available in the United States. I use a conventional home oven or an outdoor charcoal grill for my tandoori dishes.

Almond-Flavored Chicken
(Badaami Murgh)

¼ cup blanched almonds
Water, as needed
4 tablespoons vegetable oil
1 bay leaf
2 cloves
5 peppercorns
1 green chili, seeded and
   minced
1 tablespoon Ginger-Garlic Paste
   (see recipe on page 15)
8 pieces skinless, bone-in
   chicken thighs

½ teaspoon red chili powder
¼ teaspoon turmeric powder
1 teaspoon coriander powder
½ teaspoon Warm Spice Mix
   (see recipe on page 14)
Table salt, to taste
¼ cup plain yogurt, whipped
¼ cup heavy cream

Serves 4–5
Prep Time: 10 minutes
Cook Time: 35–40
minutes

The nuts add a rich creamy taste to the chicken. Serve this with the Carom-Flavored Flatbread (page 216).

1. In a blender or food processor, blend the almonds with a few tablespoons of water to make a thick, smooth paste. Set aside.
2. In a large pan, heat the vegetable oil on medium. Add the bay leaf, cloves, peppercorns, green chili, and Ginger-Garlic Paste; sauté for about 10 seconds. Add the chicken and sauté until well browned on both sides, about 5 to 10 minutes.
3. Add the red chili, turmeric, coriander, the spice mix, and salt; cook for about 5 minutes.
4. Add the yogurt and sauté until the fat begins to separate. Add about ½ cup of water. Cover and simmer until the chicken is tender and cooked through, about 10 to 15 minutes. Stir occasionally, adding a few tablespoons of water if the dish seems too dry.
5. Add the almond paste and the cream. Cook, uncovered, on medium heat for about 8 minutes. Serve hot.

Chicken Tikka Masala
(Murgh Tikka Masala)

Serves 4
Prep Time: 10 minutes
Cook Time: 20 minutes

This is probably one of the most popular Indian dishes on restaurant menus worldwide. This dish is often called the national dish of the United Kingdom!

3 tablespoons vegetable oil
1 medium-sized red onion, finely chopped
1 tablespoon Ginger-Garlic Paste (see recipe on page 15)
2 medium tomatoes, finely chopped
½ teaspoon red chili powder
¼ teaspoon turmeric powder
Table salt, to taste
½ teaspoon Warm Spice Mix (see recipe on page 14)
¾ cup heavy cream.
1 recipe Chicken Tikka (page 26)

1. In a large pan, heat the vegetable oil on medium. Add the onions and sauté until well browned, about 7 to 8 minutes. Add the Ginger-Garlic Paste and sauté for another minute.
2. Add the tomatoes and cook for about 8 minutes or until the tomatoes are cooked and the oil begins to separate from the sides of the mixture.
3. Add the red chili, turmeric, salt, and the spice mix; sauté for 1 minute.
4. Add the cream and cook for about 2 minutes. Add the Chicken Tikka and mix well. Cook for 2 minutes or until the chicken is heated through. Serve hot.

❋ Chicken Tikka Rolls

Here's another simple recipe for leftovers. Brush 1 side of a piece of Simple Indian Bread (page 204) or a flour tortilla with egg wash. Place on a hot griddle and cook it on both sides. Place a few pieces of chicken on the side of the bread with the egg, add a few slices of onions, 1 tablespoon of Mint-Cilantro Chutney (page 226), roll up, and serve.

Chicken in a Creamy Sauce
(Murgh Korma)

2 small red onions, peeled and
   chopped
1-inch piece fresh gingerroot,
   peeled and sliced
4 garlic cloves, peeled
4 dried red chilies
2 teaspoons coriander powder
Water, as needed
3 tablespoons unsalted cashew
   nuts, soaked in water for
   10 minutes
2 tablespoons white poppy
   seeds, soaked in water for
   20 minutes
2 tablespoons almonds, blanched

3 tablespoons Clarified Butter
   (see recipe on page 17)
2 (1-inch) cinnamon sticks
2 black cardamom pods, bruised
1 large bay leaf
4 cloves
2 green cardamom pods, bruised
1 teaspoon cumin powder
1 cup plain yogurt, whipped
1½ pounds boneless diced
   chicken
Table salt, to taste
1 teaspoon Warm Spice Mix
   (see recipe on page 14)
Roasted cumin seeds, for garnish

Serves 4–5
Prep Time: 25 minutes,
plus 10 minutes to soak
Cook Time: 45 minutes

The secret to
preparing the perfect
sauce is to let it
simmer slowly until it
thickens completely.

1. In a blender or food processor, blend together the onions, ginger, garlic, red chilies, coriander powder, and up to ¼ cup of water to make a paste. Set aside.

2. Process or blend together the cashew nuts, poppy seeds, almonds, and just enough water to make a smooth, thick paste. Set aside.

3. In a deep pan, heat the Clarified Butter over medium heat. Add the cinnamon sticks, black cardamom, bay leaf, cloves, and green cardamom; sauté until fragrant, about 1½ minutes. Add the onion paste and cumin. Sauté over medium-low heat, stirring constantly, until the butter separates from the onion paste. Add the yogurt and continue cooking for about 12 minutes, stirring constantly.

4. Add the chicken pieces. Simmer, covered, for 15 to 20 minutes or until the chicken is tender.

5. Add the nut paste and simmer, uncovered, for about 4 minutes. Stir in the salt and the Warm Spice Mix. Garnish with roasted cumin seeds and serve hot.

Coriander Chicken
(Dhaniye Wala Murgh)

Serves 4–5
Prep Time: 15 minutes
Cook Time: 40 minutes

Serve this with a raita of your choice (see Chapter 5, Salads) and Simple Naan Bread (page 207).

4 tablespoons vegetable oil
2 cloves
2 green cardamom pods
1 (1-inch) cinnamon stick
2 teaspoons Ginger-Garlic Paste
   (see recipe on page 15)
1½ medium tomatoes, finely
   chopped
½ teaspoon red chili powder

Table salt, to taste
2 tablespoons coriander
   powder
½ cup plain yogurt, whipped
8 skinless chicken thighs
Water, as needed
1 cup minced cilantro

1. In a large pan, heat the vegetable oil. Add the cloves, cardamom, and cinnamon. When they begin to sizzle, add the Ginger-Garlic Paste and sauté for about 15 seconds.
2. Add the tomatoes and cook for 6 to 8 minutes or until the tomatoes are cooked and the oil begins to separate from the sides of the mixture.
3. Add the red chili powder, salt, and coriander powder; fry for 1 minute.
4. Add the yogurt and mix well. Cook for about 2 minutes.
5. Add the chicken and fry, stirring constantly, for about 15 minutes. Add about ½ cup of water. Bring back to a boil, cover, and simmer until the chicken is tender and cooked through, about 15 minutes. Stir occasionally, adding a few tablespoons of water if the dish dries up too much.
6. Add the cilantro leaves and mix well. Serve hot.

❊ Handling Poultry

Be careful when handling raw poultry. Clean your preparation area thoroughly with hot, soapy water or a commercial kitchen cleaner. Ensure that you place the chicken in the fridge to marinate. This will prevent the breeding of any harmful bacteria.

Spiced Chicken in Green Curry
(Murgh Hariyali)

3 tablespoons vegetable oil
1 large onion, minced
2 teaspoons Ginger-Garlic Paste
  (see recipe on page 15)
2 green chilies, seeded and
  minced (optional)
4 tablespoons minced cilantro
4 tablespoons minced mint
5 tablespoons minced spinach

1½ pounds skinless, boneless
  chicken chunks (your choice
  of cut)
Table salt, to taste
¼ teaspoon red chili powder
Water, as needed
½ cup heavy cream

Serves 4
Prep Time: 15 minutes
Cook Time: 35–40
minutes

This dish is at its best
when fresh herbs are
used. Serve this with a
Garlic Rice (page 174).

1. In a large pan, heat the vegetable oil on medium. Add the onions and sauté until well browned, about 7 to 8 minutes. Add the Ginger-Garlic Paste and sauté for 1 minute.
2. Add the green chilies, cilantro leaves, mint leaves, and spinach leaves; fry for about 4 to 5 minutes.
3. Add the chicken, salt, and red chili powder; fry for about 5 minutes. Add ½ cup of water, cover, and cook the chicken until done, about 10 to 15 minutes. Stir occasionally to ensure that the chicken is not sticking to the pan. Add more water if needed.
4. Add the cream and cook for 1 minute. Serve hot.

❋ Dried Mint Chicken

My grandmother used to make this: Dry fresh mint (or use dried mint leaves) and crush it. Create a marinade of the mint, red chili powder, salt, pepper, and vegetable oil. Add chicken to the marinade and let it marinate for at least 4 hours. Grill or roast in an oven. Simple yet flavorful.

Cardamom Chicken
(Eliachi Murgh)

Serves 4–5
Prep Time: 10 minutes
Cook Time: 30–40 minutes

The cooking time of the chicken will depend on the cut that you choose. This dish is perfect with Simple Basmati Rice (page 162).

3 tablespoons vegetable oil
6 green cardamom pods, roughly pounded
1 medium-sized red onion, minced
2 teaspoons Ginger-Garlic Paste (see recipe on page 15)
1½ pounds skinless, boneless chicken chunks (your choice of cut)
Table salt, to taste
½ teaspoon red chili powder
¼ teaspoon turmeric powder
1 cup Hung Yogurt (see recipe on page 16)
Water, as needed

1. In a pan, heat the vegetable oil on medium. Add the cardamom pods and sauté for 10 seconds. Add the onions and sauté until well browned, about 7 to 8 minutes. Add the Ginger-Garlic Paste and sauté for 1 minute.
2. Add the chicken cubes and sauté until well browned, about 7 to 8 minutes.
3. Add the salt, red chili powder, and turmeric powder; mix well. Sauté for 1 minute.
4. Add the yogurt and mix well. Fry for another 5 minutes, stirring constantly.
5. Add about ½ cup of water, cover, and cook on low heat until the chicken is cooked through, about 10 to 15 minutes.

❊ Green Cardamoms

Green cardamoms are one of the most expensive spices in the world. In Arab countries, this aromatic spice is most often used for spicing coffee. In India, green cardamom is used as a mouth freshener.

Chicken Chettinad
(Kozi Chettinad)

3 teaspoons black peppercorns, roughly pounded

2 teaspoons Ginger-Garlic Paste (see recipe on page 15)

1 dried red chili, roughly pounded

¾ cup Hung Yogurt (see recipe on page 16)

8 skinless chicken thighs

4 tablespoons vegetable oil

8 fresh curry leaves

1 large red onion, chopped

1½ medium tomatoes, chopped

¼ teaspoon turmeric powder

Table salt, to taste

½ cup water

> **Serves 4–5**
> **Prep Time:** 10 minutes
> **Cook Time:** 40–50 minutes
>
> If you like your food milder, reduce the number of peppercorns in this dish. Serve with Simple Naan Bread (page 207).

1. In a bowl, combine the peppercorns, Ginger-Garlic Paste, red chili, and yogurt; mix well. Add the chicken thighs, making sure that the chicken is well covered in the marinade. Set aside.

2. In a pan, heat the vegetable oil on medium. Add the curry leaves; when they begin to sizzle, add the onions. Sauté until the onions are well browned, about 7 to 8 minutes.

3. Add the tomatoes and cook for about 6 to 8 minutes or until the tomatoes are cooked and the oil begins to separate from the sides of the mixture. Add the turmeric and salt; cook for 1 minute.

4. Add the chicken along with all the marinade; cook for about 6 to 8 minutes. Add the water and bring to a boil. Cover and simmer until the chicken is done, about 15 to 20 minutes. Serve hot.

☀ Prepacked Spice Mixes

If you need a spice mix in a hurry, you can buy most prepacked spice mixes (like the Garam Masala, Tandoori Masala, and Chaat Masala) at your local Indian grocery stores instead of making them yourself. I suggest the MDH brands.

Chicken Manchurian
(Murgh Manchurian)

Serves 4–5
Prep Time: 10 minutes
Cook Time: 30–40 minutes

This recipe is great with Vegetable Fried Rice (page 176). If you want to make a colorful presentation, add bell peppers in a variety of colors.

1 egg
2 tablespoons corn flour
2 tablespoons all-purpose flour
1 teaspoon Ginger-Garlic Paste (see recipe on page 15)
1 teaspoon plus 1 tablespoon red chili sauce (optional)
Water, as needed
1½ pounds skinless, boneless chicken, cubed
Vegetable oil for deep-frying, plus 3 tablespoons

1-inch piece fresh gingerroot, grated
2 green chilies, seeded and minced
2 tablespoons soya sauce
¼ teaspoon white pepper powder
Table salt, to taste
1 small red onion, thinly sliced
1 small green bell pepper, seeded and thinly sliced
1 cup chicken stock or water
3 tablespoons corn flour dissolved in ½ cup cold water

1. In a bowl, combine the egg, 2 tablespoons corn flour, the all-purpose flour, Ginger-Garlic Paste, and 1 teaspoon of the red chili sauce. Add enough water to make a thin batter; mix well. Add the chicken pieces to the batter.
2. In a deep pan, heat the vegetable oil to 350°. Add a few pieces of chicken at a time and deep-fry until the chicken is crisp and golden brown. Using a slotted spoon, remove the chicken from the oil, and drain on paper towels. Let the oil return to temperature. Continue until all the chicken pieces are fried. Set aside. Discard any remaining batter.
3. In a large skillet, heat the 3 tablespoons of vegetable oil. Add the ginger and green chilies, and sauté for about 30 seconds.
4. Add the soya sauce, remaining 1 tablespoon red chili sauce, white pepper powder, and salt; mix well. Add the onion and bell pepper; sauté for 2 to 3 minutes.
5. Add the chicken stock (*or* water), and corn flour mixture (restir the corn flour mix if you made it ahead). Bring to a boil. Lower the heat and add the chicken pieces. Simmer for 1 to 2 minutes. Serve immediately.

Goan Chicken Curry
(Goan Murgh Xcautti)

2 dried red chilies
1 tablespoon white poppy seeds
1 teaspoon black mustard seeds
2 teaspoons cumin seeds
1 tablespoon coriander seeds
¼ teaspoon black peppercorns
1 (1-inch) cinnamon stick
3 cloves
¼ cup unsweetened desiccated coconut

3 tablespoons vegetable oil
1 large red onion, minced
1 tablespoon Ginger-Garlic Paste (see recipe on page 15)
1½ pounds skinless, boneless chicken chunks
Table salt, to taste
Water, as needed
1 tablespoon fresh lemon juice (optional)

> **Serves 4–5**
> **Prep Time:** 15 minutes
> **Cook Time:** 30–35 minutes
>
> This delight from western India takes a bit of an effort to make, but the results are really rewarding.

1. In a small skillet on medium heat, dry roast the red chilies, poppy seeds, mustard seeds, cumin seeds, coriander seeds, black peppercorns, cinnamon stick, and cloves. When the spices release their aroma, remove from heat and let cool. In a spice grinder, grind the spices, along with the coconut, to a coarse powder. Set aside.
2. In a large skillet, heat the vegetable oil. Add the onions and sauté until well browned, about 7 to 8 minutes. Add the Ginger-Garlic Paste and sauté for 1 minute.
3. Add the chicken and sauté until browned, about 5 to 7 minutes. Add the reserved spice powder and the salt; sauté for 2 minutes.
4. Add about ½ cup of water and bring to a boil. Reduce the heat, cover, and simmer until the chicken is cooked through, about 10 to 15 minutes. Add 1 tablespoon of lemon juice to the dish before serving, if desired. Serve hot.

Dill Chicken
(Soa Wali Murgh)

2 tablespoons fresh lemon juice
4 tablespoons vegetable oil
1 tablespoon Warm Spice Mix
   (see recipe on page 14)
Table salt, to taste
A few sprigs of dill
2 garlic cloves, crushed
4 skinless chicken breasts
Butter for basting.

1. In a bowl or resealable plastic bag, combine all the ingredients, *except* the chicken and butter, and mix well. Add the chicken to the marinade. Make sure the breasts are well coated. Cover and refrigerate overnight.
2. Preheat oven to 350°.
3. Place the chicken in a single layer in a roasting pan. Discard any remaining marinade and the sprigs of dill. Bake for about 30 minutes or until the chicken is cooked through and the juices run clear. Baste as needed with the melted butter. Serve hot.

Creamy Chicken Kebab
(Murgh Malai Kebab)

2 teaspoons Ginger-Garlic Paste
   (see recipe on page 15)
1 teaspoon white pepper powder
2 serrano green chilies, seeded
   and minced
¾ cup heavy cream
2 tablespoons corn flour
Table salt, to taste
1½ pounds boneless, skinless
   chicken chunks
Butter for basting

1. In a bowl, combine the Ginger-Garlic Paste, white pepper powder, green chilies, cream, corn flour, and salt. Add the chicken to the marinade. Cover and refrigerate for at least 2 hours, or overnight.
2. Preheat oven to 400°. Place the chicken in a single layer in a roasting pan. Discard any remaining marinade. Bake for about 20 minutes or until the chicken is cooked through. Baste as needed with the melted butter. Brown under the broiler for 2 to 3 minutes. Serve hot.

Velvety Chicken Kebab
(Murgh Reshmi Kebab)

2 tablespoons cashews, roughly
  pounded
1 egg, whisked
½ teaspoon cumin seeds,
  roasted and roughly
  pounded
½ teaspoon Warm Spice Mix
  (see recipe on page 14)

1½ pounds minced chicken
2 teaspoons vegetable oil
½ small red onion, minced
1-inch piece fresh gingerroot,
  grated
Table salt, to taste
Butter for basting

Serves 4–5
Prep Time: 20 minutes
Cook Time: 20–25
minutes

Traditionally these are
shaped like sausages
and skewered length-
wise on long skewers.
Serve with the Mint
Chutney (page 237).

1. In a bowl, combine all the ingredients, *except* the butter, and mix
   well, using your hands.
2. Preheat oven to 350°.
3. Divide the chicken mixture into 8 portions and make equal-sized small
   patties, flattening them between the palms of your hands.
4. Place the chicken patties on a baking sheet and roast for about 10
   minutes. Turn once and baste with any remaining butter. Roast for
   another 10 minutes or until golden brown and the juices run clear.
   Serve hot.

☀ Ginger-Garlic Paste

I have provided a recipe to make this paste at home; you can also
buy this at your local Indian grocer. Many regular grocery stores
now sell ginger paste and crushed garlic, which can also be used
as a substitute.

Chili Coconut Chicken
(Mangalorian Murgh Gassi)

Serves 4
Prep Time: 15 minutes
Cook Time: 40 minutes

The coconut milk provides a nice balance to the red chilies. Serve this with Simple Basmati Rice (page 162).

½ teaspoon black mustard seeds
½ teaspoon cumin seeds
½ teaspoon coriander seeds
3 tablespoons vegetable oil
8 curry leaves
2 medium-sized red onions, finely chopped
2 teaspoons Ginger-Garlic Paste (see recipe on page 15)

3 dried red chilies, roughly pounded
½ teaspoon turmeric powder
Table salt, to taste
1½ pounds boneless, skinless chicken, cubed
Water, as needed
1 cup light coconut milk

1. In a small skillet on medium heat, dry roast the mustard seeds, cumin seeds, and coriander seeds. When the spices release their aroma, remove from heat and let cool. In a spice grinder, grind to a coarse powder. Set aside.
2. In a large skillet, heat the oil on medium. Add the curry leaves and the onions; sauté for about 1 minute.
3. Add the Ginger-Garlic Paste and red chilies. Sauté on medium heat until the onions are well browned and the oil begins to separate from the sides of the onion mixture, about 8 minutes.
4. Add the ground spices, turmeric powder, and salt; sauté for 1 minute.
5. Add the chicken pieces and sauté for about 10 minutes. Add about ½ cup of water, cover, and simmer for about 15 minutes or until the chicken is cooked through.
6. Add the coconut milk and simmer on low heat for about 5 minutes. Serve hot.

❀ Coconut Milk

Don't confuse coconut water with coconut milk. Coconut water is the liquid inside a coconut. Coconut milk is produced by steeping grated coconut in hot water and straining it. Regular coconut milk is high in saturated fat. I would advise using light coconut milk.

Fenugreek-Flavored Chicken
(Murgh Methiwala)

4 tablespoons vegetable oil
2 cloves
1 green cardamom pod,
    bruised
1 (1-inch) cinnamon stick
1 medium-sized red onion,
    finely chopped
1 tablespoon Ginger-Garlic Paste
    (see recipe on page 15)

2 tablespoons dried fenugreek
    leaves
8 skinless chicken thighs
½ teaspoon red chili powder
Table salt, to taste
½ teaspoon turmeric powder
1 cup plain yogurt, whipped
1 cup water

> **Serves 4–5**
> **Prep Time:** 5 minutes
> **Cook Time:** 30–40
> minutes
>
> A very aromatic dish,
> using either fresh or
> dried fenugreek
> leaves. Serve this with
> the Simple Naan
> Bread (page 207).

1. In a large skillet, heat the vegetable oil on medium. Add the cloves, cardamom, and cinnamon. When they begin to sizzle, add the onions and sauté for about 2 to 3 minutes.
2. Add the Ginger-Garlic Paste and the dried fenugreek leaves. Sauté on medium heat until the onions are well browned and the oil begins to separate from the onion mixture, about 3 to 4 minutes.
3. Add the chicken thighs and sauté until browned. Add the red chili powder, turmeric powder, and salt; sauté for 2 minutes.
4. Add the yogurt and fry until the fat begins to separate. Add the water, cover, and simmer until the chicken is tender and cooked through, 20 to 25 minutes. Serve hot.

☀ Green Chilies

For the recipes in this book, I use serrano chilies. You can choose another type of chili, but just make sure that you know how much heat they will add! If you like the flavor but not the heat, remove the white seeds from the chili.

Omelet Curry
(Mutta Curry)

Serves 4
Prep Time: 15 minutes
Cook Time: 20 minutes

This unusual curry is common in South India. Serve with freshly baked sliced white bread.

4 eggs
1 serrano green chili, seeded and minced
½ small red onion, minced
3 tablespoons vegetable oil
1 medium-sized red onion, finely chopped

2 teaspoons Ginger-Garlic Paste (see recipe on page 15)
2 small tomatoes, finely chopped
½ teaspoon turmeric powder
½ teaspoon red chili powder
Table salt, to taste
½ cup water

1. In a bowl, whisk the eggs; add the green chilies and minced onion.
2. In a small nonstick skillet, heat about 1 tablespoon of the vegetable oil over medium heat. Pour about ¼ of the egg mixture into the skillet and cook until the base is golden brown. Flip over and cook the other side until the omelet is firm and cooked through. Transfer to a plate. Continue until all the egg mixture is cooked. Cut the omelets into small strips. Set aside.
3. In a large pan, heat the remaining oil on medium. Add the chopped onions and sauté for 2 to 3 minutes.
4. Add the Ginger-Garlic Paste; sauté on medium heat until the onions are well browned, about 7 to 8 minutes. Add the tomatoes and cook for 7 to 8 minutes or until the oil begins to separate from the sides of the onion mixture.
5. Add the turmeric powder, red chili powder, and salt. Mix well, and sauté for 1 minute. Add the water and bring to a boil. Cover and simmer for about 8 minutes.
6. Add the omelet strips to the curry. Serve hot.

☀ Coconuts

Many recipes in the book call for coconut; you can use the unsweetened dry coconut available at your local grocery stores. If you prefer, you can use fresh coconut. A good rule of thumb is that 1 coconut yields about 1½ cups of coconut flesh.

Honey Chili Chicken
(Sahaed Wali Murgh)

3 dried red chilies, roughly
    pounded
½ cup liquid honey
Juice of 1 lemon
1 teaspoon soya sauce

2 teaspoons Ginger-Garlic Paste
    (see recipe on page 15)
1½ pounds skinless, boneless
    chicken chunks
Vegetable oil for basting

> **Serves 4–5**
> **Prep Time:** 5 minutes,
> plus 2 hours to marinate
> **Cook Time:** 20 minutes
>
> The contrasting tastes of hot red chili and the sweet honey make this dish very appealing.

1. In a bowl, combine all the ingredients *except* the oil; mix well. Cover and refrigerate for at least 2 hours.
2. Preheat oven to 400°.
3. Place the chicken on a baking sheet and roast for about 10 minutes. Turn once and baste with oil. Roast for another 10 minutes or until cooked through. Serve hot.

Easy Masala Egg
(Anda Masala)

2 tablespoons vegetable oil
½ small red onion, finely
    chopped
1 serrano green chili, seeded
    and minced

1 tablespoon minced cilantro
½ teaspoon red chili powder
¼ teaspoon turmeric powder
Table salt, to taste
4 eggs, whisked

> **Serves 4**
> **Prep Time:** 10 minutes
> **Cook Time:** 10 minutes
>
> A favorite weekend brunch dish, serve atop Spinach Bread (page 211) for a healthy and hearty meal.

1. In a large nonstick skillet, heat the vegetable oil on medium. Add the onions and sauté until transparent.
2. Add the green chili, cilantro, red chili powder, turmeric, and salt. Mix well, and sauté for 2 to 3 minutes.
3. Reduce the heat and add the eggs; cook, stirring constantly, until the eggs are done to your liking. Serve immediately.

Parsi-Style Eggs
(Akoori)

2 tablespoons vegetable oil
2 spring onions, finely chopped
2 garlic cloves, crushed
1½-inch piece gingerroot, roughly chopped
2 serrano green chilies, seeded and minced
1 small red tomato, finely chopped
½ teaspoon cumin seeds, roasted
4 eggs, whisked
2 tablespoons cream
Table salt, to taste

1. Heat the oil on medium. Add the onions and sauté until transparent.
2. Add the garlic and ginger; sauté for 30 seconds. Add the green chilies, tomatoes, and cumin seeds; sauté for 3 minutes.
3. Add the eggs and cook, stirring constantly. Add the cream. Continue cooking, stirring constantly, until the eggs are cooked to your liking. Salt to taste. Serve immediately.

Egg Curry
(Anda Curry)

3 tablespoons vegetable oil
1 medium-sized red onion, minced
1-inch piece grates gingerroot
2 small tomatoes, chopped
½ teaspoon turmeric powder
½ teaspoon red chili powder
1 teaspoon coriander powder
Table salt, to taste
1 cup whole milk
6 eggs, boiled and peeled

1. In a large skillet, heat the oil on medium. Add the red onions and sauté for about 7 to 8 minutes or until the onions are well browned.
2. Add the ginger and cook for 1 minute. Add the tomatoes, and cook until the tomatoes are soft and the oil begins to separate from the onion-tomato mixture. Then add the turmeric, red chili powder, coriander powder, and salt; mix well. Add the milk and bring to a boil. Lower heat, cover, and simmer for about 3 to 4 minutes.
3. Slice the eggs and gently fold them into the sauce. Serve hot.

CHAPTER 8
Meat Dishes (Gosht)

Meat Belli Ram
(Belli Ram Ka Gosht)

Serves 4
Prep Time: 15 minutes, plus 4 hours to marinate
Cook Time: 1 hour, 30 minutes

Belli Ram was a celebrated Indian chef from northern India. This dish, named for him, is a delicacy served on special occasions.

2 cups plain yogurt, whipped
2 medium-sized red onions, peeled and thinly sliced
3 tablespoons Ginger-Garlic Paste (see recipe on page 15)
2 cloves
2 green cardamom pods, roughly pounded
1 (1-inch) cinnamon stick
1 teaspoon red chili powder

Table salt, to taste
1½ pounds lean boneless lamb, cut in 1-inch cubes
2 tablespoons Clarified Butter (see recipe on page 17) or vegetable oil
1 tablespoon coriander seeds, roughly pounded
1 cup water

1. In a bowl or resealable plastic bag, combine the yogurt, onions, Ginger-Garlic Paste, cloves, cardamom pods, cinnamon, red chili powder, and salt; mix well. Add the lamb and coat evenly with the marinade. Refrigerate, covered, for at least 4 hours, or overnight.
2. In a deep pan, heat the butter. Add the coriander seeds. When they begin to sizzle, add the lamb and any remaining marinade.
3. Cook for about 15 minutes. Add the water and bring to a boil. Reduce heat and simmer, covered, for 1 hour or until the lamb is tender.
4. Uncover and increase heat to high. Cook until the fat begins to leave the sides of the lamb. This will take about 5 to 8 minutes, depending on the leanness of your meat. Remove from heat. Serve hot.

※ Indian Lamb Curries

Most of the curries taste even more awesome if you allow the spices to do their magic overnight. Cook the dish according to directions. Cool to room temperature. Cover and refrigerate overnight. The next day, heat the dish on high and serve.

Lamb Curry with Turnips
(Shalgam Wala Gosht)

3 tablespoons vegetable oil

2 cloves

1 bay leaf

2 medium-sized red onions, peeled and finely chopped

1 tablespoon Ginger-Garlic Paste (see recipe on page 15)

1½ pounds boneless lean lamb chunks

2 dried red chilies, roughly pounded

½ teaspoon turmeric powder

1½ teaspoons coriander powder

Table salt, to taste

½ teaspoon Warm Spice Mix (see recipe on page 14)

1 cup plain yogurt, whipped

Water, as needed

2 small turnips, peeled and diced

Serves 4
Prep Time: 10 minutes
Cook Time: 1 hour, 10 minutes

Turnips are a mild vegetable, but this dish provides them with a delicious taste. Serve with Simple Basmati Rice (page 162).

---

1. In a deep pan, heat the vegetable oil. Add the cloves and bay leaf. When the spices begin to sizzle, add the onion and Ginger-Garlic Paste. Sauté for about 5 to 7 minutes or until the onion is well browned.

2. Add the lamb and fry for about 20 minutes, stirring constantly. If the mixture starts to stick to the sides of the pan, add 1 tablespoon of water.

3. In quick succession, add the red chilies, turmeric, coriander, salt, and spice mix; sauté for 2 minutes.

4. Add the yogurt and cook for 10 minutes. Add 1 cup of water and bring to a boil. Lower the heat, cover, and simmer for about 15 minutes. Stir occasionally.

5. Add the turnips and cook covered for another 15 minutes or until the lamb has cooked through and the turnips are soft. Serve hot.

☀ Pressure-Cooking Meats

To drastically reduce the cooking time for meats, invest in a good pressure cooker. Most Indian homes have pressure cookers. They are a boon not only for meats but for lentils as well.

Fiery Lamb Vindaloo
(Gosht Ka Vindaloo)

¾ cup rice vinegar
¼ cup water
1 teaspoon black peppercorns,
   roughly pounded
1 tablespoon minced garlic
2 teaspoons red chili powder
2 serrano green chilies, minced
1½ pounds boneless lean
   lamb, cubed

3 tablespoons vegetable oil
1 tablespoon grated gingerroot
1 large red onion, peeled and
   finely chopped
6 whole dried red chilies,
   roughly pounded
1 (1-inch) cinnamon stick
½ teaspoon turmeric powder
Table salt, to taste

1. In a nonreactive bowl, combine the rice vinegar, water, black pepper, garlic, red chili powder, and green chilies. Add the lamb and coat evenly with the marinade. Refrigerate, covered, for 1 hour.
2. In a deep pan, heat the oil. Add the gingerroot and sauté for about 10 seconds. Add the onion and sauté for about 7 to 8 minutes or until golden brown.
3. Add the red chilies, cinnamon stick, and turmeric powder; sauté for 20 seconds.
4. Remove the lamb pieces from the marinade and set the marinade aside. Add the lamb and sauté on high heat for about 10 minutes or until the lamb is browned and the oil starts to separate from the mixture. Add the marinade and bring to a boil. Reduce heat and simmer, covered, for about 30 to 45 minutes or until the lamb is tender.
5. Add salt to taste. Serve hot.

❋ Selecting Lamb

Color can be a great help when buying lamb. Younger lamb is pinkish red with a velvety texture. It should have a thin layer of white fat surrounding it. If the meat is much darker in color, it means that the lamb is older and flavored more strongly.

Hot Shredded Meat
(Tala Gosht)

2 teaspoons Ginger-Garlic Paste
  (see recipe on page 15)
½ teaspoon Warm Spice Mix
  (see recipe on page 14)
¼ teaspoon turmeric powder
1 dry red chili, roughly
  pounded
1 pound boneless lean lamb
  (steak cut), shredded

3 tablespoons vegetable oil,
  plus more for deep-frying
½ cup water
Table salt, to taste
2 serrano green chilies, seeded
  and minced
Fried Onions (see recipe on
  page 18)

Serves 4
Prep Time: 10 minutes,
plus 3 hours to marinate
Cook Time: 40 minutes

Don't let this dish sit
for too long before
serving or it will lose
its texture. Serve with
Minty Potato in Yogurt
Sauce (page 66).

1. In a bowl, combine the Ginger-Garlic Paste, Warm Spice Mix, turmeric, and red chili. Add the lamb and mix well. Refrigerate, covered, for 3 hours.

2. In a medium skillet, heat the 3 tablespoons of vegetable oil. Add the lamb and fry for about 10 minutes, stirring constantly. Add the water, cover, and cook until the lamb is tender, about 15 minutes. Uncover and cook on high heat until most of the liquid dries up. Remove from heat and cool to room temperature.

3. Heat about 1 inch of vegetable oil in a deep pan to 350°. Using tongs, dip a few pieces of the lamb into the hot oil and deep-fry just until crispy. Drain on a paper towel. Continue until all the lamb is fried. Salt to taste and serve hot topped with green chilies and Fried Onions.

☀ Reruns

Many of the kebab recipes in this book lend themselves well to being used as stuffing for sandwiches. Take a pocket pita and fill with shredded lettuce, sliced tomatoes, 1 tablespoon of Hung Yogurt (page 16), ½ tablespoon of dried mint, and leftover meat from kebabs. Serve with the cooling Mango Yogurt Drink (page 44).

Kebabs from Peshawar
(Gosht Peshawari)

Serves 4
Prep Time: 10 minutes,
plus 2 hours to marinate
Cook Time: 15 minutes

Serve these kebabs
with Punjabi Onion
Salad, Mint-Cilantro
Chutney, and Fresh
Lime Soda (pages 68,
226, and 43).

1 cup plain yogurt, whipped
1 tablespoon Ginger-Garlic Paste
  (see recipe on page 15)
1 teaspoon Warm Spice Mix
  (see recipe on page 14)
½ teaspoon red chili powder
Juice of ½ lemon
1½ pounds boneless lamb chunks
Table salt, to taste
Vegetable oil for basting

In a bowl or resealable plastic bag, combine the yogurt, Ginger-Garlic Paste, spice mix, red chili powder, and lemon juice; mix well. Add the lamb and mix well. Refrigerate, covered, for about 2 hours. Preheat oven to 350°. Place the lamb in a single layer on a foil-lined baking sheet. Discard the remaining marinade. Roast in the oven for 15 minutes or until the lamb is cooked through. Baste and turn at least once. Salt to taste.

Lamb Chops with Mint Chutney
(Chutney Wali Chaampe)

Serves 4
Prep Time: 5 minutes,
plus 4 hours to marinate
Cook Time: 30 minutes

These minty lamb
chops are easy to
prepare and can be
served with the Red
Radish Salad
(page 63).

1 teaspoon cumin, roasted and
  roughly pounded
2 teaspoons Ginger-Garlic Paste
  (see recipe on page 15)
2 teaspoons Warm Spice Mix
  (see recipe on page 14)
1 cup Mint-Cilantro Chutney
  (see recipe on page 226)
Juice of ½ a lemon
1 cup Hung Yogurt (see recipe
  on page 16)
Table salt, to taste
8 lamb chops (rib or loin),
  all visible fat removed
Vegetable oil for basting

In a bowl or resealable plastic bag, combine the cumin, ginger paste, spice mix, chutney, lemon juice, yogurt, and salt; mix well. Add the lamb chops and coat evenly with the marinade. Refrigerate, covered, for 4 hours. Preheat oven to 350°. Place the lamb chops in a single layer on a foil-lined baking sheet. Bake for 10 to 15 minutes. Baste with oil. Bake for another 10 to 15 minutes or until the lamb is cooked through.

Spinach Lamb Curry
(Saag Gosht)

½ pound frozen chopped
   spinach
4 tablespoons vegetable oil
2 bay leaves
1 (1-inch) cinnamon stick
4 cloves
4 black peppercorns
2 black cardamom pods
2 medium-sized red onions,
   peeled and finely chopped
2 teaspoons Ginger-Garlic Paste
   (see recipe on page 15)

1¼ pounds boneless lean
   lamb, cut into chunks
2 small tomatoes, finely
   chopped
1 teaspoon Warm Spice Mix
   (see recipe on page 14)
½ teaspoon red chili powder
¼ teaspoon turmeric powder
Table salt, to taste
½ cup plain yogurt, whipped
½ cup water

Serves 4
Prep Time: 15 minutes
Cook Time: 1 hour,
35 minutes

This dish graces menus
at innumerable Indian
restaurants. Serve with
Simple Naan Bread
(page 207), brushed
with spiced garlic
butter.

1. Cook the spinach in boiling water until just wilted; drain. Purée in a food processor. Set aside.
2. In a large skillet, heat the vegetable oil. Add the bay leaves, cinnamon stick, cloves, black peppercorns, and cardamom pods. When the spices begin to sizzle, add the onions. Stirring constantly, fry until the onions are golden brown, about 7 to 8 minutes. Add the Ginger-Garlic Paste and sauté for 1 minute.
3. Add the lamb and fry for about 10 to 15 minutes, stirring constantly. Add the tomatoes and fry, stirring constantly, for 10 minutes or until the oil starts to separate from the mixture.
4. Add the spice mix, red chili powder, turmeric powder, and salt; mix well. Add the yogurt and cook for about 4 minutes.
5. Add the water and bring to a boil. Reduce heat to low, cover, and simmer for about 45 minutes or until the lamb is cooked through.
6. Add the spinach and cook for another 5 minutes. Serve hot.

Meatball Curry
(Kofta Curry)

4 tablespoons vegetable oil
2 bay leaves
1 (1-inch) cinnamon stick
4 cloves
4 black peppercorns
2 black cardamom pods
2 medium-sized red onions, peeled and finely chopped
2 teaspoons Ginger-Garlic Paste (see recipe on page 15)
2 small tomatoes, finely chopped
1 teaspoon Warm Spice Mix (see recipe on page 14)
$\frac{1}{2}$ teaspoon red chili powder
$\frac{1}{4}$ teaspoon turmeric powder
Table salt, to taste
$\frac{1}{2}$ cup plain yogurt, whipped
2 recipes Fenugreek-Flavored Meatballs (page 22)
$\frac{1}{2}$ cup water

1. In a large skillet, heat the vegetable oil. Add the bay leaves, cinnamon stick, cloves, black peppercorns, and cardamom pods. When the spices being to sizzle, add the onions. Stirring constantly, fry until the onions are golden brown, about 7 to 8 minutes. Add the Ginger-Garlic Paste and sauté for 1 minute.
2. Add the tomatoes and fry, stirring constantly, for 10 minutes or until the oil starts to separate from the mixture.
3. Add the Warm Spice Mix, red chili powder, turmeric powder, and salt; mix well. Add the yogurt and cook for about 4 minutes.
4. Add the water and bring to a boil. Reduce heat to low, cover, and simmer for about 10 minutes.
5. Add the meatballs and cook for 5 to 8 minutes. Serve hot.

❋ Using Bay Leaves

When using bay leaves, tear them and roughly crush them. They should be quite aromatic, sweet, and pungent. Don't use more than 1 or 2 leaves or the food will get an acrid and unpleasant taste. Always remove the bay leaves before serving—the leaf is inedible.

Peas and Minced-Meat Curry
(Kheema Mattar)

4 tablespoons vegetable oil
2 bay leaves
1 (1-inch) cinnamon stick
4 cloves
4 black peppercorns
2 black cardamom pods
2 medium-sized red onions,
    peeled and finely chopped
2 teaspoons Ginger-Garlic Paste
    (see recipe on page 15)

1¼ pounds minced lamb
2 small tomatoes, puréed
1 teaspoon Warm Spice Mix
    (see recipe on page 14)
½ teaspoon red chili powder
¼ teaspoon turmeric powder
Table salt, to taste
1 cup frozen peas, thawed

Serves 4
Prep Time: 10 minutes
Cook Time: 50–55 minutes

Make an extra batch and freeze it to make Ground Lamb, Peas, and Rice Casserole (page 170) at a later date.

1. In a large skillet, heat the vegetable oil. Add the bay leaves, cinnamon stick, cloves, black peppercorns, and cardamom pods. When the spices begin to sizzle, add the onions. Stirring constantly, fry until the onions are golden brown, about 7 to 8 minutes. Add the Ginger-Garlic Paste and sauté for 1 minute.
2. Add the lamb and sauté for about 10 to 12 minutes. Break up any lumps with the back of your spoon. Add the tomatoes and fry, stirring constantly, for 15 minutes or until the oil starts to separate from the sides of the mixture.
3. Add the spice mix, red chili powder, turmeric powder, and salt; mix well. Cook for about 2 minutes.
4. Add the peas and cook, covered, for another 15 minutes or until the peas and lamb are cooked through. Remove the cinnamon and black cardamoms. Serve hot.

Stone-Cooked Kebabs
(Pathar Pe Bane Kebab)

Serves 4
Prep Time: 20 minutes,
plus 3 hours to marinate
Cook Time: 30 minutes

Originally, this recipe required cooking the lamb on heated slabs of stone. This version can be cooked in the oven, a skillet, or on the grill.

4 tablespoons vegetable oil, divided

1 medium-sized red onion, minced

½ cup plain yogurt, whipped

½ teaspoon Warm Spice Mix (see recipe on page 14)

2 teaspoons Ginger-Garlic Paste (see recipe on page 15)

Table salt, to taste

½ tablespoon dried mint

Juice of ½ lemon

1 pound boneless lean lamb

1. In a small skillet, heat 1 tablespoon of the vegetable oil. Add the minced onion and fry until well browned. Remove from heat and place in a bowl.
2. Add the yogurt, spice mix, ginger paste, salt, mint, and lemon juice to the onion mixture. Mix well and set aside.
3. Using a mallet, flatten the lamb. Cut into slices, about 2½ inches long and 1½ inches wide. The slices should be less than ¾ inch thick.
4. Add the lamb slices to the marinade and mix well. Cover, and marinate in the refrigerator for at least 3 hours.
5. In a medium-sized skillet, heat 1 tablespoon of the oil. Shake off excess marinade from lamb slices, and place 1 or 2 slices at a time in the skillet; cook until golden brown on each side, about 6 minutes. Ensure that the lamb is cooked through. Continue until all the lamb slices are cooked. Add more oil as needed.
6. Discard remaining marinade. Keep the lamb slices warm in a 200° oven, until ready to serve.

❈ Lamb or Mutton?

In India, generally, meat means goat meat (which is also called "mutton" in India). It is much stronger in taste and flavor than lamb.

Hot Spiced Lamb
(Andhra Gosht Pittu)

1¼ pounds lean minced lamb
1 teaspoon grated fresh
  gingerroot
½ teaspoon red chili powder
1 teaspoon minced garlic
2 tablespoons plain yogurt,
  whipped
¼ teaspoon turmeric powder
1 serrano green chili, seeded
  and minced

½ cup water
3 tablespoons vegetable oil
1 large red onion, minced
¼ cup unsweetened desiccated
  coconut
Table salt, to taste
½ teaspoon Warm Spice Mix
  (see recipe on page 14)

> **Serves 4**
> **Prep Time:** 10 minutes
> **Cook Time:** 1 hour
>
> Andhra Pradesh, a state in southern India, is famous for its highly spiced meats. The Warm Spice Mix adds a nice zing to the dish.

1. In a deep pan, combine the lamb, ginger, red chili powder, garlic, yogurt, turmeric, and green chili. Add the water and bring to a boil. Cover and simmer over low heat for about 45 minutes or until the lamb is cooked through. Set aside.
2. In a large skillet, heat the vegetable oil. Add the onion and fry, stirring constantly, until well browned, about 8 minutes. Add the lamb and fry for another 4 to 5 minutes. Add the coconut and salt; sauté for another 5 minutes.
3. Serve hot, garnished with Warm Spice Mix.

❊ Green Chili Lamb Chops

Here is a really easy recipe for instant lamb chops: In a bowl, combine equal portions of Green Chili Chutney (page 238) and Mint Chutney (page 237); add lamb chops and coat evenly with the marinade. Marinate for about 2 hours, and then cook according to your preference.

Royal Lamb
(Nawabi Gosht)

Serves 4
Prep Time: 20 minutes,
plus 2 hours to marinate
Cook Time: 1 hour,
20 minutes

This typically difficult
recipe is simplified
here into easy, man-
ageable steps. Serve
hot with Simple Indian
Bread (page 204).

1 large red onion, peeled
8 dried red chilies
1½ teaspoons fennel seeds
Water, as needed
2 teaspoons Ginger-Garlic Paste
  (see recipe on page 15)
½ cup yogurt, whipped
1¼ pounds lean, bone-in lamb,
  cut into 1–1½-inch chunks
Vegetable oil for deep-frying

4 hard-boiled eggs, peeled and
  quartered
3 tablespoons Clarified Butter
  (see recipe on page 15)
Table salt, to taste
¼ teaspoon Roasted Saffron
  (see recipe on page 16)
Unsalted cashews, roasted

1. In a food processor, purée the onion, red chilies, and fennel seeds along with 1 or 2 tablespoons of water to make a paste. Set aside.
2. In a bowl, combine the Ginger-Garlic Paste, yogurt, and lamb; mix well. Refrigerate, covered, for 2 hours.
3. Heat the vegetable oil in a deep pan to about 300°. Deep-fry the eggs until crispy on the outside. Remove with a slotted spoon and place on a paper towel. Set aside.
4. In a large skillet, heat the butter. Add the paste made in step 1. Fry the paste until the oil separates from the onion mixture.
5. Add the lamb, along with the marinade, to the onion mixture. Fry, stirring constantly, for about 15 minutes. If the lamb sticks, add 1 tablespoon of water.
6. Add 1½ cups water and bring to a boil. Cover, and simmer for about 50 minutes or until the lamb is tender. Add the salt, saffron, and eggs. Cook, uncovered, for another 5 minutes. Serve garnished with unsalted roasted cashews.

Kakori Kebab
(Kakori Kebab)

1 pound minced lamb
2 tablespoons vegetable oil
  (if needed)
5 tablespoons chickpea flour
2 tablespoons Fried Onions
  (see recipe on page 18),
  roughly pounded
1 teaspoon Warm Spice Mix
  (see recipe on page 14)

$\frac{1}{4}$ teaspoon baking soda
$\frac{1}{2}$ teaspoon red chili powder
Table salt, to taste
1 tablespoon ground cashews
Butter for basting

Serves 4
Prep Time: 15 minutes,
plus 3 hours to marinate
Cook Time: 20 minutes

These kebabs are
served on special
occasions and are tra-
ditionally made in the
shape of a sausage;
I like to shape mine
into small patties.

1. In a food processor, purée the minced lamb to a smooth paste, adding up to 2 tablespoons of oil to help with the puréeing if needed. Set aside.
2. In a small skillet on medium heat, dry roast the chickpea flour until fragrant. Set aside.
3. In a bowl, combine the lamb, chickpea flour, Fried Onions, spice mix, baking soda, red chili powder, salt, and ground cashews; mix well. Refrigerate, covered, for about 3 hours.
4. Preheat oven to 350°.
5. Using your hands, create equal-sized small patties with the lamb mixture, flattening them between the palms of your hands. You should get about 8 patties. Place the lamb patties on a foil-lined baking sheet and bake for about 10 minutes. Turn once and baste with butter. Roast for another 10 minutes or until golden brown and the juices run clear. Serve hot.

Spicy Minced Lamb Kebabs
(Shammi Kebab)

Serves 4
Prep Time: 20 minutes, plus 30 minutes to soak
Cook Time: 40 minutes

You can also freeze these just prior to the frying step. Let them thaw to room temperature just before you are ready to fry.

½ cup chana dal or yellow split peas
1 pound minced lamb
3 tablespoons Ginger-Garlic Paste (see recipe on page 15)
1 medium-sized red onion, sliced
1 teaspoon cumin seeds

2 cloves
2 green cardamom pods
Table salt, to taste
1 teaspoon red chili powder
2 tablespoons chickpea flour
Vegetable oil for frying
Chaat Spice Mix (see recipe on page 16)

1. Soak the *chana dal* in hot water for about 30 minutes. Drain.
2. In a deep pan, combine the *chana dal*, lamb, Ginger-Garlic Paste, onions, cumin, cloves, cardamom, red chili powder, chickpea flour, and salt. Add enough water to cover the mixture and bring to a full boil. Cover, lower heat, and cook until the lamb is cooked through, about 30 minutes. Remove the cover and cook on high heat until all the liquid dries out.
3. Remove from heat and cool to room temperature.
4. In a food processor, grind the lamb mixture to a fine paste. Divide the mixture into 8 small patties, flattening them between the palms of your hands.
5. In a medium-sized skillet, heat about 5 tablespoons of oil. Add the patties and pan-fry until golden brown on all sides. Remove with a slotted spatula and drain on paper towels. Serve hot, sprinkled with Chaat Spice Mix.

❈ Cardamom Pods

There are two primary types of cardamom used in India—one is a smaller green one and the other is larger and black. The smaller variety is used to flavor savory and sweet dishes. The black variety is used primarily in savory dishes. Buy the pods whole and remove the seeds as needed to get the freshest flavor. Occasionally, at your grocer you will see "white cardamom"—this is nothing but the green cardamom that has been bleached.

Ginger-Flavored Lamb Chops
(Adraki Chaampe)

1 teaspoon cumin, roasted and roughly pounded
1½ tablespoons grated fresh gingerroot
2 teaspoons Warm Spice Mix (see recipe on page 14)
1 cup heavy cream
Table salt, to taste
8 lamb chops, no visible fat
Oil for basting

1. In a bowl or resealable plastic bag, combine the cumin, ginger, spice mix, cream, and salt; mix well. Add the lamb chops and mix to coat evenly with the marinade. Cover, and refrigerate for 4 hours.
2. Preheat oven to 350°. Place the lamb chops in a single layer in a roasting pan. Bake for 10 to 15 minutes. Baste with oil. Bake for another 10 to 15 minutes or until the lamb is cooked through.

> **Serves 4**
> **Prep Time:** 5 minutes, plus 4 hours to marinate
> **Cook Time:** 30 minutes

> If you like ginger, you will love these chops. Serve with Shredded Carrot Salad (page 70).

Macaroni Lamb
(Macroni Gosht Wali)

4 tablespoons vegetable oil
2 teaspoons Ginger-Garlic Paste (see recipe on page 15)
1¼ pounds minced lamb
2 small tomatoes, puréed
1 teaspoon Warm Spice Mix (see recipe on page 14)
½ teaspoon red chili powder
¼ teaspoon turmeric powder
Table salt, to taste
1 cup cooked elbow macaroni

1. In a large skillet, heat the vegetable oil. Add the Ginger-Garlic Paste and sauté for 10 seconds. Add the lamb and sauté for about 10 to 12 minutes. Add the tomatoes and fry, stirring frequently, for 25 minutes or until the oil starts to separate from the sides of the mixture.
2. Add the spice mix, red chili powder, turmeric powder, and salt. Mix well. Cook for about 2 minutes. Add the macaroni and cook, covered, for another 10 minutes or until the lamb is cooked through.

> **Serves 4**
> **Prep Time:** 20 minutes
> **Cook Time:** 50 minutes

> Try serving this with fresh French bread and a light spinach salad.

Cardamom-Flavored Lamb
(Eliachi Gosht)

Serves 4
Prep Time: 10 minutes
Cook Time: 1 hour,
30 minutes

Fragrant cardamom pods and powder perfume this dish. Adjust the amount of cardamom to your taste. Serve with warm Simple Indian Bread (page 204).

¼ cup blanched almonds
3 tablespoons vegetable oil
1 large red onion, minced
2 serrano green chilies, seeded
    and minced
4 green cardamom pods,
    bruised
1 pound lean lamb chunks

½ cup plain yogurt
1 cup water
2 tablespoons cream
Table salt, to taste
1 teaspoon cardamom powder

1. In a food processor, combine the almonds with a few tablespoons of water to make a thick, coarse paste. Set aside.
2. In a large pan, heat the vegetable oil. Add the onion and sauté until golden brown, about 7 to 8 minutes. Add the green chilies, cardamom pods, and lamb; sauté for about 25 minutes. If the lamb starts to stick to the pan, add about 1 tablespoon of water.
3. Add the yogurt and fry for 5 minutes. Add the almond paste, then add the water and bring to a full boil. Cover, lower heat, and cook for about 50 minutes or until the lamb is tender and cooked through.
4. Add the cream and mix well. Simmer for about 5 minutes. Add salt to taste. Sprinkle with the cardamom powder and serve hot.

✳ Cardamom Powder

Most stores sell this fragrant powder. Use a little at a time—it goes a long way. If you want to make your own, here is a simple recipe: Open the cardamom pods. Remove the seeds and discard the shells. In a spice grinder, grind the seeds to a fine powder. Store in an airtight jar.

Fiery Pork
(Pork Balchao)

½ teaspoon black peppercorns

5 cloves

½ teaspoon cumin seeds

6 dried red chilies

1 tablespoon Ginger-Garlic Paste (see recipe on page 15)

½ cup malt vinegar

4 tablespoons vegetable oil

1 pound lean pork, cut into chunks

1 large red onion, finely chopped

2 small tomatoes, finely chopped

1 tablespoon sugar

Table salt, to taste

> **Serves 4**
> **Prep Time:** 15 minutes
> **Cook Time:** 40 minutes
>
> This tangy pork dish will taste better a couple of days after it is prepared, once the spices are allowed to work their magic.

1. In a spice grinder, grind the black peppercorns, cloves, cumin, and red chilies. Put the spice mixture into a food processor or blender and add the Ginger-Garlic Paste and malt vinegar; process until smooth. Set aside.

2. Heat the oil in a large skillet, add the pork, and sear it until brown on all sides. Remove the pork with a slotted spoon and place on paper towels to drain. Do not discard the oil from the skillet.

3. Reheat the oil and add the onions. Sauté for about 7 to 8 minutes or until the onions are well browned. Add the tomatoes and fry, stirring constantly, until the oil starts to separate from the mixture.

4. Add the pork and mix well; stirring constantly, fry for about 6 minutes.

5. Add the sugar and salt; mix well. Fry for about 5 minutes, stirring constantly. Serve hot.

✳ The Mutiny

Pork is forbidden by many religious sects in India. During the British rule in India, there was a mutiny around the 1850s, when Indian soldiers refused to use the pork grease that was used for oiling rifles. The Christians of Goa, in western India, eat pork regularly.

Pork Bafat
(Pork Bafat)

Serves 4
Prep Time: 5 minutes
Cook Time: 30–40 minutes

Another Goan-inspired dish, this is fiery hot. Add more chilies if you like your dishes really hot!

1 tablespoon Ginger-Garlic Paste (see recipe on page 15)
4 black peppercorns
4 cloves
1 teaspoon cumin seeds
¼ teaspoon black mustard seeds
8 dried red chilies
¼ cup malt vinegar
4 tablespoons vegetable oil
1 pound pork, cubed
1 tablespoon tamarind pulp, soaked in ¼ cup hot water for 10 minutes
1 cup frozen pearl onions
Table salt, to taste
Water, as needed

1. In a food processor, grind together the Ginger-Garlic Paste, black peppercorns, cloves, cumin seeds, mustard seeds, red chilies, and malt vinegar. Set aside.
2. In a large skillet, heat the vegetable oil; add the pork and brown on all sides, about 8 to 10 minutes. Add the ground paste and sauté for 10 more minutes.
3. Strain the tamarind and discard the residue. Add the strained liquid to the pork and mix well. Add the frozen onions and salt; cook, uncovered, for about 5 minutes.
4. Add ½ cup of water. Lower the heat and simmer, uncovered, until the pork is cooked, about 10 to 15 minutes. Stir occasionally. Add more water if the dish becomes too dry or starts to stick. Serve hot.

❋ Need a Quick, Healthy Pick-Me-Up?

Try dates. The kind you eat! A single serving of dates (5 to 6 pieces) contains over 30 grams of carbohydrates, making them a powerhouse of energy.

CHAPTER 9
From the Fisherman's Net (Machwari Ke Jal Se)

Fish in a Velvety Sauce
(Bengali Doi Maach)

Serves 4
Prep Time: 20 minutes
Cook Time: 30 minutes

For this recipe, you can use tilapia or catfish. Serve this with Simple Basmati Rice (page 162).

4–5 catfish filets

¾ teaspoon turmeric powder

8 tablespoons vegetable oil, divided

1 bay leaf

½ teaspoon cumin seeds

2 teaspoons Ginger-Garlic Paste (see recipe on page 15)

1 large red onion, minced

1 teaspoon red chili powder

2 serrano green chilies, seeded and minced

½ cup plain yogurt, whipped

Table salt, to taste

Water, as needed

1. Place the catfish filets in a bowl. Rub the filets well with the turmeric and set aside for about 10 minutes. Rinse the filets and pat dry.

2. In a medium-sized skillet, heat 6 tablespoons of the vegetable oil. Add 1 filet at a time and fry until brown on both sides. Remove from heat with a slotted spoon and drain on a paper towel. Continue until all the filets are fried. Set aside.

3. In a large skillet, heat the remaining 2 tablespoons of vegetable oil. Add the bay leaf and cumin seeds. When the spices begin to sizzle, add the Ginger-Garlic Paste and onions; sauté for about 7 to 8 minutes or until the onions are well browned.

4. Add the red chili powder and green chilies; mix well. Add the yogurt and salt, and mix well. Add about ½ cup of water. Simmer, uncovered, on low heat for about 10 minutes, stirring constantly.

5. Add the fish filets and simmer for another 5 minutes. Be careful not to break the filets when you stir. Serve hot.

❉ Green Chilies

Wear gloves when handling fresh chilies. They can be quite unforgiving if they get on your hands. I often use kitchen scissors instead of a knife to snip the chilies.

Shrimp in Coconut Milk
(Chingri Maacher Malai Curry)

1 bay leaf
1 teaspoon cumin seeds
1 (1-inch) cinnamon stick
2 cloves
4 black peppercorns
1-inch piece fresh gingerroot, peeled and sliced
4 garlic cloves
Water, as needed

3 tablespoons vegetable oil
1 large red onion, minced
½ teaspoon turmeric powder
1 pound shrimp, peeled and deveined
1 (14-ounce) can light coconut milk
Table salt, to taste

> **Serves 4**
> **Prep Time:** 10 minutes
> **Cook Time:** 20 minutes
>
> A nice variation is to fry the shrimp first. It adds a nice crispness. Serve with steamed white rice.

1. In a spice grinder, roughly grind the bay leaf, cumin seeds, cinnamon stick, cloves, peppercorns, ginger, and garlic. Add 1 tablespoon of water if needed.
2. In a medium-sized skillet, heat the vegetable oil. Add the ground spice mixture and sauté for about 1 minute. Add the onions and sauté for 7 to 8 minutes or until the onions are well browned.
3. Add the turmeric and mix well. Add the shrimp and sauté for about 2 to 3 minutes, until no longer pink.
4. Add the coconut milk and salt. Simmer for 10 minutes or until the gravy starts to thicken. Remove from heat and serve hot.

❊ Defrosting Frozen Shrimp

If you are using frozen shrimp, thaw them in the refrigerator or under running cold water. It is not advisable to defrost shrimp in the microwave or at room temperature—doing so will cause the shrimp to lose a lot of flavor and texture.

Fish Fry
(Mom's Tali Macchi)

2 teaspoons turmeric powder
2 dried red chilies, crushed
2 teaspoons coriander seeds, roughly pounded
2 garlic cloves, minced
1 teaspoon Warm Spice Mix (see recipe on page 14)
Table salt, to taste

3 heaping tablespoons all-purpose flour
4 whitefish filets (such as tilapia, catfish, cod)
4 tablespoons oil
1 tablespoon fresh lemon juice

1. In a shallow dish, combine the turmeric, red chilies, coriander, garlic, and spice mix; mix well.
2. In a second dish, combine the salt and flour; mix well.
3. Coat each filet lightly, first with the spice mix and then with the flour. Discard any remaining spice mix and flour.
4. Heat the vegetable oil in a medium skillet. Fry each filet, 1 at a time, for about 3 to 4 minutes or until golden brown on each side. Drain on a paper towel. Serve immediately, sprinkled with lemon juice.

✳ Getting Rid of Fishy Smells
Soak fish for 1 hour in milk or let frozen fish thaw in milk. This will not only freshen the fish and enhance the taste but will also remove any smell.

Tandoori Fish
(Tandoori Macchi)

3 teaspoons Ginger-Garlic Paste
   (see recipe on page 15)
4 tablespoons heavy cream
1 teaspoon cumin seeds
1 teaspoon red chili powder
½ teaspoon turmeric powder
½ teaspoon Tandoori Spice Mix
   (see recipe on page 15)

½ teaspoon carom seeds
1 egg
Table salt, to taste
4 whitefish filets (such as
   tilapia, catfish, cod)
Oil for basting
Fresh lemon juice

> **Serves 4**
> **Prep Time:** 5 minutes,
> plus 1 hour to marinate
> **Cook Time:** 15 minutes
>
> Serve with the Punjabi
> Onion Salad, Green
> Chili Chutney, and an
> ice-cold Watermelon
> Cooler (pages 68,
> 238, and 47).

1. In a bowl, combine the ginger paste, cream, cumin seeds, red chili powder, turmeric, spice mix, carom seeds, egg, and salt; mix well.
2. Pour the marinade over the fish filets, turning them to ensure that they are well coated. Refrigerate, covered, for about 1 hour.
3. Preheat oven to 350°.
4. Bake for about 7 minutes on each side, basting once with oil. Serve hot, sprinkled with lemon juice.

✳ Chutney Reruns
Use leftover chutneys as a topping for grilled fish. A grilled trout topped with a Mint-Cilantro Chutney is a mouthwatering combination.

Creamy Shrimp
(Malai Jhinga)

1 pound shrimp, peeled and deveined
1 teaspoon turmeric powder, divided
3 tablespoons vegetable oil
2 teaspoons Ginger-Garlic Paste (see recipe on page 15)
2 medium tomatoes, chopped

Water, as needed
1 teaspoon red chili powder
2 teaspoons coriander powder
Table salt, to taste
4 tablespoons light cream

1. Place the shrimp in a bowl. Rub about ¾ teaspoon of the turmeric on the shrimp and set aside for about 10 minutes. Rinse them well and pat dry.
2. In a large skillet, heat the vegetable oil. Add the Ginger-Garlic Paste and sauté for about 30 seconds. Add the tomatoes and sauté for 7 to 8 minutes or until the oil begins to separate from the tomatoes. Add 1 tablespoon of water if the mixture appears to be sticking.
3. Add the remaining turmeric, the red chili powder, coriander powder, and salt; mix well. Sauté for 1 minute.
4. Add 1 cup of water and bring to a boil. Reduce the heat and simmer, covered, for about 5 minutes. Add the shrimp. Cook for about 5 to 6 minutes or until the shrimp are cooked through.
5. Remove from heat and add the light cream; mix well. Serve hot.

❋ Cilantro or Coriander?

People often confuse these two spices, but they are not the same. Cilantro is the plant, and coriander is the seeds. I store my cilantro wrapped in newspaper in the refrigerator. The newspaper helps absorb any excess moisture, keeping the cilantro fresh for a longer period of time.

Shrimp Koliwada
(Jhinga Koliwada)

1 pound medium shrimp, peeled and deveined
¾ teaspoon turmeric powder
1 teaspoon grated fresh gingerroot
1 teaspoon minced fresh garlic
1 teaspoon red chili powder
1 teaspoon Warm Spice Mix (see recipe on page 14)
½ teaspoon dried mango powder
½ teaspoon carom seeds
4 tablespoons corn flour
Water, as needed
Vegetable oil for deep-frying

Serves 4
Prep Time: 15 minutes and 20 minutes to marinate
Cook Time: 15 minutes

Named for a suburb of Mumbai, Koliwada-style dishes are a delight to the palate. Serve with your choice of chutney.

1. Place the shrimp in a bowl. Rub the turmeric on the shrimp and set aside for about 10 minutes. Rinse them well and pat dry.
2. In a bowl, combine the ginger, garlic, red chili powder, spice mix, mango powder, carom seeds, and corn flour. Add enough water to make a batter of coating consistency. Add the shrimp to the batter and marinate for about 20 minutes.
3. Heat the vegetable oil in a deep fryer or a deep pan to 300° on a deep-fry thermometer. Add a few shrimp and deep-fry until golden brown and crisp on all sides. Remove from the oil with a slotted spoon and drain on a paper towel. Let the oil return to temperature. Continue until all the shrimp are fried. Discard any remaining marinade. Serve immediately.

❋ Spices as Medicine

Indian cuisine rests on the shoulders of ancient medicine. Each spice or herb that is used is deemed to have value in the world of medicine. For example, turmeric is an antiseptic, and cumin and carom seeds aid in digestion.

Shrimp Jalfrezi Style
(Jhinga Jalfrezi)

Serves 4
Prep Time: 10 minutes
Cook Time: 10 minutes

Don't let the unusual name of the dish scare you away. You can also make this with chicken or Indian Cheese (page 14).

3 tablespoons vegetable oil
½ teaspoon cumin seeds
3 dried red chilies, broken
3 serrano green chilies, slit down the sides and seeded
1 large red onion, peeled and diced
1 large tomato, deseeded and diced

2 medium bell peppers, deseeded and diced
2-inch piece fresh gingerroot, julienned
½ cup tomato purée
1 pound medium shrimp, peeled and deveined
½ teaspoon turmeric powder
Table salt, to taste

1. In a medium-sized skillet, heat the vegetable oil. Add the cumin seeds; when they begin to sizzle, add the red and green chilies, onion, diced tomato, ginger, and bell peppers in quick succession. Sauté on high heat for about 2 minutes.
2. Add the tomato purée and cook for 3 to 4 minutes.
3. Add the shrimp, turmeric, and salt; sauté for 3 to 4 minutes or until the shrimp are cooked through. The vegetables will still have a slight crunch to them. Serve hot.

✳ Monday Night Grilled Shrimp
Marinate shrimp in yogurt along with grated ginger, Warm Spice Mix (page 14), fresh minced mint, lemon juice, salt, and red chili powder. Grill and serve hot.

Kerala Fish Curry
(Meen Moilee)

4–5 whitefish filets (such as tilapia, catfish, or cod)
1 teaspoon turmeric powder
6 tablespoons vegetable oil
½ teaspoon black mustard seeds
2 green cardamom pods, bruised
2 cloves
8 fresh curry leaves

1 large red onion, finely chopped
1 teaspoon grated fresh gingerroot
Table salt, to taste
1 teaspoon red chili powder
¼ teaspoon turmeric powder
1 teaspoon coriander powder
1 (14-ounce) can light coconut milk

Serves 4
Prep Time: 15 minutes
Cook Time: 35–40 minutes

This popular dish comes to you from the gorgeous state of Kerala on the west coast of India. Serve with Simple Basmati Rice (page 160).

1. Place the fish filets in a bowl. Rub the filets well with the turmeric and set aside for about 10 minutes. Rinse the filets and pat dry.

2. In a medium-sized nonstick skillet, heat 4 tablespoons of the vegetable oil. Add 1 filet at a time and shallow-fry until brown on both sides. Remove from the skillet with a slotted spoon and drain on a paper towel. Continue until all the filets are fried. Set aside.

3. In a large skillet, heat the remaining vegetable oil. Add the mustard seeds, cardamom, and cloves. As soon as they begin to sputter, add the curry leaves, onions, and ginger; sauté for 7 to 8 minutes or until the onions are well browned.

4. Reduce heat. Add the salt; red chili, turmeric, and coriander powder; sauté for 1 minute. Add the coconut milk and simmer for about 10 minutes. Don't let the coconut milk boil.

5. Add the fried fish to the coconut curry and spoon the sauce over the fish. Simmer for 5 to 7 minutes or until the fish is completely heated through. Serve hot.

Shrimp Patio
(Kolmino Patio)

Serves 4
Prep Time: 10 minutes
Cook Time: 15 minutes

Serve with Simple Basmati Rice (page 160). You can substitute brown sugar for jaggery if you like.

3 dried red chilies
2 teaspoons coriander seeds
1 teaspoon cumin seeds
1 teaspoon mustard seeds
4 fresh garlic cloves
¼ teaspoon black peppercorns
1 (1-inch) cinnamon stick
½ teaspoon turmeric powder
½ teaspoon red chili powder

¼ cup white vinegar
Water, as needed
3 tablespoons vegetable oil
1 large red onion, minced
1½ pounds shrimp, peeled and deveined
1 tablespoon jaggery or brown sugar
Table salt, to taste

1. In a spice grinder, grind together the red chilies, coriander seeds, cumin seeds, mustard seeds, cloves, black peppercorns, and cinnamon, as finely as possible. Place in a glass bowl and add the turmeric, red chili powder, and vinegar; mix well. If you need more liquid, add a little water. Set aside.
2. In a large skillet, heat the vegetable oil. Add the onions and sauté for about 7 to 8 minutes or until the onions are well browned. Add the spice paste from step 1 and cook for 1 minute. Add the shrimp and cook for 2 to 3 minutes.
3. Add the jaggery and salt. Add about 1 cup of water. Bring to a boil. Reduce heat and simmer for 2 minutes. Serve hot.

✳ Deveining Shrimp
To devein shrimp, run the tip of a small knife down the back of the shrimp. Use the tip of the knife or your finger to pull out the vein. Make sure you rinse all the shrimp after deveining.

Fried Fish
(Amritsari Tali Macchi)

1 cup chickpea flour
1 teaspoon carom seeds
1 teaspoon red chili powder
2 tablespoons Ginger-Garlic Paste
  (see recipe on page 15)
1½ tablespoons lemon juice
Table salt, to taste

Water, as needed
2 pounds whitefish chunks
  (such as tilapia, catfish, cod)
Vegetable oil for deep-frying
Chaat Spice Mix (see recipe
  on page 16)

Serves 4
Prep Time: 5 minutes,
plus 25 minutes
to marinate
Cook Time: 20 minutes

This crispy fish is a
North Indian favorite.
Named for the holy
city of Amritsar, it is
served garnished with
cilantro leaves and
sliced onions.

1. In a large bowl, combine the chickpea flour, carom seeds, red chili powder, Ginger-Garlic Paste, lemon juice, and salt. Add water as needed to make a thick batter. Mix well and make sure there are no lumps.
2. Add the fish pieces to the batter. Combine to ensure that the fish is well coated. Let stand for about 25 minutes.
3. In a deep pan, heat the vegetable oil to 300°. Deep-fry a few pieces at a time until crisp and golden brown. Remove with a slotted spoon (tongs also work well here) and drain on a paper towel. Continue until all the pieces are fried. Discard any remaining batter.
4. Serve immediately, sprinkled with Chaat Spice Mix.

☀ Ugadi—The Day of Creation

Raw or green mangoes hold a special significance during the Indian festival of Ugadi. Ugadi pachchadi, a dish made with jaggery, raw mango pieces, bitter neem leaves, and tangy tamarind, is said to be reflective of one's real life—a combination of sweet, sour, and bitter tastes.

Kashmiri Fish Curry
(Kashmiri Macchi)

Serves 4
Prep Time: 15 minutes
Cook Time: 20 minutes

Traditional Kashmiri cooking uses dried ginger powder, but I like the taste of fresh ginger.

4–5 whitefish filets (such as tilapia, catfish, or cod)
¾ teaspoon turmeric powder
1 teaspoon ginger, finely ground
1 teaspoon anise seeds, roughly pounded
4 tablespoons vegetable oil
1 teaspoon red chili powder
2 teaspoons coriander powder
Table salt, to taste
1 cup plain yogurt, whipped

1. Place the fish filets in a bowl. Rub the filets well with the turmeric, ginger, and anise seeds; set aside for about 10 minutes.
2. In a medium-sized skillet, heat the vegetable oil. Add 1 filet at a time and shallow-fry until brown on both sides. Remove from the skillet with a slotted spoon and drain on paper towels. Continue until all the filets are fried. Set aside. Keep the oil.
3. In the same skillet (with the oil) on low heat, add the red chili powder, coriander, and salt; mix well. Add the yogurt (it will appear to curdle a bit, but continue to cook it).
4. Simmer on low heat for about 10 minutes. The oil will begin to separate from the yogurt. Add the fried fish.
5. Cover and simmer on low heat until the fish is completely heated through. Serve hot.

※ Tips on Buying Whole Fish
When buying whole fish, look for fish with bright eyes. The flesh should be shiny and bounce back to the touch.

Grilled Yogurt-Flavored Fish
(Dahi Macchi Tikka)

1 pound whitefish, cut in chunks
¾ teaspoon turmeric powder
¾ cup Hung Yogurt (see recipe on page 16)
¼ cup heavy cream
2 teaspoons Ginger-Garlic Paste (see recipe on page 15)

1 teaspoon Warm Spice Mix (see recipe on page 14)
Table salt, to taste
Oil for basting
1 teaspoon Chaat Spice Mix (see recipe on page 16), for garnish

Serves 4
Prep Time: 15 minutes, plus 2 hours to marinate
Cook Time: 15 minutes

This delicately flavored grilled fish can be served as an appetizer or an entrée. Serve with spicy Green Chili Chutney (page 238).

1. Place the fish chunks in a bowl. Rub them well with the turmeric and set aside for about 10 minutes. Rinse and pat dry
2. In a bowl, combine the yogurt, cream, Ginger-Garlic Paste, Warm Spice Mix, salt, fish, and mix well. Refrigerate, covered, for 2 hours.
3. Preheat oven to 350°.
4. Place the fish in a single layer on a roasting pan. Bake in the oven, basting once, for 10 to 15 minutes or until the fish is cooked through. (Alternatively, you can skewer the fish and grill it.) Serve hot, sprinkled with Chaat Spice Mix.

✳ Garlic Flavor

To get the true strong flavor of garlic cloves, crush them with the flat of your knife blade or use a garlic press. Chopping or mincing them with a knife will not release the depth of flavor that you will get from crushing them.

Parsi Fish
(Patrani Macchi)

Serves 4
Prep Time: 10 minutes
Cook Time: 20–30 minutes

A perfect recipe when you have lots of leftover chutney and very little time. Serve with plain white rice.

4 (1-inch-thick) fish steaks (your choice of type)
¾ teaspoon turmeric powder

8 tablespoons Green Chili and Coconut Chutney (see recipe on page 227)

1. Place the fish steaks in a bowl. Rub the steaks well with the turmeric and set aside for about 10 minutes. Rinse and pat dry.
2. Cut 4 squares of aluminum foil large enough to accommodate the steaks. Place a steak in the center of each piece of foil. Cover the fish with 2 generous tablespoons of the chutney. Fold the foil over it as if you were wrapping a present. Leave a little room for the steam to expand.
3. Preheat the oven to 400°.
4. Place the foil packages on a baking sheet. Bake until the fish is completely cooked through (20 to 25 minutes for 1-inch-thick steaks). The timing will depend on the thickness of your steak. Serve hot.

❋ Crunchy Bread Fritters Stuffed with Tuna

Using the recipe for Crunchy Bread Fritters (page 34), stuff the fritters with tuna prior to frying. You can season the tuna with red chili powder and roasted cumin seeds prior to stuffing.

Fish Kebabs
(Kebab Macchi Ke)

2 teaspoons turmeric powder

2 dried red chilies, crushed

2 serrano green chilies, seeded
  and minced

2 eggs, beaten

Table salt, to taste

4 heaping tablespoons semolina

4 small whitefish filets

4 tablespoons oil

1 tablespoon fresh lemon juice

Serves 4
Prep Time: 10 minutes
Cook Time: 15 minutes

Refrigerating the filets for a few minutes before you fry will make the coating stay on better. Serve with Mint-Cilantro Chutney (page 226).

1. In a shallow dish, combine the turmeric, red chilies, green chilies, eggs, and salt; mix well. Place the semolina in a second shallow dish.
2. Coat each filet lightly, first with the spice mix and then with the semolina. Discard any remaining spice mix and semolina.
3. Heat the vegetable oil in a medium-sized skillet. Fry each filet, 1 at a time, for about 3 to 4 minutes or until golden brown on each side. Drain on a paper towel. Serve immediately, sprinkled with lemon juice.

❈ Semolina

Semolina, called rava or sooji in India, is used for preparing sweet and savory dishes. Buy the coarse variety. You can also substitute cream of wheat in a pinch for all the recipes indicated in this book (unless otherwise specified).

Shrimp Fritters
(Jhinge Ke Pakore)

1 pound shrimp, tail on and deveined
1 teaspoon turmeric powder
1 teaspoon red chili powder
1 serrano green chili, seeded and minced
1 tablespoon grated fresh gingerroot
1 tablespoon minced fresh garlic cloves
1 tablespoon fresh lemon juice
Table salt, to taste
2 eggs, beaten
3 heaping tablespoons all-purpose flour
Vegetable oil for deep-frying

1. Butterfly the shrimp and set aside.
2. In a shallow bowl, combine the turmeric, red chili powder, green chili, ginger, garlic, lemon juice, and salt; mix well.
3. Place the eggs in a second dish. Place the flour in a shallow dish.
4. Coat each shrimp with the spice mixture, then dip in the egg, and then coat with the flour. Continue until all the shrimp are coated. Discard any remaining eggs and flour.
5. Heat the vegetable oil in a deep fryer or a deep pan to 350°. Deep-fry the shrimp, a few at a time, until golden brown. Remove with a slotted spoon and drain on paper towels. Serve hot.

✳ Butterfly Shrimp

To butterfly the shrimp: Devein the shrimp, but leave the tail on. Using the flat blade of a knife, press down gently along the cut you made to remove the vein until the shrimp halves are opened flat, but still connected. Don't press too hard or you will split the shrimp in two!

Tamarind Fish Curry
(Imli Wale Macchi)

1½ pounds, whitefish, cut into chunks

¾ teaspoon and ½ teaspoon turmeric powder

2 teaspoons tamarind pulp, soaked in ¼ cup hot water for 10 minutes

3 tablespoons vegetable oil

½ teaspoon black mustard seeds

¼ teaspoon fenugreek seeds

8 fresh curry leaves

1 large onion, minced

2 serrano green chilies, seeded and minced

2 small tomatoes, chopped

2 dried red chilies, roughly pounded

1 teaspoon coriander seeds, roughly pounded

½ cup unsweetened desiccated coconut

Table salt, to taste

1 cup water

Serves 4
Prep Time: 15 minutes
Cook Time: 35 minutes

If you do not have tamarind, add a bit of lemon juice for a flavor that is similar. Serve with Simple Basmati Rice (page 162).

1. Place the fish in a bowl. Rub well with the ¾ teaspoon turmeric and set aside for about 10 minutes. Rinse and pat dry.
2. Strain the tamarind and set the liquid aside. Discard the residue.
3. In a large skillet, heat the vegetable oil. Add the mustard seeds and fenugreek seeds. When they begin to sputter, add the curry leaves, onions, and green chilies. Sauté for 7 to 8 minutes or until the onions are well browned.
4. Add the tomatoes and cook for another 8 minutes or until the oil begins to separate from the sides of the mixture. Add the remaining ½ teaspoon turmeric, the red chilies, coriander seeds, coconut, and salt; mix well, and cook for another 30 seconds.
5. Add the water and the strained tamarind; bring to a boil. Lower the heat and add the fish. Cook on low heat for 10 to 15 minutes or until the fish is completely cooked. Serve hot.

Chili Scallops
(Mirchi Wale Scallops)

Serves 4
Prep Time: 10 minutes
Cook Time: 25 minutes

Red chili sambal brings a fiery flavor to the scallops. If you do not have sambal, grind a few dried red chilies along with some water.

1 pound sea scallops (or cubed whitefish of your choice)
1 tablespoon red chili sambal
3 tablespoons vegetable oil
½ teaspoon mustard seeds
8 fresh curry leaves
2 teaspoons Ginger-Garlic Paste (see recipe on page 15)

2 small tomatoes, chopped
½ teaspoon turmeric powder
Table salt, to taste
Water, as needed
Coconut milk, for garnish

1. In a bowl, combine the scallops and the sambal. (If you are using dried red chilies instead, add 2 teaspoons of oil as well.) Set aside for 15 minutes.
2. While the scallops are marinating, heat the vegetable oil in a medium-sized skillet. Add the mustard seeds; when they begin to sputter, add the curry leaves, ginger paste, and tomatoes. Sauté for about 8 minutes or until the oil begins to separate from the sides of the mixture.
3. Add the turmeric and salt and stir well.
4. Add about 1 cup of water and cook, uncovered, for 10 minutes. Add the scallops (along with all the red chili sambal) and cook on medium heat until the scallops are cooked through, about 5 minutes.
5. Garnish with the coconut milk and serve hot.

※ Homemade Coconut Milk

A quick way to make coconut milk is to blend coconut cream with hot water. You can also blend unsweetened desiccated coconut or fresh coconut with hot water, but just be sure to strain before use.

Malabari Chili Fish
(Malabari Mirchi Wali Macchi)

1 pound whitefish, cut into
   1- to 1½-inch chunks
¾ teaspoon turmeric powder
Juice of ½ lemon
1 teaspoon coriander powder
1 teaspoon cumin powder
¼ teaspoon black peppercorns,
   roughly pounded

4 dried red chilies, roughly
   pounded
Table salt, to taste
Vegetable oil for deep-frying
Chaat Spice Mix (see recipe
   on page 16), optional

Serves 4
Prep Time: 15 minutes
plus 2 hours to marinate
Cook Time: 20 minutes

For an extra zing,
serve this dish with
Green Chili Chutney
(page 238).

1. Place the fish cubes in a bowl. Rub them well with the turmeric and set aside for about 10 minutes. Rinse the fish and pat dry.

2. In a bowl, combine the lemon juice, coriander powder, cumin powder, black pepper, red chilies, and salt; mix well. Add the fish and mix to ensure that all the pieces are well coated. Refrigerate, covered, for 2 hours.

3. Heat the vegetable oil in a deep fryer or a deep pan to 350°. Deep-fry a few pieces of fish at a time. Remove from the oil with a slotted spoon and drain on a paper towel. Continue until all the fish is fried. Discard any remaining marinade. Serve immediately. Sprinkle Chaat Spice Mix on the fish just prior to serving, if desired.

✷ How Hot Is This Chili Pepper?

Generally, the smaller they are, the hotter they are. The color of the peppers is not indicative of the heat of the pepper. You can deseed the peppers before using to remove the heat and retain the flavor.

Green Chili Fish
(Hari Mirch Ki Macchi)

Serves 4
Prep Time: 10 minutes
Cook Time: 20 minutes

If you are not a fan of cilantro, you can use fresh mint. Be sure to seed the chilies if you like your fish mild.

1½ pounds whitefish (such as tilapia, catfish, or cod), cut into 1- to 1½-inch chunks
¾ teaspoon turmeric powder
6 serrano green chilies
1 packed cup cilantro
2 tablespoons unsweetened desiccated coconut
Table salt, to taste
Juice of 1 lemon

¼ teaspoon red chili powder
2 teaspoons Ginger-Garlic Paste (see recipe on page 15)
4 tablespoons Hung Yogurt (see recipe on page 16)
Vegetable oil for deep-frying
1 teaspoon Chaat Spice Mix (see recipe on page 16), for garnish

1. Place the fish in a bowl. Rub well with the turmeric and set aside for about 10 minutes. Rinse and pat dry.
2. In a blender or food processor, purée the green chilies, cilantro, coconut, salt, lemon juice, red chili powder, ginger paste, and yogurt to form a paste.
3. In a bowl, combine the green chili paste with the fish. Mix well to ensure that the fish is well coated with the paste.
4. Heat the vegetable oil in a deep fryer or a deep pan to 350°. Fry the fish, a few pieces at a time, until it is crispy on all sides and cooked through. Using a slotted spoon, remove the fish from the oil and drain on paper towels. Let the oil return to temperature between batches. Continue until all the fish is fried.
5. Serve immediately, sprinkled with the Chaat Spice Mix.

❈ Hard-to-Find Spices

If you're having trouble finding some of the ingredients you are looking for, go to ✎www.namaste.com for a wonderful online selection of Indian spices, herbs, and breads. They ship all over the United States.

Portuguese Indian Shrimp Rolls
(Fofos)

2 small potatoes
1 pound shrimp, peeled and
    deveined
½ teaspoon turmeric powder
Table salt, to taste
½ cup water

2 serrano green chilies, seeded
    and minced
1 teaspoon minced garlic
2 eggs, whisked
1 cup fresh bread crumbs
Vegetable oil for deep-frying

Serves 4
Prep Time: 20 minutes
Cook Time: 15 minutes

Use fresh bread crumbs for the best results. You can also use packaged mashed potatoes as a shortcut to make this dish.

1. Peel and cut the potatoes into 1½-inch dice. Boil in water for about 8 minutes or until tender. Set aside.
2. In a deep pan, combine the shrimp, turmeric powder, salt, and water. Simmer until the shrimp just turn opaque. Drain any water and set the shrimp aside.
3. Coarsely chop the shrimp and mash the potatoes. In a bowl, combine the shrimp, potatoes, green chilies, and garlic; mix well and form into balls. You should get about 12 balls.
4. Place the eggs in a bowl and place the bread crumbs in another shallow bowl.
5. In a deep fryer or a deep pan, heat the vegetable oil to 350°. Take each shrimp roll, dip it into the eggs, and then lightly roll it in the bread crumbs. Deep-fry, 2 at a time, until golden brown. Remove from the oil with a slotted spoon and drain on paper towels. Serve hot.

❉ Fresh Bread Crumbs

To make fresh bread crumbs, remove and discard the crusts of bread slices. Cut or tear the bread into 1-inch pieces and pulse a few times in a food processor. Store in an airtight container.

Lobster in Creamy Sauce
(Lobster Ka Korma)

Serves 4
Prep Time: 15 minutes
Cook Time: 20 minutes

Keep the lobster shell
and spoon the dish
into the shell for a
lovely presentation.

3 tablespoons unsalted cashew
   nuts, soaked in water for
   10 minutes
2 tablespoons white poppy
   seeds, soaked in water for
   20 minutes
Water, as needed
2 tablespoons blanched almonds
2 teaspoons white sesame seeds
3 tablespoons Clarified Butter
   (see recipe on page 17)
1 (1-inch) cinnamon stick
1 black cardamom pod, bruised
1 small bay leaf

2 cloves
1 green cardamom pod,
   bruised
1 teaspoon Ginger-Garlic Paste
   (see recipe on page 15)
2 serrano green chilies, seeded
   and minced
½ teaspoon red chili powder
¼ teaspoon turmeric powder
1 cup yogurt, whipped
1½ pounds cooked lobster meat
Table salt, to taste
1 teaspoon Warm Spice Mix
   (see recipe on page 14)

1. Drain the cashews and poppy seeds and process or blend together
   with the almonds and sesame seeds using just enough water to make
   a thick paste. Set aside.
2. In a large skillet, heat the butter. Add the cinnamon stick, black cardamom pod, bay leaf, cloves, and green cardamom pod. When the
   spices begin to sizzle, add the Ginger-Garlic Paste, green chilies, and
   the nut paste. It will splatter a little; add 1 tablespoon of water to stop
   the splattering. Fry, stirring constantly, until the oil begins to separate
   from the mixture.
3. Add the red chili powder, turmeric, yogurt, lobster, salt, and spice mix.
   Fry, stirring constantly, until the lobster is heated through. Serve hot.

Red Chili Fish Fry
(Lal Mirchi Ki Macchi)

4 whitefish filets (such as tilapia, catfish, or cod)
¾ teaspoon turmeric powder
3 tablespoons vegetable oil
½ teaspoon black mustard seeds
8 fresh curry leaves
4 dried red chilies, roughly pounded

1 large onion, minced
2 teaspoons Ginger-Garlic Paste (see recipe on page 15)
½ teaspoon red chili powder
¼ teaspoon turmeric powder
Table salt, to taste
½ cup water

> **Serves 4**
> **Prep Time:** 15 minutes
> **Cook Time:** 20 minutes
>
> Serve with Simple Basmati Rice (page 162). For a milder version, add ½ cup of light coconut milk instead of water in step 4.

1. Place the fish filets in a bowl. Rub them well with the turmeric and set aside for about 10 minutes. Rinse the filets and pat dry.
2. In a large skillet, heat the vegetable oil. Add the mustard seeds and when they begin to sputter, add the curry leaves, red chilies, and onions. Sauté for about 6–7 minutes or until well browned. Add the Ginger-Garlic Paste, red chili powder, turmeric powder, and salt; mix well.
3. Add the fish and fry for 3 minutes. Turn and fry for another 3 minutes.
4. Add ½ cup of water and bring to a boil. Cover, lower heat, and simmer for about 6 to 8 minutes or until the fish is completely cooked through. Serve hot.

❋ Tamarind Lime Sauce

This delicious full-bodied dipping sauce takes its inspiration from a Vietnamese sauce. I love to use this sauce on grilled seafood as well as grilled chicken. The honey in this sauce balances out the tanginess of the tamarind, ginger, and lime juice. In a bowl, combine 1 tablespoon of tamarind concentrate, ¼ cup ice water, 2 teaspoons lime juice, 2 teaspoons fresh grated ginger, 2 tablespoons honey, and ½ teaspoon salt. Mix well and refrigerate until ready to use.

Salmon in Saffron-Flavored Curry
(Zaffrani Macchi)

Serves 4
Prep Time: 10 minutes
Cook Time: 10 minutes

"The king of the sea marries the queen of spices" is the best way to describe this dish. Serve with Simple Naan Bread (page 207).

4 tablespoons vegetable oil
1 large onion, finely chopped
1 teaspoon Ginger-Garlic Paste (see recipe on page 15)
½ teaspoon red chili powder
¼ teaspoon turmeric powder
2 teaspoons coriander powder

Table salt, to taste
1 pound salmon, boned and cubed
½ cup plain yogurt, whipped
1 teaspoon Roasted Saffron (see recipe on page 18)

1. In a large, nonstick skillet, heat the vegetable oil. Add the onions and sauté for 3 to 4 minutes or until transparent. Add the Ginger-Garlic Paste and sauté for 1 minute.
2. Add the red chili powder, turmeric, coriander, and salt; mix well. Add the salmon and sauté for 3 to 4 minutes. Add the yogurt and lower the heat. Simmer until the salmon has cooked through.
3. Add the saffron and mix well. Cook for 1 minute. Serve hot.

※ Saffron

Saffron is one of the most affordable luxury spices, but consider this: It takes 225,000 stigmas, picked from 75,000 violet crocuses during the 2-week fall flowering period, to produce 1 pound of saffron, which costs about $4,500 per pound.

Garlic Fish Tikka
(Lasuni Macchi)

½ cup heavy cream
1 teaspoon Warm Spice Mix
(see recipe on page 14)
½ teaspoon red chili powder
¼ teaspoon turmeric powder

Table salt, to taste
2 teaspoons minced garlic
1 pound whitefish, cut into
chunks
Butter for basting

> **Serves 4**
> **Prep Time:** 5 minutes, plus 2 hours to marinate
> **Cook Time:** 10 minutes
>
> Flaky and mild, this grilled fish is a summer favorite. Sometimes I use caramelized garlic in this recipe for a unique taste.

1. In a bowl or resealable plastic bag, combine the cream, spice mix, red chili powder, turmeric, salt, and garlic; mix well. Add the fish and coat well. Refrigerate, covered, for 2 hours.
2. Preheat oven to 350°.
3. Skewer the fish and bake for 3 to 4 minutes. Baste with butter and bake for 5 to 6 minutes or until the fish is cooked through. Serve hot.

Dried Fenugreek Fish
(Sukhi Methi Wale Macchi)

5 tablespoons fenugreek leaves
1 teaspoon red chili powder
¼ teaspoon turmeric powder
1 teaspoon Ginger-Garlic Paste
(see recipe on page 15)
Table salt, to taste

½ cup Hung Yogurt (see recipe
on page 16)
4 tablespoons heavy cream
1 pound whitefish, cut into
chunks
Butter for basting

> **Serves 4**
> **Prep Time:** 5 minutes, plus 2 hours to marinate
> **Cook Time:** 10 minutes
>
> This aromatic dish is a perfect entrée with a light salad.

1. In a bowl, mix the fenugreek leaves, red chili powder, turmeric powder, ginger paste, salt, yogurt, and cream. Add the fish and coat well. Refrigerate, covered, for 2 hours.
2. Preheat oven to 350°. Skewer the fish cubes; discard any remaining marinade. Place the fish skewers in the oven and roast for about 4 to 5 minutes. Baste with butter. Roast for another 3 to 4 minutes or until the fish is completely cooked through. Serve hot.

Chili Shrimp
(Mirchi Jhinga)

Serves 4
Prep Time: 15 minutes
Cook Time: 20 minutes

This Indian Chinese recipe is best served immediately before the shrimp soften. Serve these with the Vegetable Fried Rice (page 176).

1 egg, whisked
2 tablespoons corn flour
2 tablespoons all-purpose flour (maida)
1 teaspoon Ginger-Garlic Paste (see recipe on page 15)
1 teaspoon plus 1 tablespoon red chili sauce (optional)
Water, as needed
1½ pounds shrimp, peeled and deveined

Vegetable oil for deep-frying, plus 3 tablespoons
1-inch piece fresh gingerroot, peeled and grated
2 serrano green chilies, seeded and minced
2 tablespoons soya sauce
4 tablespoons tomato ketchup
Table salt, to taste
3 tablespoons corn flour, dissolved in ½ cup cold water

1. In a bowl, combine the egg, corn flour, all-purpose flour, Ginger-Garlic Paste, and 1 teaspoon of the red chili sauce. Add enough water to make a thin batter; mix well. Add the shrimp to the batter.
2. Pour the vegetable oil into a deep pan to about 1 inch deep, and heat to 350°. Add a few shrimp at a time and deep-fry until they are crisp and golden brown. Using a slotted spoon, remove the shrimp from the oil and drain on paper towels. Let the oil return to temperature. Continue until all the shrimp are fried. Set aside. Discard any remaining batter.
3. In a large skillet, heat the 3 tablespoons of vegetable oil. Add the ginger and green chilies, and sauté for about 30 seconds.
4. Add the soya sauce, tomato ketchup, the remaining 1 tablespoon red chili sauce, and salt; mix well.
5. Add 1 cup of water and the corn flour mixture (restir the corn flour mix if you made it ahead). Bring to a boil. Lower the heat and add the shrimp pieces. Simmer for 1 or 2 minutes to reheat the shrimp. Serve hot.

Tandoori Shrimp
(Tandoori Jhinga)

3 teaspoons grated fresh
   gingerroot
4 tablespoons heavy cream
½ teaspoon red chili powder
½ teaspoon turmeric powder
½ teaspoon Tandoori Spice Mix
   (see recipe on page 15)

½ teaspoon carom seeds
Table salt, to taste
1½ pounds shrimp, peeled and
   deveined
Lemon juice

> **Serves 4**
> **Prep Time:** 5 minutes,
> plus 1 hour to marinate
> **Cook Time:** 10 minutes
>
> You can serve this not
> only as an entrée but
> also in a bowl of
> shredded baby
> spinach, as an
> enchanting spring
> salad.

1. In a bowl, combine all the ingredients *except* the shrimp and lemon juice; mix well.
2. Add the shrimp to the marinade. Make sure that the shrimp are well coated. Refrigerate, covered, for about 1 hour.
3. Preheat oven to 350°.
4. Place the shrimp in a single layer on a foil-lined baking sheet and bake for 8 to 9 minutes or until the shrimp are cooked. Serve hot, sprinkled with lemon juice.

※ Carom Seeds

Carom seeds are said to be very powerful digestive aids. Very similar to thyme in flavor, they are quite often used when cooking seafood.

Saffron-Flavored Grilled Salmon
(Kesari Salmon)

Serves 4
Prep Time: 5 minutes
Cook Time: 10 minutes

The Saffron Mayonnaise used here is so flavorful, you need just a tiny bit to dress the salmon.

4 salmon steaks
4 tablespoons vegetable oil
1 teaspoon dried red pepper, crushed

Table salt, to taste
½ recipe Saffron Mayonnaise (page 228)

1. In a bowl, combine the salmon, vegetable oil, red pepper, and salt. Coat the salmon with the mixture.
2. Preheat oven to 400°.
3. Place the salmon steaks, along with any remaining oil, on a foil-lined baking sheet, in a single layer. Roast for 10 minutes or until the salmon is cooked through.
4. Place each piece of salmon on a plate and top with 1 or 2 heaping tablespoons (to taste) of the Saffron Mayonnaise. Serve immediately.

❋ Mango Chutney Mayonnaise

Another wonderful topping for grilled fish is mango chutney mayonnaise. Add 2 tablespoons of ready-made mango chutney (from your local grocers) to 1 cup mayonnaise. Blend together until smooth. Refrigerate until ready to use.

CHAPTER 10
Rice Dishes (Chawal)

Simple Basmati Rice
(Chawal)

Serves 4–5
Prep Time: 5 minutes
Cook Time: 25 minutes

Let the wonderful nutty flavor of the Indian basmati rice shine through. Serve this with any entrée of your choice.

2 cups basmati rice
4 cups water

1 teaspoon table salt
1 teaspoon fresh lemon juice

1. Rinse the rice at least 3 or 4 times with water. Drain and set aside.
2. In a deep pan, bring 4 cups of water to a boil.
3. Add the rice and stir for about 30 seconds. Add the salt and lemon juice and return to boiling.
4. Reduce the heat to low. Loosely cover the rice with a lid and cook for about 12 to 15 minutes or until most of the water has evaporated. You will see small craters forming on top of the rice.
5. Cover and reduce the heat to the lowest setting; cook for 5 to 6 minutes.
6. Remove from heat and let stand, covered, for about 5 minutes. Fluff with a fork before serving.

Tamarind Rice
(Pulihora)

Serves 4–5
Prep Time: 5–10 minutes
Cook Time: 10 minutes

This is a simpler version of a classic of southern India. Serve with South Indian Cucumber Salad (page 62) for a complete meal.

1 recipe Simple Basmati Rice (see above)
3 tablespoons vegetable oil
4 fresh curry leaves
½ teaspoon black mustard seeds

2 dried red chilies, broken
¼ cup salted roasted peanuts
1 cup Tamarind Chutney (see recipe on page 226)

1. Layer the warm rice on a serving platter. Set aside.
2. In a medium-sized skillet, heat the vegetable oil. Add the curry leaves and mustard seeds. When the mustard seeds begin to sputter, add the red chilies and peanuts; sauté for about 30 seconds.
3. Add the chutney. Lower the heat and simmer for about 5 minutes or until the chutney is completely heated through.
4. Spoon the chutney mixture over the rice. Just before serving, mix together the rice and chutney.

Saffron Rice
(Kesari Chawal)

1 cup basmati rice
2 cups water
2 tablespoons Clarified Butter
  (see recipe on page 17)
3 green cardamom pods,
  bruised
2 cloves
1 cinnamon stick

2 black cardamom seeds,
  bruised
2 tablespoons golden raisins
¼ cup blanched almonds
¼ teaspoon salt
3 tablespoons sugar
½ teaspoon Roasted Saffron
  (see recipe on page 18)

Serves 4
Prep Time: 5 minutes
Cook Time: 40 minutes

This rice dish can be served alongside any spicy chicken or meat curry.

1. Rinse the rice at least 3 to 4 times with water. Drain and set aside.
2. In a deep pan (with a lid), heat the butter over medium heat. Add the green cardamom pods, cloves, cinnamon stick, and black cardamom seeds. Cook for about 1 to 2 minutes.
3. Add the raisins, almonds, and salt. Stir for another minute. Add the rice and sauté for about 2 minutes. Add the sugar and the saffron; mix well.
4. Add 2 cups of water and cook, uncovered, until the water comes to a boil. Cover tightly and reduce heat to low. Cook the rice for another 8 to 12 minutes or until all the water is absorbed.
5. Remove from heat. Let stand, covered, for about 5 to 6 minutes. Serve hot. Fluff with a fork before serving.

※ Bruising or Pounding Spices

To bruise whole spices, use a mortar and pestle. You can even add the spices to a plastic bag and pound them lightly with a rolling pin. Lightly bruising a spice is an age-old technique in Indian cooking. It helps to release its aroma and flavor into the dish.

Vegetable Pulao
(Subzi Wale Chawal)

Serves 4
Prep Time: 10 minutes
Cook Time:
30–40 minutes

This is a great way to add your favorite vegetables to your meal. Serve this with a simple Creamy Walnut Salad (page 58).

1 cup basmati rice
3 tablespoons Clarified Butter (see page 17) or vegetable oil
1 small red onion, peeled and thinly sliced
1 bay leaf
2 green cardamom pods, bruised

1 cup cut frozen vegetables of your choice
1 teaspoon fresh lemon juice
2 cups of water
Table salt, to taste
Fried Onions (see page 18), for garnish

1. Rinse the rice at least 3 or 4 times with water. Drain and set aside.
2. In a deep pan, heat the butter. Add the onions, bay leaf, and cardamom pods; sauté for about 3 to 5 minutes or until the onions are soft.
3. Add the vegetables and sauté for about 5 minutes. Add ½ cup of the water and cook for 5 to 8 minutes or until the vegetables are tender.
4. Add the salt, lemon juice, and rice; mix well. Add the remaining 1½ cups of water and bring to a rolling boil. Reduce the heat and loosely cover with the lid partway off the pan so the steam can escape. Cook for about 12 to 15 minutes or until most of the water has evaporated. You will see small craters forming on top of the rice.
5. Cover tightly and reduce the heat to the lowest setting; simmer for another 5 to 6 minutes.
6. Remove from heat and let stand, covered, for about 5 minutes. Fluff with a fork before serving. Serve hot, garnished with the Fried Onions.

✳ Basmati Rice

Known as the "Queen of Fragrance," Basmati rice is a luxury. It is said to be like fine wine, getting better with age. Try Dehraduni basmati rice; it is one of the best-quality rices available in the market today.

Cumin-Scented Rice
(Jeere Wale Chawal)

1 cup basmati rice
2 tablespoons Clarified Butter (see page 17) or vegetable oil
1 small red onion, peeled and thinly sliced

1 teaspoon cumin seeds
2 cloves
1 teaspoon fresh lemon juice
2 cups water
Table salt, to taste

Serves 4
Prep Time: 5 minutes
Cook Time: 25–30 minutes

To reheat the rice, simply sprinkle some water on it, cover loosely, and heat for a few minutes in the microwave.

1. Rinse the rice at least 3 to 4 times with water. Drain and set aside.
2. In a deep pan, heat the butter. Add the onions and sauté for 3 to 4 minutes or until the onions are soft. Add the cumin seeds, cloves, salt, lemon juice, and rice; mix well.
3. Add the water and stir for 1 minute. Bring the water to a boil, then reduce the heat. Loosely cover the rice with a lid and cook for 12 to 15 minutes or until most of the water has evaporated. You will see small craters forming on top of the rice.
4. Cover tightly and reduce the heat to the lowest setting; simmer for another 5 to 6 minutes.
5. Remove from heat and let stand, covered, for about 5 minutes. Fluff with a fork before serving. Serve hot.

❋ Don't Peek!

Curiosity kills the cat! When rice is cooking, covered, resist the urge to open the cover and look inside. The rice needs the steam to cook. Also, allow the rice to rest for a few minutes before you serve it. This will help the grains to separate and will absorb any leftover water, giving you perfect rice each time.

Tomato Rice
(Tamatar Ka Pulao)

Serves 4
Prep Time: 10 minutes
Cook Time: 30–35 minutes

This lovely red-hued rice has a mild, delicious flavor. Serve with Fried Okra in Yogurt Sauce (page 60).

1 cup basmati rice
2 medium tomatoes
3 tablespoons vegetable oil
1 small red onion, roughly chopped
1-inch piece gingerroot, peeled and julienned

1½ teaspoons Warm Spice Mix (see recipe on page 14)
2 cups water
Table salt, to taste
Minced cilantro, for garnish

1. Rinse the rice at least 3 to 4 times with water. Drain and set aside.
2. Boil water and plunge the tomatoes into the pot for 30 seconds, then pull them out and run them under cold water. Peel off the tomato skins. In a bowl, roughly mash the blanched tomatoes. Set aside.
3. In a deep pan, heat the vegetable oil. Add the onion and sauté for 5 minutes or until soft. Add the gingerroot and the spice mix; mix well. Add the rice and salt; sauté for 1 minute.
4. Add the water and stir for 1 minute to remove any rice lumps. Bring the water to a boil, then reduce the heat. Loosely cover with a lid and cook for about 12 to 15 minutes or until most of the water has evaporated. You will see small craters forming on top of the rice.
5. Cover tightly and reduce the heat to the lowest setting; simmer for another 5 to 6 minutes.
6. Remove from heat and let stand, covered, for about 5 minutes. Fluff with a fork and garnish with the minced cilantro. Serve hot.

✵ Soaking Rice

To reduce the cooking time, soak rice in cold water for about 30 minutes before cooking. Keep in mind that you should use less water to cook soaked rice than you would for dry rice. The water-to-rice ratio for soaked rice is 1½ cups of water to 1 cup of rice. Soaking helps the rice absorb water and expand well during the actual cooking process. Many people like to save the soaking water and use it for cooking later.

Lemon Rice
(Nimbu Wale Chawal)

½ recipe Simple Basmati Rice (page 162)

3 tablespoons Clarified Butter (page 17) or vegetable oil

1 teaspoon black mustard seeds

8 fresh curry leaves

3 dried red chilies, broken

2 tablespoons unsalted peanuts

Table salt, to taste

½ teaspoon turmeric powder

4 tablespoons fresh lemon juice

Fresh grated coconut, for garnish

Serves 4
Prep Time: 5–10 minutes
Cook Time: 5 minutes

This is a great way to perk up leftover rice. Enjoy a Maharastrian Buttermilk (page 46) drink alongside.

1. If you are using Simple Basmati Rice that has been prepared earlier and refrigerated, warm it for a few minutes before proceeding.
2. In a large skillet, heat the butter. Add the mustard seeds. When they begin to sputter, in quick succession add the curry leaves, red chilies, and peanuts. Sauté for 1 minute. Add the salt and turmeric; mix well.
3. Add the lemon juice. It will splatter a bit, so do this carefully. Add the rice and salt; sauté for 1 minute, mixing well to evenly coat the rice with the spice mix. Serve hot garnished with fresh grated coconut.

✵ Rice and the Hindu Religion

In India, rice has a special religious significance. It is considered a symbol of fertility and prosperity. Hindu weddings use rice for many rituals. When a new bride enters her husband's home for the first time, she gently taps, with her foot, a small urn containing rice, over the threshold. This signifies that the new bride will bring wealth and prosperity to the family.

Chicken Casserole
(Murgh Ki Biryani)

Serves 4–5
Prep Time: 5–10 minutes
Cook Time: 45–55
minutes

These casseroles are
meals in themselves
and can be served
with a raita or small
salad of your choice.

1 recipe Chicken Curry
   (page 97)
2 cups basmati rice
4 cups water
2 tablespoons minced cilantro
2 tablespoons minced mint

½ cup mixed, unsalted, roasted
   nuts (slivered almonds,
   cashews, and pistachios)
1 tablespoon raisins (optional)
½ teaspoon Roasted Saffron
   (see recipe on page 18)

1. If you are using Chicken Curry that has been prepared earlier and refrigerated, warm it for a few minutes before proceeding.
2. Rinse the rice at least 3 to 4 times with water. Drain and set aside.
3. In a deep pan, combine the rice with the 4 cups of water. Bring the water to a rolling boil. Cook, uncovered, until the rice is almost cooked but still firm. This should take about 8 minutes. Drain the rice and set aside.
4. Preheat oven to 325°.
5. In a deep, ovenproof pan (with a lid), add a layer of rice (about ½ of the rice). Layer about ¼ of the Chicken Curry over the rice. Add another layer of the rice (about 1 cup), and sprinkle with 1 tablespoon each of the cilantro and mint. Add a layer of the remaining chicken curry. Add a final layer of the rice. Sprinkle with the remaining cilantro and mint. Sprinkle with the mixed nuts, raisins, and saffron.
6. Cover and cook in the oven for 30 to 40 minutes or until the rice is completely cooked and all the liquid has been absorbed. Serve hot.

❋ Raisins

Raisins are used quite often in Indian cooking. They are added to rice dishes, salads, meat dishes, and are even used to prepare chutneys.

Yogurt Rice
(Dahi Bhaat)

*1 recipe Simple Basmati Rice
(page 162)*
2 cups plain yogurt, whipped
*2 tablespoons Clarified Butter
(page 17) or vegetable oil*
*1 teaspoon black mustard
seeds*
*2 dried red chilies, roughly
pounded*

*1 serrano green chili, seeded
and minced*
8 curry leaves
*1-inch piece fresh gingerroot,
peeled and julienned*
*1 small red onion, peeled and
finely chopped*
Table salt, to taste
Fresh minced cilantro, for garnish

> **Serves 4–5**
> **Prep Time:** 5–10 minutes
> **Cook Time:** 10 minutes
>
> If you use leftover rice, ensure that the rice is heated first and then brought to room temperature before proceeding.

1. If you are using Simple Basmati Rice that has been prepared earlier and refrigerated, warm it for a few minutes before proceeding.
2. In a bowl, combine the warmed rice with the yogurt. Mix well and place in a serving bowl. Set aside.
3. In a small skillet, heat the butter. Add the mustard seeds. When they begin to sputter, in quick succession add the red chilies, green chili, curry leaves, gingerroot, onions, and salt; mix well. Sauté for about 3 to 5 minutes or until the onions are just soft.
4. Pour this spice mixture over the rice. Garnish with the fresh cilantro, and serve at room temperature.

❊ Onions and Religion

Considered an aphrodisiac, onions are avoided by many Indian Hindus for religious reasons. Some even avoid ginger and garlic. Another sect won't eat anything that grows underground!

Lentil and Rice Kedgee
(Ghar Ki Khichdee)

Serves 3–4
Prep Time: 10 minutes
Cook Time: 45 minutes

In India, there is nothing that ails you, apparently, that cannot be cured by eating khichdee.

4 tablespoons Clarified Butter (page 17) or vegetable oil
Pinch of asafetida (optional)
1 teaspoon whole cumin seeds
1 small red onion, peeled and thinly sliced
1-inch piece fresh gingerroot, peeled and julienned
2 black cardamom pods
2 cloves

Pinch of Warm Spice Mix (see recipe on page 14)
¼ teaspoon turmeric powder
¾ cup yellow mung beans, washed and drained
½ cup basmati rice, washed and drained
Salt, to taste
5 cups water

1. Heat the butter in a heavy-bottomed casserole on medium. (Make sure your casserole dish is large enough to hold the rice and mung beans, as the quantity will almost double when it is cooked.) Add the asafetida and cumin seeds. As soon as the seeds sizzle, add the onion and ginger; sauté until the onion begins to turn brown, about 5 to 6 minutes.
2. Add the cardamom pods, cloves, spice mix, and turmeric; sauté for 1 minute.
3. Add the mung beans and rice; sauté for about 1 to 2 minutes. Add the salt. Add the water and bring to a boil. Cover, turn heat to low, and cook gently for 30 minutes, stirring now and then to prevent sticking. Uncover and check to ensure that the rice and lentils have cooked completely. They should be soft to the touch and mash easily. The finished dish should have the consistency of a thick porridge. Serve hot.

❋ White Rice

Adding lemon juice when cooking rice helps the grains stay shining white. Just add a few drops during the cooking process. You can use bottled or fresh lemon juice.

Stir-Fried Peas with Rice
(Mattar Wale Chawal)

1 cup basmati rice
3 tablespoons vegetable oil
1 teaspoon cumin seeds
4 cloves
1 (1-inch) cinnamon stick
1 small bay leaf

1 cup frozen peas, thawed
Table salt, to taste
2 cups water
2 tablespoons Fried Onions
(see recipe on page 18),
optional

Serves 4
Prep Time: 10 minutes
Cook Time: 30–35 minutes

This makes a perfect side to any curry. For a more colorful presentation, add a few finely diced carrots along with the peas.

1. Rinse the rice at least 3 to 4 times with water. Drain and set aside.
2. In a deep pan, heat the vegetable oil. Add the cumin seeds, cloves, cinnamon, and bay leaf. When the spices begin to sizzle, add the peas; sauté for 1 minute. Add the salt and rice; mix well.
3. Add the water and stir for 1 minute to get rid of any lumps of rice. Bring the water to a boil, then reduce the heat. Loosely cover with a lid and cook for about 12 to 15 minutes or until most of the water has evaporated. You will see small craters forming on top of the rice.
4. Cover tightly and reduce the heat to the lowest setting; simmer for another 5 to 6 minutes.
5. Remove from heat and let stand, covered, for about 5 minutes. Fluff with a fork before serving and garnish with Fried Onions.

☀ Nuke It

A very easy way to make rice when you are in a rush is to microwave it. Wash, soak (for 30 minutes), and drain 1 cup basmati rice. Combine with 2 cups of water and salt to taste in a microwave-safe dish. Cook, uncovered, at full power for 12 to 13 minutes. Carefully stir. Cover loosely, and microwave for another 5 to 6 minutes. Let the rice stand, covered, for a few minutes. Fluff and serve. Note that microwave times may vary slightly depending on the power of the microwave.

Ground Lamb, Peas, and Rice Casserole
(Kheeme Wale Chawal)

Serves 4
Prep Time: 5–10 minutes
Cook Time: 45–55 minutes

Make extra Peas and Minced-Meat Curry (page 123) and freeze it for making this delightful dish. Serve with Fried Okra in Yogurt Sauce (page 60).

1 recipe Peas and Minced-Meat Curry (page 123)
2 cups basmati rice
4 cups water
2 tablespoons minced cilantro
2 tablespoons minced mint
½ cup mixed, unsalted, roasted nuts (slivered almonds, cashews, and pistachios)
½ teaspoon Roasted Saffron (see recipe on page 18)

1. If you are using Peas and Minced-Meat Curry that has been prepared earlier and refrigerated, warm it for a few minutes before proceeding.
2. Rinse the rice at least 3 to 4 times with water. Drain and set aside.
3. In a deep pan, combine the rice and the 4 cups of water. Bring the water to a rolling boil. Cook, uncovered, until the rice is almost cooked but still firm. This should take about 8 minutes. Drain the rice and set aside.
4. Preheat oven to 325°.
5. In a deep, ovenproof pan (with a lid), add a layer of rice (about ½ of the rice). Layer about ¼ of the minced-meat curry over the rice. Add another layer of the rice (about 1 cup), and sprinkle with 1 table-spoon each of the cilantro and mint. Add a layer of the remaining lamb curry. Add a final layer of the remaining rice. Sprinkle with the remaining cilantro and mint. Sprinkle with the mixed nuts and saffron.
6. Cover and cook in the oven for 30 to 40 minutes or until the rice is completely cooked and all the liquid has been absorbed.

❋ Mushy Rice?

Cooking rice is an art, and much depends on the age of the rice and its quality. If the rice turns out too mushy, reduce the amount of water used the next time you prepare it. Also, if you soak the rice prior to cooking it, you will need to reduce the quantity of water used.

Rice with Chutney
(Chutney Wale Chawal)

1 cup basmati rice
2 tablespoons vegetable oil
1 teaspoon sesame seeds
2 serrano green chilies, seeded and minced
1 small red onion, peeled and finely chopped

Table salt, to taste
¼ cup Mint-Cilantro Chutney (see recipe on page 224)
½ cup plain yogurt, whipped
1¾ cups water

> **Serves 4**
> **Prep Time:** 10 minutes
> **Cook Time:** 30 minutes
>
> You can substitute Green Chili and Coconut Chutney (page 227) for the Mint-Cilantro Chutney in this dish if you like.

1. Rinse the rice at least 3 to 4 times with water. Drain and set aside.
2. In a deep pan, heat the vegetable oil. Add the sesame seeds, green chilies, and onions; sauté for 3 to 5 minutes or until the onions are soft.
3. Add the salt and the chutney; sauté for 1 minute. Add the yogurt, mix well, and cook for about 2 minutes.
4. Add the rice and mix well. Sauté for about 2 minutes.
5. Add the water and stir for 1 minute. Bring the water to a boil. Reduce the heat. Loosely cover the rice with a lid and cook for about 12 to 15 minutes or until most of the water has evaporated. You will see small craters forming on top of the rice.
6. Cover tightly and reduce the heat to the lowest setting; simmer for 5 to 6 minutes.
7. Remove from heat and let stand, covered, for about 5 minutes. Fluff with a fork before serving.

❋ Texmati Rice

Texmati is a basmati hybrid cultivated in the United States; you can substitute it if you like. Follow the instructions on the box for the amount of water needed, as it varies from brand to brand.

Garlic Rice
(Lasuni Pulao)

Serves 4–5
Prep Time: 10 minutes
Cook Time: 30 minutes

This dish is a garlic lover's delight. It is best if served immediately. Garnish with Fried Onions (page 18).

1 cup basmati rice
3 tablespoons vegetable oil
6 fresh garlic cloves, peeled and crushed
1 serrano green chili, seeded and minced
¼ cup plain yogurt, whipped

Table salt, to taste
½ teaspoon Warm Spice Mix (see recipe on page 14)
1¾ cups water
1 tablespoon minced cilantro

1. Rinse the rice at least 3 to 4 times with water. Drain and set aside.
2. In a deep pan, heat the vegetable oil. Add the garlic and green chili; sauté for about 20 seconds or until the garlic turns light brown.
3. Add the yogurt, salt, and spice mix; sauté for 1 minute. Add the rice and mix well.
4. Add the water and stir for 1 minute. Bring the water to a boil. Reduce the heat. Loosely cover the rice with a lid and cook for about 12 to 15 minutes or until most of the water has evaporated. You will see small craters forming on top of the rice.
5. Cover tightly and reduce the heat to the lowest setting; simmer for another 5 to 6 minutes.
6. Remove from heat and let stand, covered, for about 5 minutes. Fluff with a fork before serving.

❋ Stronger Garlic Taste

If you want a stronger garlic taste, use a garlic press to crush the garlic. If you don't have a press, use the flat side of a large kitchen knife and press it firmly on top of the garlic. This will give you more flavor from the garlic than you will get from simply chopping it.

White Chicken Rice
(Safeed Murgh Ka Pulao)

2 cups basmati rice

4 cups water

4 tablespoons vegetable oil

1-inch piece fresh gingerroot,
   peeled and julienned

2 serrano green chilies, minced

1 small red onion, peeled and
   finely chopped

4 boneless, skinless chicken
   breasts, cubed

Table salt, to taste

½ teaspoon Warm Spice Mix
   (see recipe on page 14)

1 teaspoon red chili powder

1 tablespoon minced cilantro

1 tablespoon minced mint

½ cup whole milk

1 teaspoon Roasted Saffron
   (see recipe on page 18)

Serves 4–5
Prep Time: 10 minutes
Cook Time: 1 hour

Serve piping hot with
the Minty Potato in
Yogurt Sauce
(page 66).

1. Rinse the rice at least 3 to 4 times with water. Drain and set aside.
2. In a deep pan, combine the rice with the 4 cups of water. Bring to a rolling boil. Cook, uncovered, until the rice is almost cooked but still firm. This should take about 8 minutes. Drain the rice and set aside.
3. In a large skillet, heat the vegetable oil. Add the gingerroot, green chilies, and red onions; sauté for 7 to 8 minutes or until the onions are browned.
4. Add the chicken and sauté for 8 to 10 minutes or until the chicken is well browned and completely cooked. Add the salt, spice mix, and red chili powder; mix well. Remove from heat and set aside.
5. Preheat oven to 325°.
6. In a deep ovenproof pan (with a lid), add a layer of rice (about ½ of the rice). Layer about ¼ of the chicken mixture over the rice. Add another layer of the rice (about 1 cup); sprinkle with 1 teaspoon each of the cilantro and mint. Add a layer of the remaining chicken mixture and then a final layer of the remaining rice. Sprinkle with the remaining cilantro and mint. Sprinkle with the milk and saffron.
7. Cover and cook in the oven for about 30 to 40 minutes or until the rice is completely cooked and all the liquid has been absorbed. Serve hot.

Vegetable Fried Rice
(Sabzi Wale Chawal)

Serves 4
Prep Time: 5 minutes
(plus 2 hours for chilling
the rice, if necessary)
Cook Time: 15–20
minutes

Serve with any of the
Manchurian recipes in
this book. I would
recommend using a
mix of green beans,
carrots, broccoli, and
sweet bell peppers.

½ recipe Simple Basmati Rice
   (page 162)
3 tablespoons vegetable oil
2 green onions, finely chopped
1-inch piece fresh gingerroot,
   peeled and julienned
4 garlic cloves, minced
1 dried red chili, whole

1 cup cut frozen vegetables of
   your choice, thawed
¼ cup water
2 teaspoons soya sauce
1 teaspoon white vinegar
Table salt, to taste

1. The cooked rice needs to be cold. If you prepare it fresh for this recipe, refrigerate it for at least 2 hours prior to using it here.
2. In a large skillet, heat the vegetable oil on high. Add the green onions, ginger, and garlic; sauté for 1 minute.
3. Add the red chili and the vegetables; sauté for about 5 minutes. Add the water and cook until the vegetables are tender and most of the water has evaporated, about 8 minutes.
4. Add the soya sauce, white vinegar, and salt; mix well. Add the cold rice and mix well; sauté for about 2 to 3 minutes or until the rice has completely heated through. Serve hot.

※ Indian Vinegar Salad

Make this mild vinegar salad to serve alongside pulaos (sautéed rice dishes, usually prepared with whole spices) and heavy biryanis (rice casseroles made with meat and/or vegetables). In a small bowl, combine ½ cup diced cucumbers, ½ cup diced radish, a pinch of sugar and salt, 1 tablespoon grated ginger, and a few tablespoons of vinegar. Chill and serve.

Pork Fried Rice
(Pork Wale Chawal)

½ recipe Simple Basmati Rice
(page 162)

2 tablespoons soya sauce

1 tablespoon white vinegar

1 teaspoon cornstarch

3 tablespoons vegetable oil

2 green onions (white and
light green part only), finely
chopped

1-inch piece fresh gingerroot,
peeled and julienned

2 garlic cloves, minced

1 dried red chili, whole

¼ pound boneless pork, cut
into ½-inch dice

Serves 4–5
Prep Time: 5 minutes
(plus 2 hours for chilling
the rice, if necessary)
Cook Time: 15 minutes

Substitute your choice
of meat for this fla-
vorful stir-fry. Serve
with Chili Garlic Sauce
(page 238).

1. The cooked rice needs to be cold. If you prepare it fresh for this recipe, refrigerate it for at least 2 hours prior to using it here.
2. Combine the soya sauce, vinegar, and cornstarch; set aside.
3. In a large nonstick skillet, heat the vegetable oil on high. Add the green onions, ginger, and garlic; sauté for 1 minute.
4. Add the red chili and the pork; sauté for 7 to 8 minutes or until the pork is cooked.
5. Give the soya sauce mixture a quick stir to recombine it, and add it to the pan. Add the cold rice and mix well. Sauté for about 2 to 3 minutes or until the rice has completely heated through. Serve hot.

❊ Another Indian Chinese Favorite

Visit any Indian Chinese restaurant in India and you will be served a hot green chili sauce along with your meal. This Green Chili Vinegar Sauce adds a wonderful zing to any Chinese dish; it is generally sprinkled over a dish before it is served. To prepare about ¼ cup of this sauce: In a deep pan, combine 4 minced green chilies, ¼ cup vinegar, a pinch each of salt and sugar. Simmer on low heat for 3 minutes. Chill and serve.

Bengali Butter Rice
(Bengali Ghee Bhaat)

Serves 4
Prep Time: 5 minutes
Cook Time: 30–35 minutes

Whole spices add an amazing flavor to this aromatic and buttery rice dish. Remove the whole spices before serving.

1 cup basmati rice
3 tablespoons Clarified Butter
   (see recipe on page 17)
1 bay leaf
1 (1-inch) cinnamon stick
2 cloves

2 black peppercorns
2 green cardamom pods, bruised
2 cups water
Table salt, to taste

1. Wash the rice at least 3 to 4 times with water. Drain and set aside.
2. In a deep pan, heat the butter. Add the bay leaf, cinnamon, cloves, peppercorns, and cardamoms. When the whole spices begin to sizzle (about 1 minute), add the rice and mix well.
3. Add the water and salt; stir for 1 minute. Bring the water to a boil. Reduce the heat. Loosely cover the rice with a lid and cook for about 12 to 15 minutes or until most of the water has evaporated. You will see small craters forming on top of the rice.
4. Cover tightly and reduce the heat to the lowest setting; simmer for another 5 to 6 minutes.
5. Remove from heat and let stand, covered, for about 5 minutes. Fluff with a fork before serving.

❈ Spiced Butter

Brush your favorite Indian breads with spiced butter for an added oomph. Take a stick of butter at room temperature; add 1 teaspoon of crushed garlic and ¼ teaspoon roasted cumin; mix well. Refrigerate and use as needed.

Malabari Coconut Rice
(Thenga Choru)

1 cup basmati rice
3 tablespoons vegetable oil
1 teaspoon black mustard
  seeds
2 dried red chilies, broken
1-inch piece fresh gingerroot,
  julienned
4 garlic cloves, minced

½ teaspoon turmeric powder
Table salt, to taste
½ cup unsweetened desiccated
  coconut
½ cup light coconut milk
1½ cups water

Serves 4
Prep Time: 5 minutes
Cook Time:
30–35 minutes

This recipe comes to
you from the shores
of southwestern India.
Traditionally it is
served with hot,
spicy curries.

1. Rinse the rice at least 3 to 4 times with water. Drain and set aside.
2. In a deep pan, heat the vegetable oil. Add the mustard seeds. When they begin to sputter, add the red chilies, ginger, and garlic; sauté for about 30 seconds.
3. Add the turmeric, salt, and coconut. Mix well and sauté for 1 minute. Add the rice and mix well; sauté for 1 minute.
4. Add the coconut milk and the water; stir for 1 minute. Bring to a boil.
5. Reduce the heat. Loosely cover the rice with a lid and cook for about 12 to 15 minutes or until most of the water has evaporated. You will see small craters forming on top of the rice.
6. Cover tightly and reduce the heat to the lowest setting; simmer for another 5 to 6 minutes.
7. Remove from heat and let stand, covered, for about 5 minutes. Fluff with a fork before serving.

✻ Using Coconut Milk

Before you open a can of coconut milk, shake it vigorously to ensure that the coconut cream and the coconut water mix well together.

Eggplant and Rice
(Vangi Bhaat)

1 cup basmati rice
4 tablespoons vegetable oil
1 teaspoon black mustard
  seeds
4 dried red chilies, broken
1-inch piece fresh gingerroot,
  julienned
4 garlic cloves, minced

½ teaspoon turmeric powder
Table salt, to taste
1 small red onion, peeled and
  thinly sliced
1 (1-pound) eggplant, diced
2 cups water

1. Rinse the rice at least 3 to 4 times with water. Drain and set aside.
2. In a deep pan, heat the vegetable oil. Add the mustard seeds. When they begin to sputter, add the red chilies, gingerroot, and garlic; sauté for about 30 seconds.
3. Add the turmeric, salt, onion, and eggplant. Mix well and sauté for 7 to 8 minutes or until the eggplant and onion are well browned. Add the rice and mix well; sauté for 1 minute.
4. Add the water and stir for 1 minute. Bring to a boil, then reduce the heat. Cover loosely with a lid and cook for about 12 to 15 minutes or until most of the water has evaporated. You will see small craters forming on top of the rice.
5. Cover tightly and reduce the heat to the lowest setting; simmer for another 5 to 6 minutes.
6. Remove from heat and let stand for about 5 minutes. Serve hot. Fluff with a fork before serving.

✵ An Eggplant by Any Other Name . . .

Also called aubergine or brinjal in India, the eggplant is a native of Asia. When buying eggplant, look for the ones with firm skin. Indian eggplants tend to be less bitter than their Western counterparts.

Minty Rice
(Pudine Wale Chawal)

1 cup basmati rice
2 tablespoons vegetable oil
2 serrano green chilies, seeded
  and minced
1 small red onion, peeled and
  finely chopped

Table salt, to taste
¼ cup minced mint
½ cup plain yogurt, whipped
1¾ cups water

Serves 4
Prep Time: 10 minutes
Cook Time: 40 minutes

A refreshing dish, it is one of the most popular in my classes. You can garnish this dish with fresh grated coconut.

1. Rinse the rice at least 3 to 4 times with water. Drain and set aside.
2. In a deep pan, heat the vegetable oil. Add the green chilies and onions; sauté for 3 to 5 minutes or until the onions are soft.
3. Add the salt and the mint; sauté for 1 minute. Add the yogurt and mix well; cook for about 2 minutes.
4. Add the rice and mix well; sauté for about 2 minutes.
5. Add the water and stir for 1 minute. Bring the water to a boil, then reduce the heat. Loosely cover with a lid and cook for about 12 to 15 minutes or until most of the water has evaporated. You will see small craters forming on top of the rice.
6. Cover tightly and reduce the heat to the lowest setting; simmer for another 5 to 6 minutes.
7. Remove from heat and let stand, covered, for about 5 minutes. Serve hot. Fluff with a fork before serving.

※ Red Radish

In India, the longer white radish, called daikon, is usually used. Radish flowers are a great garnish for many Indian rice dishes. They are so easy to make. With a small paring knife, cut a zigzag pattern around the circumference of the radish. Make sure your cuts go all the way to the center. Pull the two halves apart.

Spicy Shrimp Rice
(Jhinge Ki Biryani)

1 cup basmati rice
4 tablespoons vegetable oil
1 teaspoon black mustard seeds
4 fresh curry leaves
1 pound shrimp, peeled and deveined

2 tablespoons unsweetened desiccated coconut
1 teaspoon red chili powder
½ teaspoon turmeric powder
Table salt, to taste
2 cups water

1. Rinse the rice at least 3 to 4 times with water. Drain and set aside.
2. In a deep pan, heat the vegetable oil. Add the black mustard seeds. When they begin to sputter, add the curry leaves and shrimp; sauté for about 2 to 3 minutes.
3. Add the coconut, red chili and turmeric powder, and salt; cook for about 2 minutes.
4. Add the rice and mix well; sauté for 1 minute.
5. Add the water and stir for 1 minute. Bring the water to a boil. Reduce the heat. Loosely cover with a lid and cook for about 12 to 15 minutes or until most of the water has evaporated. You will see small craters forming on top of the rice.
6. Cover tightly and reduce the heat to the lowest setting; simmer for another 5 to 6 minutes.
7. Remove from heat and let stand, covered, for about 5 minutes. Fluff with a fork before serving.

☼ Did You Say Prawns?

Most Indians refer to shrimp as prawns. Indian prawns are much bigger than the shrimp found in the United States; some are as long as the palm of your hand. Use large shrimp for most of the recipes in this book, unless otherwise indicated.

Turmeric Rice
(Peele Chawal)

1 cup basmati rice

2 tablespoons vegetable oil

2 serrano green chilies, seeded
   and minced

1 small red onion, peeled and
   finely chopped

Table salt, to taste

1 teaspoon turmeric powder

2 cups water

Serves 4
Prep Time: 10 minutes
Cook Time: 30 minutes

This simple dish has a spectacular appearance because of its stunning yellow color. Serve with any hot curry of your choice.

1. Rinse the rice at least 3 to 4 times with water. Drain and set aside.
2. In a deep pan, heat the vegetable oil. Add the green chilies and onions; sauté for 3 to 5 minutes or until the onions are soft.
3. Add the salt, turmeric, and rice; sauté for 1 minute.
4. Add the water and stir for 1 minute. Bring to a boil, then reduce the heat. Loosely cover with a lid and cook for about 12 to 15 minutes or until most of the water has evaporated. You will see small craters forming on top of the rice.
5. Cover tightly and reduce the heat to the lowest setting; simmer for another 5 to 6 minutes.
6. Remove from heat and let stand, covered, for about 5 minutes. Fluff with a fork before serving.

❈ Tri-Colored Rice

You can have a lot of fun with rice dishes. Prepare batches of Minty Rice, Tomato Rice, and Turmeric Rice (see the recipes in this chapter). Layer the rice or mound it on a plate for a spectacular presentation. Use the Minty Rice for a green layer, Turmeric Rice for yellow, and the Tomato Rice for a fiery red.

Spiced Semolina with Toasted Cashews
(Upma Kaju Wala)

Serves 4
Prep Time: 10 minutes
Cook Time: 30 minutes

Semolina is served here with toasted cashews. In South India, this is often served for breakfast. Serve sprinkled with fresh lemon juice.

1 tablespoon Clarified Butter (see recipe on page 17)

4 tablespoons unsalted cashew nuts

4 tablespoons vegetable oil

4 fresh curry leaves

½ teaspoon mustard seeds

1 small red onion, peeled and finely chopped

2 dried red chilies, broken

1 serrano green chili, minced

1 cup semolina

Table salt, to taste

2 cups hot water

1. In a small skillet, heat the butter. Add the cashews and toast them on medium heat until golden brown. Set aside.
2. In a medium skillet, heat the vegetable oil. Add the curry leaves and mustard seeds. When the mustard seeds begin to sputter, add the red onions and the red and green chilies; sauté for about 3 to 4 minutes.
3. Add the semolina and the salt; mix well.
4. Start adding the hot water, a little at a time. Stir the semolina constantly as the water is added. The semolina will begin to absorb the water. Continue until all the water has been added. Cover, lower the heat to medium low, and steam for about 5 minutes. The final consistency should be dry.
5. Remove from heat. Let the dish stand, covered, for about 10 minutes before serving. Top with the toasted cashews and serve.

✺ Clarified Butter and Religion

In India, clarified butter, or ghee, is used to light the cotton wicks of lamps. A symbol of wealth and opulence, it is used as an offering to the gods in many religious ceremonies.

CHAPTER 11
Lentil and Yogurt Dishes (Dal Aur Kadhi)

Creamy Split Peas
(Chana Dal)

Serves 4
Prep Time: 5 minutes,
plus 1 hour to soak
Cook Time: 50 minutes

To reduce cooking
times for this dahl
(dal), use a pressure
cooker. Serve this as
a side with Simple
Indian Bread
(page 204).

1 cup chana dal or yellow
   split peas, well rinsed
Water, as needed
½ teaspoon turmeric powder
3 tablespoons vegetable oil,
   divided
1 teaspoon minced garlic

1 small red onion, minced
1 teaspoon cumin seeds
Table salt, to taste
¼ cup heavy cream

1. Soak the *chana dal* in 4 cups of water for 1 hour. Drain and set aside.
2. In a deep pan, combine the turmeric powder, 1 tablespoon of the vegetable oil, the garlic, and 4 cups of water. Bring to a boil. Add the *chana dal* and cook for 20 minutes, stirring occasionally. Reduce heat to medium, cover partially, and continue to cook for about 30 minutes or until the peas are very soft. Reduce the heat to a simmer for about 8 minutes or until most of the liquid has dried up. Remove from heat and use a wooden spoon to mix well. Set aside.
3. Heat the remaining vegetable oil in a medium-sized skillet. Add the cumin seeds. When they begin to sizzle (about 30 seconds), add the onions and sauté for 7 to 8 minutes or until the onions are brown.
4. Add this mixture to the *chana dal* and mix well. Add salt and mix. Add the heavy cream and mix well. Serve hot.

❊ Cleaning Dahls

No matter what type of dahl you are cooking, rinse it well in 4 to 5 changes of water. This will get rid of any husks that might be in the dahl.

Simple Mung Bean Curry
(Tadka Dal)

1 cup yellow split mung beans (yellow moong dal), well rinsed

Water, as needed

½ teaspoon turmeric powder

4 tablespoons vegetable oil, divided

1 teaspoon cumin seeds

1 small red onion, minced

1 serrano green chili, seeded and minced

1 teaspoon grated ginger

1 small tomato, minced

Table salt, to taste

1 tablespoon minced cilantro (optional)

> **Serves 4**
> **Prep Time:** 10 minutes
> **Cook Time:** 50 minutes
>
> Tadka in Indian cooking means "seasoning." This yellow dahl (dal) is a North Indian favorite. Serve atop steamed Indian basmati rice.

1. In a deep pan, combine 4 cups of water, the turmeric, and 1 tablespoon of the vegetable oil. Bring to a boil, then add the mung beans. Reduce the heat to medium-low and cook, uncovered and stirring occasionally, for 30 minutes or until the lentils are very soft. If the water starts to dry up, you can add another ½ cup of water. Remove from heat and set aside.

2. In a medium-sized skillet, heat 3 tablespoons of vegetable oil. Add the cumin seeds; when they begin to sizzle, add the red onions. Sauté for 7 to 8 minutes or until the onions are well browned.

3. Add the ginger, green chili, and tomatoes. Cook for another 8 minutes or until the tomatoes are soft.

4. Add the salt and cilantro and mix well. Add the onion mixture and mix well. Reheat gently and serve hot.

❈ Removing Gas

Some lentils contain gas-forming compounds. In order to reduce these, rinse them well. Never cook them in the soaking water—always use fresh water.

The Five-Lentil Delight
(Paanch Dalo Ka Sangam)

4 tablespoons chana dal or yellow split peas, rinsed

4 tablespoons red split lentils (masoor dal), rinsed

4 tablespoons split black gram, or black lentils (safeed urad dal), rinsed

4 tablespoons pigeon peas (toor dal), rinsed

4 tablespoons green split mung beans (green moong dal), rinsed

Water, as needed

1 teaspoon turmeric powder

2 teaspoons table salt

5 tablespoons vegetable oil, divided

1 teaspoon cumin seeds

1 teaspoon Ginger-Garlic Paste (see recipe on page 15)

1 medium-sized red onion, minced

1 teaspoon red chili powder

½ teaspoon cumin powder

½ teaspoon Warm Spice Mix (see recipe on page 14)

1. Soak all the *dals* together in a deep pot with enough water to cover them well. Soak for about 2 hours. Drain and set aside.
2. In a deep pot, combine 6 cups of water, the turmeric powder, salt, and 2 tablespoons of the vegetable oil. Bring to a boil. Add all the drained *dals* and mix well. Bring to a full boil. Reduce heat to medium and cook, uncovered, for about 40 minutes or until the lentils are soft. If the water begins to dry out, add up to 1 cup more. (The consistency should be like a creamy soup.) Remove from heat and set aside.
3. In a medium-sized skillet, heat the remaining vegetable oil. Add the cumin seeds; when they begin to sizzle, add the Ginger-Garlic Paste. Sauté for 30 seconds and add the onions. Sauté for 7 to 8 minutes or until the onions are well browned.
4. Add the red chili powder, cumin powder, and spice mix; mix well.
5. Add the onion mixture to the *dals* and mix well. Serve hot.

Chickpea Curry
(Pindi Chane)

2 (14-ounce) cans chickpeas
4 tablespoons vegetable oil
2 teaspoons Ginger-Garlic Paste (see recipe on page 15)
1 large red onion, minced
1 teaspoon coriander powder
1 teaspoon pomegranate powder
½ teaspoon Warm Spice Mix (see recipe on page 14)
1 serrano green chili, seeded and minced
½ teaspoon red chili powder
Table salt, to taste
1 cup water

> **Serves 3–4**
> **Prep Time:** 10 minutes
> **Cook Time:** 15 minutes
>
> This time-saving recipe uses canned chickpeas (garbanzo beans), available at your local grocer. Serve with Fried Indian Bread (page 206).

1. Rinse the chickpeas well. Set aside.
2. In a deep pan, heat the vegetable oil. Add the Ginger-Garlic Paste and sauté for 1 minute, then add the onions; sauté for 7 to 8 minutes.
3. In quick succession, add the coriander powder, pomegranate powder, spice mix, green chili, red chili powder, and salt; mix well. Sauté for 30 seconds or until the spices begin to darken.
4. Add the chickpeas and mix well.
5. Add 1 cup of water and mix well. Lower the heat and simmer for about 8 minutes. Using a spoon, take out about 2 tablespoons of the chickpeas. Mash them and add them back to the pot; mix well. Remove from heat. Serve hot.

✷ Cauliflower Bites

Need something quick and yummy for those times when unexpected guests arrive? Break cauliflower into small florets. Heat oil in a deep fryer until it is almost smoking, then deep-fry the cauliflower florets, a few at a time, until they are dark brown in color and crisp. Remove from the oil using a slotted spoon and drain on a paper towel. Sprinkle with Chaat Spice Mix (page 16) and serve hot. These are the perfect accompaniment for drinks.

Indian Red Kidney Beans
(Rajmah)

Serves 4
Prep Time: 15 minutes
Cook Time: 20 minutes

Another time-saving recipe that uses canned beans. Serve it with Simple Basmati Rice (page 162) and a salad of your choice.

2 (14-ounce) cans red kidney beans
4 tablespoons vegetable oil
2 teaspoons Ginger-Garlic Paste (see recipe on page 15)
1 large red onion, minced
2 medium tomatoes, finely chopped
½ teaspoon turmeric powder

1 teaspoon red chili powder
Table salt, to taste
1 teaspoon coriander powder
1 teaspoon cumin powder
½ teaspoon Warm Spice Mix (see recipe on page 14)
Water, as needed

1. Rinse the kidney beans well and set aside.
2. In a deep pan, heat the vegetable oil on medium heat. Add the Ginger-Garlic Paste and sauté for about 20 seconds.
3. Add the onion and sauté for about 5 minutes or until well browned.
4. Add the tomatoes and sauté for about 8 minutes or until the oil begins to separate from the mixture.
5. Add the turmeric, red chili, salt, coriander, cumin, and spice mix; mix well. Add the red kidney beans and about ½ cup of water. Simmer for about 7 minutes. Remove from heat and serve hot.

❈ Storing Chutneys

Always cook and store chutneys in nonreactive pans and bowls. If cooked in other pots, the acid in the chutneys (from lemon juice, vinegar, etc.) will react to iron, copper, and brass, giving a nasty metallic taste to the chutney.

Creamy Red Lentils
(Masoor Ki Dal)

Water, as needed
½ teaspoon turmeric powder
1 teaspoon (or to taste) salt
4 tablespoons vegetable oil
1 cup red split lentils (masoor dal), well rinsed

½ teaspoon cumin seeds
2 garlic cloves, minced
½ teaspoon red chili powder

Serves 4
Prep Time: 10 minutes
Cook Time: 35 minutes

This dish tastes as beautiful as it appears. Serve with Dry Garlic Chutney (page 228) and hot Simple Naan Bread (page 207).

---

1. In a deep pot, combine 4 cups of water, turmeric powder, salt, and 2 tablespoons of the vegetable oil. Bring to a boil. Add all the lentils and mix well. Bring to a full boil. Reduce heat to medium and cook, uncovered, for about 25 minutes or until the lentils are soft. If the water begins to dry out, add up to ½ cup more. (The consistency should be like a creamy soup.) Remove from heat.
2. Using a spoon, mash the cooked lentils to a creamy consistency. Set aside.
3. In a medium pan, heat the remaining vegetable oil. Add the cumin seeds. When they begin to sizzle, add the garlic and red chili powder; sauté for about 20 seconds.
4. Remove from heat and pour over the lentils. Mix well and serve hot.

✳ A Change of "Season-ings"

Changing the final seasoning, or tadka, can completely change the taste of a dish. Take the Creamy Red Lentils above, for instance. Change the seasoning from cumin seeds to black mustard seeds and add a few fresh curry leaves, and taste the difference.

Creamy Black Gram Dahl
(Dal Makhani)

*1 cup whole black gram, or
  black lentils (urad dal), rinsed
2 tablespoons dried red kidney
  beans
½ teaspoon turmeric powder
Water, as needed
4 tablespoons butter
1 teaspoon oil*

*1 teaspoon Ginger-Garlic Paste
  (see recipe on page 15)
1 cup tomato purée (canned
  or fresh)
1 teaspoon red chili powder
Table salt, to taste
4 tablespoons heavy cream*

1. In enough water to cover, soak the *urad dal* along with the red kidney beans overnight. Drain and set aside.
2. In a heavy-bottomed pan, combine the turmeric and water; bring to a boil. Add the *urad dal* and red kidney beans and mix well. Cook on medium heat, uncovered and stirring occasionally, for about 1 hour. Check to see if the lentils are soft and if they are beginning to split. If not, continue cooking. If the lentils start to dry out, add up to 1 cup more of water. Remove from heat and set aside.
3. In a medium-sized skillet, heat the butter along with the oil. Add the Ginger-Garlic Paste and sauté for 30 seconds.
4. Add the tomatoes and cook for about 7 to 8 minutes or until the oil begins to separate from the mixture. (The tomatoes may splatter, so cover the skillet with a splatter guard or partially cover the mixture with a lid as it cooks.)
5. Add the red chili powder and salt; mix well. Remove from heat and pour over the *dal*; mix well. Just prior to serving, stir in the heavy cream. Serve hot.

❋ How Soft?

When cooking lentils, lift a few with a wooden spatula. Mash them between your fingers. If they mash easily, they are ready and cooked.

Black-Eyed Peas Curry
(Tarewale Lobhiya)

4 tablespoons vegetable oil
1 teaspoon Ginger-Garlic Paste
   (see recipe on page 15)
1 large red onion, minced
2 small tomatoes, finely
   chopped
½ teaspoon turmeric powder
1 teaspoon red chili powder

2 teaspoons coriander powder
Table salt, to taste
1 teaspoon tamarind pulp,
   concentrate
2 (14-ounce) cans black-eyed
   peas (lobhiya), rinsed
1 cup water
1 tablespoon minced cilantro

> **Serves 4**
> **Prep Time:** 10 minutes
> **Cook Time:** 30 minutes
>
> This dish is unusual and quite delicious. Serve with hot Simple Naan Bread (page 207) or your favorite bread.

1. In a deep pan, heat the vegetable oil. Add the Ginger-Garlic Paste and sauté for about 30 seconds.
2. Add the onion and sauté for about 7 to 8 minutes or until well browned.
3. Add the tomatoes and sauté for another 8 minutes or until the oil begins to separate from the sides of the mixture.
4. Add the turmeric, red chili powder, coriander, and salt; mix well. Add the tamarind and mix well.
5. Add the black-eyed peas and mix well; sauté for 2 minutes.
6. Add the water and simmer on low heat for about 6 to 8 minutes, stirring occasionally.
7. Add the cilantro and cook for 1 minute. Remove from heat and serve hot.

❈ Edible Spoons?

Indian use their bread, torn into small pieces, as spoons to scoop up yummy lentils and gravies. Try it and see the difference it makes.

Split Pea Purée
(Andhra Patoli)

1 cup chana dal or yellow split peas, well rinsed
2 serrano green chilies
1 teaspoon cumin seeds
Water, as needed
4 tablespoons vegetable oil
½ teaspoon black mustard seeds

2 dried red chilies, roughly pounded
4 fresh curry leaves
1-inch piece fresh gingerroot, grated
¼ teaspoon turmeric powder
Table salt, to taste

1. In a food processor, grind together the *chana dal,* green chilies, and cumin seeds, along with 2 to 3 tablespoons of water, to make a coarse paste. You can add more water to aid the grinding process if necessary. Set aside.
2. In a large pan (with a lid), heat the vegetable oil. Add the mustard seeds. When they begin to sputter, add the red chilies, curry leaves, and gingerroot; mix well.
3. Add the *dal* paste, turmeric powder, and salt; mix well. Add about ¼ cup of water. Cover and cook on medium heat for 7 to 8 minutes
4. Uncover, stir well, and add another ¼ cup of water. Mix well and cover. Lower the heat and cook until the lentils are soft, about 5 to 6 minutes. Serve hot.

❋ Ginger Too Dry?

If your fresh ginger has dried up, soak it in some hot water for instant revitalization. As a rule, choose young gingerroot for the recipes in this book.

Gujarati Yellow Mung Beans
(Peele Moong Ki Dal)

Water, as needed
½ teaspoon turmeric powder
2 tablespoons vegetable oil
1 cup yellow split mung beans
  (yellow moong dal), rinsed
2 packed teaspoons jaggery or
  brown sugar
Table salt, to taste

3 tablespoons vegetable oil
½ teaspoon black mustard
  seeds
5–6 fresh curry leaves
Pinch of asafetida
2 dried red chilies, roughly
  pounded

> **Serves 4**
> **Prep Time:** 10 minutes
> **Cook Time:** 45 minutes
>
> This simple dal is a staple in the western Indian state of Gujarati. Serve garnished with minced cilantro.

1. In a deep pan, heat 4 cups of water, the turmeric, and vegetable oil on high heat. Bring to a boil.
2. Add the *moong dal.* Reduce the heat to medium. Cook, uncovered, for 30 minutes or until the *dal* is soft. If the *dal* begins to dry up, add up to ½ cup of hot water.
3. Remove from heat. Using a hand mixer or the back of a wooden spoon, mash the *dal* to a coarse purée. Add the jaggery and salt; mix well. Set aside.
4. Just before serving, heat the vegetable oil in a small pan. Add the mustard seeds. When they begin to sputter (about 30 seconds), in quick succession add the curry leaves, asafetida, and red chilies. Sauté for another 30 seconds.
5. Remove from heat and pour over the *dal.* Mix well and serve hot.

✳ Jaggery

Jaggery, or gur, as it is called in India, is a beautiful caramel-colored sugar. It comes from sugar cane juice and is often used in making Indian desserts.

Maharastrian Pigeon Pea Curry
(Ambat Varan)

Serves 4
Prep Time: 10 minutes, plus 1 hour to soak
Cook Time: 55 minutes

A tangy dish from the western Indian state of Maharastra, this is traditionally served with steamed rice sprinkled with 1 tablespoon of warmed ghee.

1 cup pigeon peas (toor dal), rinsed
Water, as needed
½ teaspoon turmeric powder
4 tablespoons vegetable oil
1 teaspoon minced garlic
A pinch of asafetida

½ teaspoon cumin seeds
½ teaspoon mustard seeds
1 teaspoon tamarind pulp concentrate
1 teaspoon sugar
Table salt, to taste

1. Soak the *toor dal* in enough water to cover, for 1 hour.
2. In a deep pan, combine 4 cups of water, the turmeric, and 2 tablespoons of the vegetable oil; bring to a boil.
3. Add the *toor dal* and stir. Lower heat to medium and cook, uncovered, for about 40 minutes or until the *dals* are soft. Mash them with the back of a wooden spoon to get a smooth consistency. Remove from heat and set aside.
4. In a small skillet, heat the remaining vegetable oil. Add the garlic and sauté for 30 seconds. In quick succession add the asafetida, cumin, and mustard seeds. When the mustard seeds begin to sputter, remove from heat and pour over the *toor dal*.
5. Return the *dal* to the stovetop and add the tamarind; mix well. Add the sugar and salt, and mix well. Add ½ cup of water and bring to a boil. Remove from heat and serve hot.

❖ Reducing the Cooking Time for Dahls

Soak dahls (dals) or lentils in hot water instead of cold water. Also, add salt, lemon juice, or tamarind only at the end of the cooking process for dahls. If you add it earlier, the dahl will take a lot longer to cook. Adding a little bit of oil and turmeric powder to dahls while boiling them will also considerably shorten the cooking process.

Split Pea and Cheese Curry
(Paneeri Chana Dal)

*1 cup chana dal or yellow
  split peas, well rinsed*
½ teaspoon turmeric powder
1 teaspoon red chili powder
*3 tablespoons vegetable oil,
  divided*

*1 cup fried Indian Cheese (see
  recipe on page 73)*
4 cups water
Table salt, to taste
1 teaspoon minced garlic
1 small red onion, minced

> **Serves 4**
> **Prep Time:** 10 minutes,
> plus 1 hour to soak
> **Cook Time:** 45 minutes
>
> A cozy combination
> of creamy chana dal
> and soft paneer
> (Indian Cheese), serve
> this with warm Simple
> Indian Bread (page
> 204). Garnish with
> minced cilantro.

1. Soak the *chana dal* in enough water to cover, for 1 hour. Drain and set aside.
2. In a deep pan, combine the turmeric powder, red chili powder, 1 tablespoon of the vegetable oil, the Indian Cheese, and water. Bring to a boil. Add the *chana dal* and cook, stirring occasionally. Reduce heat to medium, cover partially, and continue to cook for about 30 minutes or until the *dals* are very soft. Reduce the heat and simmer for about 8 minutes.
3. Remove from heat and add the salt; mix well with a wooden spoon. Set aside.
4. In a medium-sized pan, heat the remaining vegetable oil. Add the garlic and sauté for 30 seconds.
5. Add the onions and sauté for 7 minutes or until the onions are browned. Remove from heat and add to the *dal*; mix well. Serve hot.

❋ Paneer Substitutes

Use tofu as a substitute when a recipe calls for firm paneer. If you're not a fan of tofu, you can also use baked ricotta in its place. To bake the ricotta: Place ricotta cheese in an ovenproof dish. Bake at 350° for 45 minutes. Cut into small pieces.

Fried Lentil Balls Stir-Fry
(Moongodi Ki Subzi)

Serves 4
Prep Time: 10 minutes
Cook Time: 10 minutes

Use freshly prepared
Fried Mung Bean Balls
for this, as this recipe
will not taste good
with defrosted balls.

4 tablespoons vegetable oil
1 small red onion, peeled and thinly sliced
1-inch piece fresh gingerroot, peeled and julienned
1 recipe Fried Mung Bean Balls (see below)

¼ teaspoon turmeric powder
Table salt, to taste
2 generous tablespoons dried fenugreek leaves (kasoori methi)

1. In a large skillet, heat the vegetable oil. Add the onions and ginger and sauté for about 3 to 5 minutes or until the onions are soft.
2. Add the Fried Mung Bean Balls and sauté for 1 minute.
3. Add the turmeric, salt, and fenugreek; sauté for 2 minutes.

Fried Mung Bean Balls
(Moongodi)

Serves 4
Prep Time: 10 minutes
Cook Time: 30 minutes

These fritters freeze
well for use in curries
at a later date. To
defrost them, add
them to a bowl of
hot water.

1 cup yellow split mung beans (yellow moong dal), well rinsed
2 serrano green chilies
Table salt, to taste

1-inch piece fresh gingerroot, roughly chopped
Water, as needed
Vegetable oil for deep-frying

1. In a food processor, purée the *moong dal,* green chilies, salt, and ginger to a smooth paste. Add up to 1 tablespoon of water to aid in the grinding process, if necessary. Transfer the mixture to a bowl, then whisk the mixture to incorporate some air into it.
2. Heat the vegetable oil in a deep pan or a deep fryer to 375°. Place a few tablespoons of the mixture, 1 at a time, into the oil. Make sure you do not overcrowd the pan. Deep-fry the pieces until golden brown on each side, about 1 minute. Remove with a slotted spoon and drain on paper towels. Let the oil return to cooking temperature. Continue deep-frying until all the mixture is used. Serve immediately.

Lemony Black-Eyed Peas
(Nimbu Wala Lobhiya)

2 (14-ounce) cans black-eyed
   peas (lobhiya), rinsed
4 tablespoons fresh lemon juice
1 teaspoon black salt
1-inch piece fresh gingerroot,
   peeled and julienned

2 tablespoons minced cilantro
2 serrano green chilies, seeded
   and minced

Serves 4
Prep Time: 10 minutes,
plus 30 minutes to chill
Cook Time: None

Lemon adds a zing to
this simple salad.
Serve this as a hearty
salad or even as a
side along with
kebabs of your
choice.

Mix together all the ingredients in a bowl. Chill, covered, for 30 minutes. Serve cold.

Black-Eyed Pea Fritters
(Lobhiya Ke Pakore)

2 (14-ounce) cans black-eyed
   peas (lobhiya), rinsed
2 tablespoons chickpea flour
1 tablespoon corn flour
1 teaspoon red chili powder

½ teaspoon turmeric powder
Table salt, to taste
2 serrano green chilies, seeded
Water, as needed
Vegetable oil for deep-frying

Serves 4
Prep Time: 15 minutes
Cook Time: 30 minutes

Whip the batter with a
spoon for a few minutes before deep-frying, for fritters that
are perfectly crunchy
outside and soft and
moist on the inside.

1. In a food processor, purée the black-eyed peas, chickpea flour, corn flour, red chili powder, turmeric powder, salt, and green chilies. Grind to a thick paste; add up to 2 tablespoons of water to aid in the grinding process if necessary. Transfer to a bowl.
2. Heat the vegetable oil in a deep pan or a deep fryer to 375°. Place a few tablespoons of the mixture, 1 at a time, in the oil. Deep-fry until golden brown on each side, about 1 minute. Remove with a slotted spoon and drain on paper towels. Let the oil return to temperature. Continue until all the mixture is used. Serve immediately.

Split Lentil Dumplings
(Urad Dal Ke Vade)

Serves 4
Prep Time: 10 minutes
plus 2 hours to
soak the dal
Cook Time: 30 minutes

These delightful
dumplings can be
served as cocktail
appetizers. Traditionally
they are served
drenched in yogurt and
topped with dollops
of Tamarind Chutney
(page 226).

1 cup skinned and split black gram (also called white lentils), rinsed
½ teaspoon fenugreek seeds (methi)
4 cups hot water

1-inch piece fresh gingerroot, peeled and coarsely chopped
2 serrano green chilies
Table salt, to taste
Vegetable oil for deep-frying

1. Soak the gram and fenugreek seeds together in the hot water for about 2 hours. Drain.
2. In a food processor, combine the soaked gram and fenugreek, ginger, chilies, and salt. Process to a smooth batter. Add up to 2 tablespoons of water if needed. Transfer to a bowl.
3. Heat the vegetable oil in a deep pan or a deep fryer to 375°. Place a few tablespoons of the mixture, 1 at a time, into the oil. Make sure you do not overcrowd the pan. Deep-fry the balls until golden brown all over, about 2 to 3 minutes. Remove with a slotted spoon and drain on paper towels. Let the oil return to temperature between batches. Continue until all the mixture is used. Serve hot.

❋ Cleaning Lentils
Always check your lentils to make sure there are no tiny stones or debris. Use a flat or shallow dish to spread out the lentils; this will make it easier to spot the stones.

Spicy Yogurt Curry
(Punjabi Kadhi)

*1 recipe Fried Mung Bean
    Balls (page 198)*
2 cups plain yogurt
4 cups water
4 tablespoons chickpea flour
1 teaspoon turmeric powder
1 teaspoon red chili powder

Table salt, to taste
2 tablespoons vegetable oil
*½ teaspoon black mustard
    seeds*
2 dried red chilies, broken
½ teaspoon cumin seeds

Serves 4
Prep Time: 10 minutes
Cook Time: 45 minutes

A staple in the North
Indian state of Punjab,
this dish is traditionally
served with steamed
Simple Basmati Rice
(page 162) and Lentil
Wafers (page 233).

1. Add the Fried Mung Bean Balls to 4 cups of *hot* water; soak for 5 minutes. Drain. Press each ball between the palms of your hands to squeeze out any water. Set aside.
2. Place the yogurt, 4 cups of water, chickpea flour, turmeric powder, red chili powder, and salt in a deep bowl. Using a hand blender or a spoon, blend well. Make sure that there are no lumps. Transfer to a deep pan.
3. Bring the yogurt mixture to a boil on medium heat, stirring constantly. Reduce the heat and continue cooking for another 20 to 30 minutes or until the mixture begins to thicken and gain a creamy consistency. Stir occasionally while cooking.
4. Add the soaked mung bean balls to the mixture and simmer for another 10 minutes. Remove from heat and set aside.
5. In a small skillet, heat the vegetable oil. Add the mustard seeds. When the seeds begin to sputter (about 30 seconds), add the red chilies and cumin seeds. Sauté for another 20 seconds. Remove from heat and pour over the yogurt mixture; mix well. Serve hot.

❋ Oily Fritters?

Oily fritters generally signal that the oil they were fried in was not hot enough. Allow the oil to heat to the required temperature between batches.

Yogurt Green Curry
(Hariyali Kadhi)

Serves 4
Prep Time: 5 minutes
Cook Time: 30 minutes

A variation on the classic Spicy Yogurt Curry (Punjabi Kadhi), serve this nutritious curry with Simple Basmati Rice (page 162).

1 (10-ounce) package chopped frozen spinach, thawed
1½ cups plain yogurt
4 tablespoons chickpea flour
2 tablespoons vegetable oil
Pinch of asafetida
2 dried red chilies, broken
1 teaspoon minced garlic
Water, as needed

1. Place the spinach in a deep pan and add enough water to cover. Boil until the leaves are cooked through, about 10 minutes. Remove from heat, drain thoroughly, and cool to room temperature. In a food processor, purée the spinach to a thick paste. Transfer to a deep bowl.
2. In a small bowl, add about 4 tablespoons of the yogurt and all of the chickpea flour. Mix well and make sure that there are no lumps. Add the rest of the yogurt and mix well. Add this mixture to the spinach purée; mix well.
3. In a deep pan, heat the vegetable oil. Add the asafetida, red chilies, and garlic; sauté for 30 seconds.
4. Add the spinach mixture to the seasoned oil. Add ½ cup of water and mix well. Cook on medium heat for about 15 minutes or until the mixture begins to thicken. Serve hot.

☀ Stinking Spice

Asafetida is a stinky resin that is used for flavoring and as a digestive aid. Don't let the smell discourage you; it dissipates during the cooking process.

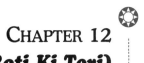

CHAPTER 12
Bread Basket (Roti Ki Tori)

Simple Indian Bread
(Chapati)

Serves 4
Prep Time: 15 minutes, plus 30 minutes for the dough to rest
Cook Time: 20 minutes

The chapati dough can be prepared up to a day in advance. Refrigerate the dough, and then let it come to room temperature before proceeding.

2 cups whole-wheat flour (atta), plus extra for dusting
1 teaspoon table salt
¾ cup warm water

Vegetable oil for greasing
2 teaspoons melted Clarified Butter (see recipe on page 17)

1. In a bowl, combine the flour and salt. Add the water slowly, kneading as you go. Make a soft dough, kneading for at least 10 minutes. The final dough should be soft and pliable. It should not be sticky; otherwise it will not roll out well.
2. Cover the dough with a damp cloth or plastic wrap and let it sit for 30 minutes.
3. Lightly dust a clean work surface with flour. Roll the dough into a log about 8 inches long. Cut into 12 equal portions and cover again with a damp cloth or plastic wrap.
4. Lightly dust the rolling surface with a bit more flour. Lightly grease your hands with oil. Take 1 portion and roll it into a ball between the palms of your hands, then flatten the ball. Place it on the prepared surface. Use a rolling pin to roll it out into a circle about 5 to 6 inches in diameter. Cover with a damp cloth or plastic wrap until ready to fry. Continue until all the portions are rolled out.
5. Heat a dry griddle on medium heat. Pick up a dough circle (keeping the remaining circles covered) and shake off any excess flour. Place it on the griddle. In about 1 minute, small blisters will begin to appear on the surface. Flip it over and cook on the other side for 1 minute.
6. Using a folded cloth to protect your fingers, press down the outer edges of the bread. This will encourage it to puff up. (If this does not happen, do not worry. It takes a good amount of practice to make the chapaties puff up.) Remove the chapati from the griddle and place in a paper towel or a cloth napkin and keep covered until ready to serve. Continue until all the chapaties are cooked
7. When you are ready to serve the chapaties, brush with a little bit of the butter. Serve hot.

Chickpea Flour Flatbread
(Missi Roti)

1 cup chickpea flour
1 cup whole-wheat flour (atta),
  plus extra for dusting
1½ teaspoons (or to taste)
  table salt
1 teaspoon carom seeds

½ teaspoon red chili powder
  (optional)
Water, as needed
Vegetable oil for greasing
4 tablespoons melted Clarified
  Butter (see recipe on page 17)

Serves 4
Prep Time: 30 minutes
Cook Time: 30 minutes

Chickpea flour and wheat flour are combined here to make this flavorful bread. Serve along with your favorite chutney.

1. In a bowl, combine the chickpea flour, wheat flour, salt, carom seeds, and red chili powder; mix well. Add water, a little bit at a time, kneading constantly. Continue kneading for at least 10 minutes or until you get a soft and pliable dough. The dough should not be sticky.
2. Cover the dough with a damp cloth or plastic wrap and let it sit for 30 minutes.
3. Lightly dust a clean surface with flour. Roll the dough into a log. Cut into 12 equal portions.
4. Lightly dust the rolling surface and rolling pin with a bit more flour. Lightly grease your hands with oil (or dust with flour). Take 1 portion of dough and roll it into a ball between the palms of your hands, then flatten the ball. Place it on the prepared surface. Use the rolling pin to roll it out into a circle about 5 to 6 inches in diameter. Cover with a damp cloth or plastic wrap until ready to fry. Continue until all the portions are rolled out.
5. Heat a dry griddle on medium heat. Pick up the circle of dough (keeping the remaining circles covered), shake off any extra flour, and place on the griddle. Small blisters will begin to appear on the surface in about 1 minute. Flip the dough over and cook on the other side for 1 more minute. Brush lightly with butter and flip over once more.
6. Remove the flatbread from the heat and place in a paper towel or a cloth napkin and keep covered until ready to serve. Continue until all the *rotis* are cooked. When you are ready to serve, brush with a little bit more of the butter. Serve hot.

Fried Indian Bread
(Bhatura)

Serves 4
Prep Time: 10 minutes, plus at least 4 hours for the dough to rest
Cook Time: 20 minutes

This puffy and crispy Indian bread tastes best when it is freshly prepared and eaten hot. It is traditionally served with Chickpea Curry (page 189).

2 cups all-purpose flour (maida), plus extra for dusting
½ teaspoon baking soda
1 teaspoon table salt
½ cup plain yogurt, whipped
Water, as needed
Vegetable oil for deep-frying and greasing

1. In a bowl, combine the flour, baking soda, and salt. Add the yogurt, slowly, and start kneading the dough. Add water as needed to form a smooth dough that is not sticky. The dough will be quite elastic.
2. Sprinkle some flour over the dough and continue to knead for at least 10 minutes.
3. Place the dough, covered, in a warm place for at least 4 hours.
4. Divide the dough into 14 equal parts. Lightly dust a clean work surface with flour.
5. Lightly grease your hands with oil. Take 1 portion of dough and roll it into a ball between the palms of your hands, then flatten the ball. Place it on the prepared surface. Use a rolling pin to roll it out into a thin disk about 5 to 6 inches in diameter. Cover with a damp paper towel until ready to fry. Continue until all the portions are rolled out.
6. In a deep pan or a deep fryer, heat the vegetable oil to 370°. Add a single disk at a time. It will begin to rise and puff up. Using the back of your slotted spoon, very lightly press the disk into the oil. Turn it over and fry for another 20 seconds or until golden brown. Using a slotted spoon, remove the fried bread from the oil and drain on paper towels. Continue until all the disks are fried. Serve immediately.

❋ Indian All-Purpose Flour

In Indian grocery stores you will find a fine white flour called maida. This is traditionally used to make Fried Indian Bread. This flour produces the right amount of elasticity in the dough to provide the spongy texture characteristic of the bread.

Simple Naan Bread
(Saada Naan)

¼ cup warm water
½ teaspoon sugar
1¼ teaspoons table salt
1 teaspoon dried active yeast
*4 cups all-purpose flour (maida),
    plus extra for dusting*

½ teaspoon baking powder
1 egg, beaten
½ cup plain yogurt, whipped
¼ cup warm milk
*5 tablespoons melted Clarified
    Butter (page 17)*

> **Serves 4**
> **Prep Time:** 20 minutes,
> plus 2 hours to rise
> **Cook Time:** 20 minutes

> Naans are traditional Indian breads prepared in clay ovens or tandoors. Fiercely popular in Indian restaurants worldwide, these are easily prepared in the conventional oven.

1. Dissolve the sugar and ¼ teaspoon of the salt in warm water and add the yeast. Set aside for 10 minutes to allow the yeast to foam.

2. Place the flour, remaining salt, and baking powder in a large shallow bowl; mix well.

3. Add the egg and yogurt and begin to knead. Begin adding the yeast mixture and the warm milk and continue kneading until you have a soft dough. If you need more liquid, add a few tablespoons of warm water. Knead for at least 10 minutes or until you have a soft dough that is not sticky.

4. Cover the dough with a damp cloth and place in a warm place for 1½ to 2 hours or until the dough has doubled in volume

5. Adjust the racks in the oven so that the top rack is 5 inches away from the top element. Preheat oven to 400°. Lightly grease a large, heavy baking sheet or cast-iron griddle and set aside.

6. Lightly dust a clean work surface and rolling pin with flour. Knead the dough again on the floured surface for about 5 minutes. Divide it into 8 equal pieces and cover with a damp towel or plastic wrap.

7. Roll each piece into a ball and flatten it with your hands. Roll it out into an oval shape about 6 to 7 inches long. Using your hands, pull at both ends of the oval to stretch it a little. Continue until you have made 8 naans.

8. Brush each oval with the butter. Place the naans on the baking sheet and bake for 5 minutes. Turn on the broiler and broil for an additional 3 minutes or until golden brown. (Depending on the size of your baking tray, you may have to do the naans in 2 batches.) Serve warm.

Almond-Coated Naan Bread
(Badaami Naan)

Serves 4
Prep Time: 20 minutes,
plus 2 hours to rise
Cook Time: 20 minutes

A more royal version
of the humble naan.
You can also top it
with grilled chicken,
dried fenugreek,
nigella seeds, or Indian
Cheese (page 14).

¼ cup warm water
½ teaspoon sugar
1¼ teaspoons table salt
1 teaspoon dried active yeast
4 cups all-purpose flour (maida),
  plus extra for dusting
½ teaspoon baking powder

1 egg, beaten
½ cup plain yogurt, whipped
¼ cup warm milk
5 tablespoons melted Clarified
  Butter (page 17)
¼ cup almonds, slivered and
  blanched

1. Dissolve the sugar and ¼ teaspoon of salt in warm water and add the yeast. Put aside for 10 minutes to allow the yeast to foam.
2. Place the flour, remaining salt, and baking powder in a large, shallow bowl; mix well. Add the egg and yogurt and begin to knead. Begin adding the yeast mixture and the warm milk and continue kneading until you have a soft dough. If you need more liquid, add a few tablespoons of warm water. Knead for at least 10 minutes or until you have a soft dough that is not sticky.
3. Cover the dough with a damp cloth and put in a warm place for 1½ to 2 hours or until the dough has doubled in volume
4. Adjust the racks in the oven so that the top rack is 5 inches away from the top element. Preheat oven to 400°. Lightly grease a large, heavy baking tray or cast-iron griddle and set aside.
5. Lightly dust a clean work surface and a rolling pin with flour. Knead the dough on the prepared surface for about 5 minutes. Divide it into 8 equal pieces and cover with a damp towel or plastic wrap.
6. Roll each piece into a ball and flatten it with your hands. Roll it out into an oval shape about 6 to 7 inches long. Using your hands, pull at both ends of the oval to stretch it a little. Continue until you have made 8 naans. Brush each oval with the butter. Sprinkle with a few almonds. Lightly press the almonds into the dough.
7. Place the naans on the baking sheet and bake for 5 minutes. Broil for 3 more minutes or until golden brown. (Depending on the size of your sheet, you may have to bake in 2 batches.)

Mint-Flavored Bread
(Pudina Paratha)

2 cups whole-wheat flour
   (atta), plus extra for dusting
4 tablespoons semolina
2 tablespoons dried mint
1½ teaspoons (or to taste)
   table salt

8 tablespoons melted Clarified
   Butter (see recipe on
   page 17)
Water, as needed
Vegetable oil for greasing

> **Serves 4**
> **Prep Time:** 30 minutes,
> plus 30 minutes to rest
> **Cook Time:** 20 minutes
>
> Serve with any raita of
> your choice (see
> Chapter 5) for a
> complete meal.

1. In a bowl, combine the wheat flour, semolina, mint, salt, and 4 tablespoons of the butter. Add the water slowly, kneading the flour as you go. Make a soft dough, kneading for at least 10 minutes. The final dough should be soft and pliable. It should not be sticky; otherwise it will not roll out well.
2. Cover the dough with a damp cloth or plastic wrap and let it sit for 30 minutes.
3. Roll the dough into a log and cut it into 10 equal portions. Lightly dust a clean work surface with flour.
4. Lightly grease your hands with oil. Take 1 portion of the dough and roll it into a ball between the palms of your hands, then flatten the ball. Place it on the prepared surface. Use a rolling pin to roll it out into a disk about 5 to 6 inches in diameter.
5. Lightly brush the disk with the butter and fold it in half. Brush again with the butter and fold in half again to form a triangle.
6. Lightly flour the work surface again, and roll out the triangle into a triangle about 5 to 6 inches in diameter at the base.
7. Heat a griddle on medium. Brush it lightly with butter and add the *paratha* to the griddle. Cook for about 2 minutes or until the bottom of the *paratha* begins to blister. Brush the top surface lightly with butter and flip over. Cook for 2 minutes.
8. Remove the *paratha* from the griddle and place on a serving platter. Cover with a paper towel. Continue until all the *parathas* are rolled out and cooked. Serve hot.

Ground Meat–Stuffed Bread
(Kheema Ka Paratha)

Serves 4
Prep Time: 25 minutes, plus 30 minutes for the dough to rest
Cook Time: 30 minutes

A great way to use leftover minced meat, these parathas are a meal in themselves. Serve with your choice of pickles and raita.

2 cups whole-wheat flour (atta)
4 tablespoons semolina
1½ teaspoons table salt
6 tablespoons melted Clarified Butter (see recipe on page 17)
Water, as needed
½ recipe Peas and Minced-Meat Curry (page 123)
Vegetable oil for greasing

1. In a bowl, combine the wheat flour, semolina, salt, and 2 tablespoons of the butter. Add the water slowly, kneading as you go. Form into a soft dough, kneading for at least 10 minutes. The final dough should be soft and pliable, but not sticky. Cover the dough with a damp cloth or plastic wrap and let it sit for 30 minutes.
2. In a medium-sized skillet on high heat, warm the Peas and Minced-Meat Curry. Sauté until all the moisture has completely dried out. Remove from heat and allow to cool. Remove any whole spices and break up any large pieces of meat with a fork.
3. Roll the dough into a log. Cut into 8 equal portions. Lightly dust a clean work surface and a rolling pin with flour. Lightly grease your hands with oil. Take 1 portion of dough and roll into a ball between the palms of your hands, then flatten the ball. Place it on the prepared work surface, then roll it out into a circle about 5 to 6 inches in diameter.
4. Lightly brush the surface of the dough circle with the butter. Add 1 tablespoon of the minced-meat filling to the center. Bring the sides together and pinch them to seal, forming a ball. Flatten lightly and dust very lightly with flour.
5. Lightly dust the work surface with flour again, and roll out the flattened ball again until it is about 5 to 6 inches in diameter.
6. Heat a griddle on medium heat. Brush it lightly with butter and add the *paratha* to the griddle. Cook for about 2 minutes or until the bottom of the *paratha* begins to blister. Brush the top lightly with butter and flip over. Cook for 2 minutes.
7. Remove the *paratha* from the griddle and place on a serving platter. Cover with a paper towel. Continue until all the *parathas* are cooked.

Spinach Bread
(Palak Ka Paratha)

1 cup frozen, chopped spinach
2 cups whole-wheat flour
*   (atta), plus extra for dusting*
2 tablespoons semolina
1½ teaspoons table salt

6 tablespoons melted Clarified
*   Butter (page 17)*
Water, as needed
Vegetable oil for greasing

Serves 4
Prep Time: 15 minutes,
plus 30 minutes to rest
Cook Time: 40 minutes

A small tea stall
hidden in the heart
of Delhi serves this
khoob khasta, which
means very flaky.
Serve with any raita
of your choice.

1. In enough water to cover, boil the spinach until wilted. Drain. Set aside to cool.
2. In a bowl, combine the spinach, wheat flour, semolina, and salt; mix well. Add 2 tablespoons of the butter. Add the water slowly, kneading the flour as you go. Make a soft dough, kneading for at least 10 minutes. The final dough should be soft and pliable. It should not be sticky; otherwise it will not roll out well.
3. Cover the dough with plastic wrap and let it sit for 30 minutes.
4. Roll the dough into a log and cut it into 10 equal portions. Lightly dust a clean work surface and rolling pin with flour.
5. Lightly grease your hands with oil. Take 1 portion and roll it into a ball between the palms of your hands, then flatten the ball. Place it on the prepared surface. Use the rolling pin to roll it out into a circle about 5 to 6 inches in diameter.
6. Lightly brush the surface of the dough circle with the butter and fold the circle in half. Brush again with the butter and fold in half again to form a triangle.
7. Lightly dust the work surface with flour again, and roll out the triangle of dough until the base of the triangle is about 5 to 6 inches wide.
8. Heat a griddle on medium heat. Brush it lightly with butter and add the *paratha* to the griddle. Cook for about 2 minutes or until the bottom of the *paratha* begins to blister. Brush the top lightly with butter and flip over. Cook for 2 minutes.
9. Remove the *paratha* from the griddle and place on a serving platter. Cover with a paper towel. Continue until all the *parathas* are rolled out and cooked. Serve hot.

Seasoned Bread
(Namak Mirch Ke Parathe)

Serves 4
Prep Time: 15 minutes, plus 30 minutes for the dough to rest
Cook Time: 20 minutes

This bread freezes well and will stay good frozen for up to three months. Serve with your favorite raita and a pickle of your choice.

2 cups whole-wheat flour (atta), plus extra for dusting
4 tablespoons semolina
1½ teaspoons (or to taste) table salt
1 teaspoon red chili powder
1 serrano green chili, seeded and finely minced
6 tablespoons melted Clarified Butter (page 17)
Water, as needed
Vegetable oil for greasing

1. In a bowl, combine the wheat flour, semolina, salt, red chili powder, green chili, and 2 tablespoons of the butter; mix well. Slowly add the water, kneading the flour as you go. Make a soft dough, kneading for at least 10 minutes. The final dough should be soft and pliable. It should not be sticky; otherwise it will not roll out well.
2. Cover the dough with a damp cloth and let it sit for 30 minutes.
3. Roll the dough into a log. Cut into 8 equal portions. Lightly dust a clean work surface and rolling pin with flour.
4. Lightly grease your hands with oil (or dust with flour). Take 1 portion of dough and roll it into a ball between the palms of your hands, then flatten the ball. Place it on the prepared surface. Use the rolling pin to roll it out into a circle about 5 to 6 inches in diameter.
5. Lightly brush the surface of the dough circle with the butter and fold the circle in half. Brush again with the butter and fold in half again to form a triangle.
6. Lightly flour the work surface again, and roll out the triangle of dough until the base of the triangle is about 5 to 6 inches wide.
7. Heat a griddle on medium heat. Brush it lightly with butter and add the *paratha* to the griddle. Cook for about 2 minutes or until the bottom of the *paratha* begins to blister. Brush the top lightly with butter and flip over. Cook for 2 minutes.
8. Remove the *paratha* from the griddle and place on a serving platter. Cover with a paper towel. Continue until all the *parathas* are rolled out and cooked. Serve hot.

Stuffed Bread
(Paratha)

*2 cups whole-wheat flour
(atta), plus extra for dusting*
4 tablespoons semolina
1½ teaspoons table salt

*6 tablespoons melted Clarified
Butter (page 17)*
1 batch, your choice of filling

Serves 4
Prep Time: 15 minutes,
plus 30 minutes for
the dough to rest
Cook Time: 30 minutes

Be careful when you
roll the bread; be
gentle so that the
filling does not break
out of the dough.
Serve with plain
yogurt.

1. In a bowl, combine the wheat flour, semolina, salt, and 2 tablespoons of the butter. Slowly add the water, kneading the flour as you go. Make a dough, kneading for at least 10 minutes. The final dough should be soft and pliable. It should not be sticky; otherwise it will not roll out well.

2. Cover the dough with a damp cloth or plastic wrap and let it sit for 30 minutes. While the dough is resting, prepare the filling of your choice.

3. Roll the dough into a log. Cut into 8 equal portions. Lightly dust a clean work surface with flour. Lightly grease your hands with oil (or dust with flour). Take 1 portion of dough and roll it into a ball between the palms of your hands, then flatten the ball. Place it on the prepared surface. Use the rolling pin to roll it out into a circle about 5 to 6 inches in diameter.

4. Lightly brush the surface of the dough circle with the butter and add 1 tablespoon of the filling to the center. Bring the sides together and pinch them together to seal, forming a ball. Flatten lightly and dust very lightly with flour.

5. Lightly dust the work surface with flour again, and roll out the flattened ball until it is about 5 to 6 inches in diameter.

6. Heat a griddle on medium heat. Brush it lightly with butter and add the *paratha* to the griddle. Cook for about 2 minutes or until the bottom of the *paratha* begins to blister. Brush the top lightly with butter and flip over. Cook for 2 minutes.

7. Remove the *paratha* from the griddle and place on a serving platter. Cover with a paper towel. Continue until all the *parathas* are cooked. Serve hot.

Potato Stuffing
(Aloo Ka Paratha)

Serves 4
Prep Time: 15 minutes, plus 30 minutes for the dough to rest
Cook Time: 30 minutes

If you tear up when chopping onions, try refrigerating them prior to use.

3 medium potatoes, peeled
Water, as needed
1 small red onion, peeled and finely minced
2 serrano green chilies, seeded and finely minced
1 tablespoon minced cilantro

1-inch piece fresh gingerroot, grated
1 teaspoon red chili powder
1 teaspoon Warm Spice Mix (page 14)
Vegetable oil for greasing

Boil the potatoes in enough water to cover for about 15 minutes. Drain. Put the potatoes in a bowl and mash them well with a fork. Add the onion, green chilies, cilantro, gingerroot, red chili powder, and spice mix; mix well. Set the filling aside to cool.

Cauliflower Stuffing
(Gobi Ka Paratha)

Serves 4
Prep Time: 15 minutes, plus 30 minutes for the dough to rest
Cook Time: 30 minutes

Be sure to squeeze out all the excess water from the grated cauliflower to keep the bread from tearing when you roll it.

Florets of 1 small cauliflower
Water, as needed
1 tablespoon minced cilantro
1-inch piece fresh gingerroot, grated

1 teaspoon red chili powder
1 teaspoon carom seeds
Vegetable oil for greasing

Using either the grater disk of a food processor or a box grater, grate the cauliflower. Squeeze handfuls of cauliflower over the sink to squeeze out any moisture. Place the cauliflower in a bowl. Add the cilantro, ginger, red chili powder, and carom seeds; mix well.

Green Peas Stuffing
(Hare Matar Ka Paratha)

*1 cup peas (fresh or frozen
    and thawed)*
Water, as needed
1 tablespoon minced cilantro
1 teaspoon red chili powder

Table salt, to taste
Vegetable oil for greasing

Serves 4
Prep Time: 15 minutes,
plus 30 minutes for the
dough to rest
Cook Time: 30 minutes

Roll the bread gently
so that the filling does
not break out of the
dough. Serve with
plain yogurt.

Boil the peas in water for 10 minutes or until tender. Drain well. Place the peas into a bowl along with cilantro, red chili powder, and salt; mash well.

✸ Cook Ahead Parathas

You can make parathas ahead of time to save some time later. Simply prepare the parathas as directed and fry them lightly until they are half cooked. Then refrigerate until you are ready to finish them. Fry them until done and serve!

Carom-Flavored Flatbread
(Ajwain Ka Paratha)

Serves 4
Prep Time: 15 minutes, plus 30 minutes for the dough to rest
Cook Time: 40 minutes

Carom, known for it legendary digestive properties, provides a savory flavoring to this bread. Serve with any raita of your choice (see Chapter 5).

2 cups whole-wheat flour (atta), plus extra for dusting
4 tablespoons semolina
1½ teaspoons (or to taste) table salt
1 teaspoon red chili powder
2 tablespoons dried fenugreek leaves, crumbled
1 tablespoon carom seeds
4 tablespoons melted Clarified Butter (see recipe on page 17)
Water, as needed
Vegetable oil for greasing

1. In a bowl, combine the wheat flour, semolina, salt, red chili powder, fenugreek leaves, carom seeds, and 2 tablespoons of the butter. Slowly add the water, kneading as you go. Make a soft dough, kneading for at least 10 minutes. The final dough should be soft and pliable. It should not be sticky; otherwise it will not roll out well.
2. Cover the dough with a damp cloth or plastic wrap and let it sit for 30 minutes.
3. Roll the dough into a log. Cut into 8 equal portions. Lightly dust a clean work surface and a rolling pin with flour.
4. Lightly grease your hand with oil (or dust with flour). Take 1 portion and roll into a ball between the palms of your hands, then flatten the ball. Place it on the prepared surface. Use the rolling pin to roll it out into a circle about 5 to 6 inches in diameter.
5. Lightly brush the surface of the dough circle with the butter and fold it in half. Brush again with the butter and fold in half again to form a triangle.
6. Lightly flour the work surface again, and roll out the triangle of dough until the base of the triangle is about 5 to 6 inches.
7. Heat a griddle on medium heat and brush it lightly with butter. Add the *paratha* to the griddle. Cook for about 2 minutes or until the bottom of the *paratha* begins to blister. Brush the top lightly with butter and flip over. Cook for 2 minutes.
8. Remove the *paratha* from the griddle and place on a serving platter. Cover with a paper towel. Continue until all the *parathas* are rolled out and cooked. Serve hot.

Onion Bread
(Pyaz Ka Paratha)

2 cups whole-wheat flour (atta),
   plus extra for dusting
4 tablespoons semolina
1½ teaspoons (or to taste)
   table salt
1 teaspoon red chili powder

1 medium-sized red onion,
   peeled and finely minced
6 tablespoons melted Clarified
   Butter (see recipe on page 17)
Water, as needed
Vegetable oil for greasing

> **Serves 4**
> **Prep Time:** 15 minutes,
> plus 30 minutes for the
> dough to rest
> **Cook Time:** 40 minutes
>
> Minced onions are
> kneaded into the
> dough to prepare this
> delightful and savory
> paratha. Serve with a
> raita of your choice
> (see Chapter 5).

1. In a bowl, combine the wheat flour, semolina, salt, red chili powder, onion, and 2 tablespoons of the butter. Slowly add the water, kneading as you go. Make a soft dough, kneading for at least 10 minutes. The final dough should be soft and pliable. It should not be sticky; otherwise it will not roll out well.
2. Cover the dough with a damp cloth or plastic wrap and let it sit for 30 minutes.
3. Roll the dough into a log and cut it into 10 equal portions. Lightly dust a clean surface and a rolling pin with flour.
4. Lightly grease your hands with oil (or dust with flour). Take 1 portion and roll into a ball between the palms of your hands, then flatten the ball. Place it on the prepared surface. Use a rolling pin to roll it out into a circle about 5 to 6 inches in diameter.
5. Lightly brush the surface of the dough circle with the butter and fold it in half. Brush with the butter and fold in half again to form a triangle.
6. Lightly flour the work surface again, and roll out the triangle until the base of the triangle is about 5 to 6 inches wide.
7. Heat a griddle on medium heat and brush it lightly with butter. Add the *paratha* to the griddle. Cook for about 2 minutes or until the bottom of the *paratha* begins to blister. Brush the top lightly with butter and flip over. Cook for 2 minutes.
8. Remove the *paratha* from the griddle and place on a serving platter. Cover with a paper towel. Continue until all the *parathas* are rolled out and cooked. Serve hot.

Puffed Bread
(Puri)

Serves 4
Prep Time: 10 minutes, plus 20 minutes for the dough to rest
Cook Time: 25 minutes

To enjoy these, serve them hot. Refrigerate rolled puris for about 15 minutes before frying; they will consume less oil and be crispier.

1 cup whole-wheat flour (atta)
1 cup all-purpose flour (maida), plus extra for dusting
1 teaspoon salt
2 tablespoons vegetable oil, plus more for deep-frying
Water, as needed

1. In a bowl, combine the wheat flour, all-purpose flour, salt, and the 2 tablespoons vegetable oil; mix well. Add the water slowly, kneading as you go. Continue to add a little water at a time and knead for about 4 to 5 minutes until you have a smooth dough that is not sticky. If the dough sticks to your fingers, add a little bit of vegetable oil and continue to knead.
2. Cover the dough with a damp cloth or a plastic cover and let rest for at least 20 minutes.
3. Divide the dough into 10 equal pieces. Roll into balls and cover with a damp cloth.
4. Heat vegetable oil in a deep fryer or a deep pan to 375°. Lightly flour a clean work surface and a rolling pin. Roll out each *puri* into a 3-inch circle.
5. Deep-fry 1 *puri* at a time. Lower it into the oil and use the back of a slotted spoon to press down lightly on the *puri*. This will make it puff up. Turn it over and fry for another 20 seconds or until golden brown.
6. Using a slotted spoon, remove the *puri* from the oil and drain on paper towels. Continue until all the *puris* are rolled out and fried. Serve immediately.

❋ Puris Too Oily?

Oily puris generally signal that the oil they were fried in was not hot enough. Allow the oil to heat to the required temperature between batches.

Puffed Bread with Peas
(Matar Ki Puri)

1 cup whole-wheat flour (atta)
1 cup all-purpose flour (maida),
*   plus extra for dusting*
1 teaspoon salt
2 tablespoons vegetable oil,
*   plus more for deep-frying*

Water, as needed
½ cup peas
1 tablespoon minced cilantro
¼ teaspoon red chili powder

Serves 4
Prep Time: 10 minutes,
plus 20 minutes for the
dough to rest
Cook Time: 25 minutes

A delicious variation
of the traditional puri,
serve these with any
pickle of your choice.

1. In a bowl, combine the wheat flour, all-purpose flour, the 1 teaspoon salt, and 2 tablespoons vegetable oil; mix well. Add the water slowly, and begin kneading. Continue to add a little water at a time and knead for about 4 to 5 minutes until you have a smooth dough that is not sticky. If the dough sticks to your fingers, add a little bit of vegetable oil and continue to knead.

2. Cover the dough with a damp cloth or a plastic cover and let rest for at least 20 minutes.

3. While the dough is resting, prepare the filling. Boil the peas in water for about 10 minutes or until tender. Drain. Place the peas into a bowl along with the cilantro, red chili powder, and salt to taste; mash well. Set aside.

4. Divide the dough into 10 equal pieces. Roll into balls. Keep them covered with a damp cloth.

5. Heat vegetable oil in a deep fryer or a deep pan to 375°. Lightly flour a clean work surface and a rolling pin. Roll out each *puri* into a 3-inch circle. Add 1 teaspoon of the pea filling to the center. Bring the sides together and pinch them to seal, forming a ball. Flatten lightly and dust very lightly with flour. Lightly flour the work surface again, and roll out the flattened ball until about 3 inches in diameter.

6. Deep-fry 1 *puri* at a time. Lower the *puri* into the oil and use the back of a slotted spoon to press down lightly on it. This will make it puff up. Turn it over and fry for another 20 seconds or until golden brown.

7. Using a slotted spoon, remove the *puri* from the oil and drain on paper towels. Continue until all the *puris* are rolled out and fried. Serve immediately.

Carom-Flavored Fried Bread
(Ajwain Puri)

Serves 4
Prep Time: 10 minutes, plus 20 minutes for the dough to rest
Cook Time: 25 minutes

This is a strongly flavored puri. Serve hot with any raita of your choice.

1 cup whole-wheat flour (atta)
1 cup all-purpose flour (maida), plus extra for dusting
1 teaspoon salt
1 teaspoon carom seeds
2 tablespoons vegetable oil, plus more for deep-frying
Water, as needed

1. In a bowl, combine the wheat flour, all-purpose flour, salt, carom seeds, and vegetable oil; mix well. Add water slowly and begin kneading. Continue to add a little water at a time and knead for 4 to 5 minutes until you have a smooth dough that is not sticky. If the dough sticks to your fingers, add a little bit of vegetable oil and continue to knead.
2. Cover the dough with a damp cloth or a plastic cover and let rest for at least 20 minutes.
3. Divide the dough into 10 equal pieces. Roll into balls. Keep them covered with a damp cloth as you begin to deep-fry.
4. Heat vegetable oil in a deep fryer or a deep pan to 375°. Lightly flour a clean work surface. Roll out each *puri* into a 3-inch disk.
5. Deep-fry 1 *puri* at a time. Lower the *puri* into the oil and use the back of a slotted spoon to press down lightly on it. This will make it puff up. Turn it over and fry for another 20 seconds or until golden brown. Serve hot.
6. Using a slotted spoon, remove the *puri* from the oil and drain on paper towels. Continue until all the *puris* are rolled out and fried. Serve immediately.

❋ Mint Puri

Making mint puri is also very easy. Add 2 generous tablespoons of dried mint leaves to the Carom-Flavored Fried Bread recipe (above) in step 1, then follow the rest of the steps in the recipe.

Baked Fenugreek Bread
(Methi Ki Puri)

1 cup whole-wheat flour (atta),
   plus extra for dusting
¼ cup semolina
2 heaping tablespoons dried
   fenugreek leaves
½ teaspoon turmeric powder
1 teaspoon red chili powder

Table salt, to taste
3 tablespoons Clarified Butter
   (see recipe on page 17)
Water, as needed
Vegetable oil for greasing

Serves 4
Prep Time: 15 minutes
Cook Time: 20 minutes

This bread keeps for
2 days stored in an
airtight container. You
can even serve this
instead of chips with
a dip of your choice.

1. Place the whole-wheat flour, semolina, fenugreek leaves, turmeric, red chili powder, salt, and 1 tablespoon of the butter in a bowl; mix well. Add water slowly, kneading the flour into a smooth dough. The dough should be a bit firm, pliable, and not sticky.

2. Lightly grease your hands with oil, and divide the dough into 10 equal portions. Roll each portion into a ball.

3. Preheat oven to 300°. Grease a baking sheet with the remaining butter. Lightly dust a clean work surface and a rolling pin with flour.

4. Roll each dough ball into a 3- to 3½-inch circle. Prick each rolled-out *puri* all over with a fork. Continue until all the *puris* are rolled out.

5. Place a few *puris* on the baking sheet and bake for about 10 minutes. Turn and bake for 2 to 3 minutes or until the *puris* are golden brown and cooked through. (Keep the uncooked *puris* covered with a damp cloth.)

6. Remove the *puris* from the oven and place on a serving platter. Serve at once.

✵ Fresh or Dried Herbs

Most Indian cooks, particularly those in India, will not use dried herbs. Dried herbs are much stronger than fresh ones. As a general rule, you need three times the quantity if you are using fresh herbs in place of dried ones.

Mixed Flour Bread
(Thalepeeth)

3 tablespoons chickpea flour
4 tablespoons rice flour
4 tablespoons whole-wheat flour
1 small red onion, peeled and minced
2 tablespoons minced cilantro
1 teaspoon turmeric powder
½ teaspoon red chili powder

Table salt, to taste
Pinch of asafetida
½ teaspoon carom seeds, crushed
Water, as needed
2 tablespoons vegetable oil

1. In a bowl, mix together all the ingredients *except* the vegetable oil. Add water, a little bit at a time, to make a very thick batter. Mix well and make sure your batter does not have any lumps.
2. Heat a medium-sized nonstick skillet on medium heat. Coat very lightly with vegetable oil.
3. Using a ladle, add about 4 tablespoons of batter to the center of the skillet (similar to a pancake). Add a few drops of vegetable oil to the sides of the bread. Lower the heat and cover for about 2 minutes. This will enable the bread to cook in its own steam.
4. Uncover and flip over. Cook until well browned on both sides, about 2 to 3 minutes.
5. Remove from heat and place on a paper towel. Continue until all the batter is used. Serve hot.

❋ Storing Chapaties

Chapaties are a classic Indian flatbread, served at almost every meal. They do take some practice to make, so don't worry if they are not perfectly round or do not puff up; they will still taste good. Chapaties can be prepared and frozen for up to 1 month. When you are ready to serve them, place them on a paper towel and microwave for a minute or so until soft.

Indian Corn Flatbread
(Makki Di Roti)

2 cups corn flour (makki ka atta)
1 teaspoon table salt
Warm water, as needed
Vegetable oil for greasing

4–5 tablespoons melted
Clarified Butter (see recipe
on page 17)

Serves 4 **Prep Time:** 10 minutes **Cook Time:** 20 minutes
Originally from the Indian state of Punjab, this bread is served with Punjabi Mustard Greens (page 74) and freshly made white butter.

1. In a bowl, combine the flour and the salt; mix well. Begin adding water, a little bit at a time, to make a soft dough. Knead for 2 to 3 minutes. The dough should be soft and not sticky.
2. Lightly grease your hands with oil. Divide the dough into 8 equal balls.
3. To prepare the *rotis*, place a ball between 2 pieces of plastic wrap, or wax paper. Using a rolling pin, roll out the dough into a circle about 3 to 4 inches in diameter and around ¼ inch thick. (This is not a thin bread.) Continue until all the *rotis* are rolled out.
4. Heat a griddle on medium heat. Brush it lightly with the melted butter. Place a flattened *roti* on the griddle. In about 1 or 2 minutes, the bottom of the *roti* will start to blister. Brush the surface of the *roti* with more butter. Flip it over and cook for 1 minute or until crisp.
5. Place the *roti* on a serving platter lined with a paper towel or cloth napkin. Continue until all the *rotis* are cooked. Serve hot.

❈ Droopy Naans

Naans get their traditional teardrop shape from the way the dough actually droops when it is applied to the extremely hot walls of the Tandoor.

CHAPTER 13
Chutney, Pickles, and Papads (Kuch Saath Me)

Mint-Cilantro Chutney
(Pudine Dhaniye Ke Chutney)

1 packed cup cilantro
½ packed cup mint
2 serrano green chilies, roughly chopped

2 fresh garlic cloves
Table salt, to taste
2 tablespoons fresh lemon juice

Blend all the ingredients in a food processor to a smooth paste. To aid in the blending process, you can add 1 tablespoon of water if needed. Chill for about 30 minutes. Serve as a dipping sauce. This chutney will keep, refrigerated, for 4 days.

Tamarind Chutney
(Imli Ki Chutney)

1 cup tamarind pulp
2 cups hot water
½ cup jaggery or brown sugar
1 teaspoon red chili powder

Table salt, to taste
½ cup dates, pitted and chopped

1. In a glass bowl, soak the tamarind pulp in the hot water for 30 minutes. Strain through a fine-meshed sieve into a bowl. Discard any residue in the sieve.
2. Add the jaggery, red chili powder, and salt to the bowl and mix well. Add the dates and purée the entire mixture in a blender. Transfer the mixture to a nonreactive cooking pan.
3. Heat on low until the chutney reaches a custardlike consistency, about 7 to 8 minutes.
4. Remove from heat and let cool to room temperature. Refrigerate for up to a week until needed.

Green Chili and Coconut Chutney
(Hari Mirch Aur Nariel Ke Chutney)

1 cup shredded coconut
4 serrano green chilies
1-inch piece fresh gingerroot, peeled
1 tablespoon fresh lemon juice
1 tablespoon minced cilantro
1 tablespoon plain yogurt (optional)

Water, as needed
1 tablespoon vegetable oil
½ teaspoon mustard seeds
2 dried red chilies, roughly pounded
4 fresh curry leaves

Yields 1 cup
Prep Time: 5 minutes
Cook Time: 5 minutes

This chutney tastes best when it is made fresh, but refrigerated it will keep for 4 days. Serve as a topping for grilled fish.

1. In a blender, purée the coconut, green chilies, ginger, lemon juice, cilantro, yogurt, and ½ cup of water to a smooth paste. Transfer to a nonreactive container with a lid and set aside.
2. In a small skillet, heat the vegetable oil. Add the mustard seeds, red chilies, and curry leaves. In less than 1 minute the mustard seeds will start to sputter. Remove from heat and pour over the coconut chutney.
3. Mix well. Refrigerate, covered, until needed.

❋ The Roots of Chutney

Chutney is the English term of the Indian word chatni. In India, chutneys are generally made fresh daily, in small quantities. They add pizzazz to any meal. They can be sweet, sour, tangy, savory, fresh, or preserved. Fresh chutneys have a bright flavor and are usually thin, smooth sauces. Cooked chutneys have a deeper, broader flavor.

Dry Garlic Chutney
(Lasan Ki Chutney)

1 cup unsweetened desiccated
  coconut
12 fresh garlic cloves, peeled

1 teaspoon red chili powder
Table salt, to taste

1. In a medium-sized skillet, roast the coconut and the garlic for about 3 to 4 minutes on low heat. The coconut and the garlic will begin to darken and release their aroma. Remove from heat and allow to cool for about 10 minutes.
2. Transfer the mixture to a blender and add the red chili powder and salt. Blend until you have a coarse powder.
3. Transfer to a container. Cover, and refrigerate until needed.

Saffron Mayonnaise
(Kesari Mayonnaise)

1 cup mayonnaise
¼ teaspoon Roasted Saffron
  (see recipe on page 18)

1 teaspoon crushed red pepper
Table salt, to taste

In a bowl, combine all the ingredients; mix well. Let the mixture chill, covered, in the fridge at least 30 minutes before serving. It will keep for up to 1 week in the refrigerator.

❄ Buying Saffron

Look for Iranian or Spanish saffron. It should be deep red in color. You should be able to see the threads clearly; if it is powdered it is not of good quality. A rule of thumb, 1 ounce of saffron is about 4 tablespoons. In India saffron (the spice and the color) has tremendous religious significance.

Carrot Chutney
(Gajar Ki Chutney)

1½ cups shredded carrot
1 teaspoon grated gingerroot
Water, as needed
1 teaspoon red chili powder

Table salt, to taste
1 tablespoon liquid honey
2 tablespoons fresh lemon juice

In a deep pan, bring the carrots, ginger, and 1 cup of water to boil. Reduce heat and cook until the carrots are tender, about 3 to 4 minutes. Drain and let cool for about 20 minutes. Add the red chili powder, salt, honey, and lemon juice; mix well. Refrigerate until needed.

> **Yields 1 cup**
> **Prep Time:** 10 minutes
> **Cook Time:** 5 minutes, plus 20 minutes to cool
>
> Serve this as an accompaniment to any meal for an added punch. Keeps for 2 to 3 days in the refrigerator.

Green Chili Pickle
(Hari Mirch Ka Achaar)

2 teaspoons fennel seeds
2 teaspoons black mustard seeds
4 teaspoons dried mango powder

25 serrano green chilies
4 tablespoons vegetable oil
4 tablespoons fresh lemon juice

1. In a medium-sized skillet, heat the fennel and black mustard seeds. When the seeds begin to sizzle (less than 1 minute), remove from heat. Allow them to cool for about 10 minutes. Using a spice grinder, grind the spices to a powder. Add the mango powder. Set aside.
2. Slit the green chilies. (If you like heat, do not seed the chilies.) Using the tip of your knife, add some of the spice mixture to each of the chilies.
3. Heat the vegetable oil in a skillet. Add the chilies and sauté for 3 to 5 minutes or until the chilies are softened. Remove from heat. Add the lemon juice. Cool to room temperature, about 15 minutes. Transfer to an airtight jar and refrigerate until ready to serve.

> **Yields 1 cup**
> **Prep Time:** 20 minutes
> **Cook Time:** 5 minutes, plus 25 minutes to cool
>
> There are innumerable variations of this pickle. This will keep for 1 week in the refrigerator.

Shredded Mango Pickle
(Aam Ka Achaar)

Yields ½ cup
Prep Time: 10 minutes
Cook Time: 10 minutes,
plus 1 day to let the
pickle marinate

Traditionally this is
made with diced
mango; my recipe
uses shredded. This is
quite hot; reduce the
amount of red chili
powder to taste.

4 tablespoons vegetable oil
1 teaspoon mustard seeds
½ teaspoon onion seeds or
 wild fennel seeds (optional)
1 cup green mango, coarsely
 shredded (with peel)
2 tablespoons red chili powder
1 teaspoon asafetida powder
Salt, to taste

1. Heat the vegetable oil in a medium-sized skillet. Add the mustard seeds and onion seeds. As soon as the seeds begin to sputter, remove from heat and cover the pan. Set aside.
2. In a clean, dry jar (with a cover), combine the mango, red chili powder, salt, asafetida, and the seasoned oil from step 1; mix together using a dry spoon.
3. Store the jar, covered, in a warm place for 1 day. Shake it intermittently to allow the spices to mix well. Refrigerate until needed.

Mango-Saffron Chutney
(Kairi Kesar Ki Chutney)

Yields 2 cups
Prep Time: 10 minutes,
plus 1 hour to stand
Cook Time: 10–15
minutes, plus 20
minutes to cool

Don't use a nonstick
skillet here, as the
sugar won't carmelize.

2 cups green mango, peeled
 and coarsely shredded
1 cup sugar
2 teaspoons grated gingerroot
2 dried red chilies, pounded
A pinch of salt
¼ teaspoon saffron, soaked in
 4 tablespoons hot water for
 10 minutes

1. In a glass bowl, combine the mango and the sugar; mix well. Let it stand for about 1 hour.
2. Heat a small skillet on medium. Add the mango-sugar mixture. Lower the heat and cook for 10 to 12 minutes or until the mangoes become very soft and the sugar begins to turn a light brown.
3. Add the ginger, red chilies, and salt; mix well. Strain the saffron and discard any residue. Add the saffron-infused water and mix well. Simmer for 1 minute. Remove from heat and let cool for about 20 minutes. Cover and refrigerate until needed.

Goan Shrimp Pickle
(Mole De Camarao)

6 tablespoons vegetable oil, divided

2 cups medium shrimp, peeled and deveined

8 curry leaves

2 serrano green chilies, minced

1 tablespoon minced garlic

6 dried red chilies, roughly pounded

2 small red onions, peeled and minced

6 tablespoons white vinegar

½ teaspoon turmeric powder

Table salt, to taste

Yields 2 cups
Prep Time: 10 minutes
Cook Time: 20–25 minutes, plus 20 minutes to cool

You can increase the quantity of this and serve it as a side dish. It will keep for up to 1 week refrigerated.

1. Heat 3 tablespoons of the vegetable oil in a medium-sized skillet. Add the shrimp and sauté for 3 to 4 minutes or until no longer pink. Transfer the shrimp to a bowl.
2. In the same skillet, heat the remaining vegetable oil. Add the curry leaves, green chilies, garlic, red chilies, and onions; sauté for 7 to 8 minutes or until the onions are well browned.
3. Add the vinegar, turmeric, and salt. Bring to a slow boil. Reduce heat.
4. Add the shrimp and simmer on very low heat for about 8 minutes.
5. Remove from heat and cool to room temperature, about 20 minutes. Transfer to a dry bowl. Refrigerate, covered, until needed.

※ Choosing Mangoes

When buying mangoes, feel the fruit. It should yield to gentle pressure. It should also be very fragrant. To ripen mangoes, place them in a brown paper bag for a few days.

Sesame Chutney
(Til Ki Chutney)

1 cup white sesame seeds
3 fresh garlic cloves
5 (or to taste) serrano green
  chilies, seeded
Table salt, to taste
2 tablespoons fresh lemon juice

Water, as needed
1 tablespoon vegetable oil
1 dried red chili, whole
¼ teaspoon mustard seeds

1. In a small skillet on low heat, roast the sesame seeds for 2 to 3 minutes. Stir constantly. When the seeds begin to darken, remove from heat. Cool for about 10 minutes.
2. In a food processor, combine the sesame seeds, garlic, green chilies, salt, and lemon juice. Grind to a fine paste. You may add up to 2 tablespoons of water to aid in the processing if needed. Transfer the chutney to a bowl. Set aside.
3. Heat the vegetable oil in a small skillet. Add the red chili and the mustard seeds. In less than 1 minute, the seeds will begin to sputter. Remove from heat and pour over the prepared chutney. Refrigerate, covered, until ready to use.

✵ Sesame Seeds

Sesame seeds are popular not only in Asia but also in the Middle East. Middle Eastern tahini, a sweet creamy sauce made from sesame seeds, is becoming very popular in North America. Because of the high oil content, sesame seeds tend to become rancid very quickly, so make sure you use fresh seeds.

Lentil Wafers
(Papads)

6 lentil wafers

Approach 1: Using tongs, hold the wafer over a low flame. Roast them until they start to change color and small black spots begin to appear on the surface. Continue until all the *papads* are roasted. Serve.

Approach 2: Microwave each wafer for about 1 minute or until it begins to crisp all over and change color. Serve.

Approach 3: Heat vegetable oil in a deep fryer to 350°. Deep-fry a single wafer at a time for less than 1 minute or until the wafer becomes crisp. Drain on a paper towel and serve hot.

✳ Move Over, Popcorn

Top your favorite papad with diced onions, green chilies, and Chaat Spice Mix (page 16), for a perfect movie-time snack. If you love popcorn, cook as you would normally, then serve sprinkled with Chaat Spice Mix.

> **Serves 4**
> **Prep Time:** None
> **Cook Time:** Few minutes
>
> Cook these just prior to serving, as they taste best freshly made. Buy prepackaged papads from your local Indian grocer to save time.

South Indian Ginger Chutney
(Allam Pachadi)

1 tablespoon tamarind pulp,
   soaked in ¼ cup hot water
   for 10 minutes
1 tablespoon vegetable oil
2 dried red chilies

¼ teaspoon fenugreek seeds
½ teaspoon mustard seeds
½ cup grated gingerroot
2 tablespoons sugar
1 teaspoon salt

1. Using a fine-meshed sieve, strain the tamarind pulp over a bowl. Discard any residue in the sieve. Set aside.
2. Heat the vegetable oil in a small skillet and add the red chilies, fenugreek seeds, and the mustard seeds. When the seeds begin to sputter (about 30 seconds), add the gingerroot. Sauté for about 2 minutes.
3. Add the strained tamarind pulp, sugar, and salt; simmer for about 5 minutes. Remove from heat and cool for about 20 minutes.
4. Transfer to a blender or food processor and blend to a smooth paste.
5. Transfer to a bowl. Cover and refrigerate until needed.

Quick Pink Ginger Pickle
(Gulabi Adrak)

¾ cup julienned ginger
½ teaspoon red chili powder
3–4 large serrano green chilies,
   slit

1 cup rice vinegar

Combine all the ingredients in a dry glass jar. Cover and let stand in the sun for about 5 to 6 hours. Refrigerate until needed. This will keep for up to 3 weeks.

Quick Carrot Pickle
(Jhatpat Gajar Ka Achar)

2 cups diced carrots
½ cup fresh lemon juice
Salt, to taste

½ teaspoon red chili powder
½ teaspoon black mustard
  seeds, roughly pounded

Combine all the ingredients in a dry glass jar. Cover and let stand in the sun for about 5 to 6 hours. Refrigerate until needed.

✻ Handling Pickles

Always use dry spoons to handle pickles or they will spoil. Moisture is the biggest enemy of pickles. Also, always store them in airtight jars to prevent spoilage.

> **Yields 2 cups**
> **Prep Time:** 10 minutes, plus 5 to 6 hours to stand
> **Cook Time:** None
>
> Serve as an accompaniment to any meal. Keeps for 3 days in the refrigerator.

Pineapple Chutney
(Ananas Ki Chutney)

1 (14-ounce) can pineapple
  chunks, drained
1 tablespoon grated fresh
  gingerroot
4 tablespoons sugar
1 tablespoon vegetable oil

½ teaspoon fennel seeds
½ teaspoon cumin seeds
2 dried red chilies, roughly
  pounded
Pinch of salt to taste

1. In a bowl, combine the pineapple, ginger, and sugar. Set aside.
2. In a small skillet, heat the vegetable oil. Add the fennel, cumin, and red chilies. Sauté for about 1 minute or until the spices begin to sizzle.
3. Remove from heat. Pour over the pineapple-ginger mixture and mix well. Transfer to a food processor and grind to a coarse paste.
4. Transfer to a covered container and refrigerate until needed.

> **Yields 1 cup**
> **Prep Time:** 5 minutes
> **Cook Time:** 5 minutes
>
> Serve this chutney with pork, turkey, or as a topping for vanilla ice cream. This chutney will keep for 3 to 4 days, refrigerated.

Papaya Chutney
(Papite Ki Chutney)

2 tablespoons vegetable oil
½ teaspoon cumin seeds
½ teaspoon fenugreek seeds
1 teaspoon fennel seeds
½ teaspoon mustard seeds
2 cups green papaya, peeled and grated

1 tablespoon grated fresh gingerroot
¼ cup sugar
½ cup water
Table salt, to taste

1. In a medium-sized skillet, heat the vegetable oil. Add the cumin, fenugreek, fennel, and mustard seeds. As soon as the seeds begin to sizzle (about 1 minute), add the papaya.
2. Add the gingerroot and sugar; mix well. Add the water and simmer on low heat until the papaya is soft, about 10 minutes. Add salt to taste. Remove from heat. Cool and refrigerate until needed.

Date Pickle
(Khajoor Ka Achar)

2 tablespoons tamarind pulp, soaked in ½ cup hot water for 10 minutes
2 cups pitted dates
1 teaspoon red chili powder
3 teaspoons coriander powder

2 teaspoons cumin powder
2 teaspoons fennel seeds, roughly pounded
Salt, to taste
4 tablespoons sugar

1. Using a fine-meshed sieve, strain the tamarind pulp over a bowl. Discard any residue in the sieve. Set the strained pulp aside.
2. In a deep pan, boil the dates in water to cover until tender, about 8 minutes. Drain.
3. Add the dates to a food processor and coarsely grind. Transfer to a bowl.
4. Add the tamarind paste, red chili powder, coriander, cumin, fennel, salt, and sugar to the dates; mix well. Transfer to a glass jar. Cover and refrigerate until needed.

Raw Mango Chutney
(Kacche Aam Ki Chutney)

*1 medium-sized green mango,
   peeled and cubed*

*6 dried red chilies
Pinch of salt*

Purée all the ingredients in a food processor. Add 1 tablespoon of water if needed to aid in the process. Serve.

❈ Tarty Starter

Slice tart green mangoes; sprinkle with Chaat Spice Mix (page 16) or black salt. Serve with cocktails as a snazzy appetizer.

> **Yields 1 cup**
> **Prep Time:** 5 minutes
> **Cook Time:** None
>
> Keeps for 2 to 3 days, refrigerated.
> Serve as a dressing for grilled fish.

Mint Chutney
(Pudine Ki Chutney)

*2 packed cups fresh mint
1-inch piece fresh gingerroot,
   peeled and coarsely
   chopped
3 tablespoons lemon juice*

*3 serrano green chilies, seeded
   and coarsely chopped
1 small red onion, peeled and
   coarsely chopped*

Combine all the ingredients in a food processor. Blend to a fine paste. Transfer to a bowl. Refrigerate, covered, until ready to serve.

> **Yields 1 cup**
> **Prep Time:** 5 minutes
> **Cook Time:** None
>
> One of the most popular Indian chutneys. A perfect dipping sauce, this even makes a unique salad dressing. This tastes best freshly made.

Green Chili Chutney
(Hari Mirch Ki Chutney)

Yield 1 cup
Prep Time: 10 minutes
Cook Time: None

Very spicy and robust. Use as a salad dressing over fresh vegetables. Don't forget to seed the chilies if you want a milder taste.

20 serrano green chilies, stemmed and coarsely chopped
½ packed cup cilantro
4 tablespoons fresh lemon juice
1 teaspoon sugar
1 teaspoon salt

In a blender, blend together all the ingredients to a fine paste. Transfer to a covered container. Refrigerate until needed.

☀ Fruit for Dinner?

Green chili, a fruit, is eaten raw with dinner in most North Indian households. (Yes, seeds and all.) If you decide to try it, ensure that the chili is properly washed and I would suggest removing the seeds at first. Drizzle with a bit of lemon juice and see if you like it!

Chili Garlic Sauce
(Mirch Aur Lasan Ki Sauce)

Yields ¼ cup
Prep Time: 5 minutes
Cook Time: 10 minutes, plus 10 minutes to cool

A perfect accompaniment to Indian Chinese dishes, this sauce keeps for up to a week in the refrigerator.

2 tablespoons vegetable oil or sesame oil
4 dried red chilies
6 fresh garlic cloves, minced
2 tablespoons white vinegar
¼ cup canned tomato sauce
Pinch of sugar

1. Heat the vegetable oil in a small skillet. Add the red chilies and sauté for about 1 minute or until they begin to change color. Remove the chilies from the skillet and drain on a paper towel. Reserve the oil in the skillet.
2. Add the garlic to the skillet and sauté for 30 seconds. Add the vinegar and tomato sauce and bring to a slow boil.
3. Remove from heat. Add the sugar and let cool for about 10 minutes.
4. In a spice grinder, grind the fried red chilies to a fine powder. Add to the tomato sauce; mix well. Refrigerate, covered, until ready to use.

South Indian Gun Powder
(Mullaga Podi)

½ cup pigeon peas (toor dal)
½ cup chana dal or yellow
   split peas
½ cup split black gram, or black
   lentils (safeed urad dal)

Pinch of asafetida
4 fresh curry leaves
6 dried red chilies
2 teaspoons table salt

1. In a medium-sized skillet, roast all the ingredients *except* the salt, stirring constantly. In 1 minute or so the *dals* will begin to change color. Remove from heat.
2. Cool for about 20 minutes. Transfer to a spice grinder and grind to a fine powder. Add the salt and mix well. Transfer to a dry jar. Cover and keep until needed. Sprinkle on steamed rice and add 1 tablespoon of hot ghee as a garnish. You can even use it to marinate vegetables, *paneer*, and meats. This will keep for up to 3 months.

> **Yields 1 cup**
> **Prep Time:** None
> **Cook Time:** 15 minutes, plus 20 minutes to cool
>
> This recipe comes from the Indian state of Tamil Nadu. A spicier version has earned the name "Gun Powder" for the heat that it adds.

Peanut Chutney
(Moongphali Ki Chutney)

1 cup salted roasted peanuts
½ teaspoon cumin powder
½ teaspoon red chili powder
1 tablespoon jaggery or palm
   sugar

2 fresh garlic cloves, peeled
   (optional)
Pinch of table salt

In a spice grinder, grind all the ingredients until powdered. As soon as the powder starts to moisten, stop grinding. Transfer to a dry bowl. Cover until ready to use.

> **Yields 1 cup**
> **Prep Time:** 5 minutes
> **Cook Time:** None
>
> Serve this with grilled chicken or even just as a spread on toast. The chutney has a shelf life of about 2 weeks without refrigeration.

Roasted Eggplant Chutney
(Bhune Baigan Ki Chutney)

1 (1-pound) eggplant
4 tablespoons vegetable oil,
  divided
1 tablespoon tamarind pulp,
  soaked in ⅓ cup hot water
  for 10 minutes
2 tablespoons unsweetened
  desiccated coconut

2 dried red chilies
1 teaspoon minced garlic
2 medium tomatoes, finely
  chopped
Table salt, to taste

1. Preheat oven to 475°.
2. Smear the eggplant with 2 tablespoons of the vegetable oil and place it on a foil-lined baking tray. Roast until the eggplant is soft and the skin is charred, about 45 to 50 minutes. Remove from the oven and let cool.
3. Peel off and discard the skin. Mash the eggplant into a smooth pulp. Set aside.
4. Using a fine-meshed sieve, strain the tamarind pulp over a bowl. Discard any residue in the sieve. Put the strained pulp in the bowl and set aside.
5. Heat a small skillet and roast the red chilies and coconut, stirring constantly. In less than 1 minute, the red chilies and coconut will begin to change color. Remove from heat and cool for about 5 minutes. Set aside.
6. In a medium-sized skillet, heat the remaining vegetable oil. Add the minced garlic and sauté for about 30 seconds. Add the tomatoes and sauté for about 7 minutes or until the tomatoes are cooked.
7. Add the eggplant pulp. Mix well and cook, uncovered, for 8 to 9 minutes or until the eggplant is completely cooked.
8. Add the red chilies mixture and strained tamarind; mix well. Remove from heat and allow to cool for about 20 minutes.
9. In a blender, blend the chutney to a smooth paste. Transfer to a bowl. Refrigerate, covered, until ready to use.

Rice Pudding
(Kheer)

3 cups whole milk
1 cup heavy cream
¼ cup basmati rice, rinsed
¾ cup sweetened condensed milk

¼ cup coconut milk (optional)
¼ teaspoon saffron threads

1. Add the whole milk and cream to a deep pan. Bring to a boil on medium heat. Stir constantly to prevent scorching.
2. Reduce the heat to medium-low. Add the rice and mix well; cook for about 20 minutes or until the milk has reduced and you obtain a creamy custardlike consistency. Stir frequently while cooking.
3. Add the condensed milk and mix well. Cook for another 5 minutes. If you are adding coconut milk, add it at this point and cook for another 5 minutes.
4. Crush the saffron threads between your fingers, and add to the rice pudding.
5. Remove from heat. Serve hot or cold. To serve cold, refrigerate, covered, for at least 2 hours before serving.

✳ Avoid Spilling Milk

Rub a little butter on the rim of the pot you are using to boil milk. When the milk begins to boil and reaches the buttered rim, it will settle back down and not boil over the pot.

Blancmange
(Phirni)

3 tablespoons ground almonds
6 tablespoons rice flour
2 cups whole milk
1 cup heavy cream
¾ cup sweetened condensed
   milk

¼ teaspoon (or less, to taste)
   cardamom powder
1 tablespoon rose water
   (optional)

> **Serves 4**
> **Prep Time:** 10 minutes
> **Cook Time:** 40 minutes
>
> Blancmange is a simple pudding that was first devised during the Middle Ages, probably in England.

1. In a deep, heavy-bottomed pan, combine the ground almonds, rice flour, whole milk, and heavy cream. Bring to a boil on high heat. Reduce heat to medium and cook, stirring constantly, for about 20 minutes or until the rice mixture obtains a creamy consistency.
2. Add the condensed milk and cook for another 10 minutes.
3. Add the cardamom and rose water and mix well. Remove from heat. Serve hot or cold.

Mango Cream
(Aamraas)

15 ounces sweetened mango
   pulp
½ cup whole milk
4 tablespoons heavy cream,
   whipped

4 tablespoons sweetened
   condensed milk

> **Serves 4**
> **Prep Time:** 5 minutes, plus 30 minutes to chill
> **Cook Time:** None
>
> Serve as a cold dessert soup garnished with mint leaves. Or serve it as a sauce over vanilla ice cream.

Combine all the ingredients in a bowl. The consistency will be sauce-like. Mix well and chill for at least 30 minutes. Serve.

❋ Sweetened Mango Pulp

Although Alphonso mangoes (the most famous of Indian mangoes) are not available here in the States, you can buy canned Alphonso mango pulp at your Indian grocer. If you use fresh mango pulp for this recipe, strain it first to remove any fibers.

Semolina Pudding
(Sooji Ka Halwa)

Serves 4
Prep Time: 5 minutes
Cook Time: 35 minutes, plus 20 minutes to cool

Served during prayer ceremonies, this pudding is very popular. Serve garnished with slivered almonds.

4 tablespoons Clarified Butter (see recipe on page 17)
1 cup semolina

3 cups hot water
1 cup sugar

1. In a large saucepan, heat the butter.
2. Add the semolina, and cook over low heat. Stir constantly and cook for about 15 minutes or until the semolina is well browned.
3. Add the water and continue cooking on low heat until all the water is absorbed, about 10 minutes. Stir constantly.
4. Add the sugar and mix well. Continue to cook for about 3 minutes. Cover and cook for another 3 to 4 minutes.
5. Remove from heat. Allow to cool for about 20 minutes. Serve.

Saffron Yogurt Pudding
(Kesari Shrikhand)

Serves 4
Prep Time: 5 minutes, plus 30 minutes to chill
Cook Time: None

This very traditional Indian dessert is generally made with saffron or mango, but I've used strawberry and kiwi for a wonderful twist.

2 cups Hung Yogurt (see recipe on page 16)
¼ teaspoon Roasted Saffron (see recipe on page 18)

¼ cup (or to taste) sugar

Place all the ingredients in a bowl and mix well. You can do this with a spatula or a handheld blender. Adjust sugar to taste. Chill for about 30 minutes, then serve.

Date Halwa
(Khajoor Ka Halwa)

*2 tablespoons Clarified Butter
(see recipe on page 17)
1–1¼ cups finely chopped
pitted dates*

*2 tablespoons heavy cream
2 tablespoons slivered almonds*

Heat the butter in a medium-sized pan. Add the dates and sauté for 30 seconds. Add the cream and mix well. Remove from heat. Add the slivered almonds. Serve immediately.

✳ Dates

If using the dates sold in a block, soak them in hot water for 10 minutes, drain, and then chop. If using loose dates, cut them with kitchen shears or chop them with a sharp knife dipped in hot water.

Serves 4
Prep Time: 5 minutes
Cook Time: 5 minutes

A power-packed dessert, serve this along with some hot Indian tea (see Chapter 4).

Opo Squash Pudding
(Dudhi Ka Halwa)

*1 cup peeled and grated opo
squash
2 cups whole milk
4 tablespoons milk powder*

*¾ cup sweetened condensed
milk
¼ teaspoon Roasted Saffron
(see recipe on page 18)*

1. Take a few handfuls of the opo squash at a time and squeeze out all the excess water. Place the squash in a deep pan.
2. Add the milk and milk powder to the pan; mix well. Bring to a boil on high heat, stirring constantly.
3. Reduce heat and continue to cook until you obtain a creamy consistency, about 35 minutes.
4. Add the condensed milk and cook for 10 more minutes.
5. Remove from heat, add the saffron, and serve warm.

Serves 4
Prep Time: 10 minutes
Cook Time: 45 minutes

This simple pudding can be made a day in advance. Serve warm garnished with roasted unsalted cashews and raisins.

Sweetened Yogurt
(Mishti Doi)

Serves 4
Prep Time: None
Cook Time: 40 minutes, plus 4 hours to set, and time to chill

This dish from the eastern Indian state of Bengal can be steamed or baked.

1 (14-ounce) can sweetened
  condensed milk
2 cups Hung Yogurt (page 16)
  or plain yogurt

Pinch of cardamom powder
  (optional)

1. Preheat the oven to 275°.
2. Blend together all the ingredients and place in an ovenproof dish. Place in the oven and bake for 40 minutes.
3. Turn off the oven and leave the dish in the oven for another 4 hours. To check for doneness, insert a toothpick into the dish; if it comes out clean, the dish is done. Refrigerate, covered, overnight.
4. Alternatively, once you blend the ingredients, place them in a small bowl. Cover with aluminum foil. Steam it in a pot of boiling water for 20 minutes or until the yogurt is set. Serve chilled.

Cheese Dessert
(Bengali Sandesh)

Yields 12 pieces
Prep Time: 5 minutes
Cook Time: 15–20 minutes

Serve as is or drizzled with a puréed raspberry sauce.

¼ pound ricotta cheese
4 heaping tablespoons milk
  powder

4 tablespoons sweetened condensed milk
Sugar, to taste (optional)

1. Blend together all the ingredients using a hand blender or by hand until you get a smooth paste. Taste the mixture. If you like your dessert sweeter, add sugar.
2. In a medium-sized nonstick pan, over very low heat, heat the cheese mixture, stirring constantly. Cook for about 15 to 20 minutes or until the mixture begins to leave the sides of the pan.
3. Remove from heat and transfer to a lightly buttered serving tray. Allow to cool for about 1 hour.
4. Cut into 12 portions. Mold into desired shapes of your choice and serve.

Mango Cheesecake
(Aam Ka Cake)

¼ cup water

1 envelope unflavored gelatin

2 cups Indian Cheese (see recipe on page 14), crumbled

1 cup ricotta cheese

4 tablespoons sweetened mango pulp

2 tablespoons sweetened condensed milk

1 cup heavy cream, whipped

1 (15-ounce) can Alphonso mango slices, drained, or fresh mango slices, coarsely chopped

Serves 4
Prep Time: 15 minutes, plus 2 hours to chill
Cook Time: 5 minutes

I love sprinkling some toasted coconut on this dessert to bring the tropics home in the sub-zero temperatures of the East Coast winter.

1. Heat the water on low in a small pan, sprinkle the gelatin on top, and heat until the gelatin completely dissolves. Set aside.
2. In a bowl, combine the Indian Cheese, ricotta cheese, mango pulp, and condensed milk. Mix well and make sure that there are no lumps. A handheld blender works well for this.
3. Slowly add the gelatin to the cheese mixture; mix well.
4. Fold in the whipped cream, and pour into a lightly buttered 6-cup mold. Chill until firm, about 2 hours.
5. When ready to serve, invert the mold onto a serving platter and top the cheesecake with the Alphonso mango.

❋ Using Paneer in Desserts

If you are using store-bought paneer (Indian Cheese), grate it while still cold, using either the grater disk of a food processor or a box grater. Let it come to room temperature before attempting to combine it with the other ingredients. When using homemade paneer, (see recipe on page 14), crumble and mash the paneer by hand to a smooth consistency before using; this will make it easier to blend with the other ingredients.

Creamy Milk Pudding
(Basoondi)

1 cup ricotta cheese
1 cup whole milk
1 cup heavy cream
½ cup (or more, to taste) sugar

1 (14-ounce) can crushed pineapple, drained and chilled

1. In a bowl, combine the ricotta cheese, milk, cream, and sugar. Mix well by hand or with a hand blender. Taste to check sweetness and add more sugar if needed.
2. Transfer the mixture to a heavy-bottomed pan. Heat on low for about 40 minutes, stirring frequently. This mixture needs to cook on a very low heat. The mixture will become creamy and have a very pale yellow color. The final consistency should be that of a creamy custard.
3. Remove from heat. Cool to room temperature, about 1 hour.
4. Fold in the chilled pineapple and serve.

❋ Vark, or Silver Foil

You will often notice Indian sweets are covered with what appears to be shining silver. It is what it appears to be—silver! Silver is beaten into very thin sheets and used as a decorative ingredient in desserts. It is edible and provides a majestic touch to dishes. It is not easily available—check with your Indian grocer.

Tapioca Pudding
(Sabudana Kheer)

¼ cup tapioca
½ cup water
1½ cups whole milk
4 tablespoons sweetened
    condensed milk

Sugar, to taste (optional)
½ teaspoon cardamom seeds

> **Serves 4**
> **Prep Time:** 1 hour
> **Cook Time:** 25 minutes,
> plus 1 hour to chill
>
> A light dessert, serve
> this garnished with
> chopped fruit of your
> choice.

1. In a large bowl, soak the tapioca in the water for about 1 hour. Drain.
2. In a deep pan on medium heat, cook the tapioca and milk for about 20 minutes or until the tapioca is cooked through.
3. Add the condensed milk and mix well. Taste to check for sweetness. Add sugar if needed.
4. Add the cardamom seeds. Cook for 5 minutes.
5. Remove from heat. Chill for about 1 hour. Serve.

Mango Mousse
(Aam Ka Meetha)

¼ cup water
1 packet unflavored gelatin
1 (15-ounce) can Alphonso
    mango slices, drained

2 tablespoons sugar
1 cup heavy cream
1 egg white
Whipped cream, for garnish

> **Serves 4**
> **Prep Time:** 5 minutes,
> plus time to chill
> **Cook Time:** None
>
> A specialty of the new
> Indian generation.
> Since fresh Alphonso
> mangoes are not
> available in the United
> States, I use the
> canned version here.

1. Add the water to a small pan on low heat. Dissolve the gelatin slowly. Set aside.
2. In a blender, blend the mango slices, sugar, and cream. Add the gelatin to the mango mixture and mix well. Set aside.
3. Whip the egg white until it forms peaks. Then fold it into the mango mixture. Transfer to a serving bowl and chill. Garnish with whipped cream before serving.

Apple Kheer
(Saeb Ki Kheer)

Serves 4
Prep Time: 10 minutes
Cook Time: 25 minutes

This is best served chilled. Garnish with silver foil (optional).

2 (red delicious) apples, cored and peeled
6 tablespoons sugar

2 cups whole milk
½ cup heavy cream

1. Grate the apples and place in a medium-sized, nonstick pan. Add the sugar and cook on low heat until the sugar has dissolved.
2. Add the milk and cream. Bring to a boil on medium heat, stirring constantly.
3. Lower the heat and continue stirring. Cook until the mixture reaches a creamy consistency, about 10 minutes.
4. Remove from heat and pour into a serving bowl. Cover and chill. Serve.

Cheese Pudding
(Paneeri Kheer)

Serves 4
Prep Time: 5 minutes
Cook Time: 1 hour, plus 5 hours to cool and chill

This recipe comes to you from my great-grandmother's kitchen. She calls this her dil khus kheer, or "heart happy pudding"! Serve chilled.

1 cup Indian Cheese (see recipe on page 14), grated
3 cups whole milk

½ cup heavy cream
½ cup (or more, to taste) sugar

1. In a bowl, combine the Indian Cheese, milk, cream, and sugar. Mix well by hand or with a hand blender. Taste to check sweetness; add more sugar if needed.
2. Transfer the mixture to a heavy-bottomed pan. Heat on very low heat for about 40 to 60 minutes, stirring constantly. The mixture will become creamy and have a very pale yellow color. The final consistency should be that of a thick custard.
3. Remove from heat and let cool to room temperature, about 1 hour. Then chill for at least 4 hours.

Vermicelli Pudding
(Seviyan Ki Kheer)

4 tablespoons Clarified Butter
  (see recipe on page 17)
  or butter
½ cup broken vermicelli
2 cups whole milk
4 tablespoons sweetened
  condensed milk

1 tablespoon raisins
1 tablespoon slivered almonds
¼ teaspoon Roasted Saffron
  (see recipe on page 18)

Serves 2–3
Prep Time: 5 minutes
Cook Time: 30 minutes,
plus 30 minutes to cool

Roasted vermicelli is
used to make this aro-
matic pudding. Serve
warm in decorative
bowls, garnished with
slivered cashews.

1. Heat a medium-sized nonstick pan on medium. Add the butter. Add the vermicelli and sauté for 1 minute or until it turns brown. Remove from heat and set aside.
2. In a deep pan, combine the milk and condensed milk. Mix well and bring to a boil. Reduce heat to medium and cook for about 15 minutes or until the milk reaches a creamy consistency. Stir constantly.
3. Add the vermicelli, raisins, and almonds. Mix well and cook for another 10 minutes or until the vermicelli is soft.
4. Remove from heat. Add the saffron and mix well. Allow to cool to room temperature (about 30 minutes) before serving.

✳ Nimish

Nimish is one of the most unusual and ethereal Indian desserts. It is prepared by churning boiled milk until foam forms on top. This foam is collected and served in terra-cotta pots. It is believed that the milk needs to be placed outside overnight and there has to be dew for this dish to achieve perfection.

Fruit Salad
(Phal Ka Salaad)

1 cup strawberries, roughly chopped
1 cup melon chunks
1 cup papaya chunks
1 cup Hung Yogurt (see recipe on page 16)
¼ teaspoon Roasted Saffron (see recipe on page 18)
1 tablespoon sweetened condensed milk

1. Combine the strawberries, melon, and papaya in a bowl. Set aside.
2. Whip together the yogurt, saffron, and condensed milk; mix well. Pour the yogurt sauce over the fruits. Chill for about 20 minutes. Serve.

Carrot Pudding
(Gajar Ka Halwa)

3 cups whole milk
½ cup heavy cream
6 tablespoons sweetened condensed milk
3 cups grated carrots
4 generous tablespoons milk powder
4 tablespoons butter
¼ cup slivered almonds

1. In a bowl, combine the milk, cream, and condensed milk; mix well. Transfer to a deep, heavy-bottomed nonstick pan, and bring to a boil.
2. Add the carrots and mix well. Cook on medium heat for about 40 minutes, stirring constantly.
3. When most of the liquid has evaporated, add the milk powder and butter. Mix well and continue to cook for another 10 minutes, stirring constantly. When the mixture begins to draw away from the pan, add the almonds. Cook, stirring constantly, for another 5 minutes. Serve hot.

Instant Saffron Ice Cream
(Kesari Kulfi)

2 (8-ounce) cans (or cartons) table cream

1 (12-ounce) can evaporated milk

1 (14-ounce) can sweetened condensed milk

½ teaspoon crushed saffron

Combine all the ingredients in a bowl and mix well. Pour into molds (should make about 16 small or 8 large servings). Cover and freeze overnight. Serve.

> **Serves 6–8**
> **Prep Time:** 2 minutes, plus overnight to freeze
> **Cook Time:** None

> If you cannot find table cream, use heavy cream. Serve this bathed in Mango Cream (page 243).

Pineapple Cake
(Ananas Ka Cake)

1 (1-pound) pound cake

½ cup pineapple juice (reserved from the drained pineapple)

1 cup whipping cream, whipped

¼ cup canned crushed pineapple, drained and chilled (juice reserved)

Slice the pound cake and set each slice on an individual serving plate. Pour 2 to 3 tablespoons of pineapple juice over each slice. Add a dollop of cream to the slices. Top each with 1 tablespoon of crushed pineapple and serve immediately.

> **Serves 4**
> **Prep Time:** 10 minutes
> **Cook Time:** None

> Although not "traditionally" Indian, this cake is very popular on Indian restaurant menus. This is an instant version of the cake, utilizing store-bought ingredients.

Mango Yogurt Pudding
(Amrakhand)

Serves 4
Prep Time: 5 minutes, plus 30 minutes to chill
Cook Time: None

A variation on Saffron Yogurt Pudding (page 244), this is tradition-ally served with hot Puffed Bread (page 218).

2 cups Hung Yogurt (see recipe on page 16)
½ cup sweetened canned mango pulp

2 tablespoons (or to taste) sugar

Place all the ingredients in a bowl and mix well. You can do this with a spatula or a handheld blender. Adjust sugar to taste. Chill for about 30 minutes, then serve.

❋ Storing Mango Dishes

Always store dishes prepared with mangoes in nonmetallic con-tainers, because mango can discolor metallic containers.

Almond Pudding
(Badam Ki Kheer)

Serves 4
Prep Time: 15 minutes, plus 2 hours to soak
Cook Time: 20 minutes

Serve garnished with silver foil (optional). You can add a few drops of amaretto fla-voring if you like.

2 cups water
¼ cup blanched almonds
¼ cup unsalted cashews

2 cups whole milk
6 tablespoons (or to taste) sugar

1. Bring the water to a boil. Remove from heat.
2. Add the almonds and cashews to the boiled water. Leave immersed in the water for at least 2 hours.
3. Drain the almonds and cashews and transfer to a blender. Add 1 cup of the milk and blend to a coarse paste.
4. In a deep pan, combine the rest of the milk and sugar; mix. Taste and add more sugar if needed. Add the nut paste.
5. Bring to a boil, stirring constantly. Reduce heat to medium and cook for 10 to 20 minutes or until the pudding is very creamy. Allow to cool for about 30 minutes. Serve.

Cream Rose Fudge
(Gulabi Malai Laddoo)

1 cup ricotta cheese, drained of any whey
1 cup Indian Cheese (see recipe on page 14), crumbled
1 (12-ounce) can sweetened condensed milk
2 tablespoons rooh afza or 2 teaspoons rose water
1–2 drops pink food color (optional)

Yields 10–12 pieces
Prep Time: 5 minutes
Cook Time: 15 minutes, plus 30 minutes to cool

Rooh afza is a fragrant syrup available at your Indian grocer. These keep for 3 days refrigerated.

1. In a bowl, combine all the ingredients and mix well by hand or using a hand blender.
2. Heat a medium-sized nonstick pan. Add the mixture and cook on low heat, stirring constantly, for about 15 minutes or until the mixture dries up and begins to pull away from the sides of the pan.
3. Remove from heat and transfer to a platter. Allow it to cool, for 30 minutes.
4. Divide into 12 pieces and roll each piece into a small ball. Serve.

Trifle

1 (4-serving-size) packet straw-berry jello
1 (4-serving-size) packet instant vanilla pudding
1 (1-pound) sponge cake
1 cup orange juice
1 cup mixed unsalted nuts, chopped
Whipped cream, for garnish

Serves 4
Prep Time: Time to prepare pudding and jello, plus 20 minutes to chill
Cook Time: None

This recipe uses instant mixes to save time, and it still makes a delightful dessert.

1. Prepare the jello according to the directions on the packet. Cut into small pieces; set aside.
2. Prepare the pudding according to directions on the packet; set aside.
3. Cut the sponge cake into small pieces of equal size. Place the cake pieces in a deep, decorative glass bowl and layer the jello over it. Then pour the juice over the jello. Finally, layer the pudding over the jello.
4. Chill for about 20 minutes. Sprinkle with the nuts and garnish with whipped cream. Serve.

Sweet Bread
(Meeti Roti)

Serves 4
Prep Time: 15 minutes, plus 30 minutes for the dough to rest
Cook Time: 40 minutes

Serve this unique dessert along with Indian tea. I usually cut this up into strips that are easy to pick up by hand.

2 cups whole-wheat flour (atta), plus extra for dusting
4 tablespoons semolina
4 tablespoons fine sugar or jaggery
1 teaspoon fennel seeds
6 tablespoons melted Clarified Butter (see recipe on page 17)
Water, as needed
Vegetable oil for greasing

1. In a bowl, combine the wheat flour, semolina, sugar, fennel seeds, and 4 tablespoons of the butter. Slowly begin to add the water, kneading as you go. Make a soft dough, kneading for at least 10 minutes. The final dough should be soft and pliable. It should not be sticky; otherwise it will not roll out well.
2. Cover the dough with a damp cloth or plastic wrap and let it sit for 30 minutes.
3. Roll the dough into a log. Cut into 10 equal portions. Lightly dust a clean work surface and a rolling pin with flour.
4. Lightly grease your hands with oil. Take 1 portion of dough and roll it into a ball between the palms of your hands, then flatten the ball. Place it on the prepared surface. Use the rolling pin to roll it out into a circle about 5 to 6 inches in diameter.
5. Lightly brush the circle with the butter and fold in half. Brush again with the butter, and fold in half again to form a triangle.
6. Lightly flour the work surface again, and roll out the triangle of dough until the base of the triangle is about 5 to 6 inches wide.
7. Heat a griddle on medium heat and brush it lightly with butter. Add the triangle of dough to the griddle. Cook for about 2 minutes or until the bottom of the bread begins to blister. Brush the top lightly with butter and flip over. Cook for 2 minutes.
8. Remove the bread from the griddle and place on a serving platter. Cover with a paper towel. Continue until all the *rotis* are rolled out and cooked. Serve hot.

Orange Cream
(Malai Santra)

2 (10-ounce) cans mandarin
  oranges
4 tablespoons heavy cream

Pinch of dried mint
¼ teaspoon Roasted Saffron
  (see recipe on page 18)

Drain the mandarin oranges; reserve the syrup. Layer the oranges on a decorative platter. Mix together the heavy cream, mint, and saffron. Add 1 tablespoon of the reserved syrup and mix well. Pour over the oranges. Chill for about 20 minutes. Serve.

> **Serves 4**
> **Prep Time:** 5 minutes, plus 20 minutes to chill
> **Cook Time:** None

> In India, cooks prepare this with the cream that forms on top of boiling milk. Try this with your favorite fruit.

Watermelon Ice
(Kalinger Ka Gola)

3 cups watermelon chunks,
  seeds removed

4 tablespoons sugar
4 tablespoons heavy cream

Put all the ingredients in a blender and blend until smooth. Transfer to popsicle molds. Add a stick to each mold. Chill overnight before serving.

> **Serves 4**
> **(8 large popsicles)**
> **Prep Time:** 10 minutes, plus overnight to chill
> **Cook Time:** None

> Growing up, I loved golas, or crushed ice popsicles, which you could buy from vendors pushing rattling carts along city roads.

Instant Fruit Cream
(Jaaldi Phal Malai)

Serves 6–8
Prep Time: 10 minutes
Cook Time: None

Try your favorite ice cream and fruits to create this simple dessert. Serve in decorative bowls topped with whipped cream and cherries.

3 cups French vanilla ice cream, softened

2 (15-ounce) cans fruit cocktail, drained

¼ cup slivered almonds

1 drop pink food coloring (optional)

Combine all ingredients in a bowl and serve.

❊ Litchi

You will find canned or fresh litchis at your local Indian grocers. Drain the canned litchis and serve chilled. Fresh litchis are covered by a leathery rind that is pink to strawberry red in color and rough in texture. The edible portion, or aril, is white, translucent, firm, and juicy.

Honey Yogurt
(Shahad Wale Dahi)

Serves 4
Prep Time: 5 minutes, plus 30 minutes to chill
Cook Time: None

This refreshing recipe is best served chilled. You can use plain yogurt for this if you like. I prefer the creamier texture of Hung Yogurt.

3 cups Hung Yogurt (see recipe on page 16)

4 tablespoons honey

¼ teaspoon Roasted Saffron (see recipe on page 18)

2 tablespoons raisins, for garnish

Combine the yogurt, honey, and saffron in a bowl; mix well. Chill, covered, for about 30 minutes. Serve topped with raisins.

Cardamom Cookies
(Eliachi Ke Biscut)

1 cup all-purpose flour
½ cup sugar
½ teaspoon cardamom powder
4 tablespoons chilled Clarified
   Butter (see recipe on
   page 17)

1 large egg
1 tablespoon milk

Yields 24 (2-in.) cookies
Prep Time: 20 minutes,
plus 2 hours to chill and
20 minutes to stand
Cook Time: 10 minutes

Tea time is very pop-
ular in India. Biscuts,
or biscuits, are served
along with a steaming
hot cup of Grandma's
Chai (page 48).

1. In a large bowl, sift together the flour, sugar, and cardamom; mix well.
2. Cut in the butter until the mixture resembles coarse crumbs.
3. In a small bowl, whisk together the egg and the milk; add to the flour mixture. Stir until a soft dough forms. (The dough will be crumbly.) Pat it together into a ball and flatten slightly. Wrap in plastic and chill for at least 2 hours.
4. Take the dough from the refrigerator and let it sit for about 20 minutes or until it is just workable.
5. Preheat oven to 375°.
6. Roll out the dough between 2 sheets of wax paper or plastic wrap to about ¼-inch thickness. Cut into desired shapes with a knife or a cookie cutter.
7. Bake on an ungreased cookie sheet for 5 to 8 minutes or until the edges turn golden brown. Remove to a cooling rack. Store in an air-tight container until ready to serve.

※ Pineapple Sauce

Here is another wonderful sauce for topping ice cream, fruits, or yogurt: In a blender, purée 1 cup of pineapple chunks, 1 tablespoon of fresh grated ginger, 2 tablespoons honey, and a few mint leaves. Chill and serve.

CHAPTER 15
A Royal Feast (Raj Khana)

Chicken Kebabs
(Sindhi Murgh Kebabs)

Serves 4
Prep Time: 10 minutes
Cook Time: 15 minutes

These hasty, tasty kebabs require no oven or grill or special utensils. The soya and brandy in the sauce give it an oriental flavor.

¾ cup water

1 tablespoon soya sauce

1 teaspoon red chili powder, divided

2 tablespoons brandy

1 pound ground chicken

1 large red onion, peeled and finely chopped

3 serrano green chilies, seeded and finely chopped

1-inch piece fresh gingerroot, peeled and grated

2 garlic cloves, minced

Table salt, to taste

2 teaspoons coriander powder

1 tablespoon minced cilantro

1 teaspoon Warm Spice Mix (see recipe on page 14)

2 tablespoons vegetable oil

1. In a bowl, combine ¼ cup of the water, the soya sauce, ½ teaspoon of the red chili powder, and the brandy. Set the sauce aside.
2. In another bowl, combine the chicken, onion, green chilies, ginger, garlic, salt, coriander, cilantro, Warm Spice Mix, and remaining red chili powder; mix well. Divide into 8 equal portions and roll into small round balls.
3. In a deep pan, bring the remaining water to a boil. Add the kebabs to the water. Reduce the heat and cook for about 3 to 4 minutes on each side. The kebabs will begin to darken as they absorb the water. Remove the kebabs from the water and place on a paper towel.
4. Heat a medium-sized nonstick skillet. Add the oil to it. Add the kebabs and sauté until golden brown.
5. Add the sauce. Mix well and cook for another minute. Serve with Mint Chuntey (page 237).

❋ Ceremonial Food

Kheer, or pudding, is served in India during many religious ceremonies as an offering to the gods. During the research for this book, I also discovered that rice kheer in particular is served in some parts of western India at funerals.

Lemon Chicken
(Nimbu Wali Murgh)

2 tablespoons butter
1 tablespoon oil
4 skinless bone-in chicken
   thighs
Juice of 2 lemons

¼ cup water
2–3 teaspoons Warm Spice Mix
   (see recipe on page 14)
Table salt, to taste

Serves 4 **Prep Time:** 10 minutes **Cook Time:** 35 minutes
You can use your choice of chicken cuts—adjust the cooking time accordingly. Serve warm, garnished with minced cilantro and thinly sliced lemons.

1. In a large nonstick skillet, heat the butter and oil. Add the chicken and cook for 3 to 4 minutes per side or until each side is well browned.
2. Add the lemon juice and water. Reduce heat to medium, cover, and cook until the chicken is done, about 7 minutes (depending on the thickness of the cut).
3. Remove the cover and increase the heat to high. Add the spice mix and salt. (If you like your dish milder, add only 2 teaspoons of garam masala.) Mix well. Cook until all the water has dried off. Serve hot.

✳ Salting Chicken

Don't salt chicken before you cook it. The salt forces the juices out and impedes browning. Instead, salt the chicken toward the end of the cooking process.

Royal Rice
(Shahi Chawal)

Serves 4
Prep Time: 10 minutes, plus 3 hours to soak
Cook Time: 20 minutes

This spectacular dish can be served garnished with raisins.

¼ cup dried dates, pitted and chopped
¼ cup dried apricots, pitted and chopped
1 cup whole milk
1 cup cream
3 tablespoons vegetable oil
4 tablespoons cashews
4 tablespoons slivered almonds
2 green cardamom pods, bruised
1 bay leaf
1 black cardamom pod
2 cups basmati rice, rinsed
Table salt, to taste
2 cups water

1. Place the dates and apricots in a bowl. Add the cream and milk, and let soak for 3 hours.
2. In a deep pan, heat the vegetable oil. Add the cashews and sauté for 20 seconds. Add the almonds and green cardamom; sauté for another 20 seconds.
3. Add the bay leaf, black cardamom, and rice; sauté for 1 minute.
4. Add the salt, water, and the apricot-date mixture. Bring to a boil.
5. Reduce heat. Cover and cook until the rice is done, about 15 minutes. Serve hot.

✳ Frying Nuts

When frying almonds, cashews, or other nuts at the same time, first fry the cashews, then the almonds, as the almonds will discolor the oil.

Minty Potato Salad
(Pudine Wale Aloo)

*4 medium potatoes, peeled
  and cubed
Juice of 1 lemon
1 cup fresh mint
¼ cup fresh cilantro
2 fresh garlic cloves, crushed
Table salt, to taste
1 tablespoon vegetable oil*

*Water, as needed
½ cup canned chickpeas
  (garbanzo beans)
1 small red onion, peeled and
  chopped
1 small cucumber, peeled and
  chopped*

Serves 4
Prep Time: 10 minutes
Cook Time: 15 minutes,
plus time to chill

This chilled dish can
be served as a salad
or a hearty appetizer.
Serve garnished with
diced cherry toma-
toes and slit green
chilies.

1. Boil the potatoes, in enough water to cover, for 7 to 8 minutes or until tender. Drain and set aside.
2. In a blender or food processor, blend together the lemon juice, mint, cilantro, garlic, salt, and vegetable oil. Add a few tablespoons of water to aid in blending. The final consistency should be that of a salad dressing. Set aside.
3. In a bowl, combine the potatoes, garbanzo beans, red onion, and cucumber. Pour the dressing over the potato mixture. Chill and serve.

☀ Oil-Free Green Chili Pickle

Here is a simple recipe to create a healthy green chili pickle: Mince green chilies; add salt, red chili powder, a pinch of turmeric, and lemon juice (enough to cover the chilies). Let it sit for about 2 hours. Your tangy pickle is ready to eat.

Rose Lemonade
(Gulabi Nimbu Pani)

Serves 4
Prep Time: 5 minutes
Cook Time: None

This lemonade is perfect to serve on hot summer nights. Serve this chilled, garnished with pink rose petals.

4 cups cold water
Juice of 2 large lemons

4 tablespoons sugar
1 teaspoon rose water

In a blender, blend all the ingredients until the sugar is dissolved. Serve over crushed ice.

Mango Ice Cream
(Aam Ki Kulfi)

Yields about 16 pieces
Prep Time:
Overnight to freeze
Cook Time: None

Topped with fresh mango chunks and mint sprigs, this dessert is a gourmet's delight.

2 (8-ounce) cans table cream or half-and-half
1 (12-ounce) can evaporated milk

1 (14-ounce) can sweetened condensed milk
1 cup canned mango pulp

Combine all the ingredients in a bowl and mix well. Pour into your choice of ice cream molds (should make about 16). Cover and freeze overnight. Serve.

Introduction to the Spice of Mexico

▶ Mexican cooking is known for its combinations. It's a rare dish that uses just one or two ingredients. Meats, for example, are marinated then drenched in sauces containing dozens of ingredients. Fish may be broiled or baked but it is always topped with a unique sauce. Even something as simple as a salad of melon balls will have a tart sauce draped over it.

And, to the dismay of many a traveler, the ingredients often don't seem to make sense to anyone but a Mexican. A favorite candy, for example, combines sweetened milk, cocoa, pistachio nuts, and chili powder. Fruits will be marinated in vinegar and chili peppers. Beef steaks will be cooked with sweet fruits and even drinks will contain cornmeal, peanuts, and chopped vegetables. Poultry will be marinated in a cocoa sauce.

So get your taste buds ready, and have a great time in the kitchen cooking these fabulous Mexican recipes for your own family.

Chapter 16

Getting Started

Spicy, messy, and mushy. If those are the three words that come to mind when you think of Mexican cooking, you're likely not alone. For many people living north of Mexico, Mexican food has gotten a tainted reputation. We think that it has to be hot, that it must have tons of chili peppers in it, and that everything has to be slopped onto one plate so that the beans, red rice, and tortillas all mush together.

Myths and Misconceptions

Unfortunately, overeager restaurateurs striving to bring some small bit of Mexican cuisine into our lives perpetuate some common misconceptions about Mexican food. In their efforts to create meals that appeal to a palate not accustomed to spicy foods, they have eliminated the subtle blending of flavors and the wonderful textures in Mexican meals. They quickly reproduce cuisine that takes hours if not days of "management" to reach its true potential. And they don't even bother to give us some of the most unusual taste treats the country has to offer.

Blend, Blend, Blend

Mexican cuisine has actually changed very little over the several thousand years that the country has been settled. Europeans brought new varieties of meats, vegetables, and cheeses, but the basic tenets of Mexican cooking are the same today as in the days of sun goddesses and tall pyramids.

Mexicans blend everything. There is absolutely no mixture of foods and spices they won't try. While Europeans and people in the United States tend to remain firm in their beliefs about what foods go together, Mexicans like to throw those ideas back at us. Separate flavors are good, but when they are combined, they create something so unusual, so mouthwateringly wonderful, that you just have to try adding another combination of ingredients. Marinate the steak in garlic and olive oil? Sure, but can't we add just a little oregano, a few peppers, and some green tomatoes?

At first, the tastes might seem odd, but you will quickly get used to the idea of appreciating the melded flavor as something new in and of itself. Don't ask, "What's in this sauce," but instead appreciate it for the complete flavor that it offers.

Don't worry that you find mussels and lobster tidbits alongside pork hocks and chicken cubes. It's Mexican. Don't fret when you find chocolate in your meat sauce or wine in your eggs. It's Mexican. And don't cringe when you see specks of chili powder in your candy or peanuts and beets floating in your water. The blend of flavors is tantalizingly, uniquely Mexican.

Never fill a blender more than halfway and never seal the cover completely. Cover the top with a towel to prevent spills while blending. A combination of half liquids and half solids is the best mix. Begin blending by pulsing a few times to make sure the blades are clear. If something gets stuck in the blades, use a wooden spoon to loosen it. Never put your hand inside the blender.

As a result, you will quickly find that Mexican cooking uses just a few basic main ingredients—meat, beans, tortillas, and vegetables—but combines them in a multitude of different ways:

- **Soups:** These may be blended together or they can be European style with larger chunks of meat.
- **Dry Soups:** These are more like casseroles. They start with a soup consistency but use tortillas or white bread to soak up the ingredients.
- **Stews:** These are exactly like their European counterparts, mixing large chunks of meats, fruits, and vegetables.
- **Moles:** These slightly chunky, heavy gravies can be eaten as is or they can be used as stuffing for tamales. They can also be used as toppings for whole pieces of meat such as chicken breasts.
- **Salsas:** Salsa literally means "sauce" and can be used to describe anything from a watery salad dressing to a thick mixture of tomatoes, onions, and spices.

Common Spanish Cooking Terms

You'll find many terms in this cookbook, some that you've heard before, and probably some that you haven't. Here's a list of definitions to keep in mind as you cook:

- **Verde:** green, usually meaning the recipe uses green tomatoes or tomatillos
- **Picadillo:** shredded meat, vegetable, and/or fruit filling
- **Salsa:** sauce

- **Relleno:** stuffed
- **Arroz:** rice
- **Pollo:** chicken
- **Nopale:** cactus paddle
- **Carne:** meat, usually beef
- **Raja:** roasted chili strip
- **Lomo:** pork

You can also refer to the glossary (see Appendix D) for more listings.

Tortillas

Of course, the more you blend your ingredients, the more you need something to put them in. Enter the tortilla. Be it rolled, folded, fried, baked, or soaked, it's still a tortilla.

History of the Tortilla

The corn tortilla is distinctly associated with Mexico. The ancient people of Mexico made tortillas by letting the corn kernels dry on the ears in the fields. The kernels were soaked in lime water until the skins could be rubbed off. The wet corn then was ground on a flat stone until it was a fine powder that could be used to make dough. The dough was made into thin patties, then baked over open fires.

Today, true Mexican food aficionados will still make their tortillas this way. However, the Mexican homemaker is more likely to buy masa harina, dehydrated masa flour. Although some people substitute cornmeal, masa harina is actually made from white corn, as opposed to the yellow corn more popular in the northern climates.

Healthy Tortillas

Health-conscious people also have altered the traditional Mexican tortilla. Today, it is just as common to use baked tortillas made from wheat flour as it is to use corn tortillas. Some people will also add ingredients such as tomatoes, spinach, or spices to the masa flour to create a more flavorful tortilla.

As with any culture's cuisine, Mexican food is always changing. Most Mexican cooks now use flour tortillas for some dishes and many are experimenting by adding spices or other flavors. Relax. If you like sun-dried tomato tortillas, it's OK. You will still be eating authentic Mexican cuisine. You won't be eating it in the style of ancient civilizations, but you will be eating it as the people of Mexico eat it today.

Chili Peppers

After the tortilla, probably the one food most often associated with Mexican cooking is the hot chili pepper. Unfortunately, most people assume this means that the dish must be hot, when the opposite is often true. The chili peppers are added for flavor and sometimes for spice, but even a large dish will often contain only a couple chili peppers, along with a similar amount of onion.

Capsaicin, the chemical combination that gives chili peppers their "heat" is the ingredient in many commercial cold medicines that is used to make people cough so that they don't stay congested. Peppers also contain vitamins C, A, and E, while being good sources of potassium and folic acid. Some people eat hot peppers to clear their sinuses when they have a cold.

In ancient times, the chilies were added partly to help preserve food but also to add unique tastes to the ubiquitous turkey meat they ate. As a result, one common cooking technique is to change the type of chili peppers added to a sauce. By doing this, you can create a completely different dish.

And it's not hard to do. There are nearly seventy varieties of chilies, ranging in size from large peas to nearly a foot long. They come in every color from red, purple, and green to yellow. As a general rule, color has no effect on flavor, but size does: the smaller the chili, the hotter it tends to be.

If you don't like the spice chili peppers add to your foods, don't leave them out completely. Just add less. Or, instead of chopping the pepper into small pieces, add it whole and remove it before serving the meal. That will provide some of the flavor without adding any unwelcome bits to the dish.

Seven Chilies You Need to Know

1. **Jalapeños:** These chilies are almost universal. Either red or green, they reach about three inches and have a medium heat.
2. **Poblanos:** These are dark green, medium-sized peppers that are often used for roasting or stuffing. They are relatively hot.
3. **Chilies de arbol:** These dried red chilies are long and thin with a papery skin. They are very hot.
4. **Chipotles:** These are dried or smoked red jalapeños. They are usually dark reddish brown and add a smoky flavor to dishes. They are relatively mild.
5. **Moritas:** These are dried, smoked jalapeños. They are small and brown with a spicy taste. They are not as smoky as chipotles but are hotter.
6. **Habaneros:** This is the hottest of the chilies. They are lantern-shaped and can be orange, red, or green.
7. **Serranos:** These are small, thin chilies that taste similar to jalapeños but are a little hotter. The red ones are a little sweeter than the green.

Spices

Mexican cooking uses a number of spices that are unique to the cuisine. However, it's more common to see a combination of more common spices working together with chili peppers to create the unique Mexican flavor. There is very little that you can't find in a well-stocked grocery store. And, if you really want to try a dish that calls for something unique, it's likely you can find it at a specialty store such as a food co-op.

Mexicans take their flavorings seriously. Many recipes call for you to roast the spices first. Some will have you using only fresh spices because the dried variety will either lose their flavor or create a totally different flavor. Some recipes will call for specific types of a spice, such as Mexican oregano or Mexican cinnamon. The tastes differences in most cases are minor from the American versions, but they are noticeable. However, if you can't find the Mexican variety, don't worry. The food will still taste great.

Following are spices you should know how to obtain before you start any Mexican recipe:

- **Cinnamon:** Look for the rough-edged variety from Sri Lanka as opposed to the tightly wound variety used in the United States.
- **Cilantro:** Also known as *coriander*, it has a unique, strong flavor. Fresh is always better tasting but dried can be substituted.
- **Oregano:** More than a dozen different varieties grow in Mexico and it's the most common spice in the Mexican kitchen. You will need both fresh and dried, as they are used in different ways.
- **Cumin:** This lends a distinctly Mexican flavor to many dishes. Buy the seeds whole and grind them as needed. Some people add whole seeds to a dish to get a burst of flavor when they're bitten into.
- **Epazote:** This herb's strong, bitter flavor can dominate any dish, and for this reason, it is the one herb most often used alone in Mexican cooking. It actually is treated as a weed in North America but can be hard to find in a grocery store. Use fresh whenever possible because dried loses much of the flavor.
- **Anise:** This is used in many dishes. The leaves are used to wrap food in, but dried, ground anise can flavor anything from candy to stews.
- **Cocoa:** This is not sweetened. The sweetened variety is never used, not even semisweet chocolate. Traditionally, Mexicans used ground cocoa beans.
- **Cloves:** These are often used as part of a spice mixture for moles and sauces.
- **Nutmeg:** This also is used as part of a spice mixture.
- **Corn husks:** Dried corn husks are most often used to make tamales. They are first soaked in water. They are actually considered a spice

because the flavor is transferred to the corn flour when steamed.

- **Annatto seeds:** Also called *achiote,* these are the seeds from a tropical tree. They have a musky, earthy flavor. It is used as a commercial dye to add orange tints to cheeses and other foodstuffs.
- **Tamarind:** This is a tough brown seedpod that produces a sticky paste. It is the main ingredient in Worcestershire sauce.
- **Chili powder:** There are as many different types of chili powder as there are chilies. Most are simply dried, ground versions of chili peppers although some contain mixtures of different chili peppers It's best to experiment to find your favorite. Note that chili powder is usually added for its flavor, not to make the dish hotter tasting.

Nuts

Nuts are used as both a spice and a thickening agent in many Mexican dishes. Among the most common you will find in Mexican recipes are:

- **Pepitas:** a pumpkin seed.
- **Pistachios:** a wrinkly green nut (Do not use the white or red dyed types.)
- **Cashews:** use unsalted, fresh-roasted when possible
- **Peanuts:** skinless, unsalted are the best, if available

Beans

In ancient times, when the only source of meat protein came from turkeys, Mexicans turned to beans for both variety and to provide other proteins. As a result, the bean was a staple of the Mexican diet long before the Spanish arrived. And they continue to be popular today.

Most of us associate either black beans or the pinkish pinto beans with Mexican cooking. However, there are more than twenty different varieties of beans that are commonly used in Mexican dishes. A Mexican kitchen has as many different types of beans as the Italian kitchen has pasta shapes.

There is no one right bean for any recipe. In the countryside, the Mexican cook will have her own garden and plant the varieties her family likes. In the city, people will buy what they like or what the grocery store has in stock that day.

However, the various beans do taste different, so it's worth experimenting. The milk lima bean, for example, will give a totally different flavor to a refried bean dish than the heartier black bean. In the end, though, if you like it, that's all that counts.

No one really knows why the Mexicans started creating refried beans. Perhaps it was a way to make a quick dish out of their staple food. They could prepare the beans days and even weeks beforehand, then just recook them as needed.

Chances are you will want to make your refried beans fresh. Resist the urge to serve them right out of the pot though. Letting them sit in the refrigerator for a day or two before mashing them with spices and reheating them lets the true flavor of the beans emerge.

Cheese

Cheese didn't exist in Mexico until the Spanish conquistadors brought milk animals to the land. In nearly 500 years, though, Mexican cooks have embraced both the flavor and nutrition in cheese by adding it to many of their dishes. They also have developed some of their own unique cheeses that have yet to be exported from the country in large amounts.

However, most Mexican cheeses have either a similar European counterpart or they don't play a crucial role in the dish. As a result, many Mexican cooks will substitute a common European cheese from time to time. Also remember that Mexican cooking is known for being able to adapt to the ingredients available. If you can't find an authentic cheese, don't be concerned. A transplanted Mexican would just use what was available!

Cheese Substitutes

Following are some of the common cheeses in Mexican recipes along with their European substitutes. Note that in this book we did the work for you and just list the substitute in the ingredients.

- **Queso añejo:** This means "aged cheese." Parmesan and Romano are good substitutes.
- **Queso panela:** This is a semisoft cheese that looks like mozzarella but does not melt well. Cottage cheese and ricotta are good substitutes.
- **Queso fresco:** This means "fresh cheese." Fresh ricotta or a mild fresh goat cheese is a good substitute. Cottage cheese also works well.
- **Queso manchego:** This is a semisoft cheese that melts easily. Monterey jack is usually substituted for it.
- **Queso Chihuahua and queso menonita:** These are hard, aged cheeses that have a mild flavor. Mild or medium-sharp Cheddar is a good substitute. Colby also works well.
- **Queso de bola, quesillo de Oaxaca, and asadero:** These are made by cooking the curds and pulling them into long strings. Although they have a unique flavor, mozzarella is a good substitute.

Meats

Poultry, red meat, fish, and seafood are important ingredients in Mexican cooking, but they more often are on the receiving end of the spicy sauces. As a result, they don't get a great deal of attention in most Mexican recipes. In fact, a typical recipe will call for "carne," or simply beef. Even when making seafood meals, the authentic recipes usually don't specify what main ingredient to use.

As in most poor cultures, when red meat is used, the entire animal is used. As a result, tripe (intestines), heads, tongues, and hocks (feet) are common ingredients in many Mexican meat dishes. If you've never tried any of these food items, it's worth the venture. The unique textures and interesting flavors can be delightful and they are rarely as unusual as you might expect.

Still, there are things to keep in mind. Mexico is a large exporter of beef, so it is readily available in Mexico. However, many people don't have refrigerators and beef is still relatively expensive. As a result, it is often reserved for special meals. Pork is more common than beef in daily meals but lamb is actually the most common red meat. Poultry is still the protein of choice for most Mexicans.

For people who live on the coasts, seafood is a common meal. Interestingly, it has as many variations as the red and white meats in terms of sauces and mixtures, but fish is actually grilled more often than meat. It's common to serve a grilled lobster tail with absolutely no sauce, while beef or pork is never served "naked."

It's important to know your fish when using it in cooked meals, especially the moles or picadillos. You need a fish that will keep its consistency, not turn rubber, or, worse yet, disintegrate into the mix. Most recipes do well with bass or flounder. If you have a wide variety of fish available in your area, it's best to ask the fish seller how the fish holds up to long cooking before you try it.

Vegetables and Fruits

With a subtropical climate, there are no shortages of fresh vegetables and fruits in the Mexican diet. Perhaps the only truly unique item in this arena is cactus. Mexicans put *napoles,* or cactus paddles, in a number of different recipes, treating it almost as those in the United States treat string beans or broccoli. Napoles aren't difficult to cook, but, unless you live in the southwest, it can be very difficult to find fresh ones.

While many people will substitute green or unripe tomatoes in recipes that call for tomatillos, the two are not the same. Tomatillos are actually a member of the gooseberry family. However, green tomatoes give a very similar flavor when substituted in cooked dishes.

Today, it's very easy to find fresh tropical fruits in even the northern-most grocery stores. It can take a little bit of time to learn how to peel or deseed these fruits, but it can be well worth the effort to gain a taste of the real thing. Canned fruits virtually never taste the same as the fresh variety.

Putting It All Together

Mexicans like to eat. In fact, they eat more meals than most of the rest of the world. If you're putting together a true Mexican feast, it might be fun to devote an entire day to the Mexican style of eating. Here's what you would do:

- **Desayuno** is served early in the morning and usually consists of coffee with milk and tortillas.
- **Almuerzo** is served in midmorning and includes eggs, beans, tortillas, chili sauce, and coffee.
- **Comida** is served in midafternoon during the siesta period, when the sun is at its peak. Many businesses close so people can go home for this meal. It begins with appetizers and is followed by soup. The next course is a dry soup followed by fish or meat with a salad and vegetables. The dessert is a sweet or fruit.
- **Merienda** is served in the early evening. It is usually a cup of hot chocolate or coffee with tortillas.
- **Cena**, or supper, is served any time after 8 P.M. If *comida* was a large meal, this will be a light meal. However, if it is a fiesta, the meal will start as late as midnight and rarely before 10 P.M. In this case it might be served more as a buffet or, in the case of a formal gathering, it will have even more courses than the *comida*.

Now that you've learned the background information, let's get started!

CHAPTER 17
THE BASICS

TOMATO SALSA

4 medium tomatoes
1 medium-sized yellow onion
1 (4-ounce) can green chilies
   or 2 fresh green chilies

$\frac{1}{4}$ cup fresh cilantro
$\frac{1}{2}$ cup canned or frozen corn
1 small green or red bell
   pepper

1. Dice the tomatoes into $\frac{1}{4}$-inch pieces.
2. Remove the skin from the onion and cut into $\frac{1}{4}$-inch pieces.
3. If using fresh chilies, remove the stem and seeds and cut into $\frac{1}{4}$-inch pieces.
4. Chop the cilantro into $\frac{1}{4}$-inch pieces.
5. Remove the stem and seeds from the bell pepper and chop the pepper into $\frac{1}{4}$-inch pieces.
6. Combine all the ingredients and let sit overnight in a covered container in the refrigerator.

GREEN TOMATO SALSA

1 large white onion
2 fresh habanero peppers
   ($\frac{1}{4}$ cup canned or 2 fresh
   jalapeños may be substituted)

8 medium-sized green tomatoes
1 bunch fresh cilantro
2 teaspoons salt
1 teaspoon ground black pepper

1. Remove the skin from the onion and chop into $\frac{1}{4}$-inch pieces.
2. Remove the stems from the peppers and chop into $\frac{1}{4}$-inch pieces.
3. Remove the stems from the green tomatoes and place the tomatoes in a food processor or blender; blend on medium setting for 30 seconds.
4. Roughly chop the cilantro so the pieces are about $\frac{1}{2}$-inch long.
5. Combine all the ingredients; mix well.
6. Refrigerate for at least 12 hours before using.

CHILI CON QUESO

1 medium-sized yellow onion
2 garlic cloves
5 fresh chipotle chili peppers
2 fresh jalapeño peppers
2 medium tomatoes

½ pound Monterey jack cheese
½ pound Colby cheese
2 tablespoons vegetable oil
1 cup sour cream

1. Remove the skin from onion and garlic; chop into ¼-inch pieces.
2. Remove the stems and seeds from the peppers; chop into ¼-inch pieces.
3. Chop the tomatoes into ¼-inch pieces. Grate the cheeses.
4. Heat the oil at medium temperature in a large skillet. Sauté the onions and garlic until tender but not brown. Add the peppers and tomatoes; cook for 3 minutes, stirring constantly.
5. Turn the heat to medium-low. Add the cheeses to the pan and cook, stirring constantly, until the cheese melts. Stir in the sour cream.

> **Serves 16**
>
> This is the perfect dip for tortilla chips. It also makes an excellent sauce to pour over enchiladas.

BASIC CORN TORTILLAS

2 cups cornmeal or masa harina
1½ cups warm water
1 teaspoon salt

1. Mix the ingredients to form a soft dough. The dough should not stick to your hands. If it is sticky, add cornmeal 1 teaspoon at a time until it doesn't stick any longer.
2. Divide the dough and roll it into balls about the size of golf balls.
3. Flatten the balls between 2 sheets of wax paper. If they stick, scrape them off, add more cornmeal, and start over. Flatten to about ¼-inch thick.
4. Place each tortilla separately in an ungreased frying pan and cook over medium heat until slightly brown, usually 1 to 2 minutes. Flip and cook on the other side until slightly brown.

> **Makes 8–20 depending on size**
>
> As the basic ingredient in Mexican cooking, you may want to make large batches of these ahead of time and freeze them.

FLOUR TORTILLAS

2 cups flour
1 teaspoon salt
1 teaspoon baking soda

1 tablespoon lard or margarine
½ cup cold water

1. Preheat oven to 350°.
2. Mix together all the ingredients well. If the dough sticks to your hands, add more flour, 1 teaspoon at a time, until it doesn't stick.
3. Divide the dough and roll into balls about the size of golf balls.
4. Flatten the balls between 2 sheets of wax paper. If they stick, scrape them off, add more flour, and start over. Flatten to about ¼-inch thick.
5. Place the tortillas on an ungreased baking sheet and bake in the oven for about 2 minutes. Flip and bake for 2 more minutes, or until lightly browned.

REFRIED BEANS

2 cups dried pinto beans
8 cups water, divided
1 large white onion

½ cup lard
2 teaspoons salt
1 teaspoon ground black pepper

1. Soak the beans overnight in 4 cups water.
2. Drain off the water and rinse the beans. Bring 4 cups water to boil in a medium saucepan. Add the beans and cover; boil for 5 minutes. Lower heat to medium and simmer for 2 hours.
3. Remove the skin from the onion and chop into ¼-inch pieces.
4. Melt the lard in a large frying pan over medium heat. Add the onion, salt, and pepper; sauté on medium heat for about 10 minutes or until the onion is tender.
5. Mash the beans with a potato masher. Add the mashed beans to the lard and onion; stir lightly to combine.
6. Cook on medium heat until the liquid evaporates.

TOSTADAS

½ cup vegetable oil
1 recipe Corn Tortillas (see
    recipe on page 283)

½ teaspoon salt

1 recipe Corn Tortillas (see recipe on page 283)

1. Spread the oil evenly over the bottom of a large frying pan. Preheat to medium-high temperature.
2. Place the tortillas in hot oil, 1 at a time, and fry until crisp. Flip the tortillas when 1 side is brown to ensure even cooking.
3. Sprinkle with salt while cooking.
4. Place on paper towels to drain.

> **Makes 8–20 depending on tortilla size**
>
> For taco chips, simply break the tostadas into chip-sized pieces. For a unique taste, sprinkle with dry ranch dressing mix.

BASIC PICANTE SAUCE

1 large white onion
1 fresh jalapeño pepper or ¼
    cup canned jalapeños
6 medium-sized ripe tomatoes
6 tablespoons vegetable oil

1 teaspoon salt
¼ teaspoon granulated sugar
1 tablespoon fresh, crushed
    cilantro or 1 teaspoon dried
    cilantro

1. Remove the skin from the onion and chop into ¼-inch pieces.
2. Remove the stems from the jalapeño (if using fresh) and tomatoes and chop into ¼-inch pieces.
3. Preheat the oil to medium temperature in a large frying pan. Add the onions and sauté for about 10 minutes or until tender but not brown.
4. Add the remaining ingredients. Turn heat to medium-low and simmer for about 10 minutes.

> **Yields about 3 cups**
>
> For a less spicy sauce, keep the jalapeño whole and remove it after simmering the mixture.

RED RICE

Serves 8

Add some spice to this recipe by including ¼ cup of your favorite hot peppers chopped into small pieces.

3 cups water
1 cup short-grain white rice
2 medium-sized red tomatoes
1 bunch fresh green onions or scallions

1 tablespoon vegetable oil
1 teaspoon salt
1 teaspoon ground black pepper

1. Bring the water to a boil in a medium saucepan. Add the rice, cover, and boil for 5 minutes. Reduce heat to medium-low and simmer for 15 minutes or until the rice is tender. Drain off remaining water from the rice.
2. Remove and discard the stems from the tomatoes. Place the tomatoes in a food processor and blend on medium setting for about 30 seconds.
3. Remove the skins from the onions and chop into ¼-inch pieces.
4. Heat the oil to medium-high in a large frying pan. Add all the ingredients; stir well. Cover and simmer for 10 minutes.

CHICKEN STOCK

Yields 3 quarts

Add almost any mix of meats and vegetables to this basic broth to make a healthy, hearty soup. You also can substitute turkey for the chicken.

1 medium-sized yellow onion
2 celery ribs
2 large carrots
2–3 pounds chicken bones (leftovers are great)

2 teaspoons salt
1 teaspoon ground black pepper
1 tablespoon dried parsley
1 gallon water

1. Remove the skin from the onion and chop into 1-inch pieces. Clean the carrots and chop into ½-inch rounds. Chop the celery into 1-inch pieces.
2. Add all the ingredients to a large stockpot; bring to a boil. Reduce heat, cover, and let simmer for 3 hours.
3. Strain the broth and discard the vegetables.

GUACAMOLE

2 large, ripe avocados
1 medium-sized red tomato
1 small yellow onion
½ cup canned jalapeño peppers

1 tablespoon lime juice
1 teaspoon salt
½ teaspoon ground black
  pepper

1. Cut the avocados in half lengthwise and pry out the pits. Remove the peels and cut the avocados into 1-inch pieces. Mash with a fork.
2. Cut the tomato into ½-inch pieces. Remove the skin from the onion and cut into ¼-inch pieces. Drain off the liquid from the jalapeño peppers and cut the peppers into ¼-inch pieces.
3. Combine all the ingredients; mix well.

Serves 8

This is a wonderful topping for potatoes and meat dishes as well as a popular dip for tostadas and raw vegetables.

SHREDDED BEEF

2 garlic cloves
4 medium tomatoes
3 fresh jalapeño chili peppers
1 bunch fresh cilantro
1 bay leaf

4 pounds top sirloin
2 teaspoons salt
2 teaspoons ground black pepper
1 (8-ounce) bottle Italian salad
  dressing

1. Peel and mince the garlic. Cut the tomatoes into 1-inch pieces, reserving the juice. Remove the stems and seeds from the chili peppers. Remove the stems from the cilantro.
2. Place all the ingredients in a heavy pot. Cover and cook over medium heat for about 5 hours.
3. Remove the meat from the broth, let cool, and cut into 2-inch cubes. Shred with forks or in a food processor. Discard broth.

Yields 4–5 pounds

Shredded beef can be used in enchiladas, tacos, and many other dishes that call for either beef chunks or ground beef.

GREEN CHILI SAUCE

Yields 2 cups

Use as a green sauce for tacos, enchiladas, or any other dish.

1 cup fresh green chilies (the type of your choice), roasted
1 cup canned tomatillos with juice
1/4 cup fresh parsley
1/4 cup onion
1 garlic clove
1/4 cup canned jalapeño peppers, drained
1 teaspoon salt
1/2 teaspoon ground black pepper
1/4 cup olive oil

1. Remove the skin, stems, and seeds from the green chilies.
2. Combine the chilies, tomatillos with their juice, parsley, onion, garlic, jalapeños, salt, and pepper in a blender or food processor; purée.
3. Heat the oil in a medium-sized frying pan over medium heat. Add the sauce and cook for about 5 minutes, stirring constantly.

RED CHILI SAUCE

Yields 2½ cups

This is the classic enchilada or burrito sauce. It can also be made with other chilies.

12 dried red ancho chilies
1 small white onion
3 garlic cloves
3 large red tomatoes
4 cups water
1/4 teaspoon salt
1 teaspoon granulated sugar

1. Preheat oven to 250°. Toast chilies on a baking sheet in the oven for 8 minutes. Transfer the chilies to a bowl filled with cold water. Remove the stems and seeds.
2. Peel the onion and chop into 1/4-inch pieces. Peel the garlic cloves. Chop the tomatoes into 1/4-inch pieces.
3. Combine all the ingredients in a medium pot. Cover and simmer on medium heat for 30 minutes. Every 5 minutes, remove the cover and push the chilies back down into the liquid.
4. Add mixture to blender; purée. Strain to remove the skins.
5. Heat the sauce on medium in a frying pan. Then simmer for 5 minutes.

SPICY CHICKEN

2 garlic cloves
4 medium tomatoes
3 fresh jalapeño chili peppers
1 bunch fresh cilantro
1 bay leaf
2 teaspoons salt

2 teaspoons ground black
  pepper
1 (8-ounce) bottle Italian salad
  dressing
1 fryer chicken (about 2½
  pounds)

Yields 4 to 5 pounds

Spicy Chicken can be used in enchiladas, tacos, and many other dishes that call for either beef chunks or ground beef.

1. Peel and mince the garlic. Cut the tomatoes into 1-inch pieces, reserving the juice. Remove the stems and seeds from the chili peppers. Remove the stems from the cilantro.
2. Combine all the ingredients in a heavy pot. Cover and cook over medium heat for about 5 hours.
3. Remove the meat from the broth and let cool. Remove and discard the skin and bones, and shred the meat with forks or in a food processor. Discard the broth.

Where There Are Chickens . . .

Chickens are perhaps the most plentiful food animal in Mexico. They are easy to raise and can feed off bits of discarded grain. They also provide eggs. When they stop laying eggs they invariably become chicken stock, a standard ingredient in many Mexican recipes.

CITRUS SALSA

2 large ripe tomatoes
1 medium-sized white onion
3 garlic cloves
1 fresh or canned jalapeño pepper
1/4 teaspoon fresh cilantro or 1/8 teaspoon dried cilantro
1/4 cup lime juice

1 teaspoon lemon juice
1 tablespoon dry cooking white wine
1 teaspoon chili powder
1/2 teaspoon ground black pepper

1. Cut the tomatoes into 1/4-inch pieces. Remove the skins from the onion and garlic, and mince. Remove the stem and seeds from the pepper and cut into 1/4-inch pieces. Chop the cilantro into 1/8-inch pieces.
2. Combine all the ingredients in a medium-sized mixing bowl; stir until well mixed.
3. Cover and refrigerate overnight. Let stand at room temperature for 1 hour before serving.

How to Use a Blender
Using a blender can be a messy business. Cover the top of the blender with a dishtowel while using. Never fill a blender more than halfway. Always have about half liquid in the blender to offset the solids. Always leave a crack open at the top. Start blending by "pulsing" a few times to make sure the blades are running freely.

ROASTED RED PEPPER SALSA

2 large red bell peppers
12 scallions
3 tablespoons fresh cilantro
¼ cup black olives
⅓ cup grated Parmesan cheese
¼ cup olive oil

4 tablespoons lime juice
½ teaspoon salt
½ teaspoon ground black
    pepper

<table>
<tr><td>Serves 12</td></tr>
<tr><td>While salsas are always delicious with tortilla chips, try something different and serve dollops of salsa on toasted French bread or use garlic bagel chips for dipping.</td></tr>
</table>

1. Preheat oven to 350°.
2. Remove the core and seeds from the red peppers. Slice into 12-inch-wide strips. Coat the insides with olive oil and bake for 1 hour or until lightly brown. Let cool, then chop into ¼-inch pieces.
3. Remove the skin from the scallions and discard all but 2 inches of the white and light green part; chop into ¼-inch pieces. Chop the cilantro into ⅛-inch pieces. Remove the pits from the olives and slice into ¼-inch pieces.
4. Combine all the ingredients in a medium-sized mixing bowl. Cover and refrigerate for 12 hours. Let stand until mixture reaches room temperature before serving.

Stocking Up on Ethnic Staples

If your local grocery store doesn't carry certain ethnic spices or ingredients, you may be able to find them on the Internet or at specialty shops. Just make sure to stock up on shelf-stable necessities so you can make these dishes whenever you like.

PINEAPPLE, MANGO, AND CUCUMBER SALSA

Serves 8

Serve with
Grilled Swordfish
(page 380).

½ cup fresh pineapple
½ cup fresh mango
½ cup cucumber
1 medium tomato
3 tablespoons green onions

⅓ cup red bell pepper
1 fresh jalapeño chili pepper
3 tablespoons fresh cilantro
½ teaspoon salt

1. Remove the top, core, and rind from the pineapple; cut the fruit into ½-inch pieces. Remove the skin and seeds from the mango; cut the fruit into ½-inch pieces. Peel the cucumber and cut into ½-inch pieces. Cut the tomato into ½-inch pieces. Reserve the juice from the pineapple, mango, cucumber, and tomato.
2. Remove the roots and cut the green onions into ½-inch pieces. Remove the stem and seeds from the red bell pepper and cut into ½-inch pieces. Remove the stem from the jalapeño and cut into ½-inch pieces. Remove the stems from the cilantro and cut the leaves into ½-inch pieces.
3. Combine all the ingredients, including the reserved juices; mix well.
4. Refrigerate for at least 4 hours before serving.

Green Onions and Scallions
Scallions are small yellowish onions that have a relatively mild flavor. Green onions are elongated white onions that grow no bigger than your index finger. It's common to eat the stems of green onions as you would chives.

CUCUMBER AND LIME SALSA

2 medium cucumbers
2 key limes
1 clove garlic
1 medium-sized white onion
2 sprigs parsley

¼ cup lime juice
1 teaspoon salt
1 teaspoon granulated sugar
½ teaspoon ground black
  pepper

1. Peel the cucumbers and cut into ½-inch cubes. Peel the key limes and cut into ½-inch squares. Peel and mince the garlic. Peel the onion and cut into ¼-inch pieces. Chop the parsley into ¼-inch pieces.
2. Combine all the ingredients in a medium-sized mixing bowl. Cover and refrigerate for 3 to 4 hours before using.

> **Yields 2 cups**
>
> This is a wonderful salsa served with chicken or veal because its light flavors don't over-power the meat.

DRIED FRUIT SALSA

¼ cup golden raisins
¼ cup dried apples
¼ cup prunes
¼ cup dried apricots
¼ cup dried pears

¼ cup dried peaches
¼ cup pecans
1 small green onion
1 cup dry white wine

1. Cut all the fruits into ¼-inch pieces. Chop the pecans into ¼-inch pieces. Peel the green onion and remove the roots; chop the onion and stem into ¼-inch pieces.
2. Combine all the ingredients in a mixing bowl. Mix well so the wine covers everything.
3. Cover and refrigerate for 8 to 10 hours before serving.

> **Yields 2 cups**
>
> This makes an excellent sauce for chicken, but it also works well as a dessert when put into warm Flour Tortillas (page 284).

GREEN ALMOND SALSA

Yields 1–1½ cups

This makes an excellent tostada chip dip but also can be used as a sauce when cooking chicken or pork.

3 tablespoons olive oil, divided
1 slice white bread
1 cup blanched almond slivers
3 green tomatoes
½ cup fresh green bell pepper
½ cup canned green serrano chilies (canned jalapeños can be substituted)
3 garlic cloves
½ cup fresh cilantro
½ teaspoon dried coriander seeds
½ teaspoon salt
½ teaspoon ground black pepper

1. Heat 2 tablespoons of the olive oil in a frying pan on medium-high heat and fry the bread on both sides until it is medium brown. Set on paper towels to soak up the remaining oil. When the bread is dry and cool, chop it into ¼-inch pieces.
2. Add the remaining olive oil and the almond slivers to the skillet. Reduce the heat to medium and sauté the almonds until they are medium brown. Drain off the grease.
3. Cut the tomatoes into quarters. Remove the stem and seeds from the green bell pepper and cut into ¼-inch pieces. Drain the chilies. Remove the skin from the garlic and cut into quarters. Remove the stems from the cilantro.
4. Add all the ingredients to a blender or food processor. Blend on medium speed until all the ingredients are well melded. Small pieces may remain.
5. Pour the mixture into a medium-sized saucepan and simmer on low heat for 10 minutes.
6. Refrigerate for at least 4 hours before serving.

What's Hot
The hottest parts of a chili pepper are the seeds and the pith, the fleshy interior that attaches to the seeds. The flesh contains less heat than the interior of the chili. Although chilies can be red, yellow, or green, the color is not an indication of how hot they are.

CHIPOTLE SALSA

6 chipotle chili peppers
½ cup water
1 medium-sized yellow onion
3 medium-sized red tomatoes
3 garlic cloves
2 tablespoons olive oil

½ teaspoon dried oregano
½ teaspoon granulated sugar
½ teaspoon salt
½ teaspoon pepper
1 tablespoon lime juice

Yields 2 cups

Use this as a unique enchilada or taco sauce. It also makes an excellent marinade for pork chops.

---

1. Remove the stems from the chili peppers and place them in a small saucepan with the water. Turn the temperature to low and simmer for 15 minutes or until the chili peppers are puffy. Drain off the water and chop the chilies into ¼-inch pieces.
2. Peel the onion and chop into ¼-inch pieces. Cut the tomatoes into ¼-inch pieces. Peel and mince the garlic.
3. Heat the olive oil in a medium-sized frying pan at medium heat. Add the onion, garlic, and chili peppers. Sauté until the onion is clear and limp, not brown. Drain off excess olive oil.
4. Add the tomatoes, oregano, salt, pepper, and sugar to the frying pan; stir well. Cover and simmer on low heat for 20 minutes.
5. Remove from heat and let cool. Stir in the lime juice. Refrigerate for at least 4 hours before serving.

Choosing the Right Pan
When choosing a pan for cooking on a stovetop, make sure the food comes no closer than 2 inches from the top of the pan when all the ingredients are added. If the food fills the pan more than that it won't cook evenly.

CRIMSON PRICKLY PEAR SAUCE

16 fresh prickly pears (avoid those with yellow-gray green rinds)

½ cup granulated sugar
1 tablespoon lime juice
1 tablespoon orange liqueur

1. Remove the rind from the prickly pears by cutting off both ends and running a slice down both sides. If ripe, the rind will pull off easily.
2. Chop the prickly pear fruit into approximately 1-inch pieces and place in a blender. Blend on medium-high until you have a purée. Strain through cheesecloth or a fine-meshed strainer. Reserve both the juice and purée. Remove the seeds from the purée.
3. Put 2 cups of the prickly pear juice in a medium-sized saucepan with the sugar. Cook over medium heat until the mixture is reduced by half.
4. Remove from heat. Add 1 cup of puréed prickly pear, the lime juice, and orange liqueur; stir well.
5. Refrigerate for at least 4 hours before serving.

What's a Prickly Pear?
These egg-shaped fruit come from the same prickly-pear cactus that gives us the cactus paddles used as a vegetable. The flesh is very watery and tastes a bit like watermelon and strawberries, although one variety (with yellow-gray green rinds) tastes very sour. When ripe, the rind yields slightly to the touch.

ROASTED MORITA CREAM SAUCE

½ cup whipping cream
½ cup plain yogurt
2 fresh morita chilies
1 cup whole milk

2 tablespoons olive oil
1½ tablespoons flour
1 teaspoon salt

Makes 2 cups

Serve warm over potatoes or fresh vegetables.

1. Make thick cream by pouring the whipping cream into a small saucepan and cooking it on low heat until it is lukewarm. (It must not go above 100°.)
2. Remove from heat and stir in the yogurt. Pour into a clear glass jar and cover with a loose cap or clear plastic food wrap. Place in a warm place (80° to 90°), such as the top of the refrigerator.
3. Let the cream develop for 12 to 24 hours. Stir gently and chill for 4 to 8 hours.
4. Remove the stems and seeds from the chilies and cut into 1-inch pieces.
5. Put the chilies and milk in a food processor or blender and blend on medium setting until smooth.
6. Heat the milk and chili mixture in a medium-sized saucepan over medium-low heat.
7. In another saucepan, blend the olive oil and flour. Cook over medium heat, stirring constantly for 2 to 3 minutes. After about 3 minutes, begin gently whisking in the heated milk and chili mixture. Continue to cook and stir until smooth and thickened.
8. Whisk in the thick cream.

PUMPKIN SEED SALSA

Makes 2 cups

This sauce can be used like this for dipping, or you can add 2 more cups of chicken stock and use it as a sauce when baking chicken.

1 heaping cup hulled pepitas
   (pumpkin seeds)
1 small white onion
2 garlic cloves
½ cup fresh cilantro leaves
2 large radish leaves
3 small romaine lettuce leaves

3 serrano chilies
1½ cups Chicken Stock (see
   recipe on page 286)
1 tablespoon olive oil

1. Place the pumpkin seeds in a large skillet over medium heat. Spread out the pumpkin seeds and toast them, stirring regularly, until nearly all have popped and turned golden. Spread on a plate to cool.
2. Peel the onion and cut into quarters. Peel the garlic. Remove the stems from the cilantro, radish, and romaine leaves. Tear the leaves into 2-inch pieces. Remove the stem and seeds from the serrano chilies and chop into 1-inch pieces.
3. Put all the ingredients *except* the olive oil in a blender or food processor. Blend on medium setting until you have a smooth purée.
4. Pour the olive oil into a large frying pan. Add the purée. Cook on medium setting, stirring constantly, until the sauce is very thick.

Roasting Nuts

Roasting nuts must be done slowly or else the nuts will taste bitter. After you have roasted any nuts, pick out those that have dark brown or even black places. If roasting them to eat, add a tablespoon of sugar to each cup of nuts to make your own pralines.

JICAMA SALSA

1 medium carrot
1 small zucchini
½ cup fresh green beans
4 fresh radishes
1 medium-sized white onion
4 garlic cloves
2 tablespoons fresh cilantro
  leaves
1 medium jicama (about 2
  pounds)

1 chipotle chili pepper
1 cup boiling water
1 teaspoon dried oregano
½ cup white vinegar
½ cup water
½ cup olive oil
1 tablespoon lime juice

> **Yields 2 cups**
>
> This makes an excellent condiment for grilled fish or chicken.

1. Peel the carrot and zucchini, and dice into ¼-inch pieces. Snap off the ends of the green beans and cut into ¼-inch pieces. Remove the roots and tops from the radishes and cut into ¼-inch pieces. Peel the onion and cut into ¼-inch pieces. Peel and mince the garlic. Remove the stems from the cilantro and dice finely. Remove the skin from the jicama and dice into ¼-inch pieces.
2. Place the carrots, green beans, radishes, and chili pepper in a small pot containing the boiling water. Cook for 2 to 3 minutes, then drain. Remove the stem and seeds from the chili pepper; chop the pepper into ¼-inch pieces.
3. Mix together all the ingredients in a large mixing bowl. Cover and refrigerate for 4 hours.
4. Let warm to room temperature before serving.

Paprika

Paprika is made from red peppers, which are dried and powdered into a coarse-grained spice. It is used in many Spanish recipes and a handful of Mexican recipes. Interestingly, paprika comes in many different strengths. What's typically sold in the United States is the most mild.

PEAR-GINGER SALSA

1½ cups canned pears
½ red bell pepper
⅓ cup golden raisins
2 scallions
1 tablespoon canned jalapeño peppers

1 tablespoon white wine vinegar
2 teaspoons fresh-grated gingerroot
1 teaspoon salt

1. Drain off the juice from the pears and cut into ¼-inch pieces. Remove the stem and seeds from the red bell pepper and cut into ¼-inch pieces. Remove the peels, roots, and stems from the scallions and mince. Mince the gingerroot. Drain off the juice from the jalapeño pepper and mince.
2. Combine all the ingredients in a medium-sized mixing bowl.
3. Cover and refrigerate for 8 to 12 hours.

JALAPEÑO JELLY

6 fresh jalapeños
5½ cups granulated sugar
1½ cups cider vinegar
2 tablespoons fresh lemon juice

1 bottle pectin
green food coloring

1. Remove the stems and seeds from the jalapeños and cut into ¼-inch pieces.
2. Combine the jalapeños, sugar, cider vinegar, and lemon juice in a large pot over medium-high heat; bring to a boil. Boil for 5 minutes, stirring occasionally.
3. Stir in the pectin and boil for 1 minute.
4. Remove from heat and stir in 8 drops of green food coloring.
5. Pour into sterilized jars, seal, and place in a hot water bath for 5 minutes.

GARLIC SALSA

20 garlic cloves
1 small white onion
2 medium-sized red tomatoes
1 fresh serrano pepper
3 lemons
½ cup fresh parsley leaves

½ teaspoon salt
½ teaspoon ground black
 pepper
½ teaspoon paprika
1 tablespoon dried oregano
½ cup olive oil

Yields 2 cups

This is an excellent substitute for tomato salsa or even picante sauce, especially for people who prefer lots of garlic in their recipes.

1. Peel and mince the garlic and onion. Cut the tomatoes into ¼-inch pieces. Remove the stem and seeds from the serrano and cut into ¼-inch pieces. Juice the lemons. Cut off the stems from the parsley and mince the leaves.
2. Combine all the ingredients; mix well.
3. Cover and refrigerate for 8 to 12 hours before using.

ROOSTER'S BILL (PICO DE GALLO)

1 medium jicama
1 large orange
1 small yellow onion
1 tablespoon lemon juice

1 teaspoon salt
1 teaspoon medium-hot red
 chili powder
½ teaspoon dried oregano

Serves 4

Use as a sauce for tacos or as a side dish for a meal such as Mexican Meat Loaf (page 419).

1. Wash, pare, and chop the jicama into ½-inch chunks. Pare and section the orange, reserving the juice. Peel the onion and cut into ⅛-inch pieces.
2. Combine the orange and jicama in a medium-sized bowl. Pour the orange juice over the mixture. Add the onion, lemon juice, and salt. Stir until evenly mixed.
3. Cover and refrigerate for at least 1 hour before serving.
4. Sprinkle with chili powder and oregano before serving.

ADOBO SAUCE

Yields 2½ cups

This is typically served over meat. If making a pork or beef dish, reserve some of the stock and replace the chicken stock with that.

6 dried ancho chilies
1 large white onion
2 garlic cloves
1 cup canned tomatoes
½ teaspoon dried oregano
½ teaspoon ground cumin

2 tablespoons vegetable oil
1½ cups Chicken Stock (see recipe on page 286)
1 teaspoon salt
½ teaspoon ground black pepper

1. Remove the stems from the chilies and chop the chilies into ¼-inch pieces. Peel the onion and chop into ¼-inch pieces. Peel and mince the garlic. Drain the tomatoes.
2. Combine the chilies, onion, garlic, tomatoes, oregano, and cumin in a blender or food processor; blend to a thick purée.
3. Heat the oil in a medium-sized skillet to medium heat. Add the purée and cook for about 5 minutes. Stir in the stock, salt, and pepper.

NOGADA SAUCE

Yields 1¼ cups

Heat and serve over anything from pork chops to cheese-stuffed jalapeño peppers.

1 cup walnuts
1 garlic clove
5 peppercorns
¼ cup bread crumbs

2 tablespoons cider vinegar
2 tablespoons granulated sugar
½ teapsoon salt
6 tablespoons water

1. Peel the garlic.
2. Add the walnuts, garlic, peppercorns, and bread crumbs to a food processor or blender. Blend until finely ground.
3. Add the vinegar to the mixture; stir well. Stir in the sugar and salt. Add just enough water to make a thick sauce.

MOLE POBLANO

6 dried ancho chilies
1 large onion
1 garlic clove
1 Basic Corn Tortillas
 (see recipe on page 283)
2 cups canned tomatoes, with juice
½ cup salted peanuts
⅓ cup raisins
2 tablespoons sesame seeds
¼ cup oil
1 tablespoon granulated sugar

¼ teaspoon anise seeds
¼ teaspoon ground cinnamon
¼ teaspoon ground cloves
¼ teaspoon ground coriander seeds
¼ teaspoon ground cumin
1 cup Chicken Stock (see recipe on page 286)
1 ounce unsweetened chocolate
1 teaspoon salt
1 teaspoon ground black pepper

> **Serves 8**
>
> Use as a sauce for poultry or red meat. Use as a filling for tortillas or tamales by adding 3 cups of chopped, precooked chicken, beef, or turkey to the sauce and warming it thoroughly.

1. Remove the stems and seeds from the chilies. Peel and quarter the onion and garlic. Tear the tortilla into 1-inch pieces.
2. Combine the chilies, onion, garlic, tomatoes with their juice, tortilla, peanuts, raisins, and sesame seeds in a blender. Blend on medium speed until you have a thick purée.
3. Heat the oil to medium temperature in a large frying pan. Add the purée and cook, stirring constantly, for about 5 minutes. Stir in the sugar, anise, cinnamon, cloves, coriander, cumin, and stock; bring to a boil. Reduce heat to low and simmer uncovered for 10 minutes.
4. Add the chocolate and continue simmering, stirring constantly, until the chocolate melts and blends into the sauce. Add the salt and pepper.

Mole Poblano

Legend has it that the nuns of Santa Rosa received a surprise visit from their archbishop in the late 1500s. They had little time to prepare dinner for such an esteemed guest, so they added everything in their kitchen to their mole sauce. Today, this is one of the most famous—and most used—sauces in Mexican cooking.

CHAPTER 19
APPETIZERS

BRIE AND PAPAYA QUESADILLAS

Serves 6

Serve as an appetizer with Guacamole (page 287), sour cream, and Pico de Gallo (page 303). Or add some spicy chicken to the quesadillas to create an easy, 1-dish meal.

½ medium-sized yellow onion
2 large red chili peppers
1 ripe papaya
1 pound brie
½ cup water

12 Flour Tortillas (see recipe on page 284)
4 tablespoons butter
4 tablespoons oil

1. Remove the peel from the onion and cut into ¼-inch-thick slices. Remove the stems from the chilies and dice the chilies into pieces about ⅛-inch square. Peel and deseed the papaya; dice into pieces about ⅛-inch square. Cut the brie into ¼-inch strips.
2. Heat the water on high in a medium-sized skillet until boiling. Remove from heat and add the onions; let stand for 10 to 15 minutes. Drain and set aside.
3. Warm the tortillas by placing them in the oven for 10 minutes at 250°. Melt the butter in a small saucepan over low heat. Add the oil to the butter and stir until mixed. Remove the tortillas from the oven but leave the oven at 250°.
4. Place a few strips of cheese on each tortilla. Add several onion strips, ¼ teaspoon of diced chili peppers, and 1 tablespoon of diced papaya. Add another tortilla to make a sandwich, then brush the top tortilla with the butter and oil mixture.
5. Place the quesadillas 1 at a time in a large skillet on medium heat. Brown both sides. Place the quesadillas on a baking sheet in the oven to keep warm while the others are being made.
6. Cut the quesadillas into 6 triangular wedges to serve.

FRIED PLANTAINS

12 plantains
¼ cup vegetable oil
½ teaspoon salt
¼ cup ground horseradish

¼ cup sour cream
¼ cup honey
¼ cup brown sugar

1. Remove the skins from the plantains and cut into 2-inch lengths. Using a heavy spatula, press down on each piece, round end up, until it is ¼-inch to ½-inch thick. They should be about the size of a 50-cent piece.
2. Pour the oil into a medium-sized skillet and turn to medium heat. Fry the plantain patties until they are lightly browned on each side.
3. Make a sauce by combining the horseradish, salt, and sour cream. Make another sauce by combining the brown sugar and honey. Use the sauces for dipping the hot plantain patties.

Serves 4

If you can't find plantains, try this same technique with bananas. Use bananas that are just starting to ripen, as they hold up better during the cooking process.

SPINACH CON QUESO

1 (10-ounce) package frozen, chopped spinach
1 small white onion
1 medium-sized red tomato

1 pound Velveeta cheese with jalapeños
½ cup whole milk
1 (2-ounce) jar diced pimientos

1. Thaw the spinach and squeeze the water from it until the spinach is as dry as possible.
2. Remove skin from the onion and chop into ¼-inch pieces. Chop the tomato into ¼-inch pieces.
3. Combine the onion, cheese, milk, and pimientos in a medium-sized pot over low heat (or in a slow cooker set on the lowest temperature setting). Cook, stirring periodically, until the cheese melts. Stir in the spinach and tomato.

Serves 8

Serve with broken, warm Tostadas (page 285) for dipping.

QUESO FUNDIDO

Serves 8

Serve this with broken fresh Corn Tostadas (page 285).

½ pound Cheddar cheese
½ pound Monterey jack cheese
3 medium eggs

½ cup Green Tomato Salsa
(see recipe on page 282)

1. Preheat oven to 350°.
2. Grate the cheeses. Mix together and place in a large baking dish.
3. Beat together the eggs and salsa; pour over the cheeses.
4. Bake for 30 minutes.

MEXICAN ROLL-UPS

Serves 6

Serve with an assortment of fresh salsas for an interesting treat.

2 fresh jalapeño chili peppers
1 bunch green onions
½ cup pitted black olives
16 ounces cream cheese
½ teaspoon garlic salt

½ teaspoon medium-hot red
chili powder
6 Flour Tortillas (see recipe on
page 284)

1. Remove the stems and seeds from the jalapeño peppers and chop the peppers into ¼-inch pieces. Remove the roots from the green onions and chop the onions and stems into ¼-inch pieces. Chop the olives into ¼-inch pieces.
2. Combine all the ingredients and mix until well blended.
3. Spread on tortillas. Roll up and serve.

CAULIFLOWER TORTAS

1 head cauliflower
2 eggs
2 tablespoons flour
1 teaspoon salt

½ teaspoon ground black
*   pepper*
4 cups vegetable oil

Serves 8

Serve with an assortment of salsas.

1. Rinse the cauliflower, remove the outer leaves, and separate into florets. Cook in boiling water until almost tender, about 8 to 10 minutes. Drain.
2. Separate the eggs. Beat the egg whites until they form rounded peaks. Beat the egg yolks until smooth. Pour the yolks into the whites gradually, beating lightly with a fork to combine.
3. In a separate small bowl, combine the flour, salt, and pepper. Roll the cooked cauliflower in the flour, then dip in the eggs, coating well.
4. Heat the oil to 375° in a frying pan. Add a few cauliflower florets at a time and fry until brown on all sides.

TOMATO EMPANADAS

½ pound butter
8 ounces cream cheese
2 cups flour

2 medium-sized red tomatoes
1 small yellow onion

Serves 6

These can be made ahead of time and frozen. They can be reheated in a microwave.

1. Mix together the butter and cream cheese until creamy. Add the flour and mix well. Roll into a ball, cover, and chill for at least 4 hours.
2. Preheat oven to 350°.
3. Cut the tomatoes into ¼-inch pieces. Peel the onion and cut into ¼-inch pieces. Mix together the tomatoes and onion.
4. Roll out the dough to about ¼-inch thick. Cut into circles about 3 inches across.
5. Put 1 teaspoon of tomato and onion mixture in the center of each circle. Fold in half and seal the edges with a fork. Prick the top of each empanada with a fork.
6. Place on a baking sheet and bake for 15 to 20 minutes.

CABBAGE TAMALES

Makes 36

Serve as an appetizer before any traditional Mexican meal, such as Mexican Pot Roast (page 412).

1 fresh cabbage
1 pound lean ground beef
1 pound patty sausage
1 cup condensed tomato soup

1 cup dry rice
4 tablespoons chili powder
½ teaspoon salt

1. Preheat oven to 300°. Remove the core from the cabbage. Separate the leaves and place in a pan of warm water.
2. Combine the ground beef, sausage, soup, rice, chili powder, and salt. Mix well with your hands so that all the ingredients are blended.
3. Remove the cabbage leaves from the water and pat dry. Place about 2 tablespoons of the meat mixture in the middle of each cabbage leaf. Roll up and secure with a toothpick.
4. Place the rolls in a 9" × 12" baking dish. Bake with foil cover for 1½ hours.

SPINACH BALLS

Makes 24

In addition to being used as an appetizer, these often are added to a basic Chicken Stock (page 286) to make an interesting soup.

½ cup cooked ham
½ cup Cheddar cheese
3 eggs
¼ cup flour

2 pounds fresh spinach
½ teaspoon salt
1 cup vegetable oil

1. Cut the ham into ½-inch cubes. Cut the cheese into ½-inch cubes. Separate the egg yolks from the egg whites.
2. Wash the spinach and remove the hard stalks. Place the spinach in a medium-sized saucepan and add 1 inch of water. Cook on medium heat until the spinach is thoroughly cooked; drain. Let cool slightly, then form into balls about the size of golf balls.
3. Push a piece of ham or cheese into the center of each ball.
4. Beat the egg whites until stiff. Gradually beat in the yolks, flour, and salt. Coat the spinach balls with the egg batter.
5. Heat the oil to medium-high. Fry 1 layer of spinach balls at a time until lightly browned.

TOTOPOS

1 small yellow onion
2 avocados
¼ head of lettuce, shredded
3 dill pickles
1 fresh red tomato
2 cups Spicy Chicken (see
   recipe on page 289)
1 tablespoon butter
2 cups canned kidney beans,
   undrained

1 teaspoon salt
½ teaspoon ground black
   pepper
1⅓ cups vegetable oil, divided
12 small Corn Tortillas (see
   recipe on page 283)
2 tablespoons white wine vinegar
1½ teaspoons granulated sugar
¼ teaspoon garlic salt
¾ cup crumbled goat cheese

> **Serves 6**
>
> Change the ingredients
> to suit your whims.
> Hot peppers, beef,
> and guacamole also
> make good toppings.

1. Peel the onion and chop finely. Peel and pit the avocados and slice into crescents ¼-inch thick. Shred the lettuce. Slice the pickles into ¼-inch rounds. Remove the stem from the tomato and cut into ¼-inch slices. Warm the chicken in a small pan on low heat.
2. Melt the butter in a medium-sized frying pan on medium heat. Add the onion and sauté until limp but not brown. Add the kidney beans with their liquid and the salt and pepper. Cook until the liquid is reduced by half.
3. Heat 1 cup of the vegetable oil in a large skillet to medium-high. Fry tortillas 1 at a time. Drain and cool.
4. Mix together the vinegar, sugar, garlic salt, and the ⅓ cup remaining vegetable oil in a small container with a cover. Cover and shake until well mixed.
5. Combine the lettuce, avocado, pickles, and chicken in a medium-sized bowl. Mix with the vinegar and oil dressing.
6. Spread the beans about ½-inch thick on the tortillas. Pile the salad mixture on top. Add the tomato slices and sprinkle with cheese.

Totopos
Totopos literally means "toppers." It's also the word used for the condiments served with tacos or when serving "make your own" tostadas.

SWEET CHILI RELLENOS

12–18 fresh, large hot peppers
2 garlic cloves
1 small white onion
2 large ripe tomatoes
1 teaspoon capers
1/4 cup chopped green olives
2 tablespoons candied lemon
   peel
1/4 cup almonds
2 eggs
4 whole cloves
5 peppercorns

1/2 pound ham
3 tablespoons shortening
1 pound lean ground pork
2 tablespoons snipped parsley
3 tablespoons cider vinegar
1/2 teaspoon vanilla extract
2 tablespoons granulated sugar
1/4 teaspoon ground nutmeg
1/8 teaspoon powdered saffron
1/4 cup seedless raisins
1/2 cup flour
1 cup vegetable oil

1. Cut out the stems of the peppers, leaving the peppers whole. Scoop
   out the seeds and membrane. Place the peppers in a large saucepan.
   Cover with boiling water, bring to a boil, and cook for about 2 minutes. Drain and invert the peppers on a paper towel.
2. Peel and mince the garlic. Peel the onion and chop into 1/4-inch pieces.
   Remove the stems from the tomatoes and chop into 1/4-inch pieces.
   Finely chop the capers, green olives, lemon peel, almonds. Beat the
   eggs and set aside. Crush the cloves and peppercorns. Grind the ham
   using a meat grinder.
3. Heat the shortening in a large frying pan. Add the garlic, onion and
   both meats. Cook until the meat is browned, stirring occasionally.
4. Mix together the tomatoes, parsley, vinegar, vanilla extract, sugar,
   cloves, peppercorns, nutmeg, and saffron; add mixture to the meat
   along with almonds, raisins, capers, lemon peel, and olives. Stir. Cook
   over low heat, stirring frequently, until the mixture is almost dry, about
   30 to 40 minutes. Spoon the filling into the peppers, packing lightly so
   the mixture will remain in the pepper cavities during frying.
5. Roll the peppers in flour, coating entire surface. Dip in the beaten eggs.
6. Heat the oil to medium-high in a large frying pan. Fry peppers until
   golden. Place on paper towels to drain off grease.

Chapter 20
SOUPS

JALAPEÑO AND POTATO SOUP

Serves 8

Add a dollop of sour cream and sprigs of fresh cilantro before serving.

5 pounds red potatoes
¼ cup fresh or ⅛ cup canned jalapeño peppers
1 medium-sized yellow onion
¼ cup butter
8 cups Chicken Stock (see recipe on page 286)
1 teaspoon ground cumin
¼ teaspoon baking soda
4 cups evaporated milk
½ teaspoon ground black pepper

1. Clean the potatoes and cut into quarters (do not peel). Remove the stem and seeds from the jalapeño and cut into ⅛-inch pieces. Remove the skin from the onion and cut into ¼-inch pieces.
2. Sauté the onions in butter until the onions are clear but not brown.
3. Combine the potatoes, onions, stock, and cumin in a large stockpot. Cook uncovered for about 30 minutes, until the potatoes are tender.
4. Coarsely mash the potatoes with a potato masher. Stir in the jalapeños, soda, and evaporated milk; stir well.
5. Simmer on low heat for 15 minutes, stirring constantly.

Jalapeño Chili Peppers
Jalapeños are perhaps the most common hot pepper sold in the United States. They come in both green and red colors that taste only slightly different. When in doubt, use jalapeños, because they definitely add heat and spice but they are mild enough that most people can tolerate them.

MEXICAN ONION SOUP

3 large yellow onions
2 cloves garlic
¼ cup butter
2 cups tomato juice
2 cups beef broth (canned or
    homemade)
1 cup water

½ cup Tomato Salsa (see
    recipe on page 282)
1 cup grated Monterey jack
    cheese

Serves 6

Serve with Brie and Papaya Quesadillas (page 308) for a light yet filling lunch.

1. Remove the skins from the onions and slice into thin rings. Remove the skin from the garlic cloves and mince.
2. Melt the butter over medium-low heat in a large frying pan. Add the onions and cook for about 20 minutes, stirring frequently. Onions should be tender and light brown.
3. Stir in the tomato juice, broth, water, and salsa. Bring to a boil. Reduce heat to low.
4. Simmer uncovered for 20 minutes. Top with grated cheese before serving.

Let's Hear It for Green Tomatoes

Although we tend to think of green tomatoes as unripe, therefore not fit to eat, the opposite is true. Because they have a firmer flesh and more tart taste, they add a distinctly different flavor from their ripe counterparts. Eating green tomatoes also means we get to enjoy the fresh garden tomatoes for a longer season.

ASPARAGUS AND PISTACHIO SOUP

1 medium onion
2 cups fresh asparagus tips
    (about 1 inch long)
½ cup natural pistachio meats
1 tablespoon butter
6 cups Chicken Stock (see
    recipe on page 286)
½ teaspoon salt

1 teaspoon ground black
    pepper
¼ cup cooking sherry
½ cup heavy cream

1. Remove the skin from the onion and chop into ¼-inch pieces.
2. Cook the asparagus tips in water on medium heat until slightly tender.
3. Cover the pistachio meats with boiling water and let sit for 10 minutes. Remove the skins and let the meats dry.
4. Sauté the pistachio meats in the butter on medium heat until golden. Set the pistachio meats aside and add the onion to the butter; sauté until limp.
5. Combine 1 cup of the stock, the pistachio meats, onion, salt, black pepper, and cooking sherry in a blender and mix until it's a smooth paste.
6. Place the mixture in a medium-sized pot over medium heat. Add the remaining stock and stir until well mixed. Add the asparagus tips and cook for 20 minutes on low heat.
7. Stir in the cream right before serving.

The Green Nut

Pistachios are a very common treat in Mexico. When walking the streets of virtually any town, you're likely to have a young child come up to you offering fresh roasted pistachios. Be sure to avoid the red and white dyed pistachios sold in the United States, as the dye will discolor your food.

CHICKEN TORTILLA SOUP

1 *whole chicken (precooked)*
1 *cup dry black beans*
1 *medium-sized white onion*
4 *garlic cloves*
1 *red bell pepper*
3 *medium-sized red tomatoes*
2 *tablespoons chili powder*
2 *teaspoons salt*
1 *tablespoon ground cumin*
½ *teaspoon ground red pepper*

1 *teaspoon granulated sugar*
2 *cups canned (and drained) or frozen corn*
6 *cups Chicken Stock (see recipe on page 286)*
¼ *cup lime juice*
4 *Tostadas (see recipe on page 285)*
1 *bunch fresh cilantro leaves*

Serves 8

An alternative for cooking this soup is to put all the ingredients except the lime juice, tostada, and cilantro in a slow cooker, cover, and cook on low setting for 8 to 10 hours.

---

1. If necessary, roast the chicken for 3 hours in 350° oven.
2. Soak the beans overnight in 3 cups water.
3. Remove the skin from the onion and garlic. Chop the onion into ¼-inch pieces. Mince the garlic. Remove the stem and core from the red bell pepper and chop into ¼-inch pieces. Chop the tomatoes into 1-inch pieces.
4. Remove the skin from the chicken and cut into 1-inch cubes, discarding the bones.
5. Combine all the ingredients *except* the lime juice, tostadas, and cilantro in a large stockpot. Bring to a boil and cook for 20 minutes. Reduce heat to low, cover, and simmer for 2 hours. Stir in the lime juice right before serving.
6. Break the tostadas into small pieces. Cut the stems from the cilantro. Sprinkle the tostada pieces and cilantro leaves on the soup before serving.

ROASTED RED PEPPER AND CABBAGE SOUP

2 red bell peppers
1 tablespoon olive oil
1 large white onion
2 large carrots
4 garlic cloves
1 medium cabbage
2 medium zucchini (8–12 inches long)

2 cups canned (and drained) or frozen corn
2 teaspoons salt
1 teaspoon ground black pepper
6 cups Chicken Stock (see recipe on page 286)

1. Preheat oven to 350°.
2. Remove the stems and seeds from the red bell peppers. Cut the peppers into 2-inch-wide strips. Place skin-side down on a baking sheet. Spread the olive oil over the pepper strips. Place in oven and bake for 30 minutes or until the peppers are lightly blackened on the edges.
3. Remove the skin from the onion and chop into ¼-inch pieces. Clean the carrots and chop into ¼-inch rounds. Remove the skin from the garlic and mince. Tear the cabbage leaves into pieces about 3 inches square. Clean the zucchini and cut into ½-inch pieces. Cut the roasted red pepper pieces into 1-inch squares.
4. Add all the ingredients to a large stockpot. Bring to a boil, cover, and cook for 20 minutes. Reduce heat to medium-low and simmer for 2 hours.

Where Are the Hot Peppers?
While many people think Mexican food must have hot chili pepper in it to be traditional, that is absolutely not true. Mexican food is known for its use of fresh fruits and vegetables and a variety of spices, both mild and unusual. Hot peppers are just one of many interesting things to discover with this cuisine.

COLD AVOCADO SOUP

1 medium-sized yellow onion
3 garlic cloves
1 medium-sized green tomato
2 ripe avocados
2 fresh habanero chilies (¼ cup canned jalapeños can be substituted)
½ cup fresh cilantro leaves

4 cups Chicken Stock (see recipe on page 286)
1 teaspoon salt
½ teaspoon ground red pepper
1 cup sour cream
¼ cup lime juice

Serves 8

This makes a wonderful summer lunch served with a fresh fruit salad.

1. Remove the skin from the onion and chop into ¼-inch pieces. Remove the skin from the garlic and mince. Remove the skin from the tomato and mash with a potato masher. Peel and pit the avocados, then cut into 2-inch pieces. Remove the stems and seeds from the chilies and chop into ¼-inch pieces.
2. Combine all the ingredients *except* the sour cream and lime juice in a food processor or blender. You may need to do it in 2 or 3 batches. Blend on medium setting for 3 minutes or until the ingredients are well melded. Strain and discard any chunks.
3. Refrigerate for 3 hours. Remove any fat that has congealed on the top of the soup. Stir and refrigerate for an additional hour.
4. Top with a dollop of sour cream and a sprinkle of lime juice before serving.

What's an Avocado?

An avocado actually is a fruit that comes in several different varieties. It is fairly high in calories (about 300 for an average avocado). Although many people think otherwise, avocados contain only monounsaturated fat, which may help reduce bad cholesterol. When choosing a ripe avocado, the flesh should give slightly to your touch.

CREAMY CORN SOUP

1 large white onion
3 medium-sized red tomatoes
3 cups canned (and drained) or frozen whole-kernel corn
4 cups Chicken Stock (see recipe on page 286)

1 teaspoon salt
½ teaspoon ground black pepper
1 cup heavy whipping cream

1. Remove the skin from the onion and cut into quarters. Remove the skin from the tomatoes and cut into quarters.
2. Put the corn, onion, tomatoes, and 1 cup of the stock in a food processor or blender. Blend on medium setting for 3 minutes or until all the ingredients are melded. They do not have to be liquefied—small pieces of corn, onion, and tomato are fine.
3. Place the remaining stock in a large saucepan on medium-low heat. Stir in the blended mixture. Add the salt and pepper. Heat thoroughly, but do not boil.
4. Stir in the whipping cream and cook on low heat, stirring constantly, for 5 minutes.

Peeling Tomatoes

Although a tomato can be peeled cold, the easiest way to peel it is to drop it in boiling water for 20 seconds. Then cool it by running it under cold water. The peel will easily strip off with a paring knife.

CORNBALL SOUP

1 small yellow onion
1 garlic clove
2 cups masa harina or cornmeal
1 cup milk
2 eggs
¼ cup fresh-grated Parmesan
  cheese
1 teaspoon dried cilantro

2 large red tomatoes
¼ cup vegetable oil
8 cups Chicken Stock (see
  recipe on page 286)
2 teaspoons salt
1 teaspoon ground black pepper

Serves 8

This can also be made using a beef stock with beef and vegetable chunks.

1. Peel and mince the onion and garlic.
2. Combine the onion, garlic, cornmeal, milk, eggs, Parmesan cheese, and cilantro. Roll into balls about the size of golf balls.
3. Remove the skin from the tomatoes and cut into quarters. Put in blender or food processor and blend on medium setting until thick and creamy.
4. Heat the vegetable oil on medium-high in a medium-sized frying pan. Add the cornmeal balls and fry until lightly brown. (Cut one open to make sure they are cooked into the center.) Keep them warm by putting them in a warm oven.
5. Heat the stock. Stir in the tomato purée, salt, and black pepper. Add the cornmeal balls. Serve immediately.

Cross-Cultural Soups
It's interesting how soups travel through different cultures, changing to fit the available ingredients and tastes of different peoples. This soup seems awfully similar to matzo ball soup, yet it has a distinctly Mexican touch with the tomatoes, cilantro, and garlic.

SPICY VEGETABLE SOUP

Serves 8

Serve this soup with
Jalapeño Corn Bread
(page 62.)

2 large carrots
1 large yellow onion
2 celery ribs
2 medium zucchini (8–10
   inches long)
2 cups fresh or frozen green
   beans
1 pound fresh spinach
4 medium-sized red tomatoes
½ red bell pepper
4 garlic cloves
2 medium potatoes

3 hot chili peppers (type of
   your choosing)
8 cups Chicken Stock (see
   recipe on page 286)
1 cup fresh or frozen peas
1 cup fresh or frozen corn
1 teaspoon salt
½ teaspoon ground red pepper
½ teaspoon medium-hot red
   chili powder
4 tablespoons vegetable oil

1. Peel the carrots and cut into ¼-inch rounds. Remove the skin from the onion and cut into ¼-inch pieces. Cut the celery into ¼-inch pieces. Cut the zucchini into 1-inch pieces. Remove the stems from the green beans and cut into ½-inch pieces. Remove the stems from the spinach. Cut the tomatoes into quarters. Remove the stem and seeds from the red bell pepper and cut half the pepper into ¼-inch pieces. Remove the skin from the garlic cloves and slice thinly. Peel the potatoes and cut into 1-inch pieces. Remove the stem and seeds from the hot peppers and cut into ¼-inch pieces.
2. Put the chicken stock in a large stockpot on high heat. Add the carrots, onion, celery, green beans, garlic, peas, corn, potatoes, salt, ground red pepper, and chili powder; stir well. Bring to a boil, cover, and reduce heat to medium.
3. Heat the vegetable oil to medium temperature in a medium-sized frying pan. Add the bell pepper, spinach, tomatoes, and zucchini; sauté for 5 minutes. Drain off the oil and add the sautéed vegetables to the stockpot.
4. Simmer for 2 to 3 hours.

TURKEY AND FILBERT SOUP

1 medium-sized white onion
2 cups skinless turkey meat
¼ cup butter
½ cup filberts
8 cups Chicken Stock (see recipe on page 286)
¼ cup dry red wine

½ teaspoon ground nutmeg
1 tablespoon dried parsley flakes
1 teaspoon salt
1 teaspoon ground black pepper

Serves 8

This is a great way to use leftover turkey. It also works well with chicken.

1. Remove the skin from the onion and chop into ¼-inch pieces. Cut the turkey meat into ½-inch pieces.
2. Melt the butter in a small frying pan at medium heat and sauté the filberts for 5 minutes. Drain off the butter and discard.
3. Place the filberts, ½ cup of the turkey meat, the onions, and 1 cup of the stock in a blender or food processor. Blend at medium speed until you have a purée—a thick substance with all the ingredients melded.
4. Combine the mixture with the remaining chicken stock in a large stockpot. Add the remaining ingredients. Heat on medium temperature for 30 minutes, stirring frequently.

Edible Soup Bowls

Use squash as a soup bowl. Many small squashes make excellent complements to soups and stews. Cut them in half, remove the seeds, and prebake in the microwave or oven. Ladle your soup or stew into the squash for a festive look.

MEXICAN CHICKEN CHOWDER

Serves 4

Serve with
Jalapeño Corn Bread
(page 330).

1½ pounds boneless, skinless
   chicken breasts
2 medium-sized white onions
2 garlic cloves
2 celery ribs
½ cup canned, chopped
   jalapeño peppers, or 3
   fresh jalapeños
½ pound Monterey jack cheese
1 tablespoon olive oil

4 cups Chicken Stock (see
   recipe on page 286)
1 package dry chicken gravy
   mix
2 cups whole milk
2 cups Tomato Salsa (see
   recipe on page 282)
1 (32-ounce) bag frozen hash
   brown potatoes

1. Preheat oven to 300°.
2. Cut the chicken into ½-inch cubes. Peel the onion and cut into ¼-inch pieces. Peel and mince the garlic. Cut the celery into ¼-inch pieces. Drain the chilies and cut into ⅛-inch pieces. Cut the cheese into ½-inch cubes.
3. Combine the chicken, onions, garlic, celery, oil, and stock in a large mixing bowl; stir until well blended. Pour into a casserole dish, cover, and bake in oven for 1 hour.
4. Dissolve the gravy mix in the milk in a medium-sized mixing bowl. Stir into the cooked chicken mixture. Add the salsa, potatoes, chilies, and cheese; mix well. Cover and cook for an additional hour.

Hold the Salt
Resist the urge to salt. Salt draws flavors and juices out of meat and vegetables. Let the flavors release on their own time for the best results. Guests can salt their own dishes if they prefer. They'll also use less than if you add it while cooking.

MARKET BASKET SOUP

2 pounds smoky link sausages

1 small white onion

¼ cup canned jalapeño chili
   peppers

2 celery ribs

4 medium-sized red tomatoes

1 green bell pepper

1 medium zucchini (8–12
   inches long)

1 cup black olives

1 cup canned or frozen whole-
   kernel corn

1 cup canned green lima beans

2 cups canned pinto beans

4 ounces Bloody Mary mix

2 cups water

1 package dry onion soup mix

2 teaspoons salt

2 teaspoons ground white
   pepper

1 teaspoon dried oregano

> **Serves 8**
>
> This soup is also called wastebasket soup, probably because it is often made at the end of the week when the refrigerator and cupboards are being cleaned out.

1. Cook the sausages in a medium-sized frying pan on medium-low heat until lightly browned. Cut into 1-inch pieces.
2. Peel the onion and chop into ¼-inch pieces. Drain the jalapeños and cut into ¼-inch pieces. Cut the celery into ¼-inch pieces. Cut the tomatoes into 1-inch pieces. Remove the stem and seeds from the bell pepper and cut into ¼-inch pieces. Cut the zucchini into 1-inch pieces. Cut the black olives into ¼-inch pieces.
3. Add all the ingredients to a large stockpot and stir well. Bring to a boil, then lower the temperature to medium-low and simmer uncovered for 1 hour.

Lower the Cholesterol

When frying, sautéing, or browning foods, you don't have to use oil. Many chefs simply use a little bit of water to cook these items. When browning a fatty meat, such as sausages, start cooking them at a low temperature to cook some of the fat out before you turn up the temperature for browning.

CREAMY GAZPACHO WITH AVOCADO

4 eggs
5 medium-sized fresh red tomatoes
1 large cucumber
1 medium-sized white onion
1 ripe avocado
¼ cup vegetable oil
1 tablespoon prepared yellow
   mustard

1 tablespoon Worcestershire
   sauce
¼ cup lime juice
1 teaspoon garlic salt
½ teaspoon ground black
   pepper
1 cup sour cream

1. Boil the eggs in water for about 10 minutes. Cool and peel. Slice the
   eggs in half and remove the yolk. Set the whites aside. Peel the tomatoes. Set 1 tomato aside and chop the other 4 into quarters. Pare and
   seed the cucumber. Chop ¾ of the cucumber into 1-inch pieces and
   set aside the rest. Peel the onion and cut into quarters. Peel the avocado and remove the pit; set aside half.
2. Put the chopped tomatoes, cucumber, onion, and half of the avocado
   in a blender or food processor; blend until smooth.
3. Put the egg yolks in a small bowl and mash with a fork. Blend in the
   oil, mustard, Worcestershire sauce, lime juice, garlic salt, and pepper.
   Add the mixture to the blender and blend until thoroughly mixed. Add
   the sour cream gradually, blending well.
4. Pour the mixture into a medium-sized container with a cover. Chop
   the remaining tomato, cucumber, and hard-cooked egg whites and add
   to soup. Slice the remaining avocado half thinly and add to the soup.
   Stir in lightly.
5. Cover and refrigerate for at least 8 hours before serving.

CHAPTER 21
BREADS

JALAPEÑO CORN BREAD

Serves 4

Serve with Mexican
Pot Roast (page 412).

1 small yellow onion
2 garlic cloves
2 tablespoons canned chopped
    jalapeños
1½ cups bread flour
¾ cup masa harina or corn-
    meal
¼ cup granulated sugar
4½ teaspoons baking powder

1 teaspoon salt
1 egg
1 cup whole milk
½ teaspoon vegetable oil
½ cup canned cream-style corn
½ cup grated Cheddar cheese

1. Preheat oven to 350°.
2. Remove the skin from the onion and chop into ¼-inch pieces.
   Remove the skin from the garlic and mince. Drain off the water
   from the jalapeños.
3. Mix all the ingredients together in a medium-sized mixing bowl.
4. Pour the mixture into a greased bread pan.
5. Bake for 30 to 45 minutes or until lightly brown on top.

Know When Bread Is Done
*Bread that is fully cooked will spring back when you lightly
touch the top with your finger. In addition, a toothpick inserted into
the center of the bread should come out clean. Most breads will
also be lightly browned on top when they are done.*

PINEAPPLE SOPAPILLAS

2 cups flour
1 tablespoon baking powder
1 teaspoon salt
4 cups peanut oil
¾ cup water

3 cups canned pineapple, drained
1 cup white granulated sugar
2 tablespoons ground cinnamon

Makes 20
These can be made using any jam or heated fruits.

1. Mix together the flour, baking powder, and salt in a medium-sized mixing bowl.
2. Blend the oil into the dry ingredients. Stir in just enough water to make a soft dough.
3. Divide the dough into 4 parts. Roll out 1 part at a time to about ¼-inch thick. Cut into triangles about 4 inches by 2 inches.
4. In a large skillet, heat the peanut oil to about 385°. Add 3 to 4 pieces of dough at a time. Stir the oil until the sopapillas puff up like pillows. Fry until light brown. Lay on paper towels to drain off excess grease.
5. Chop the pineapple into ½-inch pieces. Drain off juice. Heat the pineapple to lukewarm in a small saucepan over medium-low heat.
6. Open a small hole in the side of each sopapilla and spoon about 2 tablespoons of pineapple inside it.
7. Mix together the cinnamon and sugar. Sprinkle on the top of each sopapilla.

Browning Fruit

To keep fruit such as bananas and apples from turning brown once they have had their peels removed, sprinkle them with a small amount of lemon juice. The acid in the juice stops the sugars in the fruits from reacting with the air to produce the brown color.

EASY MEXICAN SWEET ROLLS

2 eggs
⅔ cup flour
½ cup white granulated sugar
¼ cup softened butter
1 (10-ounce) can refrigerator
  flaky biscuits

1 tablespoon whole milk
½ teaspoon shortening

1. Preheat oven to 375°.
2. Separate the egg yolks from the egg whites.
3. Combine the flour and sugar in a bowl. Cut in the butter until the mixture resembles coarse crumbs. Add the egg yolks and mix until well blended. Set aside ¼ cup of this mixture.
4. Separate the canned biscuits into 10 pieces. Press or roll each to a ³/₅-inch oval. Crumble 1 to 2 tablespoons of the sugar and flour mixture over each oval to ¼ inch from the edge.
5. Roll the biscuit, starting at the shorter side, wrapping the dough around the filling and rolling to the opposite side.
6. Place the seam side down on a baking sheet lightly greased with shortening.
7. Beat the egg whites with the milk. Brush over the rolls with a pastry brush. Sprinkle evenly with the reserved ¼ cup of sugar and flour mixture. Press lightly into the rolls.
8. Bake for 13 to 17 minutes or until medium brown.

Separating Eggs
If you don't have an egg separator in your kitchen, break the egg neatly in half and transfer the yolk back and forth, catching the egg white in a small bowl underneath. In some recipes even the smallest amount of yolk in an egg white can cause the recipe to fail, so don't break that yolk!

MANGO CORN BREAD

1 tablespoon active dry yeast
¼ cup warm water
1 medium-sized white onion
1 mango
1 fresh jalapeño chili pepper
*3 cups masa harina or corn-
   meal*
1½ cups grated Cheddar cheese

½ cup vegetable oil
1 cup canned cream-style corn
3 tablespoons granulated sugar
⅓ cup whole milk
⅓ cup buttermilk

Serves 6
Serve for breakfast to accompany Huevos Bogotano (page 359).

1. Preheat oven to 425°.
2. Dissolve the yeast in the warm water. Peel the onion and chop into ¼-inch pieces. Remove the skin and seeds from the mango; cut into ¼-inch pieces. Remove the stem and seeds from the jalapeño and cut into ¼-inch pieces.
3. Combine all the ingredients in a large mixing bowl. Mix until well blended.
4. Pour into a greased bread pan and bake for 35 minutes.

About Yeast

Yeast is a live entity that grows when it gets warm. However, if it's added to boiling water, you can kill it. You can make a heavy, dense bread by leaving out the yeast and substituting baking soda.

ROSQUILLAS FRITAS

4 cups vegetable oil
2 teaspoons active dry yeast
$\frac{1}{4}$ cup warm water
$\frac{1}{2}$ cup roasted almonds
2 eggs
3 cups flour
$1\frac{1}{4}$ cups white granulated sugar
1 teaspoon baking soda
$\frac{1}{2}$ teaspoon salt

$\frac{1}{2}$ teaspoon cinnamon
$\frac{1}{2}$ teaspoon almond extract or flavoring
2 tablespoons butter
$\frac{1}{4}$ cup whole milk
$\frac{1}{2}$ cup white sugar, confectioners' sugar, or sugar and cinnamon mixed, to taste

1. Pour the vegetable oil into a medium-sized skillet. The oil should be about 2 inches deep. Heat to about 370°. Dissolve the yeast in the warm water. Chop the almonds into small pieces.
2. Mix the eggs with half of the flour, the sugar, dissolved yeast, almonds, baking soda, salt, cinnamon, almond extract, butter, and milk. Beat until the dough begins to thicken. Add the remaining flour and mix well. If the dough is not stiff enough to knead, add more flour, $\frac{1}{4}$ cup at a time.
3. Flour a flat surface and remove the dough from the bowl. Knead the dough until it is pliable and smooth. Roll out the dough about $\frac{1}{2}$-inch thick and cut into doughnut shapes.
4. Put 2 to 3 fritas in the hot oil at a time. Fry for 2 to 3 minutes or until golden brown. Flip and fry for 2 to 3 minutes on the other side. Place on paper towels to absorb the excess oil.
5. Sprinkle with white sugar, confectioners' sugar, or a mixture of sugar and cinnamon.

Extracts and Flavorings
Extracts are flavorings that have actually been extracted from the fruit or seed by squashing it and removing the oil. Flavorings are usually artificially produced and added to a water base.

KINGS' BREAD RING

2 cups candied fruits (citron, cherries, orange peel)
3 eggs
2 teaspoons (or 1 package) active dry yeast
½ cup warm water
½ cup milk
⅓ cup white granulated sugar
⅓ cup shortening

2 teaspoons salt
4 cups all-purpose flour
Tiny china doll (approximately 1 inch high)
½ cup melted butter
1⅓ cups confectioners' sugar
4 teaspoons water
½ teaspoon vanilla extract

> **Serves 8**
>
> Served on January 6, Three Kings' Day, the person who gets the small china doll is expected to host a Candlemas Day party on February 2.

1. Chop candied fruits into ¼-inch pieces. Beat the eggs until the yolks and whites are blended. Dissolve the yeast in the warm water. Heat the milk in a small saucepan at medium-high temperature until scalded.

2. Combine the granulated sugar, shortening, and salt in a large bowl. Pour in the scalded milk and mix until sugar is dissolved and the shortening is melted. Let cool to lukewarm.

3. Beat in 1 cup of the flour, the eggs, and yeast. Add more flour until a stiff dough is formed. Stir in 1½ cups of the candied fruits.

4. Turn the dough onto a floured surface and knead until smooth and satiny. Roll the dough to form a long rope; shape into a ring, sealing the ends together. Transfer to a greased baking sheet. Push the tiny china doll into the dough so that it is completely covered. Melt the butter in a small saucepan over low heat. Brush the ring with butter.

5. Cover with a towel and let rise in a warm place until it doubles in size, about 1½ hours.

6. Preheat oven to 375°.

7. Bake for 25 to 30 minutes or until golden brown. Cool on a wire rack.

8. Blend together the confectioners' sugar, 4 teaspoons water, and vanilla extract to make an icing. When the bread is cool, spread the icing over the top.

MOLLETES

Makes 16 large rolls

Serve as a breakfast treat with Easy Huevos Rancheros (page 359).

4 eggs
2 teaspoons (or 1 package) active dry yeast
½ cup warm water
½ cup butter
½ cup granulated sugar
½ teaspoon salt
1 tablespoon anise seeds
4½ cups (approximately) all-purpose flour
2 tablespoons light corn syrup

1. Leave the eggs out until they reach room temperature. Add the warm water to a large bowl and sprinkle the yeast on top. Stir until it dissolves. Melt the butter in a small pan on low heat.
2. Add 3 of the eggs, the melted butter, the sugar, salt, anise seed, and 2 cups of the flour to the bowl with the yeast; beat until smooth. Stir in enough additional flour to make a soft dough.
3. Turn the dough onto a lightly floured surface; knead until smooth and elastic, about 10 minutes.
4. Put the dough into a greased bowl and turn the dough over to grease the top. Cover and let rise in a warm place until the dough doubles in size, about 1 hour.
5. Punch the dough down and turn onto a lightly floured surface. Roll into a 12-inch square. Cut into fourths and cut each square into 4 triangles.
6. Place the triangles on a greased baking sheet, allowing space for rising. Cover and let rise in a warm place until they double in size, about 1 hour.
7. Preheat oven to 350°.
8. Separate the yolk and white of the remaining egg. Discard the white. Beat the egg yolk and corn syrup together until well blended. Generously brush over the triangles.
9. Bake for 10 to 15 minutes or until lightly browned. Serve warm.

PASTELITOS

1 cup dried apricots
1 cup water
½ cup granulated sugar
1 teaspoon vanilla extract,
  divided
2 cups all-purpose flour
¾ teaspoon salt

½ teaspoon baking powder
⅔ cup shortening
5 tablespoons ice water
1 cup confectioners' sugar
3 tablespoons cream

**Makes about
24 pastries**

For variety, use any dried fruit in this recipe. Peaches and pears make an especially tasty pastry.

1. Put the apricots and 1 cup of water into a medium-sized saucepan. Cover and bring to a boil. Reduce to a simmer and cook for 20 minutes. Pour the mixture into a blender or food processor and blend until smooth.
2. Combine the blended apricots and the granulated sugar in a saucepan. Cook on medium heat until thick, about 5 minutes. Let cool slightly. Stir in ½ teaspoon of the vanilla extract.
3. Preheat oven to 400°.
4. Mix together the flour, salt, and baking powder in a bowl. Cut in the shortening until crumbly. Add the cold water, 1 tablespoon at a time. Toss with a fork until the dough holds together. Divide the dough in half.
5. Roll out each half of dough into a 14" × 10" rectangle on a lightly floured surface.
6. Line a 13" × 9" × 2" baking pan with 1 rectangle of dough. Spread the apricot mixture evenly over the dough. Place the remaining dough on top. Seal the edges. Prick the top crust with a fork.
7. Bake for 25 minutes or until lightly browned. Let cool slightly.
8. Combine the confectioners' sugar and the remaining vanilla extract. Blend in the cream. Use as a frosting for the baked pastry. When cool, cut the pastry into squares.

TORREJAS DE COCO

1½-pound loaf cooked egg
    bread
¼ cup blanched almonds
4 cups granulated sugar
1½ cups water
2 cups shredded coconut
3 eggs

1 tablespoon flour
1 cup shortening
1 cinnamon stick
3 tablespoons raisins

1. Slice the egg bread into 24 slices. Chop the almonds into small pieces.
2. Dissolve 1 cup of the sugar in ½ cup of the water in a saucepan over medium heat. Bring to boil and boil for 3 minutes. Add the shredded coconut. Cook for about 15 minutes. Remove from heat and let cool slightly.
3. Spread the coconut paste on 12 slices of egg bread. Cover each with another slice of egg bread.
4. Beat the eggs with the flour. Dip both sides of the sandwiches in the egg.
5. Heat the shortening in a large frying pan to medium-high heat. Fry the sandwiches on each side for about 1 minute. Set on paper towels to cool.
6. Make a syrup by heating the remaining sugar and water with the cinnamon stick in a large frying pan; boil for 5 minutes. Add the browned sandwiches, reduce heat, and simmer for 5 minutes. Turn the sandwiches over and simmer for an additional 5 minutes.
7. Arrange the sandwiches on a serving dish. Garnish with raisins and almonds. Top with strained syrup.

PAN DE MUERTO

1 tablespoon (or 1 package)
  active dry yeast
½ cup warm water
5 eggs
1 tablespoon anise seed

¼ cup butter
½ cup granulated sugar
½ teaspoon salt
½ teaspoon ground nutmeg
2½ cups flour

Makes 1 loaf

This bread is tradition-ally served on the Day of the Dead, November 1, although you can exclude the gruesome decoration and make it any time of the year.

1. Dissolve the yeast in ¼ cup of the warm water. Separate 2 of the eggs' yolks from their whites. Beat together 2 eggs plus the 2 egg yolks. Steep the anise seed in the remaining ¼ cup warm water for 10 to 15 minutes. Melt the butter in a small saucepan on low heat.
2. Combine the dissolved yeast and 1 tablespoon of the sugar in a large mixing bowl; stir gently. Let sit for about 10 minutes or until it appears foamy.
3. Stir in the salt, ⅓ cup of the sugar, the nutmeg, the melted butter, the anise seed and water mixture, and the beaten eggs and yolks. Mix well while slowly adding the flour. The dough should be slightly sticky. Knead for 10 to 15 minutes.
4. Lightly coat a large mixing bowl with oil or shortening. Place the dough inside and cover with a towel. Place in a warm place and let rise until it is double in size, usually 1 to 2 hours.
5. Punch the dough down and place it on a floured surface. Remove a handful of dough and set aside. Shape the remaining dough into a round loaf about 1-inch thick and place it on a greased baking sheet.
6. Make a deep indentation in the center of the loaf with your fist. Form the small piece of dough set aside into 2 "bone" shapes about 4 inches long and 1 "skull" shape. Place these in the center indentation.
7. Cover the dough with a towel and place in a warm place to rise for 45 minutes to 1 hour. The dough should hold a fingerprint when pressed.
8. Preheat oven to 375°.
9. Bake for 30 minutes or until golden brown.
10. Beat the remaining egg and use it as a wash on the bread while the bread is still warm. Sprinkle with the remaining sugar.

MEXICAN SPOON BREAD

Serves 6

This is used as a side
dish to meals that
don't have tortillas.
Spoon it out
as you would
mashed potatoes.

½ cup shortening
1 pound Cheddar cheese
¼ cup canned jalapeño chili
  peppers
1 cup cornmeal or masa
  harina
2 eggs

15-ounce can cream-style corn
1 teaspoon salt
½ cup milk
½ teaspoon baking soda

1. Preheat oven to 350°.
2. Melt the shortening in a small saucepan on medium heat. Grate the Cheddar cheese. Cut the chili peppers into ¼-inch pieces.
3. Mix together the cornmeal and eggs until well blended. Add the shortening, corn, salt, milk, and baking soda; mix well.
4. Pour half of the mixture into a greased 9" × 9" casserole. Add a layer of jalapeños and half of the cheese. Add the remaining mixture and top with the rest of the cheese.
5. Place in the oven and bake for 45 to 50 minutes or until lightly browned.

Low-Fat Milk Products
Low-fat cheese and sour cream can be substituted in most recipes. However, they do not melt as well and do not hold up over a long time of heating, so they do not work well in dips and baked dishes.

CHAPTER 22
SALADS

FRESH CAULIFLOWER SALAD

1 head cauliflower
2 celery ribs
1 large red onion
1 garlic clove
6 slices bacon

1 cup Tomato Salsa (see recipe on page 282)
1 teaspoon salt
1 teaspoon ground cumin
½ cup sour cream

1. Break the cauliflower florets into bite-sized pieces. Slice the celery into ⅛-inch-thick slices. Peel the onion and chop into ¼-inch pieces. Peel and mince the garlic. Cook the bacon until crisp; drain off the bacon grease and discard. Crumble the bacon.
2. Combine the salsa, salt, and cumin. Add the cauliflower florets, celery, onion, garlic, and bacon; mix well. Chill covered for 2 hours.
3. Right before serving, combine the sour cream and salsa. Pour over vegetable mixtures and toss lightly.

BLACK BEAN AND CORN SALAD

1 red bell pepper
1 fresh habanero pepper
1 medium Vidalia onion
1 celery rib
¼ cup sour cream

¼ cup mayonnaise
2 (15-ounce) cans black beans, drained
2 (15-ounce) cans kernel corn, drained

1. Remove the stem and seeds from the red bell pepper and cut into ½-inch pieces. Remove the stem and seeds from the habanero pepper and cut into ¼-inch pieces. Remove the skin from the Vidalia onion and cut into ½-inch pieces. Cut the celery into ¼-inch pieces.
2. Combine the sour cream and mayonnaise until well blended.
3. Combine the beans, corn, red pepper, habanero, onion, and celery in a large mixing bowl. Stir in the dressing until well coated.
4. Cover and refrigerate overnight. Serve chilled.

MEXICAN POTATO SALAD

1 pound small red potatoes
1 quart water
1 large tomato
½ cup ripe olives
6 green onions
1 tablespoon fresh cilantro
¼ cup Tomato Salsa (see
  recipe on page 282)

1 tablespoon olive oil
2 tablespoons lime juice
½ teaspoon salt
½ teaspoon ground black
  pepper

Serves 8

Use this as a side
dish to complement
a spicy fish or
poultry meal.

1. Clean and quarter the potatoes. Boil in 1 quart of water until tender but not mushy. (They may also be cooked in the microwave.) Drain and set aside.
2. Cut the tomato into ½-inch cubes. Remove the pits from the olives and slice into ¼-inch pieces. Remove the skins from the onions and slice into ¼-inch pieces. Remove the stems from the cilantro.
3. Combine all the ingredients *except* the tomatoes and cook uncovered on low heat for 5 minutes.
4. Pour the sauce over the potatoes and store in a covered bowl in the refrigerator for 8 to 12 hours before serving.

What's a Potato?

Most of us eat a great deal of potatoes but are we aware of how many different types there are? New potatoes are usually very small brown potatoes that have a sweet flavor. Red potatoes can be either new or larger and have a mild flavor. Bakers are large, tough potatoes. New varieties such as golden-fleshed and purple-fleshed potatoes offer other tastes.

SHRIMP SALAD

Serves 6

This works well as a main course, especially for lunch. Serve with Jalapeño Corn Bread (page 330).

3 cups baby shrimp
3 eggs
1 small white onion
2 large red tomatoes
1 avocado
½ cup pimento-stuffed green
  olives
1 bunch fresh cilantro

½ cup olive oil
¼ cup lime juice
1 teaspoon salt
1 teaspoon ground black
  pepper

1. Boil the shrimp for 5 minutes in 6 cups water. Drain and rinse with cold water. Remove shells if necessary.
2. Boil the eggs in 4 cups of water for 10 minutes. Rinse with cold water. Peel and chop into small pieces.
3. Remove the skin from the onion and chop into ¼-inch pieces. Chop the tomatoes into ½-inch pieces. Peel and pit the avocado and chop into ½-inch pieces. Chop the olives into quarters. Remove the stems from the cilantro and chop the leaves roughly.
4. Combine the olive oil, lime juice, salt, and pepper; mix well.
5. Combine the shrimp, eggs, onion, tomatoes, avocado, olives, and cilantro in a large mixing bowl. Pour the lime juice and olive oil dressing over the top. Stir gently until the ingredients are well blended.
6. Chill before serving.

Clean Those Shrimp

After you've boiled a shrimp and taken off its shell, look at the back and you will see a large vein running up the middle of the back. This is the equivalent of the shrimp's intestines. If you don't remove this membrane, you will be eating shrimp poop!

CRAB SALAD

2 cups precooked crabmeat
1 medium jicama
1 celery rib
1 cup cucumber
½ cup pitted black olives
1 small white onion
1 fresh jalapeño pepper

⅓ cup mayonnaise
⅓ cup sour cream
1 teaspoon salt
1 teaspoon cayenne pepper

Serves 4

You can easily turn this into a mixed seafood salad by adding cooked shrimp, lobster meat, and scallops.

1. Shred the crabmeat. Peel the jicama and cut into ½-inch pieces. Cut the celery into ¼-inch pieces. Peel the cucumber and cut into ½-inch pieces. Cut the black olives in half. Remove the skin from the onion and cut into ¼-inch pieces. Remove the stem and seeds from the jalapeño and cut into ¼-inch pieces.
2. Mix together the mayonnaise and sour cream.
3. Combine the crabmeat, jicama, celery, cucumber, black olives, onion, jalapeño, salt, and cayenne pepper in a large mixing bowl. Add the mayonnaise and sour cream mixture. Mix until well blended.
4. Serve chilled.

Jicama

Jicama is a root vegetable with a crisp, white flesh. It has a very mild flavor that will pick up the flavor of dressings or spices. It's an excellent addition to salads because it looks so beautiful nestled among all the other colored foods!

BROCCOLI SALAD

Serves 6

Serve on a bed of lettuce with a cold meat and cheese tray for a complete, summertime meal.

4 cups broccoli florets
1 medium-sized yellow onion
1 cup yellow raisins
1 cup dry cooking sherry
1 cup canned mandarin oranges, undrained
½ cup lime juice
½ cup olive oil
1 tablespoon dried cilantro
1 teaspoon salt
1 teaspoon ground white pepper
½ cup blanched almond slivers

1. Cut the broccoli florets into bite-sized pieces. Remove the skin from the onion and cut into ¼-inch pieces. Place the raisins in the sherry and let soak for 15 minutes.
2. Combine the juice from the mandarin oranges, the lime juice, cilantro, olive oil, salt, and white pepper; mix well.
3. Combine the broccoli, onion, raisins, mandarin oranges, and blanched almond slivers; mix until well blended.
4. Pour dressing on top of the broccoli mixture and stir until well blended.
5. Refrigerate for at least 1 hour before serving.

Coriander
Coriander is an herb of the parsley family. The fresh leaves of the plant, called "cilantro" or "Chinese parsley," are commonly used in Mexican cooking. The leaves produce a flavor that is completely different from that of coriander seeds. The seeds are the dried ripe fruits of the herb, and they come either whole or ground. It is considered an aromatic spice because it gives off a wonderful smell in addition to a strong flavor. It is especially good when the whole seeds are slightly roasted in a small frying pan before being ground and added to a dish.

CACTUS SALAD

2 cups canned cactus strips
2 large red tomatoes
½ cup pitted black olives
2 tablespoons fresh cilantro
4 medium-sized red radishes
¼ cup olive oil
¼ cup red wine vinegar

1 teaspoon garlic salt
1 teaspoon ground white
  pepper
½ teaspoon cayenne pepper

> **Serves 6**
>
> Canned cactus strips are available at most large grocery stores today, although you can substitute any vegetable such as broccoli or cauliflower.

1. Drain off the water from the cactus strips. Cut the tomatoes into 1-inch pieces. Cut the black olives in half. Remove the stems from the cilantro and chop. Remove the stems and roots from the radishes and cut into ½-inch pieces. Combine these ingredients in a large mixing bowl.
2. In a small container with a cover, mix the olive oil, vinegar, garlic salt, white pepper, and cayenne pepper; shake well to mix.
3. Pour the dressing over the vegetables and toss until well mixed.
4. Chill before serving.

What about the Stickers?

For those of us in northern climates, the idea of eating cactus is, well, terrifying. However, it really is quite juicy and flavorful. Many people in the southwestern United States will simply pick their own backyard cactus. The canned variety is much mushier and loses some of its flavor but is a good place to start for those new to this delicacy.

MIXED VEGETABLES WITH HOT PEPPER DRESSING

Serves 6

Experiment by adding smoked or pickled peppers to the dressing instead of fresh peppers.

1 cup broccoli florets
1 cup cauliflower florets
1 cup fresh green beans
1 carrot
4 radishes
½ cup pimiento-stuffed green olives
1 cup canned or frozen corn kernals

2 large red tomatoes
2 fresh or canned serrano chili peppers
2 garlic cloves
1 cup dry red wine
1 cup olive oil
½ teaspoon dried oregano
½ teaspoon salt
½ teaspoon cayenne pepper

1. Cut the broccoli and cauliflower florets into bite-sized pieces. Cut the ends off the green beans and cut the beans in half. Peel the carrot and cut into ¼-inch rounds. Cut the roots and stems from the radishes and cut the radishes into ¼-inch rounds. Cut the green olives into quarters. Drain off the water from the corn. (Thaw if using frozen corn.) Cut the tomatoes into 16 wedges each.
2. Mix these ingredients in a large mixing bowl.
3. Remove the stems (but not seeds) from the chili peppers and mince. Remove the skin from the garlic cloves and mince. Mix together the chilies, garlic, red wine, and olive oil. Add the oregano, salt, and cayenne pepper. Place in a small container with a cover. Cover and shake until well mixed.
4. Pour the dressing over the other ingredients; toss gently until well mixed.
5. Best if chilled before serving.

What Happened to the Salad?

Mexicans typically don't serve a salad course with their meals. If a green salad is served, it typically takes the place of the vegetable. As a result, many of their salads feature a wide variety of vegetables.

CARROT AND CHILI PEPPER SALAD

1 large carrot
2 celery ribs
3 green onions or scallions
1 fresh jalapeño pepper

1 cup canned pineapple
   chunks, drained
1 cup light mayonnaise

Serves 4
Serve with Empanaditas de Carne (page 496).

1. Grate the carrot. Cut the celery into ¼-inch pieces. Remove the roots from the green onions and chop into ¼-inch pieces, including the green tops. Remove the stem and seeds from the jalapeño and cut into ¼-inch pieces.
2. Combine the carrot, celery, green onions, jalapeño, and pineapple in a medium-sized mixing bowl; stir until well mixed.
3. Add the mayonnaise and stir until all the ingredients are covered.

The Food Processor

As with all electrical gadgets, a food processor simply saves time. Several decades ago, our grandmothers achieved the same—and sometimes better—dishes by cutting, grinding, and mashing by hand. Remember, you never have to use a food processor, blender, or nut grinder. Just count on it taking more time if you don't.

CUCUMBER MOUSSE

Serves 4

Use as the salad course when serving Chicken Tablecloth Stainer (page 404).

1 small white onion
1 medium cucumber
1 (3-ounce) package lime-flavored gelatin
¾ cup boiling water
1 cup cottage cheese
1 cup mayonnaise
1 cup slivered almonds

1. Peel the onion and grate until you have 2 tablespoons. Grate the cucumber until you have ¾ cup.
2. Dissolve the gelatin in the boiling water. Stir in the onion, cottage cheese, and mayonnaise until well blended.
3. Fold in the cucumber and almonds.
4. Pour the mixture into a 1-quart mold. Refrigerate until set.

CARROT SALAD

Serves 4

This makes an excellent first course to Southwestern Fried Chicken (page 510).

6 large, fresh carrots
½ cup golden raisins
¾ cup orange juice
1 teaspoon granulated sugar
⅛ teaspoon salt
¼ cup pistachio meats

1. Peel and grate the carrots.
2. Combine the carrots, raisins, orange juice, sugar, and salt in a medium-sized bowl. Cover and refrigerate for 3 to 4 hours before serving.
3. Right before serving, mix in the pistachio meats.

ZESTY CHEESE SALAD

1 medium-sized red onion
4 garlic cloves
2 small poblano chilies
1 large avocado
1 medium jicama
2/3 cup fresh cilantro leaves
1 pound mozzarella cheese
1 teaspoon ground cumin

1/2 teaspoon fresh oregano
  (or 1/4 teaspoon dry)
2/3 cup olive oil
1/2 teaspoon salt
1/2 teaspoon ground black
  pepper
1/2 cup lime juice

Serves 12

Serve with Grilled
Swordfish (page 380).

1. Peel the onion and cut into 1/4-inch pieces. Peel and mince the garlic. Remove the stem and seeds from the chilies and cut into 1/4-inch pieces. Peel and pit the avocado and slice into 2-inch lengths about 1/4-inch thick. Peel the jicama and cut into pieces about the size of matchsticks. Remove the stems from the cilantro and chop the leaves into 1/4-inch pieces. Cut the mozzarella into 1/2-inch cubes.
2. In a large mixing bowl, combine the onion, chilies, avocado, jicama, and cheese; toss until well mixed.
3. In a medium-sized container with a lid, combine the garlic, cumin, oregano, olive oil, salt, black pepper, and lime juice. Cover and shake until well mixed.
4. Pour the dressing over the vegetables and cheese; toss lightly

How to Substitute Dry Spices

Because dry spices have the water taken out of them, you usually substitute half the amount of dry for the fresh variety. However, many spices lose their flavor when dried, so it's best to use what the recipe calls for if at all possible.

MEXICAN COLESLAW

Serves 6

Serve as a salad with
Barbecued Pork Ribs
(page 416).

3 tablespoons salad oil
½ cup cider vinegar
2 tablespoons white granulated
   sugar
1½ teaspoons salt
1 teaspoon paprika
½ teaspoon dry mustard
1 teaspoon celery seeds

1 large cabbage
1 green bell pepper
1 small yellow onion
¼ cup canned diced pimientos
½ cup pitted black olives

1. In a small container with a cover, combine the salad oil, cider vinegar, white sugar, salt, paprika, dried mustard, and celery seed. Cover and shake until well mixed.
2. Remove the outer leaves of the cabbage and discard. Shred the remaining cabbage into pieces about the size of wooden matchsticks.
3. Remove the seeds and stem from the bell pepper and cut into ¼-inch pieces. Peel the onion and cut into ¼-inch pieces. Dice the pimientos if necessary. Cut the black olives into ¼-inch rounds.
4. In a large serving bowl, combine the cabbage, bell pepper, onion, pimientos, and black olives; toss gently until well mixed.
5. Pour the dressing on top and toss gently until well covered.
6. Cover and refrigerate for at least 1 hour before serving.

Watch the Dirt
Clean root vegetables thoroughly by scrubbing them with a nail brush or scouring pad designated for that purpose. Because they grow in fertilized soil, they can harbor bacteria on their skins.

VEGETABLE-STUFFED AVOCADOS

1 head cauliflower
2 tablespoons red wine vinegar
1½ teaspoons granulated sugar
¼ teaspoon salt
⅓ cup vegetable oil

1 cup canned green peas
½ cup black olives
¼ cup canned pimiento
3 large ripe avocados

Serves 6
Use as the main course for a summer luncheon or serve as the salad course for a large dinner.

1. Cut the cauliflower florets into pieces about the size of a dime until you have about 2 full cups. Chop black olives into ¼-inch pieces. Chop pimiento into ¼-inch pieces.
2. Combine the red wine vinegar, sugar, salt, and vegetable oil in a small container with a cover. Cover and shake until well mixed.
3. Combine the cauliflower, peas, olives, and pimiento in a medium-sized bowl. Cover with vinegar and oil dressing; mix well. Cover and refrigerate for 4 to 6 hours.
4. Peel, halve, and remove the pits from the avocadoes. Fill with cauliflower salad.

Appetizer Advice

Appetizers should complement the meal to come, not overpower it. Serve items that have milder but similar flavors to the main dish. Remember not to have so many appetizers that the guests aren't hungry for the main meal.

SPINACH SALAD

1 large bunch of spinach
1 large red onion
4 medium-sized red radishes
2 serrano chilies
½ cup goat cheese
½ cup hulled pepitas (pumpkin seeds)

½ cup olive oil
¼ cup dry white wine
3 tablespoons lime juice
1 tablespoon Tabasco sauce

1. Remove the stems from the spinach, wash leaves, and dry.
2. Remove the skin from the onion and cut into ¼-inch rounds. Remove the stems and roots from the radishes and cut into ¼-inch rounds. Remove the stems and seeds from the chilies and cut into ½-inch pieces. Crumble the goat cheese.
3. Combine the spinach, onion, radishes, chilies, and *pepitas* in a large mixing bowl.
4. In a small container with a cover, combine the olive oil, wine, lime juice, and Tabasco sauce. Cove and shake until well blended.
5. Pour the dressing over the salad and toss until well coated. Top with crumbled goat cheese.

When Did the Greeks Arrive?

Yes, the Mexicans do use feta cheese. It is very similar to many goat cheeses that have been used since ancient times. In addition, it complements many of their hot, spicy dishes very well, so they have adopted this traditionally Greek cheese.

CHAPTER 23
EGGS

CHILI RELLENO SOUFFLÉ

1 pound mild Cheddar cheese
1 pound Monterey jack cheese
½ cup canned green chili peppers

4 eggs
1 cup evaporated milk
⅔ cup flour
1 (8-ounce) can tomato sauce

1. Preheat oven to 350°.
2. Grate the cheese. Cut the chili peppers into ¼-inch strips.
3. Mix together the eggs, milk, and flour.
4. Layer ⅓ of the cheese, then ½ of the egg mixture, and ½ of the chilies in a rectangular baking pan. Repeat layers. Top soufflé with the tomato sauce.
5. Bake uncovered for 30 to 45 minutes. Cover with the remaining cheese and bake for 15 minutes.

SPINACH EGG BAKE

2 cups cooked ham
1 (10-ounce) package chopped spinach
8 ounces fresh mushrooms
1 small white onion
¼ cup canned jalapeño peppers

¾ pound Cheddar cheese
6 eggs
2 cups small-curd cottage cheese
½ cup butter
6 tablespoons flour

1. Preheat oven to 350°.
2. Cut the ham into 1-inch pieces. Thaw the spinach and squeeze out the water. Cut the mushrooms into thin slices. Remove the skin from onion and chop into ¼-inch pieces. Drain off the water from the jalapeños. Grate the cheese. Beat the eggs until the whites and yolks are well blended.
3. Mix together all the ingredients in a large mixing bowl. Stir well until all ingredients are blended. Pour into a 9" × 13" baking dish. Bake for 1 hour. Let stand for 10 minutes before cutting.

MEXICAN FRITTATA

3 cups whole milk
1½ cups flour
½ teaspoon salt
6 eggs
1 tablespoon vegetable oil
1½ pounds fresh chili peppers
   (type of your choosing)

1½ pounds medium Cheddar
   cheese
1½ pounds Monterey jack
   cheese
1 avocado
1 red bell pepper

Serves 4

This is a perfect breakfast meal served with Mexican Coffee (page 545).

1. Preheat oven to 375°.
2. Blend the milk, flour, salt, and eggs.
3. Spread the oil over the bottom and sides of a 9" × 13" pan.
4. Remove the stems and seeds from the chili peppers and cut into 1-inch pieces.
5. Shred the cheeses and mix.
6. Place half of the chili peppers in a layer on the bottom of the pan. Top with half of the cheese. Add the rest of the chili peppers. Add the rest of the cheese. Pour the egg mixture over the top.
7. Bake for 40 minutes.
8. Remove the skin and seed from the avocado and cut into slices. Remove the seeds and stem from the red pepper and cut into 1-inch pieces. Use the avocado and red pepper as garnish.

All about Eggs

Egg yolks contain all of the fat and cholesterol in an egg. Use egg whites instead of whole eggs when making pasta, cakes, and other dishes. Usually 2 egg whites can be substituted for 1 whole egg.

EGG-STUFFED ROLLS

2 quarts water

6 eggs

2 pounds Velveeta cheese

15-ounce can pitted black olives

1 medium-sized yellow onion

½ cup canned jalapeño peppers, or 4 fresh jalapeños

1 cup Tomato Salsa (see recipe on page 282)

1 cup vegetable oil

¼ cup vinegar

1 tablespoon garlic salt

3 dozen small French rolls

1. Bring the water to boil in a medium-sized pot. Add the eggs and cook at a boil for 6 minutes. Turn off the heat but keep the eggs in the water for 4 more minutes. Run cold water over the eggs. When the eggs are cool enough to handle, remove the shells and chop the eggs into ¼-inch pieces.
2. Grate the cheese. Cut the black olives into ¼-inch pieces. Peel the onion and cut into ¼-inch pieces. Drain off the juice from the jalapeños and cut into ¼-inch pieces.
3. Combine the eggs, cheese, olives, onions, jalapeños, tomato salsa, vegetable oil, vinegar, and garlic salt in a medium-sized mixing bowl. Cover and refrigerate for 8 to 12 hours.
4. Preheat oven to 300°.
5. Cut off the tops of the French rolls and dig out some of the bread. Fill with the egg mixture and wrap the stuffed rolls with waxed paper.
6. Place on a baking sheet and bake for 1 hour.

Dealing with Sticky Cheese
To save money, buy blocks of cheese and grate them yourself. To keep the cheese from sticking together, add a little cornstarch and toss the cheese until mixed through.

EASY HUEVOS RANCHEROS

1 avocado
1 tablespoon vegetable oil
4 eggs
4 Corn Tortillas (see recipe on page 283)

1 cup Tomato Salsa (see recipe on page 282)

Serves 4

Serve with a side of Extra-special Frijoles Refritos (page 451).

1. Peel the avocado and remove the pit. Slice the fruit into ½-inch-thick slices.
2. Heat the oil to medium temperature in a medium-sized frying pan. Add the eggs. Fry to your liking.
3. Remove the eggs and put the tortillas in the frying pan. Fry for 30 seconds on each side. Place 1 egg on top of each flattened tortilla. Cover the egg with salsa. Garnish with avocado slices.

HUEVOS BOGOTANO

½ pound ground sausage
½ pound fresh or frozen corn
12 eggs

¼ teaspoon onion powder
½ teaspoon salt
½ teaspoon ground black pepper

Serves 6

Spice this dish up any way you would like. Add hot peppers, oregano, or dill weed, for example.

1. Crumble the sausage and sauté over medium heat in a medium-sized frying pan until cooked but not browned, stirring frequently. Remove the sausage and spread on a paper towel to absorb excess fat. Wipe the grease from the frying pan with a paper towel.
2. In a small saucepan, heat the corn at medium temperature until thoroughly warmed.
3. Crack the eggs into a medium-sized mixing bowl. Add the onion powder, salt, and pepper. Beat until light and fluffy.
4. Pour the eggs in the frying pan and stir in the sausage and corn. Cook over low heat, stirring frequently, until the eggs are done.

EGGS IN POTATO SHELLS

Serves 2

Serve with a side of fresh fruit to make this a complete meal.

1 large baking potato (at least 8 ounces)
2 tablespoons sour cream
1 small yellow onion
2 tablespoons fresh green bell pepper

1 tablespoon canned jalapeño pepper, or 1 fresh jalapeño
1 medium-sized red tomato
1 teaspoon butter
2 eggs
1 cup grated Cheddar cheese

1. Preheat oven to 350°.
2. Cut the potato in half lengthwise. Using a spoon, scoop out the inside of the potato, leaving ¼-inch-thick shell.
3. In a small mixing bowl, combine the potato pulp and 1 tablespoon of the sour cream; mash and set aside.
4. Peel and mince the onion. If using a whole green bell pepper, remove the stem and seeds; cut into ¼-inch pieces. Drain off the juice from the jalapeño pepper and mince. Remove the skin from tomato; cut into ¼-inch pieces.
5. In a small frying pan, melt the butter. Add the onion and pepper. Sauté over medium-high heat, stirring frequently, until the vegetables are tender.
6. Add the tomatoes and continue cooking, stirring frequently. Cook for about 3 minutes.
7. Add about half of the sautéed vegetables to the potato pulp mixture and stir to thoroughly combine. Spoon half of mixture into each reserved potato shell.
8. Place the potato halves in a 1-quart casserole dish. Using the back of a spoon, make a deep indentation in the center of each potato. Break 1 egg into a small dish, then slide it into the indentation. Repeat with the second potato.
9. Place in the oven and bake for 50 minutes. Top with Cheddar cheese and return to the oven for 5 minutes or until the cheese is melted. Top each egg with the remaining vegetable mixture and sour cream right before serving.

ROYAL EGGS

¼ cup raisins
½ cup dry sherry
12 eggs
2 cups granulated sugar
1 cup water

1 cinnamon stick
¼ cup slivered almonds

Serves 6

Serve this as a dessert at your next traditional Mexican meal.

1. Preheat oven to 325°.
2. Soak the raisins in ¼ cup of the sherry. Separate the eggs and discard the whites.
3. Beat the egg yolks until they form a ribbon when poured from the beater. Pour into a buttered shallow pan. Set this pan in another larger pan with about 1 inch of water in it.
4. Bake for 20 to 25 minutes, or until set. Remove from oven and cool on a wire rack. When cool, cut into 1-inch cubes.
5. While the eggs are cooling, combine the sugar, water, and cinnamon stick in a saucepan and bring to boil. Reduce heat to medium-low and simmer for about 5 minutes, stirring until all the sugar is dissolved. Remove the cinnamon stick.
6. Carefully place the egg cubes in the sauce. Continue simmering over very low heat until the cubes are well-saturated with the syrup. Add the soaked raisins and remaining sherry. Sprinkle with slivered almonds.

Finding Fresh Eggs

Fresh eggs will be translucent when held up to the light. When you break the egg, the white should be clear and the yolk should be shiny. Yolks can vary in color, depending on the diet and breed of chicken the egg came from.

EGGS CHILAQUILES

Serves 4

Serve with fresh cantaloupe and honeydew melon slices.

4 Corn Tortillas (see recipe on page 283)
2 medium-sized red tomatoes
1 small white onion
2 tablespoons butter or margarine
4 eggs
½ teaspoon salt
¼ teaspoon ground black pepper
½ teaspoon Tabasco or other hot sauce
½ cup grated Parmesan cheese

1. Cut the tortillas into ½-inch strips. Destem the tomatoes and chop into ¼-inch pieces. Peel the onion and chop into ¼-inch pieces. Beat the eggs.
2. Melt the butter in a skillet. Fry the tortilla strips until golden brown.
3. Stir in the tomatoes and onion and heat to boiling.
4. Stir in the eggs, salt, pepper, and Tabasco sauce; cook until the eggs are set, stirring frequently.
5. Top with Parmesan cheese. Serve immediately.

SCRAMBLED EGG TACOS

Serves 4

Serve with Pastelitos (page 337).

1 teaspoon butter
½ cup Tomato Salsa (see recipe on page 282)
8 eggs
⅓ cup cream
½ teaspoon salt
4 Corn Tortillas (see recipe on page 283)
½ cup shredded Monterey jack cheese

1. Melt the butter in a large frying pan. Add the tomato salsa and heat until the onion is soft.
2. Beat the eggs with the cream and salt. Pour the egg mixture into the salsa and cook over medium heat, stirring constantly, until the eggs are set.
3. While the eggs are cooking, heat the tortillas in an ungreased medium-hot skillet or griddle, turning frequently.
4. Place a hot, soft tortilla on a plate and spoon eggs on top. Sprinkle with cheese. Serve immediately.

CHILI EGG NOODLES

6 eggs
½ teaspoon chili powder
½ teaspoon salt
1 cup flour
2 dried ancho chilies

1 cup whipping cream
1 cup grated Cheddar cheese
½ teaspoon paprika

Serves 6

Serve as a side dish
for Mexican Meat Loaf
(page 419).

1. Separate the eggs and discard the whites. Combine the egg yolks, chili powder, and salt in a small bowl. Mix, adding the flour until you have a workable dough.
2. Roll out the dough on a flat, floured surface. Let air dry about 1 hour. Cut into noodles by drawing a knife through the dough.
3. Bring 2 quarts of water to a boil in a large saucepan. Add the noodles; boil for 10 minutes. Drain and rinse in cold water.
4. Preheat oven to 350°.
5. Wash, peel, and seed the chilies. Cut into quarters and put in a blender or food processor. Add the whipped cream and blend until the chilies are finely chopped.
6. In a greased 2-quart casserole dish, layer the noodles, cheese, then sauce. Sprinkle the top with paprika.
7. Bake for 30 minutes or until bubbling hot.

Different Eggs

While Americans typically only eat chicken eggs, other birds' eggs can provide some interesting taste sensations. Try duck or goose eggs when baking to give more fluffiness to your cakes and dessert bars. They also have a sweeter taste in casseroles and even as scrambled eggs.

CHAPTER 24
STEWS AND MOLES

BEEF MOLE

3 pounds stewing beef
3 fresh jalapeño peppers
2 medium-sized white onions
2 garlic cloves
3 medium-sized red tomatoes
3 tablespoons vegetable oil

4 medium potatoes
1 medium zucchini (about
  10 inches long)
2 teaspoons salt
1 teaspoon ground black
  pepper

1. Place the beef in a large saucepan and fill with water to about 2 inches from the top of the pan. Bring to a boil, cover, and reduce heat to medium. Cook for 2 hours. Drain and set aside.
2. Remove the stems and seeds from the jalapeños and cut into quarters. Remove the skin from the onion and cut into quarters. Remove the skin from the garlic cloves. Remove the skin from the tomatoes and cut into quarters. Place these ingredients in blender or food processor and blend on medium until all the ingredients are puréed. They should look as though they are chopped into very small pieces, but not blended into a paste.
3. Heat the oil on medium-high setting in a large frying pan. Add the purée and cook, stirring constantly for 5 minutes.
4. Peel the potatoes and cut into 1-inch cubes. Place in a medium-sized saucepan, cover with water, and boil until tender. Drain and set aside.
5. Cut the zucchini into 1-inch cubes.
6. Combine all the ingredients in a frying pan; stir gently. Heat on medium setting for 10 minutes.

Can You Really Eat a Mole?

Moles (pronounced mo-LAY) are actually stews made with thick, intensely flavorful sauces, usually featuring different chili peppers and nuts. Sometimes the mole is poured over uncut pieces of meat, such as chicken, so the meat can stew that way. Most often, however, the meat is cut up and made part of the sauce.

BEEF AND CACTUS STEW

2 pounds beef steak
2 tablespoons olive oil
1 medium-sized yellow onion
4 garlic cloves
1 cup canned cactus pieces
4 fresh jalapeño chilies
2 chipotle chilies

4 green tomatoes
2 medium-sized red tomatoes
1 teaspoon dried oregano
1 teaspoon salt
1 teaspoon ground black
  pepper

> **Serves 4**
>
> This is excellent
> served with Red Rice
> (page 286).

1. Cut the beef into 1-inch pieces. Place in a large frying pan with the olive oil. Heat to medium temperature. Cook beef until brown on all sides.
2. Remove the skin from the onion and cut into 1-inch pieces. Remove the skin from the garlic and mince. Drain off the water from the cactus and cut into 1-inch pieces. Remove the stems and seeds from the chilies and cut into ¼-inch pieces. Cut the green and red tomatoes into 1-inch pieces.
3. Add all the ingredients to the beef and reduce the heat to low. Cover and cook for 1 hour, stirring periodically.

 What Oil to Use?

In most recipes you can substitute virgin olive oil for the veg-etable oil. It gives a slightly more tangy taste. Sunflower and soy oil have the lightest flavors and are the healthiest. Corn oil is slightly heavy and gives a heartier feel to a dish. Traditionally, Mexican cooking uses lard, which adds a beefy flavor but contributes to heart disease.

CHICKEN DRY SOUP

Serves 4

Serve with Extra-special Frijoles Refritos (page 451).

4 boneless, skinless chicken breasts
1 medium-sized yellow onion
2 garlic cloves
1 tablespoon olive oil

1 cup Tomato Salsa (see recipe on page 282)
4 cups Chicken Stock (see recipe on page 286)
5 Corn Tortillas (see recipe on page 283)

1. Cut the chicken breasts into 1-inch cubes. Remove the skin from the onion and cut into ¼-inch pieces. Remove the skin from the garlic and cut into thin slices.
2. Heat the olive oil in a large frying pan on medium. Add the chicken, onion, and garlic to the frying pan and cook until the chicken is brown on all sides.
3. Reduce the heat to low and add the salsa and stock; mix well. Cook for 30 minutes, uncovered, stirring periodically.
4. Tear the tortillas into 1-inch pieces. Add to the frying pan and stir well. Cover and simmer for 1 hour.
5. Remove cover and simmer until the dish is moist but not runny.

Onion Varieties

Onions vary in sweetness. Vidalia tend to be the sweetest, followed by red, then yellow. White onions are the least sweet and are better in meat dishes than in soups.

MEXICAN CHICKEN CASSEROLE

4 boneless, skinless chicken
    breasts
1 small onion
12 Flour Tortillas (see recipe
    on page 284)
1½ cups grated Cheddar
    cheese
1 (10¾-ounce) can cream of
    mushroom condensed soup

1 (10¾-ounce) can cream of
    chicken condensed soup
1 cup sour cream
½ cup canned chopped
    jalapeño peppers, drained
    (or 4 fresh jalapeños)
1 cup Tomato Salsa (see
    recipe on page 282)

> **Serves 4**
>
> Serve over a bed of
> lettuce with fresh
> Tostadas (page 285).

1. Preheat oven to 300°.
2. Cut the chicken into 1-inch cubes. Peel the onion and grate using the fine side of a vegetable grater. Tear the tortillas into eighths.
3. Combine the onion, cheese, soups, sour cream, and jalapeños in a medium-sized bowl. Make layers in a casserole dish using ⅓ of the corn tortillas, soup mixture, chicken, then salsa. Repeat twice, in that order.
4. Cover and bake for 2 hours.

Nuns as Cooks
Many of the Mexican recipes that combine European ingredients such as sherry with traditional Mexican ingredients such as eggs actually were invented by Spanish nuns who first came to Mexico as missionaries.

BEEF AND BEAN STEW

2 pounds round steak
1 yellow onion
4 red tomatoes
1 beef bouillon cube
2 cups canned kidney beans
½ cup canned chopped
   jalapeño peppers

¼ teaspoon ground black
   pepper
½ teaspoon garlic salt
1 tablespoon chili powder
1 tablespoon prepared yellow
   mustard

1. Cut the beef into 1-inch cubes. Peel and chop the onion into ¼-inch
   pieces. Cut the tomatoes into quarters. Crush the bouillon cube. Drain
   the kidney beans and jalapeños.
2. Mix together the meat, pepper, garlic salt, chili powder, and mustard
   in a large pot. Cover with the onion, tomatoes, crushed bouillon cube,
   beans, and jalapeños; mix well.
3. Cover the pot, and cook on medium-low temperature for 2 hours.
   Stir periodically.

Tomato Types

*All tomatoes are not alike. Substitute plum tomatoes for a more
robust flavor. Choose golden tomatoes for a more mellow taste.
Reserve pricier hot-house tomatoes for recipes in which tomatoes are
the main ingredient.*

CALDO DE REZ

1½ pounds beef stew meat
1 medium cabbage
1 small white onion
1 celery rib
4 medium-sized red tomatoes
½ green bell pepper
4 medium baking potatoes
1 teaspoon dried cilantro

1 teaspoon salt
½ teaspoon ground black
  pepper
1 teaspoon Tabasco or other
  hot sauce.

Serves 6

Serve with Pineapple
and Coconut Salad
(page 462).

1. Remove any fat from the stew meat. Cut the cabbage into wedges. Peel the onion and chop into ¼-inch pieces. Chop the celery into ¼-inch pieces. Cut the tomatoes into 1-inch pieces. If using a fresh green bell pepper, remove the stem and seeds, then chop into ¼-inch pieces. Peel the potatoes and cut into 1-inch cubes.
2. Place all the ingredients into a large pot and stir until well mixed. Cover and bring to a boil; reduce temperature to medium-low and simmer for 30 minutes.

Too Salty?

If the dish tastes too salty, add a teaspoon each of cider vinegar and sugar to the recipe. They will neutralize the salt without adding additional flavor.

PORK POSOLE

4 medium-sized yellow onions
6 medium-sized red tomatoes
12 fresh serrano chilies
5 garlic cloves
4 pounds lean pork roast
2 pounds fresh or frozen
  hominy
¼ cup granulated sugar

3 tablespoons salt
1 teaspoon ground black pepper
2 cups fresh or canned tomato
  sauce
2 tablespoons lemon juice

1. Peel the onions and chop into ¼-inch pieces. Cut the tomatoes into ¼-inch pieces. Remove the stems and seeds from the chili peppers. Peel the garlic and chop into ¼-inch pieces.
2. In a large stew pot, combine the roast, onions, chili peppers, garlic, hominy, sugar, salt, and pepper. Cover with water and bring to a boil. Turn heat to medium-low and cook until the meat is done and the hominy is tender but not mushy, about 3 hours. Stir occasionally and add more water if necessary.
3. Remove the meat and shred. Return the meat to the pot.
4. Add the tomatoes and tomato sauce. Cook uncovered at medium temperature for 30 minutes.
5. Stir in the lemon juice right before serving.

What Is Posole?

Mexican cooking has many dishes with no European equivalents. Although this is a stew because many ingredients are mixed with liquids, posole tends to be heavier and thicker than a traditional stew. If the hominy is not overcooked, it will be a bit crunchy, adding a unique texture to what most North Americans think of in a stew.

BEEF PICADILLO

1 small white onion
2 garlic cloves
1 medium Granny Smith apple
1 pound ground beef
1 cup canned or fresh tomato
    sauce
½ cup raisins
¼ cup toasted almond slivers
1 tablespoon vinegar

1 teaspoon granulated sugar
1 teaspoon salt
¼ teaspoon ground cinnamon
¼ teaspoon ground cumin
⅛ teaspoon ground black
    pepper

Serves 6

This is excellent served with Broccoli Salad (page 346).

1. Peel the onion and cut into ¼-inch pieces. Peel and mince the garlic. Peel and remove the core and stem from the apple; cut into ¼-inch pieces.
2. Place the ground beef, onion, and garlic in a medium-sized frying pan. Cook on medium heat until the ground beef is browned.
3. Stir in the remaining ingredients.
4. Continue cooking on medium heat, stirring periodically, until all the ingredients are well blended.

Substitute Mushrooms

To turn any meat dish into an instant vegetarian entrée, substitute morel mushrooms for the meat. Be sure to substitute by volume, not weight, because even these heavier mushrooms weigh less than meat.

MEXICAN MEATBALL STEW

Serves 6

Serve with fresh Corn Tortillas (page 283) and Tomato Salsa (page 282).

1 large white onion
6 carrots
6 new potatoes (small)
15-ounce can plum tomatoes or
    4 fresh plum tomatoes
2 large fresh jalapeño peppers
3 garlic cloves
1½ pounds lean ground beef
½ pound ground sausage
1 teaspoon dried cilantro
1 teaspoon salt

1 teaspoon ground black
    pepper
1 teaspoon ground cumin
1 teaspoon celery salt
1 teaspoon garlic powder
2 tablespoons vegetable oil
1 cup canned hominy
15-ounce can red kidney beans
6 cups water
3 beef bouillon cubes, crushed

1. Peel the onion and cut into ¼-inch pieces. Peel the carrots and cut into quarters. Wash the potatoes and quarter. If using fresh tomatoes, cut into quarters. Remove the stems and seeds from the jalapeño peppers and cut into ¼-inch rounds. Peel and mince the garlic.
2. Combine the ground beef and ground sausage. Add the cilantro, salt, black pepper, cumin, celery salt, and garlic powder. Mix well with your hands. Form meatballs slightly smaller than golf balls.
3. Heat the oil in a large skillet at medium-high. Add the meatballs and garlic. Cook until browned, flipping meatballs so all sides are browned. Drain off the grease. Set the meatballs on paper towels to soak up excess grease.
4. Transfer to a large stew pot. Add the onions, carrots, potatoes, jalapeños, hominy, kidney beans, and water. Cook for 1 hour on medium-low heat or until the potatoes and carrots are tender.
5. Add the bouillon and tomatoes.

TOMATO DRY SOUP

1 large white onion
2 garlic cloves
2 cups canned tomatoes, with juice
10–12 stale Corn Tortillas (see recipe on page 283)
½ cup vegetable oil, divided
1 teaspoon salt

½ teaspoon ground black pepper
½ teaspoon dried oregano
1 cup whipping cream
1 cup grated Parmesan cheese
1 teaspoon paprika

Serves 6

Use Flour Tortillas (page 284) for a slightly different taste.

1. Preheat oven to 350°.
2. Peel the onion and chop into ¼-inch pieces. Peel and mince the garlic. Roughly chop the tomatoes, reserving the juice. Cut the tortillas into ½-inch-wide strips.
3. In a large saucepan, heat 2 tablespoons of the oil to medium temperature. Add the onion and garlic. Cook until the onion is soft but not brown. Add the tomatoes, salt, pepper, and oregano, and stir until blended. Heat to simmering and cook for about 10 minutes.
4. Heat the remaining oil in a large frying pan. Fry the tortilla strips until limp, not crisp. Set on paper towels to absorb excess grease.
5. In an ovenproof casserole, arrange layers as follows: a little tomato sauce, a handful of tortilla strips, some cream, then cheese. Repeat until all the ingredients are used, ending with cheese. Sprinkle the paprika on top.
6. Bake for 20 minutes, uncovered, or until the dish is bubbling.

PIG FEET STEW

1 pound pork roast
3 medium potatoes
1 large white onion
3 medium carrots
8 garlic cloves

6 pigs feet
2 quarts water
1 teaspoon salt
1 teaspoon dried oregano
1 cup fresh or frozen peas

1. Cut the pork roast into 1-inch cubes. Peel the potatoes and cut into 1-inch cubes. Peel the onion and chop into ¼-inch pieces. Peel the carrots and cut into ¼-inch rounds. Peel the garlic and slice thinly.
2. Put the pigs feet and onion into a large stockpot with the water. Add the salt and oregano; stir well. Bring to a boil. Boil uncovered for 30 minutes.
3. Add the remaining ingredients. Reduce heat to medium and simmer uncovered for 3 to 4 hours or until the carrots are soft and the meat is tender.

CASHEW CHILI

1 medium-sized white onion
1 small green bell pepper
2 celery ribs
6 large tomatoes
1 tablespoon vegetable oil
1 teaspoon dried oregano

1 teaspoon ground cumin
1 teaspoon garlic powder
1 tablespoon chili powder
4 cups canned (or precooked) kidney beans
2 cups cashews

1. Peel the onion and cut into ¼-inch pieces. Remove the seeds and stem from the green pepper and cut into ¼-inch pieces. Cut the celery into ¼-inch pieces. Dice tomatoes, reserving the juice.
2. Heat the oil to medium heat. Add the onion, green pepper, and celery. Cook until the onion is browned. Add the spices; stir well.
3. Transfer the mixture to a soup kettle. Add the tomatoes and beans. Simmer on low for 3 hours, stirring periodically. Add the cashews and heat through just before serving.

CHAPTER 25
FISH AND SEAFOOD

SEA BASS WITH FILBERTS

Serves 6

This is excellent served with Zucchini with Jalapeños (page 427).

1 (5- to 6-pound) whole sea bass
1 tablespoon lemon juice
1 medium-sized white onion
12 pitted green olives
¼ cup olive oil
¼ cup canned, chopped pimientos
1 teaspoon ground black pepper

½ teaspoon salt
½ teaspoon crushed coriander seeds
2 tablespoons orange juice
½ cup crushed filberts
¼ cup chopped fresh parsley

1. Preheat oven to 375°.
2. Remove the head and guts from the fish and slice in half. (You might ask the meat department manager to do this for you!) Lay the fish in an ovenproof baking pan, skin-side down. Sprinkle with lemon juice.
3. Remove the skin from the onion and chop into ¼-inch pieces. Chop the olives into ¼-inch pieces.
4. Sauté the onions in olive oil on medium heat in a small skillet for 3 minutes. Add the olives, pimientos, salt, black pepper, and coriander seeds, and sauté for an additional 3 minutes.
5. Remove from heat and add the orange juice and filberts; stir well.
6. Pour the mixture over the fish and place in the oven for 30 minutes or until the fish flakes easily. Sprinkle with parsley before serving.

How to Store Spices
Store ground spices, dried herbs, and seeds in airtight containers away from light. Keep spices away from all heat and humidity sources to retain their integrity.

GARLICKY SEAFOOD SAUTÉ

½ pound medium-sized fresh
   shrimp
½ pound fresh lobster tail
½ pound fresh squid, cleaned
½ pound fresh scallops
4 medium tomatoes
2 medium carrots
1 medium-sized white onion

16 garlic cloves
½ pound fresh spinach
½ cup vegetable oil
½ teaspoon white ground
   pepper
1 bunch fresh cilantro (parsley
   may be substituted for a
   milder flavor)

Serves 4

This is best served
with plain white rice
or pinto beans. It
also goes well with
fresh fruit.

1. Preheat oven to 300°.
2. Remove the shells from the shrimp and lobster tail. Place all the seafood in a large pot of boiling water for 10 minutes. Drain and rinse with cold water. Cut the squid into 1-inch lengths. Devein the shrimp by running a fork tine along the back of each shrimp to remove the black-colored membrane. Cut the lobster tail into ½-inch pieces.
3. Cut the tomatoes into ½-inch pieces. Clean the carrots and cut into ¼-inch rounds. Remove the skin from the onion and chop into ¼-inch pieces. Remove the skin from garlic and mince. Remove the stems from the spinach.
4. In a large frying pan heat the oil to medium temperature. Add the onions and garlic; sauté until the onion is limp but not brown. The garlic should be light brown by this time. Drain off the oil and discard.
5. Lay the seafood in a 9" × 9" baking pan. Cover with the garlic and onion mixture. Bake for 20 minutes.
6. While the seafood is in the oven, combine the spinach, cilantro, white pepper, tomatoes, and carrots in a vegetable steamer and cook until the spinach has wilted and the carrots are tender, about 10 minutes. (If you don't have a vegetable steamer, put 1 inch of water in the bottom of the pan and simmer the vegetables until tender.)
7. Right before serving, mix the steamed vegetables together and spread a layer on each plate. Lay a scoop of the seafood on top.

GRILLED SWORDFISH

4 large swordfish fillets (about 6 ounces each)
1 teaspoon chili powder
2 tablespoons lime juice
1 teaspoon dried oregano
1 teaspoon dried cilantro

¼ cup canned anchovies
½ teaspoon ground cayenne pepper
1 teaspoon salt
1 cup Basic Picante Sauce (see recipe on page 285)

1. Preheat grill to medium-high heat.
2. Add the chili powder, lime juice, oregano, cilantro, anchovies, cayenne pepper, and salt to the picante sauce.
3. Place the fillets on the grill and baste liberally with the sauce, reserving about ¼ cup for serving. Turn once and baste again.
4. When the fillets are done, drizzle the remaining sauce over the top.

SHARK STEAK WITH GREEN TOMATO SAUCE

4 medium shark steaks (about 6 ounces each)
½ teaspoon salt
½ teaspoon ground black pepper
1 teaspoon olive oil
4 garlic cloves

4 scallions
2 habanero chilies
2 teaspoons dried cilantro
1 cup Green Tomato Salsa (see recipe on page 282)

1. Preheat oven to 350°.
2. Sprinkle both sides of the shark steaks with the salt and pepper. Grease the bottom of a 9" × 13" baking pan with the olive oil. Place the steaks in the pan.
3. Remove the skin from the garlic cloves and scallions; slice thinly. Remove the stem and seeds from the chilies and slice thinly. Top the steaks with the garlic, scallion, and chili peppers. Sprinkle cilantro on top.
4. Pour the green tomato salsa over the steaks evenly. Bake for 20 minutes.

SOUSED LANGOUSTINES

6 garlic cloves
6 capers
½ cup fresh lime juice
½ cup dry white wine
½ teaspoon cayenne pepper
½ teaspon salt

2 pounds langoustines lobster
   (If you must substitute lobster
   tails, cut them into 1-inch
   slices)

> **Serves 4**
>
> While this is excellent served with white rice for a light dinner, it is good served cold atop a bed of mixed greens, too.

1. Peel and mince the garlic. Mince the capers.
2. Combine the lime juice, white wine, capers, garlic, cayenne pepper, and salt.
3. Put the lobster in a medium-sized frying pan and pour the liquid mixture over the top. Slowly bring the mixture to a simmer at medium heat. Simmer for 5 minutes or until the langoustines are opaque.
4. Remove from heat and pour the entire mixture into a bowl; refrigerate for 24 hours.
5. Drain off the liquid and reheat the langoustines by placing in a medium-sized, covered pot on medium-low heat for five minutes. Stir and test by eating a small piece. If not hot enough, add ¼ cup water, cover and raise heat to medium for 2 more minutes.

What Are Langoustines?
Langoustines are small lobsters commonly found in tropical climates. They are excellent for cooking in stews and soups because the pieces of flesh are so small that they easily take up the spices. You likely won't find langoustines in the shell anywhere except the southern coastal states, but fresh or freshly frozen usually work just fine in a recipe.

SMOTHERED SHRIMP

2 pounds medium-sized fresh
   shrimp
1 small white onion
4 garlic cloves
3 medium-sized red tomatoes
1 cup canned, stewed green
   tomatoes, with juice

½ cup canned or fresh
   jalapeño peppers
½ cup olive oil
¼ cup dry cooking sherry

1. Boil the shrimp for 10 minutes in 1 gallon of water. Rinse with cold water. Remove the shell and use a fork tine to remove the back vein.
2. Peel and mince the onion and garlic. Chop the tomatoes into ¼-inch pieces, reserving the juice from the green tomatoes. Remove the stem and seeds from the jalapeños and mince.
3. Heat the olive oil in a medium-sized frying pan. Add the onion, garlic, and jalapeños; sauté on medium heat until the onions are limp but not brown. Add the red and green tomatoes, including the juice from the green tomatoes. Continue cooking at medium heat, stirring constantly, for 15 minutes. Stir in the cooking sherry.
4. Preheat oven to 300°.
5. Arrange the shrimp in a large baking pan. Pour the sauce over the shrimp. Place the pan in the oven for 15 minutes.

What Fish Tastes Best?

Because most Mexican fish recipes call for adding sauces and spices to the fish, look for a firm, mild-flavored, white-fleshed fish that holds up well to cooking. Bass, flounder, shark, swordfish, and red snapper all work well. Some fish can have surprisingly strong flavors so if you want to try a new fish, take a small piece home and steam it to see if you like the flavor before putting it in your recipe.

RED SNAPPER WITH PECAN SAUCE

1 cup Chicken Stock (see
    recipe on page 286)
1 cup water
4 (6- to 10-ounce) red snapper
    fillets
1 small yellow onion
2 garlic cloves

1 cup pecans
1 teaspoon salt
1 teaspoon saffron powder
2 key limes

recipe on page 286

> **Serves 4**
>
> This unique blend of flavors is suitable for almost any white fish. It also works for seafood such as shrimp and scallops.

1. Combine the stock and water in a large frying pan and bring to a boil. Add the fish fillets. Reduce heat to medium-low and cook until the fish flakes easily with a fork. Lift the fish out and place on a serving platter. Reserve ½ cup of the cooking liquid.
2. Remove the skin from the onion and garlic cloves. Cut the onion into quarters.
3. Put the onion, garlic cloves, ½ cup of reserved cooking liquid, ¾ cup of the pecans, salt, and saffron powder into a blender or food processor; blend at medium speed for about 2 minutes or until you have a smooth purée.
4. Heat the sauce in a medium-sized saucepan at medium heat. *Do not let it boil.* Pour the sauce over the fish fillets.
5. Top with the remaining whole pecans. Squeeze the juice from the limes on the top right before serving.

Use Saffron Sparingly

Pure saffron is one of the rarest spices in the world. It has a very subtle yet distinctive flavor that is brought out in fish dishes. Saffron powder is usually diluted with other ingredients that help carry the flavor of the saffron throughout the food.

TUNA STEAKS WITH CHILI SAUCE

Serves 4

To add some color to this dish, garnish the fish with fresh sprigs of parsley or cilantro.

1 cup Chicken Stock (see recipe on page 286)
1 cup water
4 (6- to 10-ounce) tuna steaks
1 medium-sized yellow onion
2 garlic cloves

8 chili peppers (type of your choosing)
½ teaspoon cayenne pepper
1 teaspoon salt
1 teaspoon ground white pepper

1. Combine the stock and water in a large frying pan and bring to a boil. Add the tuna steaks. Reduce heat to medium-low and cook until the fish flakes easily with a fork. Lift the fish out and place on a serving platter. Reserve ½ cup of the cooking liquid.
2. Remove the skin from the onion and garlic cloves. Cut the onion into quarters. Remove the seeds and stems from the chilies. Cut into quarters.
3. Put the onion, garlic, chilies, ½ cup reserved cooking liquid, salt, cayenne pepper, and white pepper into a blender or food processor and blend at medium speed for about 2 minutes or until you have a smooth purée.
4. Heat the sauce in a medium-sized saucepan at medium heat. Do not let it boil. Pour the sauce over the fish.

Choosing Chili Peppers

Chili peppers can be fun to experiment with, as there are so many varieties available today. Don't hesitate to try something new. (See Chapter 16 for a guide to their hotness.) You will soon get beyond the heat of the first bite and discover a wide range of flavors to match the many shapes, colors, and sizes available.

FRIED FLOUNDER WITH SPICY GREEN SAUCE

4 (6- to 10-ounce) flounder fillets
1 cup flour
3 tablespoons vegetable oil
½ small white onion
2 garlic cloves
8 fresh chili peppers (type of
    your choosing)
6 green tomatoes
¼ teaspoon ground cloves
½ teaspoon ground cinnamon

½ teaspoon ground nutmeg
½ teaspoon dried oregano
½ teaspoon ground cumin
½ teaspoon dried thyme
½ teaspoon dried rosemary
1 teaspoon dried parsley flakes
¼ cup lime juice

Serves 4

Try adding some freshly grated Parmesan cheese on top of the fish fillets during the last 10 minutes of baking for an additional flavor treat.

1. Wash the fillets with warm water and cover with the flour.
2. Heat the oil to medium-high heat in a large frying pan. Add the fillets and fry on both sides until golden brown. Drain off the oil and place the fillets in a baking dish.
3. Remove the skin from the onion and garlic. Remove the stems and seeds from the chili peppers. Cut the green tomatoes into quarters.
4. Preheat oven to 350°.
5. Place the onion, garlic, cloves, cinnamon, nutmeg, oregano, cumin, thyme, rosemary, parsley flakes, tomatoes, and lime juice in a food processor or blender. Blend at medium speed until you have a smooth purée.
6. Pour the sauce over the fish. Place the fish in the oven and bake for 1 hour or until the fish flakes easily with a fork.

Pearl Onions

When using pearl onions, cook them first in boiling water for 3 minutes. Plunge them into cold water. Remove them from the water and cut off the ends before easily removing the stems.

CRAB WITH SPINACH AND RICE

4 cups Chicken Stock (see recipe on page 286)
2 cups dry white rice
1 small yellow onion
2 garlic cloves
1 fresh jalapeño pepper
2 cups frozen or canned spinach
2 pounds crabmeat
1 teaspoon salt
1 teaspoon ground black pepper
1 cup grated mozzarella cheese

1. Bring the stock to a boil in a medium-sized saucepan. Add the rice. Cover and boil for 5 minutes. Reduce heat to medium-low and cook for 20 minutes or until the rice is tender.
2. Remove the skin from the onion and garlic. Cut the onion into ¼-inch pieces. Mince the garlic. Remove the stems and seed from jalapeño pepper and mince.
3. Preheat oven to 350°.
4. In a large mixing bowl, combine the rice, onion, garlic, jalapeños, spinach, crabmeat, salt, and black pepper until well mixed.
5. Spread the mixture evenly in a large baking dish. Top with cheese. Bake for 1 hour.

Crabby or Not?

Many people try to substitute "imitation crab" for the real thing. These inexpensive "sea legs" are actually a fine substitute if you are eating the meat right away. However, they quickly lose their flavor and soon taste like gummy noodles. You're better off paying for the real thing.

MUSSEL CEVICHE

1 pound fresh shelled mussels
½ cup lime juice
1 small Vidalia onion
2 habanero chilies
3 green tomatoes
½ cup tomato juice

½ cup clam juice
1 teaspoon salt
3 key limes

Serves 4

Serve atop a bed of lettuce with fresh Tostadas (page 285).

1. Combine the mussels and lime juice in a small glass or ceramic container. Cover and refrigerate for 1 hour.
2. Remove the skin from the onion and cut into ¼-inch pieces. Remove the stem and seeds from the chilies and cut into ¼-inch pieces. Chop the tomatoes into ¼-inch pieces; reserve the juice.
3. Drain off and discard the lime juice and put the mussels in a medium-sized mixing bowl. Add the onions, chilies, green tomatoes with their juice, red tomato juice, clam juice, salt, and fresh-squeezed juice from the key limes; stir well.
4. Refrigerate in a glass or ceramic container for 4 to 12 hours.

Mussels with Muscle
Fresh mussels will not smell fishy. The water they sit in will be clear and the shells will be bright, not filmy. Frozen and canned mussels simply don't have the same flavor as the fresh ones. However, some people substitute canned oysters for fresh mussels and consider it a good tradeoff.

HALIBUT CEVICHE

Serves 4

Serve with Black Bean and Corn Salad (page 342) for a wonderful mix of flavors.

1½–2 pounds fresh halibut
½ cup lime juice
1 small red onion
2 serrano chilies
1 large red tomato
½ cup fresh cilantro leaves
¼ cup pimiento-stuffed green
  olives
½ cup orange juice
1 teaspoon salt

1. Cut the halibut into ½-inch cubes. Combine the fish and lime juice in a small glass or ceramic container. Cover and refrigerate for 1 hour.
2. Remove the skin from the onion and cut into ¼-inch pieces. Remove the stem and seeds from the chilies and cut into ¼-inch pieces. Chop the tomato into ¼-inch pieces; reserve the juice. Chop the cilantro into ¼-inch pieces. Slice the olives in ¼-inch rounds.
3. Drain off and discard the lime juice and put the fish in a medium-sized mixing bowl. Add the onions, chilies, tomatoes with their juice, olives, cilantro, orange juice, and salt; stir well. Refrigerate in a glass or ceramic container for 4 to 12 hours.

Do I Have to Eat It Raw?

Ceviche is always served with raw fish because the lime juice effectively cooks the outside layer of flesh. However, if you're squeamish about eating raw fish, steam the fish chunks for 5 minutes to make sure they are fully cooked. You will lose some of the authentic flavor of a true ceviche, but it will still taste marvelous.

SHRIMP IN VINAIGRETTE

2 small red onions
½ teaspoon cayenne pepper
2 pounds fresh medium-sized
* shrimp*
1 jalapeño chili pepper
1–2 cups red wine vinegar

1 teaspoon granulated sugar
½ teaspoon salt
½ teaspoon ground white
* pepper*

> **Serves 4**
>
> This makes an excellent substitute for a salad course for a formal meal. It is also a good lunch on a hot summer day when served with a green lettuce salad.

1. Remove the skin from the onions. Cut 1 onion into ½-inch rings and add it to 2 gallons of water in a large stockpot. Add the cayenne pepper. Bring to a boil and add the shrimp. Cook for 10 minutes. Drain and discard the onions. Run the shrimp under cold water. Remove the shells and back vein.
2. Chop the other onion into ¼-inch pieces. Remove the stem and seeds from the jalapeño and chop into ¼-inch pieces.
3. Mix together 1 cup of the red wine vinegar, the chopped onions, chilies, sugar, salt, and ground white pepper.
4. Put the shrimp in a large glass or ceramic dish. Pour the sauce over the top, making sure all the shrimp are covered. If you need more sauce, add the remaining cup of red wine vinegar.
5. Chill in the refrigerator for 4 to 12 hours before serving.

Canned or Fresh?

Canned jalapeños are mushy, so they blend better with the other ingredients. If you prefer to use fresh jalapeños, you could substitute 1 small pepper, removing the seeds and stem.

SCALLOPS WITH SESAME SEED SAUCE

Serves 4

Serve with Eggplant Casserole (page 435).

1½ pounds fresh scallops
1 garlic clove
½ cup plain hulled pepitas (pumpkin seeds)
3 tablespoons sesame seeds
2 tablespoons vegetable oil
¾ teaspoon chili powder
¼ teaspoon ground cinnamon
⅛ teaspoon ground cloves
¾ cup Chicken Stock (see recipe on page 286)
½ teaspoon salt
1½ tablespoons lime juice

1. Put the scallops in a medium-sized saucepan. Add ½-inch water. Cover and heat on low until the scallops are opaque and firm.
2. Peel the garlic. Combine the *pepitas*, sesame seeds, garlic, and oil in a saucepan. Stir and cook over medium heat until the sesame seeds are light golden brown.
3. Remove from heat and stir in the chili powder, cinnamon, and cloves. Put the sauce in an electric blender or food processor and grind. Add the broth and salt. Grind again.
4. Transfer the mixture to a saucepan. Mix in the lime juice and heat over low heat, stirring until thickened.
5. Arrange the scallops on a platter and spoon the sauce over them.

Fresh or Frozen Fish?
Many people prefer frozen fish because they can be assured that it is clean and fresh. However, frozen fish can lose some of its flavor and texture in the freezing process. Finding good fresh fish doesn't have to be scary. Just look for a fish with clear eyes that doesn't smell too fishy.

SEAFOOD PAELLA

1 small rock lobster tail
24 fresh clams in shells
1½ pounds medium-sized
shrimp
1 pound scallops
1 pound fresh crabmeat
1 small yellow onion
2 garlic cloves

2 medium-sized ripe tomatoes
1 cup fresh or frozen green peas
1 cup whole pimientos
¼ cup parsley
1 cup olive oil
1½ teaspoons salt
2 cups uncooked rice
1 quart hot water

Serves 8

Enjoy this with fresh fruit and a Spinach Salad (page 354).

1. Boil the lobster, clams, shrimp, scallops, and crab for about 10 minutes. Remove the shells and devein the shrimp. Cut the lobster into 1-inch cubes. Cut the crabmeat into 1-inch pieces.

2. Peel and mince the onion and garlic. Remove the stems from the tomatoes and chop into ¼-inch pieces. Thaw the peas if using frozen. Cut the pimientos into ¼-inch wide strips. Remove the stems from the parsley and chop roughly.

3. Heat the oil in a large frying pan. Add the onion and garlic. Cook until the onion is limp, about 2 minutes. Add the shrimp, clams, scallops, tomatoes, and salt.

4. Add the hot water, rice, peas, and parsley; mix well. Cover and cook, stirring occasionally, for about 20 minutes or until the rice is tender.

5. Mix in the lobster, half of the pimientos, and the clams. Heat until very hot. Serve garnished with remaining pimientos.

CHAPTER 26
POULTRY

CHICKEN-STUFFED AVOCADO

2 medium avocados
¼ cup fresh lime juice
2 cooked boneless chicken
  breasts
2 medium tomatoes
4 scallions or green onions
1 cup lettuce
12 pimiento-stuffed green olives

½ teaspoon salt
1 teaspoon black pepper
2 tablespoons red wine vinegar
½ cup shredded Cheddar
  cheese

1. Peel the avocados. Slice in half and remove the pits. Sprinkle with lime juice.
2. Remove the skin from the chicken and chop into ½-inch pieces to yield about 1 cup of meat.
3. Chop the tomatoes into ¼-inch pieces. Remove the skin from the scallions and chop into ¼-inch pieces. Tear the lettuce into ½-inch pieces. Cut the olives into quarters.
4. Combine all the ingredients *except* the avocados and cheese in a medium-sized bowl.
5. Place ¼ of the mixture into each avocado half. Sprinkle the cheese on top.

A Word about Oregano

Oregano is one of the most common herbs found in the Mexican kitchen. It comes in many different varieties, although we usually see just one fresh variety in the United States. Unlike many spices, dried oregano is used by Mexicans even when fresh is available.

KEY LIME CHICKEN

1 chipotle chili
6 key limes
¼ cup lemon juice
¼ cup orange juice
1 cup Green Tomato Salsa
  (see recipe on page 282)

2 tablespoons vegetable oil
1 teaspoon salt
4 skin-on chicken breasts

Serves 4

This is wonderful served with Refried Beans (page 284) or Red Rice (page 286).

1. Remove and discard the rind from 4 of the key limes. Remove and discard the stem and seeds from the chili pepper.
2. Combine the peeled key limes, chili, lemon juice, orange juice, salsa, oil, and salt in a blender or food processor. Blend on medium until you have a nice purée—it should be thick with no obvious chunks.
3. Transfer the blend to a medium-sized pot and cook on medium heat for about 15 minutes. Let cool.
4. Debone the chicken breasts and place in a large mixing bowl. Pour the sauce over the top. Cover and refrigerate for 6 to 12 hours.
5. Preheat the broiler. (These also are great cooked on the grill.)
6. Place on the broiler and use the marinade to baste the chicken every few minutes. Turn the chicken over when the first side gets brown and cook again. Chicken breasts take from 10 to 20 minutes to cook thoroughly. Cut into the center of 1 of the breasts to make sure it is cooked through before serving.
7. Cut the remaining 2 key limes in half. Before serving, squeeze the juice of ½ a lime onto each breast.

The Chipotle Chili

Chipotle chilies are dried, smoked red jalapeño peppers. There is no other chili pepper like them. Although spicy, the flavor that lingers is the smoky taste. As a result, you should know what you are doing when you put them into a dish. They will flavor something more than any other chili pepper.

CINNAMON FRIED CHICKEN

If there is extra room in the roasting pan, wash potatoes, leaving the skin on, and quarter them. Place them in with the chicken to bake.

4 skin-on chicken breasts
1 cup milk
1 cup flour
2 tablespoons ground cinnamon
1 teaspoon cayenne pepper
1 tablespoon salt
1 teaspoon ground nutmeg
1 teaspoon ground cloves
4 tablespoons vegetable oil

1. Preheat oven to 300°.
2. Wash the chicken thoroughly. Pour the milk into a soup bowl and dunk the chicken breasts in milk until completely coated. Discard the remaining milk.
3. In another soup bowl, mix together the flour, cinnamon, cayenne pepper, salt, nutmeg, and cloves. Roll each breast in the flour mixture until well coated.
4. Put the vegetable oil in a roasting pan. Place the chicken breasts skin-side down in the roasting pan and bake for 30 minutes.
5. Flip the chicken so that the skin side is up and put back in the oven for 1 hour.

The Subtler Spices

Mexican cooking abounds in its use of subtle spices. Cinnamon, nutmeg, and cloves, for example, are common ingredients in many recipes that don't contain an abundance of hot chili peppers.

FRUIT-STEWED TURKEY

4 cups precooked turkey meat
   (leftovers are great)
1 small yellow onion
1 cup pineapple chunks, drained
6 pitted prunes
¼ cup dried apricots
1 tablespoon olive oil
½ cup fresh raspberries
1 teaspoon salt
1 teaspoon ground white pepper

Serves 4

This simple dish is wonderful served over white rice with a side of Zucchini with Jalapeños (page 427).

1. Cut the turkey into 1-inch chunks. Remove skin from onion and cut into quarters. Cut the pineapple into 1-inch chunks if necessary. Cut the prunes and apricots in half.
2. In a large frying pan preheat the olive oil to medium temperature. Add the turkey chunks and fry until lightly browned on all sides.
3. Drain off the oil and add the onion, pineapple, apricots, prunes, raspberries, salt, and pepper to the pan. Turn heat to low and cook for 1 hour, stirring periodically.

NUTTY CHICKEN

1 (2½- to 3½-pound) whole
   chicken
½ cup olive oil
¼ cup hulled pepitas (pumpkin
   seeds)
¼ cup sesame seeds
¼ cup pecans
¼ cup slivered almonds
¼ cup pistachio meats
¼ cup filberts

Serves 4

Because this is a mild entrée, it goes well with a spicy vegetable or rice dish.

1. Preheat oven to 350°. Wash the chicken and cut it into 8 serving pieces. Brush each piece with some of the olive oil.
2. Combine all the nuts. In a food processor or nut grinder, grind the nuts into small pieces. Place the nut mixture in a soup bowl and roll each piece of chicken in the nuts. Reserve the remaining nuts.
3. Put the remaining olive oil in a baking pan. Place the chicken, skin-side down, in the pan. Bake for 30 minutes. Flip the chicken and sprinkle with the remaining nuts. Bake for an additional 1 hour.

CHICKEN TACOS

Serves 6

Authentic Mexican
tacos are usually
served with just meat
and salsa. However,
you can add the
American fixing such
as cheese and lettuce
if you'd like.

6 cups water
1 medium-sized yellow onion
4 garlic cloves
1 carrot
1 green bell pepper
1 celery rib
4 chicken breasts (with skin
    and bones)

1 teaspoon salt
1 teaspoon black pepper
12 Flour Tortillas (see recipe
    on page 284)

1. Place the water in a large stockpot and bring to a boil.
2. Remove the skin from the onion and cut into 1-inch pieces. Remove the skin from the garlic cloves and cut into thin slices. Peel the carrot and cut into ½-inch rounds. Remove the core and seeds from the green pepper and cut into 1-inch pieces. Cut the celery into 1-inch pieces.
3. Place the chicken breasts, onion, garlic, carrot, green pepper, salt, black pepper, and celery in the boiling water; boil for 20 minutes. Skim the foam from the top, reduce heat to medium, and continue cooking until the meat falls off the bones when picked up with a fork.
4. Pour the contents of the stockpot into a strainer. Pull out the chicken breasts. Remove the bones and skin. Discard all the vegetables, chicken bones, and skin.
5. Shred the meat. Use as a filling for the tacos.

Fruit and More Fruit

Being a warm-weather culture, Mexican dishes frequently use a great deal of fresh fruits. Although those in the United States tend to think of tropical fruits as distinctly Mexican, it's only because most of us don't get them that often. Berries and citrus fruits are common in Mexican diets, too.

SOUSED CHICKEN

1 (2½- to 3½-pound) whole
   chicken
1/2 cup prunes
1/2 cup dried pears
1 large green apple
1 medium-sized red onion
4 garlic cloves
½ cup black olives
3 cups dry white wine

½ cup raisins
1 teaspoon salt
1 teaspoon ground black
   pepper
1 tablespoon dried cilantro
1 cup whole roasted almonds

> **Serves 4**
>
> Serve with white rice.
> Ladle the fruit onto
> the top of the chicken
> and the rice before
> serving.

1. Preheat oven to 300°.
2. Wash the chicken and cut into 8 serving pieces. Remove the skin.
3. Remove the pits from the prunes and cut in quarters. Cut the pears into quarters. Remove the stem and core from the apple; cut into 1-inch pieces. Remove the skin from the onion and cut into ¼-inch rounds. Remove the skin from the garlic cloves and cut into quarters. Cut the black olives into quarters.
4. Put the chicken in an oven-safe pot. Pour the wine over the top. Add the raisins, prunes, pears, apple, onion, garlic, olives, salt, pepper, and cilantro to the pot.
5. Cover and bake for 2 hours. Remove the cover, add the almonds, and bake for 30 minutes.

Is It Soused or Potted?

Mexican dishes that have meat soaking in a sauce, especially an alcohol-based sauce, are often called soused or potted dishes. Funny that those two words have come to mean someone who is drunk, too!

CHICKEN IN NUTTY GREEN SAUCE

Serves 4

Have fun with this dish by experimenting with different types and amounts of chili peppers.

1 (2½- to 3½-pound) chicken
2 cups Chicken Stock (see recipe on page 286)
6 habanero chilies
1 medium-sized yellow onion
4 garlic cloves
6 green tomatoes
1 green bell pepper
1 bunch fresh cilantro

½ cup blanched almond slivers
½ cup chopped walnuts
1 teaspoon salt
1 teaspoon ground black pepper
1 tablespoon olive oil
½ cup cooking sherry

1. Preheat oven to 300°.
2. Wash the chicken and cut into 8 serving pieces.
3. Place the chicken and stock in an ovenproof casserole dish with a lid. Cover and cook for 30 minutes.
4. Remove the stems and seeds from the chilies. Peel the onion and garlic, and cut into quarters. Remove the stems from the tomatoes and cut into quarters. Remove the stems and seeds from the green bell pepper and cut into quarters. Remove and discard the stems from the cilantro.
5. Combine the chilies, onion, garlic, tomatoes, bell pepper, cilantro, almonds, walnuts, salt, black pepper, olive oil, and cooking sherry in a mixing bowl. Scoop out about 1 cup at a time and place in a blender or food processor. Blend until all the ingredients are melded but not puréed. Repeat until all the ingredients are blended.
6. Drain off and discard the chicken stock from the chicken. Pour the sauce over the chicken, cover, and replace in the oven. Cook for 1½ hours.

COCOA TURKEY

1 (8- to 10-pound) turkey
1 medium-sized red onion
4 garlic cloves
¾ cup vegetable oil
2 cups powdered cocoa

1 teaspoon ground cinnamon
¼ teaspoon anise seeds

1. Preheat oven to 350°.
2. Thaw the turkey, remove the neck and giblets from the cavities, and wash the cavities thoroughly.
3. Remove the skin from the onion and chop into ¼-inch pieces. Peel and mince the garlic. Stir the onion and garlic into ¼ cup vegetable oil and, using a paper towel, rub the inside of the turkey cavity with the garlic and onion mixture. Leave all the garlic and onion pieces inside the cavity.
4. Mix together the cocoa, cinnamon, and anise into the remaining ½ cup vegetable oil. Use this to baste the turkey.
5. Place the turkey in the oven and baste every 15 minutes for 3 hours.
6. Remove the turkey and let it rest for 30 minutes before serving.

Cocoa as a Spice
While Americans think of cocoa only in terms of chocolate, many Mexican dishes use it as a main spice. They will mix it with cheeses, meats, and even vegetables. Although it can take some getting used to, it's definitely worth trying.

FIVE-PEPPER CHICKEN STEW

4 chicken breasts
4 fresh jalapeño chilies
4 fresh mulato chilies
4 fresh ancho chilies
1 fresh poblano chili
4 fresh habanero chilies
4 medium tomatoes
1 large yellow onion

4 garlic cloves
4 medium baking potatoes
2 large carrots
½ cup hulled pepitas (pumpkin seeds)

1. Remove the skin and bone from the chicken breasts. Cut the chicken meat into 1-inch pieces.
2. Remove the stems and seeds from the chilies and chop chilies into ¼-inch pieces. Cut the tomatoes into quarters. Remove the skin from the onion and chop into ¼-inch pieces. Remove the skin from the garlic cloves and cut into thin slices. Peel the potatoes and carrots, and cut into 1-inch pieces.
3. Combine all the ingredients in a large pot, cover, and cook on medium-low heat for 3 hours. Stir occasionally.

The Poblano Chili
Poblano chilies are one of the largest and mildest-tasting green peppers in the chili category. They are meaty and relatively juicy, which makes them excellent for roasting and baking. Because they are fairly large, they also work well for stuffing.

CHICKEN ACHIOTE

1 (2½- to 3½-pound) whole
  chicken
4 garlic cloves
1 medium-sized red onion
4 jalapeño chili peppers
½ cup white grapefruit juice

1 cup green seedless grapes
½ cup red cooking sherry
2 tablespoons achiote paste

Serves 4

Serve with Pineapple
and Coconut Salad
(page 462).

1. Cut the chicken into 8 serving pieces. Remove the skin, but not the bones.
2. Remove the skin from the garlic and onion. Cut the onion into quarters. Remove the stems (but not the seeds) from the jalapeños. Combine the garlic, onion, chili peppers, grapefruit juice, sherry, and achiote paste in a blender or food processor. Blend on medium setting until all the ingredients are melded.
3. Place the chicken in a large mixing bowl. Cover with sauce. Cover the bowl and place in the refrigerator for 6 to 12 hours.
4. Preheat oven to 350°.
5. Cut the grapes in half.
6. Remove the chicken from the bowl and place in a baking dish; discard the sauce. Cover with grapes.
7. Cook, uncovered, for 1 hour.

Achiote
Achiote is a blend of ground annatto seeds, garlic, black pepper, other spices, and vinegar. It is most common in Yucatan cooking but has migrated into middle Mexican cooking as well. It leaves food (as well as clothing, plastic cookware, and anything else it touches) a bright orange color.

CHICKEN TABLECLOTH STAINER

Serves 8

Serve with Turnip and
Mustard Leaf Rolls
(page 431).

2 fryer chickens (about 2½
  pounds each)
½ cup canned pineapple
  chunks
1 medium-sized red apple
1 large, firm banana
1 medium-sized white onion
1 garlic clove
½ pound link sausages
1 tablespoon chili powder
2 cups canned tomatoes

½ cup whole blanched
  almonds
¼ teaspoon ground cinnamon
⅛ teaspoon ground cloves
2 cups Chicken Stock (see
  recipe on page 286)
2 teaspoons salt
1 teaspoon ground black
  pepper

1. Cut each chicken into 8 serving pieces. Drain off the juice from the pineapple. Peel, core, and slice the apple into ¼-inch-thick crescents. Peel the banana and cut into ¼-inch-thick rounds. Peel the onion and slice in half. Peel the garlic.

2. Fry the sausage until brown in a medium-sized frying pan. (Reserve the grease in the pan.) Put the chicken and sausages in a large, heavy kettle. Add the pineapple, apple, and banana on top.

3. Combine the chili powder, onion, garlic, tomatoes with their juice, almonds, cinnamon, and cloves in a blender or food processor; blend to a purée.

4. Heat the grease in the skillet in which the sausages were cooked. Add the blended sauce and cook about 5 minutes, stirring constantly. Stir in the stock. Add the salt and pepper.

5. Pour the sauce over the chicken. Cover and simmer over low heat for 1 hour or until the chicken is tender.

Oh, That Stained Linen

Mexicans love to have whimsical names for their meals. Note Rooster's Bill in Chapter 18. This one obviously got its name from the wonderful red color the chili powder gives it.

MARINATED CHICKEN

2 fryer chickens (about 2½ pounds each)
1 cup canned or frozen sliced carrots
2 celery stalks
1 large white onion
1 garlic clove
1½ cups vegetable oil

⅛ teaspoon thyme
⅛ teaspoon marjoram
1 bay leaf
12 peppercorns
1 teaspoon salt
3 cups vinegar

Serves 8
Serve this dish cold, garnished with pickled vegetables.

1. Cut each chicken into 8 serving pieces. Thaw the frozen carrots *or* drain canned carrots. Chop the celery into 1-inch pieces. Peel the onion and cut into 1-inch pieces. Peel and mince the garlic.
2. Heat the oil to medium temperature in a large skillet. Brown the chicken pieces, then place them in a large pot. Top with the carrots, onions, celery, garlic, thyme, marjoram, bay leaf, peppercorns, and salt. Pour the vinegar over the top.
3. Remove from heat and let cool to room temperature. Cover and refrigerate for 3 to 4 hours.

Key Limes Go

Mexicans love key lime juice in almost everything. They squirt fresh key lime juice into soups, onto salty tostadas, and into their drinking water. The secret is that key limes—tiny golf-ball–sized fruits—are actually very sweet and mild tasting as compared to the Florida and California limes that people in the United States are used to.

DUCK IN PRUNE SAUCE

Serves 6

Serve with Green Beans with Pine Nuts and Feta Cheese (page 428).

2 cups pitted prunes
¼ cup raisins
1 cup dry sherry
1 (4–5 pound) duckling
1 cup flour
1 large white onion
2 garlic cloves
4 tomatillos

½ cup butter
1 teaspoon salt
½ teaspoon ground black pepper
½ teaspoon ground nutmeg

1. Cut the prunes into ¼-inch pieces. Combine the prunes and raisins in a small bowl and add the sherry; let soak for at least 2 hours.
2. Preheat oven to 325°.
3. Cut the duck into serving pieces and roll in flour. Peel the onion and chop into ¼-inch pieces. Peel and mince the garlic cloves. Peel the tomatillos and chop into ¼-inch pieces.
4. Melt the butter in a large frying pan over medium heat. Add the duck pieces and cook until browned on both sides. Sprinkle with salt and pepper during the last couple minutes of browning. Place the duck pieces in a large ovenproof casserole. Do not drain the grease from the frying pan.
5. Put the onions in the frying pan and cook on medium heat until they are limp but not brown. Stir in the garlic, tomatillos, and nutmeg; pour over the duck. Cover the casserole and cook for 1½ hours. Pour the prune and raisin mixture over the duck, cover, and cook for an additional 15 minutes.

Nuts Galore

Mexico's subtropical climate means a large variety of nuts grow easily here, making nuts very easy to buy and cook with. As a result, Mexicans often use them as the equivalent of flour, as a thickening agent for sauces or as a batter.

SQUABS IN ORANGE SAUCE

1 medium-sized white onion
1 garlic clove
2 medium-sized red tomatoes
2 tablespoons pecans
4 squabs
½ cup butter
1 cup freshly squeezed orange
   juice

½ cup dry white wine
½ teaspoon thyme
1 tablespoon grated orange
   rind

Serves 4

Use the juice in the bottom of the pan as a dipping sauce for the meat.

1. Preheat oven to 325°. Peel the onion and cut into ¼-inch rounds. Peel and mince the garlic. Remove the stems from the tomatoes and chop into ¼-inch pieces. Chop the pecans finely.
2. Split each squab in half lengthwise, leaving it in 1 piece. Melt the butter in a large frying pan on medium heat. Sauté each squab until golden brown on all sides. Do not drain grease. Place the squabs in an ovenproof casserole. (It's fine if they overlap.)
3. Put the onion and garlic in the frying pan and sauté until the onion is limp but not brown. Reduce heat to low. Add the tomatoes, pecans, orange juice, wine, and thyme; cook for 5 minutes, stirring occasionally. Pour over the squabs.
4. Cover the casserole and bake for 1½ hours.
5. Arrange the squabs on a serving platter. Sprinkle with orange rind.

GREEN CHICKEN WITH ALMOND SAUCE

1 fryer chicken
4 fresh tomatillos
4 fresh serrano chilies
1 large white onion
1 handful fresh cilantro
1 handful fresh parsley
1 cup blanched almonds
1 cup flour
1 teaspoon garlic salt

1 teaspoon ground white
* pepper*
2 tablespoons olive oil
1 cup white cooking sherry
1 cup Chicken Stock (see
* recipe on page 286)*

1. Preheat oven to 350°.
2. Cut the chicken into 8 serving pieces. Peel and quarter the tomatillos. Remove and discard the stems from the chilies and quarter. Peel and quarter the onion. Cut the thick stems off the cilantro and parsley. Chop the almonds into small pieces.
3. Combine the flour, garlic salt, and white pepper. Moisten the chicken with water and roll in the flour.
4. Heat the olive oil to medium temperature in a large frying pan. Add the chicken. Fry until the chicken is golden brown on all sides. Place chicken in an ovenproof casserole.
5. Put the tomatillos, chilies, onion, coriander, parsley, sherry, and stock in a blender. Blend on medium speed until puréed. Stir in the almonds. Pour the mixture over the chicken. Bake for 1 hour.

Remove the Alcohol
If you don't want alcohol in your noncooked recipe, take slightly more than you need for the recipe and sauté it over medium heat for a few minutes. The alcohol will evaporate but you will be left with all the flavor.

CREAMY RED CHICKEN WITH MUSHROOMS

*1 pound fresh white button
    mushrooms
1 large red onion
1 garlic clove
2 medium-sized red tomatoes
1 red bell pepper
2 fresh jalapeño chilies
4 boneless, skinless chicken
    breasts*

*2 cups Chicken Stock (see
    recipe on page 286)
1 sprig epazote
½ cup heavy cream*

Serves 4

Serve with Cucumber
Mousse (page 350)
for an interesting
blend
of flavors.

---

1. Preheat oven to 350°.
2. Clean the mushrooms and slice thinly. Peel the onion and slice into ¼-inch rounds. Peel and quarter the garlic. Peel the tomatoes and remove the stems; cut into quarters. Remove the stem and seeds from the red pepper; cut the pepper into quarters. Remove the stems and seeds from the jalapeños and cut into ¼-inch rounds.
3. Place the chicken breasts in an ovenproof casserole. Add the mushrooms and onion slices on top. Pour 1 cup of the chicken broth over the top. Cover and bake for 1 hour.
4. In the meantime, combine the remaining 1 cup chicken stock, garlic, tomatoes, red pepper, jalapeño peppers, and epazote in a blender; blend on medium speed until puréed.
5. Pour the mixture into a medium-sized skillet over medium heat. Gently stir in the heavy cream until it is well mixed, making sure the mixture does not boil.
6. Pour the creamy mixture over the chicken. Replace the cover and bake for an additional 15 minutes.

JALAPEÑO CHICKEN

1 (2½- to 3½-pound) whole
  chicken
4 garlic cloves
4 fresh jalapeño peppers
1 cup orange juice
1 cup honey

¼ cup lime juice
1 teaspoon cayenne pepper
1 teaspoon salt

1. Preheat oven to 350°.
2. Wash the chicken and cut it into eight serving pieces.
3. Remove the skin from the garlic. Remove the stem and seeds from the jalapeño peppers.
4. Put the garlic, peppers, orange juice, honey, lime juice, salt, and cayenne pepper in a blender or food processor; blend on medium setting for 5 minutes or until the peppers and garlic are well chopped up.
5. Place the chicken in a roasting pan. Brush the glaze on the chicken liberally but save about half for later.
6. Cook for 1½ hours. After 30 minutes, turn the chicken and again glaze liberally. After another 30 minutes, turn the chicken over again and use the remaining glaze.

Cayenne Pepper
We often overlook cayenne pepper as a spice, but it does some interesting things, especially when added to chocolate. It loses most of its flavor while retaining the heat. And, most interesting, it literally heats up a person's body. It was the secret ingredient of the chocolatier in the movie Chocolate.

CHAPTER 27

BEEF AND PORK

MEXICAN POT ROAST

3 tablespoons olive oil
3-pound pot roast
½ cup flour
1 large yellow onion
1 garlic clove
6 medium-sized red tomatoes

4 fresh morita chilies
¼ teaspoon dried oregano
1 teaspoon salt

1. Preheat oven to 350°.
2. Heat the olive oil in a large skillet on medium. Dredge the beef in the flour by pounding the flour into the meat until no more flour will stick. Place the beef in the skillet. Cook, turning until the meat is brown on all sides.
3. Peel the onion and garlic clove. Cut the onion into ¼-inch-thick rings and mince the garlic. Cut the tomatoes into 1-inch pieces. Stem and seed the chilies and cut into ¼-inch pieces.
4. Place the pot roast in a roasting pan. Sprinkle with oregano and salt, and cover with the remaining ingredients.
5. Cook, covered, for 2 hours.

The Morita Chili Pepper

Morita chilies are a type of jalapeño that has been dried and smoked. They tend to be a bit hotter than regular jalapeños and less smoky than chipotles.

CITRUS VEAL

4 veal cutlets
¼ teaspoon ground cinnamon
¼ teaspoon ground cloves
1 teaspoon salt
1 large white onion
2 garlic cloves

2 oranges
1 tablespoon vegetable oil
1 cup orange juice
¼ cup lime juice

Serves 4

Serve this with a fresh fruit salad to carry through the fruity flavor of the dish.

1. Preheat oven to 350°.
2. Season both sides of the veal cutlets with cinnamon, cloves, and salt.
3. Remove the skin from the onion and cut into 1-inch pieces. Remove the skin from the garlic and cut thinly. Cut the oranges into ¼-inch rounds with the rind remaining on the oranges.
4. Pour the oil into the bottom of a medium-sized baking dish. Place the veal cutlets in the dish so that they don't overlap. Pour the orange juice and lime juice over the veal. Place the onions, oranges, and garlic on top.
5. Cover, and cook for 1 hour.

Choosing Good Veal

A good veal steak will be nearly as white and textureless as chicken breasts. It should have less than a half inch of fat around the edges.

PORK ROAST WITH APPLES

Serves 6

Serve with Turnip and Mustard Leaf Rolls (page 431) for a unique combination of flavors.

3-pound pork roast
½ teaspoon dried oregano
½ teaspoon dried thyme
½ teaspoon dried cilantro
1 teaspoon salt
1 teaspoon ground black pepper
2 tablespoons vegetable oil
1 medium-sized yellow onion

4 garlic cloves
3 medium-sized green apples (such as Granny Smith)
1 cup apple juice
½ cup dry white wine
1 envelope unflavored gelatin

1. Preheat oven to 350°.
2. Season the pork roast with the oregano, thyme, coriander, salt, and black pepper.
3. Heat the vegetable oil in a large frying pan. Add the pork roast. Cook on medium heat, turning the pork roast until all sides are browned.
4. Remove the skin from the onion and cut into 1-inch pieces. Remove the skin from the garlic and cut into thin slices. Remove the stem and core from 2 of the apples and cut into ½-inch slices.
5. Put the pork roast in a large baking dish. Cover with the apple juice and white wine. Sprinkle the apple pieces, onion, and garlic on top. Cover and bake for 1 hour.
6. Remove the peeling, stem, and core from the remaining apple. Place in a food processor or blender and blend until puréed.
7. Boil 1 cup of water. Add the gelatin. Stir in the apple purée. Cool in the refrigerator for 15 minutes.
8. Remove the meat from the oven. Cut into ½-inch pieces and arrange on a platter. Top with the gelatin mixture right before serving.

HOT AND SPICY TRIPE

1 medium-sized yellow onion
4 garlic cloves
6 fresh habanero peppers
½ cup filberts
2 pounds fresh beef tripe
1 quart water
1 tablespoon salt

1 tablespoon olive oil
1 teaspoon dried oregano
1 teaspoon ground black
  pepper
1 cup canned pinto beans

Serves 4

Serve with broken
Tostadas (page 285)
in bowls, much as you
would serve Chinese
soft noodles.

1. Remove the skin from the onion and chop into ¼-inch pieces. Remove the skin from the garlic and cut into thin slices. Remove the stem and seeds from the peppers and cut into ¼-inch pieces. Chop the filberts into small pieces.
2. Place the tripe into the water. Add the salt and stir until well mixed. Let stand for 2 to 3 hours.
3. Place the onion, garlic, and peppers in a large frying pan. Add the olive oil. Cook on medium heat until the onion and garlic are browned. Reduce heat to low, and add the tripe, oregano, and pepper. Cover and simmer for 1 hour.
4. Add the beans. Cover and simmer for 15 minutes.
5. Add the filberts right before serving.

Trying Tripe

Although many people find the idea of eating tripe a bit scary, it really can be an excellent meal because it picks up the flavor of the ingredients it is cooked with. Expect the tripe itself to be fairly tasteless and rubbery, but enjoy the mingling of flavors that are carried with the tripe.

BARBECUED PORK RIBS

Serves 4

Serve with Jalapeño Corn Bread (page 330) and Grilled Corn on the Cob (page 430).

1 small red onion
12 garlic cloves
8 fresh chipotle chilies
½ cup water
¼ cup red wine vinegar
1 cup honey
½ cup Dijon mustard
1 tablespoon dried oregano

1 teaspoon salt
1 teaspoon ground black
  pepper
4 pounds pork ribs

1. Preheat grill to medium setting.
2. Peel the onion and cut into ¼-inch pieces. Peel and mince the garlic. Remove the stems from the chilies.
3. Place the chilies in a small saucepan with the water; cover and simmer on low setting for 10 minutes or until the chilies are plump. Drain off the water. Cut the chilies into ¼-inch pieces.
4. Combine all the ingredients *except* the ribs in a medium-sized saucepan; stir well. Bring the mixture to a boil. Cover and simmer for 10 minutes.
5. Use as a basting sauce while grilling the ribs. Reserve ½ cup to be served as a dipping sauce with the meal.

Cooking Ribs
Ribs must be cooked very slowly to ensure that they get done. If the cooking temperature is too hot, the meat will burn off. Some people boil the ribs in beer or water for 10 minutes before grilling to ensure the meat doesn't dry out.

SALPICON

*3 cups Shredded Beef (see
recipe on page 287)
1 bottle Italian salad dressing
1 cup cooked garbanzo beans*

*½ pound Monterey jack cheese
1 cup canned jalapeños
2 avocados
1 bunch parsley*

Serves 6

This can be used as a
dip, as filling for tacos,
or as a side dish.

1. Arrange the beef in a 9" × 11" casserole dish. Marinate with salad dressing, cover, and refrigerate overnight.
2. Preheat oven to 300°.
3. Drain the garbanzo beans. Shred the cheese. Drain the chili peppers and cut into ¼-inch pieces. Remove the skin and nut from the avocado and cut the avocado into ½-inch slices. Remove the stems from the parsley and roughly chop the leaves.
4. Spread layers over the beef in this order: garbanzo beans, cheese, jalapeño chilies, avocados, parsley. Place in the oven for 20 minutes

CHORIZO (MEXICAN SAUSAGE)

*2 pounds ground pork
2 tablespoons paprika
1 teaspoon ground black pepper
1 teaspoon dried oregano
1 teaspoon ground cumin
¼ teaspoon ground coriander
seeds*

*⅔ cup vinegar
1 teaspoon garlic powder
2 tablespoons salt
2 tablespoons cayenne pepper*

Makes 2 pounds

This goes very well
with Huevos
Rancheros (page 359)
or any other egg dish.

1. Place all the ingredients in a large mixing bowl. Mix with your hands until all the ingredients are well blended.
2. Place in an airtight container. Refrigerate for at least 2 days.
3. Form into patties for frying.

FIDEO CON CARNE

2 medium-sized red tomatoes
¼ head cabbage
3 garlic cloves
¼ cup vegetable oil
8 ounces vermicelli noodles
1 pound lean ground beef
¼ teaspoon ground cumin
¼ teaspoon salt
¼ teaspoon ground black
   pepper
2 quarts water

1. Chop the tomatoes into ¼-inch pieces. Chop the cabbage into 1-inch pieces. Peel and mince the garlic.
2. Heat the oil to medium temperature in a large frying pan. Add the vermicelli noodles; sauté until the noodles are lightly browned. Remove the noodles and set aside.
3. In the same pan, sauté the garlic and beef until the beef is browned. Drain off the oil.
4. Add the tomatoes, vermicelli, cumin, salt, and ground pepper; stir until all the ingredients are mixed. Add the water. Bring to a simmer, cover, and cook for 10 minutes.
5. Add the cabbage and stir to combine. Simmer, uncovered, for 15 minutes.

Sausage

Virtually every culture that slaughters animals has invented some type of sausage. Traditionally it is made with the little pieces of meat that are left over from the slaughter—ears, nose, and so on. Spices are added for both flavor and preservation. Many cultures, including the Mexicans, force the meat mixture into cleaned-out intestines to make links.

MEXICAN MEAT LOAF

1 large white onion
1/4 cup pimiento-stuffed green
    olives
3 eggs
1 pound ground beef
1/2 pound ground pork
2/3 cup uncooked oats

1 teaspoon salt
1/4 teaspoon ground black
    pepper
1 cup Red Chili Sauce (see
    recipe on page 288)

Serves 4
Serve with Pineapple and Coconut Salad (page 462).

1. Preheat oven to 350°.
2. Peel the onion and chop into 1/4-inch pieces. Slice the olives into 1/4-inch rounds. Boil 2 of the eggs for 10 minutes. When cool, slice into 1/4-inch rounds. Beat the remaining egg until the white and yolk are well mixed.
3. Combine the ground beef, ground pork, onion, oats, salt, pepper, 1/2 cup of the chili sauce, and the beaten egg. Mix with your hands until well blended.
4. Pack half of the meat mixture into an 8" × 4" × 2" loaf pan. Arrange the hard-cooked eggs in a row down the center of the loaf. Arrange the olive slices on either side of the eggs. Press the eggs and olives slightly into the meat mixture. Cover with the remaining half of the meat mixture. Pour the remaining 1/2 cup chili sauce on top.
5. Bake for 1 hour.

What Makes a Pepper Hot?

The heat of a chili pepper is caused by the presence of a volatile oil called capsaicin, which can burn the skin and eyes. As a result, if you are handling a lot of chilies, such as picking them fresh from your garden, it's important to wear rubber gloves. Always wash your hands with lots of soap after handling even a small amount of chili pepper.

ALBONDIGAS (MEATBALLS)

Makes 24–30 large meatballs

Serve with Eggplant Casserole (page 435) and Pistachio-Coconut Flan (page 476).

1 medium-sized yellow onion
1 garlic clove
4 canned chipotle chilies
3 eggs
¼ cup vegetable oil
1 cup canned tomato sauce
2 cups canned or fresh beef broth
2½ teaspoons salt
½ teaspoon dried oregano

½ teaspoon ground cumin
¼ pound ham
1 medium-sized white onion
1 pound ground beef
½ pound ground pork
2 slices stale bread
¼ cup milk
¼ teaspoon ground black pepper

1. Peel the yellow onion and chop into ¼-inch pieces. Peel and mince the garlic clove. Chop the chipotles into ¼-inch pieces. Boil 2 of the eggs in water for 10 minutes. When cool, chop into ¼-inch pieces.
2. Heat the vegetable oil to medium temperature in a large frying pan. Cook the onion and garlic in the oil until the onions are clear and tender. Add half the chilies, the tomato sauce, beef broth, oregano, cumin, and 1 teaspoon of the salt; heat to boiling, stirring constantly. Reduce heat and let simmer.
3. Cook the ham by boiling or frying, then grind with a meat grinder. Peel the white onion and chop into ¼-inch pieces. Combine the ham, onion, beef, and pork; mix with your hands until well blended.
4. Break the bread into ½-inch pieces or smaller. Put the bread chunks and milk into a small bowl and mix well.
5. Beat the remaining egg slightly and add the remaining 1½ teaspoons salt, the black pepper, and the remaining chopped chilies.
6. Add the egg mixture and bread-milk mixture to the meat; mix until well blended. Form into balls about 1½ inches in diameter. Press 2 to 3 chunks of hard-cooked egg into the center of each meatball.
7. Add the meatballs to the simmering sauce, cover, and simmer for 1 hour.

PORK PICADILLO

1½-pound pork roast
1 large white onion
2 garlic cloves
¼ cup canned jalapeño chilies,
   or 2 fresh jalapeños
1 cup frozen or canned peas
1 cup frozen or canned carrots
1 bay leaf
¼ cup vegetable oil

1 cup Green Chili Sauce
   (see recipe on page 288)
½ cup Chicken Stock (see
   recipe on page 286)
¼ teaspoon dried ginger
1 teaspoon salt
¼ teaspoon ground black
   pepper

Serves 6

Serve as a stew over white rice or use as a filling for enchiladas.

1. Place the pork roast in a large stew pot and add just enough water to cover. Cook the meat on medium temperature for 1 to 3 hours or until tender. Shred the meat by pulling it apart into strips.
2. Peel the onion and chop into ¼-inch pieces. Peel the garlic and chop into ¼-inch pieces. Stem, seed, and chop the jalapeños. If using frozen vegetables, thaw and warm to room temperature. If using canned vegetables, drain off the water. Crumble the bay leaf but discard stem.
3. Heat the vegetable oil to medium-high temperature in a large frying pan. Add the onions and garlic. Sauté until the onion is limp but not brown.
4. Add all the ingredients to the frying pan; stir well. Reduce heat to low, cover, and cook for 30 minutes.

Picadillo

Picadillo literally means "meat and vegetable hash." As a result, the variations are endless. Some versions call for vegetables while others call for fruits and nuts. Get creative and see if you can discover your own unique variation.

TONGUE IN ALMOND SAUCE

1 medium-sized yellow onion
2 whole cloves
1 veal tongue (about 2½ pounds)
1 celery stalk, with leaves
1 bay leaf
6 black peppercorns
2 teaspoons salt
2 dried ancho chilies
½ cup canned tomatoes, with juice

½ cup whole blanched almonds
½ cup raisins
2 tablespoons vegetable oil
1 slice white bread
¼ cup blanched slivered almonds

1. Peel the onion and stick the cloves in it. Put the tongue, onion, whole celery stalk, bay leaf, peppercorns, and salt into a kettle. Cover with water. Bring to a boil. Reduce heat to medium and cook for about 2 hours or until the meat is tender. Allow the meat to cool in the liquid.
2. Remove the skin from the cooled tongue, trim off the roots, and cut the meat into ½-inch slices. Strain the stock and save 1 cup of the liquid. Return the meat to the kettle.
3. Remove the skin, seeds, and stem from the dried chilies. Put the chilies, tomatoes with juice, whole almonds, and ¼ cup of the raisins in a food processor or blender; blend to a thick purée.
4. Heat the vegetable oil to medium temperature in a medium-sized frying pan. Add the puréed mixture and cook for about 5 minutes. Stir in the reserved tongue stock and the remaining ¼ cup of raisins. Cook for 5 more minutes.
5. Pour the sauce over the meat in the kettle. Heat to medium and simmer until the meat is heated through.
6. Garnish with slivered almonds.

PORK WITH PINEAPPLE

3-pound pork loin
1 large white onion
1 large red tomato
⅓ cup sliced pimientos
1 tablespoon vegetable oil
2 cups canned pineapple
   chunks, with juice
1 cup canned beef stock (or 1
   beef bouillon cube dissolved
   in 1 cup water)

¼ cup dry sherry
½ teaspoon chili powder
1 teaspoon salt
½ teaspoon black pepper
2 tablespoons flour

> **Serves 8**
>
> Serve with Red Rice
> (page 286).

1. Cut the meat into 2-inch chunks. Peel the onion and chop into ¼-inch pieces. Remove the stem from the tomato and chop into ¼-inch pieces. If using fresh pimientos, cut into ¼-inch strips.
2. Heat the vegetable oil in a large frying pan. Add the meat and brown well on all sides. Add the onion and cook for about 5 minutes or until soft.
3. Add the tomato, pimientos, the pineapple with juice, beef stock, sherry, and chili powder to the skillet; stir until well mixed. Bring to a boil, reduce heat to a simmer, and add the salt and pepper.
4. Cover and simmer until the meat is tender, about 1½ hours. Stir occasionally.
5. Just before serving, sprinkle the flour over the simmering sauce and stir in. Cook and stir until the sauce is thickened.

Use Fresh Garlic

Beware of prepared garlic. While preminced garlic looks like a good buy and certainly sounds easier, it releases an oil while stored after chopping. This affects both the taste and consistency in your recipes. Fresh garlic is always best.

BAKED NOODLES WITH CHORIZO

¼ pound Chorizo Sausage (see recipe on page 417) or any hot, spicy sausage
1 small yellow onion
4 tablespoons vegetable oil
7 ounces small egg noodles
2 cups Chicken Stock (see recipe on page 286)
1 cup cottage cheese
1 cup sour cream
1 teaspoon Tabasco or other hot sauce
1 teaspoon salt
½ teaspoon ground black pepper
½ cup grated Parmesan cheese

1. Preheat oven to 350°.
2. Fry the sausage in a large frying pan until cooked through. Crumble the sausage as it fries. Remove meat from frying pan and set aside. Peel the onion and chop into ¼-inch pieces.
3. Add the oil to the frying pan to about 1 inch deep. Stir in the onion and uncooked noodles; fry until the noodles are lightly browned and the onion is soft. Stir often to prevent burning.
4. Return the chorizo to the frying pan and stir in the stock.
5. Transfer the mixture to an ovenproof casserole dish. Bake uncovered for about 15 minutes or until all the liquid is absorbed by the noodles.
6. Remove from the oven. Stir in the cottage cheese and sour cream. Add the hot sauce, salt, and pepper. Sprinkle the Parmesan cheese on top. Return to the oven and bake uncovered for about 10 minutes or until bubbling hot.

HOME-CANNED SPICY TOMATILLOS

30–40 small tomatillos
8 jalapeño peppers
4 celery ribs
4 teaspoons dill weed
2 teaspoons dried oregano

1 quart cider vinegar
½ cup granulated pickling salt

1. Wash the tomatillos, jalapeño peppers, and celery. Remove the stems from the tomatillos and jalapeño peppers.
2. Place 2 of the jalapeño peppers, 2 ribs of celery, 1 teaspoon of dill weed, and ½ teaspoon of oregano into each of 4 hot canning jars.
3. Finish packing the jars with the tomatillos.
4. Combine the cider vinegar and pickling salt in a saucepan. Bring to a boil and stir until the salt dissolves. Pour the mixture into the jars to ½ inch from the top.
5. Place the lids tightly on the jars and put the jars into a boiling water bath for 5 minutes. Let sit at least 1 month before using.

Tomatillos
Tomatillos are an essential ingredient in many Mexican dishes. They are pale green or yellow and encased in a papery husk, which is removed before cooking. Avoid any with shriveled husks. Don't hesitate to substitute these for green tomatoes in any recipe, although they are slightly more tart than tomatoes.

ZUCCHINI WITH JALAPEÑOS

4 medium zucchini (8–10 inches long)
2 medium tomatoes
1 medium-sized yellow onion
2 garlic cloves
1 small green bell pepper

4 canned or fresh jalapeño peppers
½ teaspoon salt
½ teaspoon ground black pepper
1 tablespoon butter

1. Chop the zucchini and tomatoes into 1-inch pieces.
2. Remove the skins from the onions and garlic and chop into ¼-inch pieces.
3. Remove the stems and seeds from the bell pepper and jalapeños and chop into ¼-inch pieces.
4. Add all the ingredients to a medium-sized frying pan and sauté on medium heat until the zucchini is tender but not limp.

> **Serves 8**
>
> This is excellent served with a mild meat or fish dish.

JALAPEÑO MASHED POTATOES

1 quart water
4 medium potatoes
2 fresh jalapeño peppers
1 teaspoon salt
1 tablespoon butter

½ cup plain yogurt
1 teaspoon ground white pepper
1 teaspoon fresh epazote

1. Place the water in a large cooking pot and bring to a boil on medium-high heat.
2. Peel the potatoes and cut into 1-inch cubes. Remove the stems and seeds from the jalapeño peppers and cut into ¼-inch pieces.
3. Place the potatoes, peppers, and salt in water and boil for about 15 minutes or until potatoes are easily pierced with a fork. Drain the potatoes.
4. Combine the butter, yogurt, white pepper, and epazote in a small mixing bowl. Add to the potatoes and jalapeño peppers. Mash with a potato masher or hand mixer on low speed.

> **Serves 4**
>
> You can try almost any peppers in this recipe to complement the main dish being served.

GREEN BEANS WITH PINE NUTS AND FETA CHEESE

1½ pounds fresh green beans
4 quarts water
1 large red onion
1 garlic clove
½ cup fresh spearmint leaves, packed (substitute ¼ cup dried spearmint if fresh is unavailable)
1 cup pine nuts

¾ cup olive oil
¼ cup white vinegar
¾ teaspoon salt
½ teaspoon ground black pepper
1 cup crumbled feta cheese

1. Wash the green beans in cold water. Remove the stems and cut the beans in half. Bring the water to a boil in a large saucepan on medium-high heat. Add the green beans and cook for about 4 minutes or until tender but still crisp. Drain and immerse in ice-cold water for 2 minutes. Remove and spread on paper towels to dry.
2. Remove the peel from the onion and finely chop. Remove the peel from the garlic and mince. Remove the stems from the mint leaves and finely chop the leaves. Finely chop the pine nuts.
3. Combine the garlic, mint, oil, vinegar, salt, and pepper in a food processor or blender; blend until the ingredients are melded together. Cover and refrigerate for at least 2 hours.
4. Pat the beans to remove any remaining water. Place the beans in a serving bowl. Sprinkle the pine nuts and onions on top. Pour the dressing over the top and toss gently.

YAMS WITH MANGO

4 medium-sized fresh yams
1 fresh ripe mango
½ cup honey
½ cup unflavored yogurt

1 tablespoon cinnamon
1 tablespoon butter

1. Preheat oven to 350°.
2. Peel the yams and cut into ¼-inch-thick rounds. Peel and seed the mango; cut the mango into ¼-inch slices.
3. Mix together the honey, yogurt, and cinnamon.
4. Grease a medium-sized baking dish (that has a lid) with the butter. Layer half the yams, then the mangoes, then the remaining half of the yams in the dish. Cover with the sauce.
5. Cover and place in the oven for 1 hour. Remove cover and place back in the oven for 30 minutes.
6. Drain the remaining liquid from the pan before moving the yams and mango to a serving dish. Lightly toss before serving.

Serves 4

If you prefer mashed yams, don't bother layering the ingredients; instead, combine everything and then mash the yams and mango right before serving.

Yams or Sweet Potatoes?

Many people think yams and sweet potatoes are the same thing, but they are definitely different. Sweet potatoes are shaped more like a potato and have a brighter, orange flesh. Yams are more elongated and have stringy hairs on their skin. Their flesh is more pale and less sweet.

PEPPERED CORN

2 (10-ounce) cans whole-kernel sweet corn
2 poblano chilies
1 ancho chili
2 serrano chilies
1 small white onion
2 tablespoons butter
1 tablespoon dried cilantro
1 teaspoon ground black pepper

1. Pour the corn into a medium-sized pan and place on medium-low heat.
2. Remove the stems and seeds from the chilies and cut into ¼-inch pieces. Remove the skin from onion and cut into ¼-inch pieces.
3. Add the chilies and onion to the corn and cook until well-heated.
4. Remove from stove and drain off the liquid. Add the butter, cilantro, and black pepper; mix well, making sure the butter is melted.

GRILLED CORN ON THE COB

8 ears fresh sweet corn
4 tablespoons butter
1 tablespoon cayenne pepper
1 teaspoon ground black pepper
1 teaspoon onion salt
1 teaspoon dried cilantro

1. Preheat the grill to medium temperature.
2. Peel back the corn husks and remove the hairs, leaving the husks attached.
3. Mix together the butter, cayenne pepper, black pepper, onion salt, and cilantro.
4. Use the mixture to coat the corn. Fold the husks back up over the corn cob.
5. Place on the grill, turning frequently. Check every few minutes to make sure the corn is not burning. The corn is done when a few kernels on each cob begin to turn light brown.

TURNIP AND MUSTARD LEAF ROLLS

1 bunch turnip leaves
1 bunch mustard leaves
4 tablespoons butter
¼ cup fresh epazote leaves

1 teaspoon salt
1 teaspoon ground black
  pepper

1. Remove the stems from the turnip and mustard leaves and wash the leaves thoroughly. Pat dry with a paper towel.
2. Remove the stems from the epazote leaves and mince the leaves.
3. Layer 1 turnip leaf then 1 mustard leaf. Add ½ teaspoon of butter in the center of the mustard leaf. Sprinkle with epazote leaves, salt, and black pepper. Roll up the leaves. Repeat with remaining leaves.
4. Place the leaf rolls in a frying pan with a small amount of water. Cover and turn heat on low. Cook for 10 minutes on low heat.

> **Serves 6**
>
> Any combination of leaves works well. If your local store has a small supply of exotic leaves, try spinach and beet leaves.

MASHED CHARD

1 bunch chard leaves
1 small white onion
½ cup water
2 tablespoons butter
½ cup sour cream

1 tablespoon dried oregano
1 teaspoon salt
1 teaspoon ground black
  pepper

1. Remove the stems from the chard and wash the leaves thoroughly. Do not dry. Remove the skin from the onion and cut into ¼-inch pieces.
2. Put the chard and onion in a medium-sized pot on the stove on low heat. Add the water. Cook for about 15 minutes or until the chard is very limp.
3. Drain off the water. Add the butter, sour cream, oregano, salt, and black pepper to the pot. Mash with a potato masher.

> **Serves 4**
>
> Virtually any green works well in this recipe. If you live in a chemical-free area, try using dandelion leaves.

MUSHROOM-AND-NUT-STUFFED CHAYOTE

Serves 4

Chayote can be hard to find in northern climates, but you can substitute acorn squash for an equally good treat.

2 chayote squash
1 cup button mushrooms
¼ cup pistachio meats

¼ cup pecans
¼ cup roasted almonds
½ cup honey

1. Preheat oven to 350°.
2. Cut the squash in half and remove the seeds. Poke holes in the squash meat with a fork. Do not pierce the rind. Clean the mushrooms and cut into quarters.
3. Combine the pistachios, pecan, and almonds. Grind in a food processor or nut grinder until you have small pieces.
4. Combine the mushrooms, nuts, and honey; mix well. Add ¼ of the mixture to the cavity of each squash half.
5. Bake directly on the oven rack for 1 to 2 hours or until the squash is easily pierced with a fork.

TOMATOES WITH GUACAMOLE

Serves 8

Serve as the salad course to complement a spicy beef or pork dish.

1 ripe avocado
1 small yellow onion
2 garlic cloves
4 large ripe tomatoes
2 tablespoons lime juice
1 teaspoon chili powder
4 tablespoons mayonnaise

1 cup whipping cream
½ teaspoon salt
½ teaspoon ground black pepper
Fresh cilantro sprigs (substitute dried cilantro if fresh isn't available)

1. Peel the avocado and remove the nut. Peel the onion and garlic cloves. Cut into quarters. Slice the tomatoes ¼-inch thick.
2. Put the avocado, onion, garlic, lime juice, chili powder, mayonnaise, whipping cream, salt, and black pepper in a food processor or blender; blend on medium until smooth.
3. Pour the sauce over the tomatoes and garnish with cilantro sprigs.

BROCCOLI WITH WALNUTS AND GOAT CHEESE

1½ pounds fresh broccoli
4 quarts water
1 large red onion
1 garlic clove
½ packed cup fresh chives
1 cup chopped walnuts

1 cup crumbled goat cheese
¾ cup olive oil
¼ cup white vinegar
¾ teaspoon salt
¼ teaspoon ground black
    pepper

> **Makes 2 cups**
>
> Serve as a salad before a heavier dish such as Pork Roast with Apples (page 414).

1. Cut off the broccoli florets and cut into bite-sized pieces. If desired, cut the stems into ¼-inch pieces. Bring the water to a boil in a large saucepan. Add the broccoli and cook for 4 to 5 minutes. Drain and immerse in cold water. Remove from cold water and pat dry.
2. Peel the onion and garlic. Cut the onion into ¼-inch pieces. Cut the chives into 2-inch lengths. Chop the walnuts into small pieces and crumble the goat cheese, if necessary.
3. Combine the garlic, chives, oil, vinegar, salt, and pepper in a food processor and blend until smooth. Place in a bowl, cover, and refrigerate for at least 4 hours.
4. Place the broccoli in a serving bowl. Sprinkle with the onions, nuts, and cheese.
5. Just before serving, pour the dressing over the broccoli and toss.

Cutting Boards

Although many chefs prefer wooden cutting boards, plastic is actually more sanitary. Meat and vegetable juice can soak into wood, allowing bacteria to grow.

PASTEL DE ELOTE (CORN PIE)

Serves 6

This dish often is served as a side dish for meals such as Cinnamon Fried Chicken (page 396).

Shortening
¼ pound Monterey jack cheese
¼ pound sharp Cheddar cheese
½ cup canned jalapeño chili peppers
1½ cups frozen corn
½ cup butter
3 large eggs

15-ounce can cream-style corn
½ cup masa harina or cornmeal
1 cup sour cream
½ teaspoon salt
¼ teaspoon Worcestershire sauce

1. Preheat oven to 350°. Grease a pie plate with shortening.
2. Cut the cheeses into ½-inch cubes. Drain the jalapeños and cut into ¼-inch pieces. Thaw the frozen corn. Melt the butter in a saucepan over low heat or in the microwave.
3. In a large mixing bowl, beat the eggs until frothy.
4. Add all the remaining ingredients; stir until thoroughly mixed. Pour into the prepared pie plate.
5. Bake for 20 minutes.

Glazed Vegetables

For a quick and easy glaze for fresh vegetables, use equal parts brown sugar and honey. Add a pinch of salt and some grated orange peel.

CALABACITAS
(ZUCCHINI WITH CHEESE AND CORN)

3 small zucchini
1 large red tomato
2 fresh jalapeño peppers

1 garlic clove
½ pound mild Cheddar cheese
2 cups canned whole-kernel corn

Serves 4

Serve as a side dish to Salpicon (page 417).

1. Cut the zucchini into 1-inch chunks. Chop the tomatoes into ¼-inch pieces. Remove the stems and seeds from the jalapeños and chop into ¼-inch pieces. Peel and mince the garlic. Cut the cheese into ½-inch chunks.
2. Combine the squash, tomatoes, peppers, and garlic in a large saucepan. Turn heat to medium-low. Heat slowly until the ingredients are hot.
3. Add the corn and cheese. Cover and continue to cook until the cheese is melted.

EGGPLANT CASSEROLE

1 medium eggplant
½ teaspoon garlic salt
½ cup canned jalapeño peppers
2 cups canned tomato sauce

½ cup sour cream
½ teaspoon ground cumin
1½ cups grated Cheddar cheese

Serves 6

This goes very well as a side dish for Pork Roast with Apples (page 414).

1. Preheat oven to 350°.
2. Remove the stem from the eggplant. Wash the rind but do not peel. Slice into ½-inch-thick rounds. Arrange the rounds in a 9" × 9" lightly greased baking pan. Sprinkle with the garlic salt.
3. Combine the jalapeño peppers, tomato sauce, sour cream, and cumin; mix well. Pour over the eggplant rounds. Layer the cheese over the top.
4. Bake for 45 to 60 minutes or until the cheese is melted and the eggplant is soft.

MEXICAN STUFFED PEPPERS

Serves 4

Serve as the vegetable course with a mild-flavored poultry dish.

8 fresh, large jalapeño peppers
2–3 cups Refried Beans (see recipe on page 284)
1/4 cup shredded mild Cheddar cheese
1 tablespoon olive oil

1. Preheat oven to 300°.
2. Remove the stems from the peppers and cut in half lengthwise. Remove the seeds.
3. Brush the cavities of the peppers with olive oil.
4. Place enough refried beans in each cavity to fill just to the top. (Don't heap the beans over the top.)
5. Sprinkle a small amount of cheese on top of each stuffed pepper.
6. Place on a baking sheet or in a baking pan. Bake for 30 minutes.

TOMATILLOS WITH ZUCCHINI

Serves 6

This mild dish is the perfect accompaniment for a spicier main course such as Hot and Spicy Tripe (page 415).

3 medium zucchini
4 medium tomatillos
1 large yellow onion
2 tablespoons butter
1/2 teaspoon dried oregano
1/2 teaspoon salt
1 tablespoon water
1/4 cup grated Parmesan cheese

1. Remove the stem from the zucchini (do not peel). Cut the zucchini into thin slices. Remove the skin from the tomatillos and chop into 1/4-inch pieces. Peel the onion and chop into 1/4-inch pieces.
2. Melt the butter in a large frying pan at medium heat. Add the onion and cook until limp but not brown.
3. Add the zucchini, tomatillos, oregano, salt, and water; stir well.
4. Cover, bring to a boil, then reduce heat. Cook until the zucchini is tender but still slightly crisp, about 6 minutes.
5. Stir in the cheese before serving.

PICKLED CHILIES

4 pounds mixed chili peppers
2 large red onions
20 garlic cloves
1 (2-inch piece) fresh ginger
12 tablespoons olive oil
12 cloves
1 tablespoon fresh-ground
  cinnamon

2 teaspoons dried thyme
2 teaspoons dried oregano
8 cups distilled white vinegar
2 tablespoons sea salt

> **Makes 8 pints**
>
> If you're planning to eat these within 6 months, you can simply seal them and keep them in the refrigerator.

1. Rinse the chilies in cold running water to clean. Remove the stems. Prick each chili 3 or 4 times with a fork. Peel the onions and slice into ¼-inch rounds. Peel the garlic cloves. Slice the ginger thinly.
2. Heat the olive oil to medium-high in a very large saucepan. Add the garlic. Sauté until golden, then smash the garlic into the oil with the back of a spoon or spatula. Add the onions, ginger, cloves, cinnamon, thyme, and oregano. Cook for 2 to 3 minutes or until the onion just turns clear. Add the chilies and cook for 5 to 6 minutes, stirring constantly.
3. Heat the vinegar to boiling in a large saucepan. Add it to the chili mixture. Bring everything to a boil for about 5 minutes. Stir in the salt until dissolved.
4. Pour into sterilized jars and seal.

Using a Double Boiler

A double boiler consists of two pots, one sitting on top of the other. The food to be cooked goes in the top pot while the boiling water goes in the bottom. The steam from the boiling water cooks the food. By not having direct contact with the heat source, you eliminate the possibility of burning the food, while still being able to get it very hot.

CACTUS PADDLES

Serves 4

Try topping this with a sprinkling of ground pistachio meats.

2 pounds fresh cactus paddles
1 small yellow onion
4 garlic cloves

2 tablespoons butter
1 teaspoon dried oregano
1 cup sour cream

1. Clean the cactus paddles and pat dry. Cut into 1-inch pieces. Remove the skin from the onion and cut into ¼-inch pieces. Remove the skin from the garlic and cut into thin slices.
2. Melt the butter in a skillet on low heat. Add the cactus pieces, onion, garlic, and oregano; cook, stirring periodically, until the onion is clear.
3. Drain off excess butter. Stir in the sour cream.

GRILLED ZUCCHINI

Serves 8

This is perfect served with Barbecued Pork Ribs (page 416) or any other grilled meat.

4 medium zucchini
2 garlic cloves
1 fresh habanero pepper
½ cup olive oil

1 teaspoon dried oregano
1 teaspoon chili powder
1 teaspoon salt
½ teaspoon ground black pepper

1. Preheat grill to medium heat.
2. Remove the stems from the zucchini (do not peel) and slice in half lengthwise. Peel and mince the garlic. Remove the stem and seeds from the habanero pepper and mince.
3. Combine the garlic, habanero, oil, oregano, chili powder, salt, and black pepper in a small covered container; shake until well mixed.
4. Place the zucchini flesh side down on the grill for 10 minutes. Then turn fresh side up and grill until the zucchini is soft. Use the oil and spice sauce to baste the zucchini as it cooks.

CHAPTER 29
RICE AND BEAN DISHES

RED, WHITE, AND GREEN RICE SALAD

2 cups uncooked brown rice
1 medium-sized green bell pepper
2 small pimientos
2 medium tomatoes
3 green onions
2 eggs
1 teaspoon fresh marjoram
½ teaspoon fresh basil
1 tablespoon fresh parsley
¼ cup vegetable oil
¼ cup olive oil
¼ cup wine vinegar
1 teaspoon salt

1. Bring 4 cups of water to a boil. Add the rice; boil for 5 minutes. Reduce heat to medium-low and let cook for 20 minutes or until the rice is tender.
2. Remove the stem and seeds from the green pepper and pimientos. Slice into ¼-inch strips. Cut the tomatoes into ½-inch cubes. Remove the skin and roots from the green onions; slice into ¼-inch pieces. Hard-boil the eggs and chop into ¼-inch pieces.
3. Combine the rice, pepper, pimientos, tomatoes, green onions, and eggs in a medium-sized bowl; toss until well mixed.
4. Chop the marjoram, basil, and parsley into small pieces. Combine in a small bowl. Add the vegetable oil, olive oil, vinegar, and salt; stir well.
5. Pour the dressing over the salad. Cover and chill for at least 1 hour before serving.

GORDO

1 cup uncooked white rice
1 garlic clove
1 medium yellow onion
2 medium fresh jalapeños
1 cup sour cream

½ cup grated Parmesan cheese
1½ cups grated Cheddar cheese
1 teaspoon salt
¼ teaspoon ground black pepper

Serves 4

This is an excellent complement to a poultry or red meat dish.

1. Add the rice to 2 cups of water in a medium-sized saucepan. Cover and bring to a boil. Boil for 5 minutes, then reduce heat to low and simmer for 20 minutes or until the rice is tender.
2. Preheat oven to 300°. Lightly butter or grease a square baking dish.
3. Remove the skin from the onions and garlic and chop into ¼-inch pieces.
4. Mix together all the ingredients in a large mixing bowl. Spoon the mixture into the prepared baking dish and bake, covered, for 35 minutes. Remove cover and bake for an additional 5 minutes.

JALAPEÑO RICE

1½ cups uncooked white rice
½ pound Monterey jack cheese
¼ cup fresh green chilies or ⅛ cup canned green chilies

2 cups sour cream
½ teaspoon salt
¼ cup butter

Serves 6

Serve as a side dish to any fish or chicken meal.

1. Preheat oven to 350°. Grease a 9-inch-square baking pan.
2. Bring 6 cups of water to a boil. Add the rice and salt. Cover and boil for 5 minutes. Reduce heat to medium-low and cook for 20 minutes or until the rice is tender.
3. Grate the cheese. If using fresh chilies, remove the stem and seeds. Chop the chilies into ¼-inch pieces.
4. Layer the rice, sour cream, cheese, and chilies in pan in that order. Dot with butter on top. Bake for about 30 minutes.

CASA GRANDE

1½ cups uncooked white rice
1 large bunch fresh spinach
1 large yellow onion
2 tablespoons butter
1½ cups Colby cheese
¼ teaspoon garlic salt

4 eggs
½ cup milk
2 teaspoons salt
½ teaspoon ground black pepper

1. Add the rice to 3 cups water in a medium-sized pan. Cover, bring to a boil, and cook for 5 minutes. Turn the heat to low and simmer for 20 minutes or until the rice is tender.
2. Remove the stems from the spinach and wash well. Pat dry. Place in a medium-sized pot with 1 cup water. Cover and cook on low heat until the spinach is limp and has diminished in size to about 1 cup. Drain off the water from spinach.
3. Preheat oven to 350°.
4. Peel the onion and chop into ¼-inch pieces. In a large frying pan, melt the butter. Add the onion and cook until clear and tender but not brown. Add the rice, spinach, ½ cup of the cheese, and the garlic salt; mix well.
5. Combine the eggs, milk, salt, and pepper; mix well. Stir into the rice mixture.
6. Pour into a casserole dish and bake, uncovered, for 30 minutes.

Experimenting with Rice

There are many types of rice available in today's markets. Most are fairly easy to cook with, although you will need to experiment with the amount of water and cooking time each one needs. Generally, the less processed the rice, the more water it will take up and the more cooking time it will need.

COLD RICE AND BEANS

1½ cups dry white rice
1 cup frozen peas
2 cups canned pinto beans
2 cups canned black beans
3 celery ribs
1 medium-sized red onion
1 cup canned jalapeño chili
    peppers, or 8 fresh jalapeños
1 bunch fresh cilantro

⅓ cup white wine vinegar
¼ cup olive oil
1 teaspoon salt
½ teaspoon garlic powder
½ teaspoon ground black
    pepper
¼ teaspoon cayenne pepper

Serves 6

Serve as a summer luncheon with fresh Flour Tortillas and Jasmine and Rose Hips Tea (see recipes on pages 284 and 541).

1. Bring 3 cups water to a boil in a medium-sized pot. Add the dry rice. Cover and boil for 5 minutes. Reduce heat to medium-low and simmer for 20 minutes. Drain off excess water.
2. Thaw the peas. Rinse and drain the beans. Cut the celery ribs into ¼-inch pieces. Peel the onion and cut into ¼-inch rounds. Drain the jalapeño peppers and cut into ¼-inch pieces. Remove the stems from the cilantro and roughly chop the leaves into ½-inch pieces.
3. Combine the rice, peas, pinto beans, black beans, celery, onion, jalapeño peppers, and cilantro in a large serving bowl; toss lightly to mix.
4. In a small glass jar, combine 2 tablespoons water, the white wine vinegar, olive oil, salt, garlic powder, black pepper, and cayenne pepper. Cover and shake until well mixed. Pour over the salad. Toss until all the ingredients are covered.
5. Cover and refrigerate for at least 24 hours before serving.

RICE WITH SAUTÉED PORK

Serves 4

Serve with Tropical
Gelatin (page 478)
and fresh Flour
Tortillas (page 284).

1½ cups dry white rice
1-pound pork loin
1 medium-sized yellow onion
2 cups canned pinto beans
2 tablespoons olive oil
¼ teaspoon garlic powder
¾ cup canned tomato paste

2 teaspoons salt
½ teaspoon dried oregano
½ teaspoon ground cumin
1½ teaspoons medium-hot red
   chili powder

1. Bring 3 cups of water to a boil in a medium-sized pot. Add the rice; boil for 5 minutes. Reduce temperature to medium-low and simmer for 20 minutes. Drain off excess water.
2. Cut the pork into thin slices. Peel the onion and cut into ¼-inch pieces. Rinse and drain the pinto beans.
3. Heat the oil to medium temperature in a large frying pan. Add the pork and cook until browned. Add the onions, garlic powder, salt, oregano, cumin and chili powder; sauté lightly until the onions are soft and clear but not brown. Stir in the tomato paste and 1 cup of water.
4. Turn heat to low. Cover and simmer for 30 minutes.
5. Add the beans and stir lightly. Cover and simmer for 15 minutes longer.
6. Stir in the rice. Cook, uncovered, for 10 minutes.

Slicing Meat Thin
To easily cut meat into small cubes or strips, thaw it only partially, then use a large kitchen knife and cut the meat as you would a brick of cheese. It should have about the same consistency.

RICE AND CHICKEN WITH GUACAMOLE

2 large chicken breasts
1 tablespoon vegetable oil
1½ cups dry white rice
1 cup frozen peas
1 medium-sized yellow onion
3 celery ribs
¼ cup canned pimientos
1 teaspoon salt
1 teaspoon ground black
* pepper*

1 cup mayonnaise
1½ teaspoons Tabasco or
* other hot sauce*
1 large avocado
½ teaspoon Worcestershire
* sauce*
1 cup sour cream
½ teaspoon dried onion flakes
½ teaspoon garlic salt
½ teaspoon onion salt

Serves 4
Serve as a summer luncheon with Brie and Papaya Quesadillas (page 308).

1. Remove the skin and bones from the chicken breasts. Bring the vegetable oil to medium temperature in a medium-sized frying pan. Add the chicken breasts and cook until the meat is lightly browned on all sides. Cut the breasts with a knife to make sure they are thoroughly cooked. Set on a paper towel to cool.

2. In a medium-sized pan, bring 3 cups of water to a boil. Add the rice; boil for 5 minutes, then lower temperature to low. Cover and simmer for 20 minutes. Drain off excess water.

3. Cut the chicken breasts into 1-inch cubes. Thaw the peas. Peel the onion and cut into ½-inch pieces. Cut the celery into ¼-inch pieces. Drain the pimientos and cut into ¼-inch pieces.

4. In a large serving bowl, combine the rice, chicken, peas, onion, celery, pimientos, salt, black pepper, ½ cup of the mayonnaise, and 1 teaspoon of the hot sauce; toss lightly until well mixed.

5. Peel the avocado and then remove pit. Mash until no chunks remain.

6. Combine the avocado, remaining ½ cup mayonnaise, Worcestershire sauce, sour cream, onion flakes, garlic salt, onion salt, and the remaining ½ teaspoon hot sauce; mix well.

7. Pour the dressing over the salad and mix until all the ingredients are covered. Cover and refrigerate for at least 4 hours before serving.

ARROZ CON POLLO

1 large fryer chicken
2 teaspoons salt
1 medium onion
4 large tomatoes
1 garlic clove
4 tablespoons shortening

1½ cup uncooked brown rice
1 teaspoon black pepper
1 teaspoon cumin seeds
2–3 cups warm water

1. Cut the chicken into 8 serving pieces. Sprinkle the salt over the chicken pieces. Remove the skin from the onion and slice into ¼-inch rings. Cut the tomatoes into eighths. Remove the skin from the garlic and mince.
2. Melt the shortening in a large frying pan over medium heat. Add the rice and stir constantly until the rice is browned.
3. In a separate frying pan, brown the chicken over medium heat.
4. Place the chicken pieces over the top of the rice. Add the tomatoes, onion, garlic, spices, and warm water.
5. Cover and simmer over low heat until the rice is tender and fluffy. If the mixture dries before the rice is cooked, add more warm water.

The Types of Arroz

Arroz is simply the Spanish word for "rice." As with most other warm-weather cultures around the world, the Mexicans have adopted rice as a staple of their diet. Although they usually use white rice in their cooking, brown rice is favored when seeking a more hearty dish.

BAKED GREEN RICE

1½ cups dry white rice
2 fresh green chilies
4 tomatillos
1 bunch green onions
1 bunch parsley
½ pound mild Cheddar cheese
2 eggs

⅓ cup butter
1 teaspoon salt
½ teaspoon ground black
   pepper
1 cup milk

Serves 8

Serve as a side dish
for Cinnamon Fried
Chicken (page 396).

1. Preheat oven to 350°.
2. Put the rice in a medium-sized saucepan with 3 cups of water and bring to a boil. Reduce heat to low, cover, and simmer for 20 minutes or until the rice is tender.
3. Remove the stems, membranes, and seeds from the chilies. Remove the skins from the tomatillos and chop into ¼-inch pieces. Chop the green onions and their stems into ¼-inch pieces. Cut off the stems from the parsley and chop the leaves into small pieces. Grate the cheese. Beat the eggs.
4. Combine the hot rice with the cheese and butter; toss until well mixed. Add the chilies, tomatillos, onions, parsley, salt, and pepper; mix well. Add the beaten eggs and milk; stir well.
5. Transfer the mixture to a greased 2-quart baking dish. Cover and bake for 30 minutes. Uncover and bake for an additional 10 minutes.

ARROZ CON QUESO

Serves 8

Serve with Mexican
Pot Roast (page 412).

2 cups dry white rice
¾ pound Monterey jack cheese
⅛ pound Cheddar cheese
¼ cup canned, diced green
    chilies
1 pint sour cream

1. Preheat oven to 350°.
2. Bring 4 cups of water to a boil in a medium-sized saucepan. Add the rice; cover and boil for 5 minutes. Reduce heat to low and simmer for 20 minutes or until the rice is tender. Drain off any excess water.
3. Grate the cheeses. Drain the chilies and mix into the sour cream.
4. In a 1-quart casserole, layer the ingredients in the following order: ½ the rice, ½ the sour cream with jalapeños, ½ the Monterey jack cheese, the remaining rice, sour cream with jalapeños, and Monterey jack cheese.
5. Bake for 30 minutes. Top with Cheddar cheese and broil for 2 to 3 minutes before serving.

CUMIN RICE

Serves 8

Serve with Pork
Roast with Apples
(page 414).

1 small onion
1 medium-sized red bell pepper
1 medium-sized green bell
    pepper
1 garlic clove
2 tablespoons butter
1 teaspoon ground cumin
1½ cups uncooked white rice
1½ cups hot Chicken Stock
    (see recipe on page 286)

1. Peel the onion and chop into ¼-inch pieces. Remove the stems, seeds, and membranes from the peppers and cut into ¼-inch pieces. Peel and mince the garlic.
2. Heat the butter to medium temperature in a saucepan. Add the peppers and onion; cook until the onion is limp but not brown. Add the garlic, cumin, rice, and hot stock. Mix well and cover the saucepan.
3. Bring to a boil, reduce heat, and cook for about 20 minutes or until the rice is tender and the liquid is absorbed.

SHERRIED RAISIN AND RICE PUDDING

²/₃ cup golden raisins
¼ cup dry red sherry
1 egg
1 cup uncooked white rice
1 teaspoon grated lemon peel

½ teaspoon salt
1½ cups water
3 cups whole milk
1 cup granulated sugar
½ teaspoon ground cinnamon

> **Serves 6**
>
> Add whipped cream and coconut to each dish right before serving for a festive atmosphere.

1. Soak the raisins in the sherry for 15 minutes. Beat the egg and set aside.
2. Put the rice, lemon peel, salt, and water in a saucepan; bring to a boil. Reduce heat to low, cover, and cook until all the water is absorbed, about 15 minutes.
3. Stir in the milk, sugar, and cinnamon; cook over very low heat, stirring frequently, until all the milk has been absorbed.
4. Stir in the soaked raisins, then the beaten egg. Continue to heat, stirring constantly, until the egg is cooked, about 1 to 2 minutes.
5. Transfer the pudding to a serving dish. Chill in the refrigerator for 2 to 3 hours before serving.

To Mash or Not to Mash?

Often in Mexico when you order refried beans you receive a bowl of warm beans and onions in water with a triangle of dry toast. In short, they don't have to be mashed to be refried. They also don't have to be pinto beans. Any bean that is cooked twice is considered refried.

CREAMED RICE WITH CHILIES

Serves 4

Serve with fried
Chorizo (page 417).

2 cups dry white rice
4 cups water
4 habanero chilies
1 small yellow onion
2 garlic cloves
1 cup frozen or fresh peas

1 cup frozen or fresh corn
 kernels
½ pound Monterey jack cheese
2 tablespoons butter
2 cups sour cream

1. Bring the water to a boil in a medium-sized saucepan. Add the rice and bring back to a boil. Reduce heat to medium-low and simmer, covered, for 20 minutes or until the rice is tender. Drain off excess water and set the rice aside.
2. Preheat oven to 350°.
3. Remove the stems and seeds from the chilies and cut into ¼-inch pieces. Peel the onion and cut into ¼-inch pieces. Peel and mince the garlic. Thaw the peas and corn if necessary. Grate the cheese.
4. Melt the butter in a medium-sized frying pan on medium heat. Add the onions and garlic; sauté until the onions are limp but not brown. Reduce heat to medium-low. Add the chilies, peas, and corn; cook until thoroughly heated. Stir in the sour cream and cheese. Cook, stirring often, until the cheese is melted.
5. Add the rice to the vegetable and cheese mixture; stir until well blended. Pour into an ovenproof casserole dish. Bake for 30 minutes or until it is slightly brown on top.

What Makes a Salsa?

Salsa actually means "sauce." It can be hot, cold, chunky, or runny. Except when you use it as a dip for chips, salsa invariably is used as a topping for a dish or as a basic ingredient to complement the other ingredients in a recipe.

EXTRA-SPECIAL FRIJOLES REFRITOS

2½ cups uncooked pinto beans
5 slices bacon
1 large white onion
2 garlic cloves
4 large tomatoes
1 teaspoon salt

1 teaspoon ground black pepper
1 teaspoon dried oregano
1 teaspoon ground cumin
1 cup beef broth

> **Serves 6**
>
> This is traditionally served with tortillas or dry toast triangles. However, it also makes an excellent meat substitute in tacos or enchiladas.

1. Soak the beans overnight in 5 cups of water. Drain and place in a large saucepan on medium heat. Add 4 cups of water. Cover and cook until tender but not mushy (about 2 hours). Remove from heat and drain.
2. In a large frying pan, fry the bacon until crisp. Set the bacon on a paper towel to drain grease. Chop roughly.
3. Remove the skin from the onion and chop into ¼-inch pieces. Remove the skin from the garlic and mince. Add the onion and garlic to the bacon grease and sauté on medium heat until golden brown.
4. Cut the tomatoes into ½-inch pieces. Add the tomatoes and beans to the onions and garlic in the frying pan; stir together. Add the salt, pepper, oregano, and cumin; mix thoroughly. Stir in the chopped bacon. Stir in the beef broth. Cover and simmer on medium-low heat for 20 minutes.

Tortilla or Tostada

Although many North Americans associate crispy corn tortillas with tacos, the tostada is the only item that calls for frying the tortilla until it is crisp and hard. Mexicans rarely use the formed, fried tortillas we see at Mexican restaurants. Instead, they heat the soft corn tortilla, place the meat in the middle, and fold it over.

BLACK BEAN AND AVOCADO BURRITOS

½ cup dry black beans (or 1 cup canned black beans)

½ cup dry brown rice

4 Flour Tortillas (see recipe on page 284)

1 small onion

1 medium avocado

¼ cup canned or frozen whole-kernel corn

2 tablespoons fresh cilantro

¼ cup canned green chilies or 2 fresh green chilies

¼ teaspoon salt

½ teaspoon black pepper

½ cup shredded Monterey jack cheese

½ cup Tomato Salsa (see recipe on page 282)

½ cup shredded lettuce

1. To cook the black beans, soak the dry beans in water overnight. Drain and rinse the beans. Bring 1½ cups of water to a boil. Add the beans, cover, and boil for 5 minutes. Reduce heat to medium-low and cook for 1 hour. Drain off remaining water before using.

2. To cook the brown rice, bring 1½ cups of water to a boil. Add the rice. Cover and boil for 5 minutes. Reduce heat to medium-low and cook for an additional 30 minutes. Drain off remaining water before using.

3. Preheat oven to 350°. Place the tortillas in a covered container in the oven for 5 to 10 minutes.

4. Remove the skin and chop the onion into ¼-inch pieces. Remove the skin and pit from the avocado and chop the avocado meat into ½-inch pieces. Drain or thaw the corn. Remove the stems from the cilantro and roughly chop the leaves. Roughly chop the lettuce.

5. Combine the beans, rice, onion, corn, cilantro, lettuce, green chilies, salt, and pepper in a medium sized-bowl. Mix well.

6. Remove the tortillas from the oven and place ½ cup of the rice-bean mixture in the center of each tortilla. Top each with ¼ of the avocado, 2 tablespoons cheese, and 1 tablespoon salsa.

7. Roll up each tortilla. Fold over the ends before serving.

MIXED BEAN SALAD

1 (15-ounce) can cooked gar-
banzo beans
1 (15-ounce) can cooked pinto
beans
1 (15-ounce) can cooked black
beans
1 (15-ounce) can cooked green
beans
1 medium-sized red onion
2 garlic cloves

1 medium carrot
1 medium cucumber
1 cup vegetable oil
½ cup white vinegar
¼ cup lemon juice
1 teaspoon salt
1 teaspoon ground black pepper
½ cup roasted pecans

> **Serves 6**
>
> For some added zing, add a chopped hot pepper to the salad and some cayenne pepper to the dressing.

1. Drain off the water from all the beans and rinse with cold water. Combine in a large mixing bowl.
2. Remove the skin from the onion and cut into ¼-inch rounds. Remove the skin from the garlic and cut into thin slices. Peel the carrot and cut into ¼-inch rounds. Peel the cucumber and cut into ¼-inch rounds. Mix these ingredients with the beans.
3. In a small container with a lid, mix together the vegetable oil, vinegar, lemon juice, salt, and ground black pepper. Cover and shake until well blended. Pour on the bean and vegetable mixture and toss gently until well mixed.
4. Chill overnight before serving. Right before serving, sprinkle pecans on top.

MIXED BEAN SOUP

1 cup each dried pinto, kidney,
   and black beans
1 large yellow onion
2 garlic cloves
2 medium-sized red tomato
1 large carrot
1 fresh jalapeño or habanero
   pepper

1 teaspoon chili powder
½ teaspoon red chili pepper
   flakes
2 teaspoons salt
2 cups Chicken Stock (see
   recipe on page 286)

1. Soak the beans overnight in 6 cups of water.
2. Remove the skin from the onion and chop into ¼-inch pieces. Remove
   the skin from the garlic and mince. Remove the stems from the tomatoes and chop into ½-inch pieces. Peel the carrot and chop into
   ¼-inch pieces. Remove the stem and seeds from the pepper.
3. Add all the ingredients *except* the chicken stock to a large stockpot.
   Bring to a boil for 5 minutes. Reduce heat to medium-low and
   simmer, uncovered, for 3 hours.
4. Drain off the water and transfer the mixture to a blender. (You may
   need to divide it into 2 or 3 groups.) Blend on medium setting for
   2 minutes or until the mixture becomes a paste.
5. Stir in the chicken stock. Reheat to serving temperature.

Blend at Will
*Mexicans love to use their blenders and mashers. While similar
dishes in other cultures leave the ingredients in chunky bites, the
Mexican versions often have them blended together to create a
unique meld of flavors.*

BEER BEANS

2 cups dry pinto beans
2 cups dark Mexican beer
2 pieces bacon
1 medium onion
3 garlic cloves
2 large red tomatoes

4 pickled jalapeño chilies
1 teaspoon salt
1 teaspoon ground black pepper

Serves 6

Serve as a side dish to Barbecued Pork Ribs (page 416) or another meat dish.

1. Soak the pinto beans in 6 cups of water overnight. Drain and rinse. Put the beans into a large pot and cover with water. Bring to a boil, then reduce heat. Simmer for 30 minutes or until the beans are cooked but still firm. Drain off water and add the beer. Stir and continue to cook on low heat.

2. Fry the bacon until very crisp. Reserve the grease in the frying pan. Transfer the bacon to a paper towel to cool. When cool, crumble into pieces about ¼-inch square.

3. Peel the onion and chop into ¼-inch pieces. Peel and mince the garlic. Remove the stems from the tomatoes and chop into ½-inch pieces. Remove the stems from the jalapeños and chop the chilies into ¼-inch pieces.

4. Add the onion and garlic to the bacon grease. Cook until the onion is clear and limp. Add the tomato and jalapeños; stir to blend. Cook for about 5 minutes.

5. Add the tomato mixture to the beans. Stir in the crumbled bacon, salt, and pepper. Bring to a boil, reduce heat to low, and simmer for about 15 minutes.

BEAN BURRITOS

Serves 6

Serve with fresh Tostadas (page 285) and Guacamole (page 287).

2 teaspoons ground cumin
3 cups Refried Beans (see recipe on page 284)
¼ cup sour cream
1 cup Tomato Salsa (see recipe on page 282)
6 large Flour Tortillas (see recipe on page 284)
½ cup grated Monterey jack cheese

1. Place the cumin in a small frying pan on low heat. Heat until toasted and fragrant, stirring constantly.
2. Place the beans in a blender or food processor and blend on medium speed until smooth. Add the cumin and sour cream; blend until well mixed. Remove from blender and stir in the tomato salsa.
3. Add about ⅔ cup of the mixture to the center of each tortilla. Sprinkle cheese on top. Fold over ends and roll up.

BEAN-STUFFED PEPPERS

Serves 6

Serve as a side dish for Jalapeño Chicken (page 410).

2 eggs
6 red bell peppers
3 cups Refried Beans (see recipe on page 284)
¼ cup flour
1 cup shortening
½ cup cream
¼ pound Monterey jack cheese

1. Preheat oven to 350°.
2. Separate the eggs. Beat the egg yolks until thick. Beat the whites until they are shiny and stiff. Fold the egg whites into the egg yolks. Remove the stems and seeds from the bell peppers. Stuff with refried beans. Dust the peppers with flour, then dip into the egg mixture.
3. Melt the shortening in a medium-sized frying pan. Put 2 or 3 peppers in the pan at a time and fry on all sides.
4. Arrange the peppers in an ovenproof casserole dish. Cover with the cream. Grate the cheese and sprinkle on top. Bake for about 20 minutes.

BEAN-STUFFED ZUCCHINI

2 medium zucchini (about
    10 inches long)
2 medium onions
1 green bell pepper
½ pound Monterey jack cheese
3 tablespoons butter or
    margarine
2 teaspoons ground cumin

1 teaspoon dried basil
2 teaspoons Red Chili Sauce
    (see recipe on page 288)
2 cups Refried Beans (see
    recipe on page 284)
¾ cup sour cream

Serves 4

Serve with Jalapeño Corn Bread (page 330).

1. Preheat oven to 350°.
2. Wash the zucchini and slice off the ends. Slice each squash lengthwise and scoop out the centers. Place the squash in a 9" × 12" baking pan. Chop the squash centers and set aside.
3. Peel the onions and chop into ¼-inch pieces. Remove the stem and seeds from the green pepper and chop into ¼-inch pieces. Grate the cheese.
4. Melt the butter in a large frying pan at medium heat. Add the onion and green pepper; sauté until onion is clear and tender. Add the cumin, basil, chili sauce, and squash centers; sauté for an additional 5 minutes. Add the beans, stir well, and cook another 5 minutes. Add the cheese. Stir and cook until the cheese melts. Turn off the heat and stir in the sour cream.
5. Stuff the zucchini shells with the cooked mixture. Bake for 30 minutes or until the mixture is hot and bubbly.

Making a Dressing

Americans and most Europeans prefer an oily dressing, using about twice as much oil as vinegar. Mexicans, however, enjoy a stronger vinegar taste in their dressings. They also frequently add a bit of citrus juice, such as lime, to their dressing to give it an added zing.

ENROLLADOS

1 medium-sized yellow onion
2 medium-sized red tomatoes
3 cups Refried Beans (see recipe on page 284)
1 cup Red Chili Sauce (see recipe on page 288)
12 Flour Tortillas (see recipe on page 284)

1½ cups shredded Monterey jack cheese
½ cup vegetable oil
2 eggs
½ cup flour

1. Peel the onion and chop into ¼-inch pieces. Remove the stems from the tomatoes and chop into ¼-inch pieces.
2. Heat the beans on low in a medium-sized saucepan. Add the onion, tomatoes, and chili sauce; heat through.
3. Spoon about ⅓ cup of the mixture into the center of each tortilla. Add about 2 tablespoons of the cheese. Roll up the tortilla as you would an enchilada.
4. Heat the oil to medium-high in a large frying pan. Beat the eggs in a medium-sized bowl. Roll each tortilla in the flour and then in the beaten eggs. Place in the frying pan and fry until golden brown on all sides.

Canned or Fresh Peppers?
A stop at a local Wal-Mart in the northern United States found no fewer than seven varieties of fresh chili peppers—showing that you will likely be able to find fresh chilies to meet your needs virtually anywhere. However, if you must use canned, plan to use about half as much as you would of fresh, because they become more packed during the canning process.

MEXICAN PORK AND BEANS

¼ pound sliced bacon
¼ pound boneless pork
* tenderloin*
¼ pound ham
1 large white onion
1½ cups canned diced tomatoes

1 teaspoon chili powder
½ teaspoon ground cumin
½ teaspoon dried oregano
2 cups canned pinto beans
1 cup tequila

Serves 4
Serve as a stew with fresh Flour Tortillas (page 284).

1. Cut the pork and ham into 1-inch cubes. Peel the onion and slice into ¼-inch rounds.
2. Cook the bacon on medium heat in a frying pan until crisp. Reserve the grease in the pan and transfer the bacon to paper towels to drain. When cool, crumble.
3. Brown the pork and ham in the bacon fat. Add the onion. Turn the heat to medium. Cover and cook until soft, about 5 minutes.
4. Add the tomatoes, chili powder, cumin, oregano, and the crumbled bacon, stir well. Add the beans. Bring to a boil. Gradually stir in the tequila.
5. Continue to cook, uncovered, for 1 hour or until the pork is well done and the mixture is the consistency of a rich stew. Stir occasionally.

Dry Soup?

Many Mexican dishes feature bread or tortillas that are soaked in a sauce until the dish resembles more of a casserole or heavy stew than a soup. In Mexico, they refer to these dishes as dry soups. It's not certain where this name came from, but it's an apt description.

GARBANZOS WITH SAUSAGE

Serves 4

This makes an excellent accompaniment to Citrus Veal (page 413).

1 medium-sized white onion
1 garlic clove
2 cups canned garbanzo beans
½ cup canned pimientos
½ pound pork sausage

1 teaspoon chili powder
½ teaspoon salt
¼ teaspoon dried oregano
½ teaspoon ground black pepper

1. Peel the onion and chop into ¼-inch pieces. Peel and mince the garlic. Drain the garbanzo beans and rinse. Drain the pimientos and cut into ¼-inch-wide strips.
2. Brown the sausage in a frying pan on medium heat. Add the onion, garlic, and chili powder; cook until the onion is soft.
3. Add the garbanzos and pimientos; stir well. Bring to a simmer. Add the salt, oregano, and pepper.

LIMA BEAN CASSEROLE

Serves 6

Serve with fresh fruit for a well-balanced meal.

1 pound dried lima beans
1 large white onion
¼ pound spicy sausage
¼ pound ham
¼ cup vegetable oil

1 cup Red Chili Sauce (see recipe on page 288)
½ cup grated Monterey jack cheese

1. Put the lima beans in a large pot. Add water to cover them. Soak for 1 hour. Bring to a boil, reduce heat, and cook until tender, about 1 hour. If the beans seem dry after 30 minutes, stir in 1 cup more of water.
2. Peel the onion and cut into ¼-inch rings. Cut the ham into ½-inch cubes.
3. Heat the oil to medium temperature in a medium-sized skillet. Add the onion and sausage; cook until the sausage is browned. Add the ham and chili sauce. Cover and cook for about 30 minutes.
4. Skim off excess fat. Add the cooked beans and cook another 15 minutes. Sprinkle with cheese before serving.

Chapter 30
FRUIT

PINEAPPLE AND COCONUT SALAD

1 fresh pineapple (substitute canned if necessary)
1 fresh coconut (substitute 2 cups preshredded if necessary)
1 medium-sized fresh cabbage (or 2 cups preshredded)

1 cup mayonnaise
1 teaspoon lemon juice
6 large lettuce leaves

1. Remove the rind, core, and top from the pineapple. Cut into ½-inch cubes. Remove the shell from the coconut and shred until you have 2 cups. Shred the cabbage until you have 2 cups.
2. Combine the pineapple, coconut, cabbage, mayonnaise, and lemon juice in a large serving bowl; toss gently until well mixed.
3. Cover and chill for at least 1 hour before serving. Serve by scooping onto lettuce leaves.

MANGO PASTE

2 ripe mangoes

4 cups (approximately) granulated sugar

1. Peel the mango and remove the seeds.
2. Place the fruit in a food processor or blender and mix on medium setting until you have a purée—the mixture should be free of large lumps.
3. Weigh the mango and measure out an equal weight of sugar.
4. Put the mango and sugar in a large pot on low heat; mix well. Cook, stirring often, until the mixture has the consistency of jelly. This usually takes 1 to 3 hours.
5. Remove from the heat and beat with a large spoon for about 10 minutes or until you have a heavy paste.
6. Pour the paste onto wax paper and set in a sunny area for at least 24 hours.

FRUITY TAMALES

2 cups masa harina or cornmeal
1 teaspoon salt
1 teaspoon baking powder
⅓ cup shortening
1 cup granulated sugar
1 cup water
1 teaspoon lime juice

24 corn husks
½ cup dried peaches
½ cup dried apricots
½ cup raisins
½ cup slivered almonds

Serves 8
These are a favorite to take to the beach. Put the just-steamed tamales in a small cooler to keep them warm.

1. Soak the corn husks in warm water for 1 hour. Drain off the water and pat the husks dry with a paper towel.
2. Mix together the cornmeal, salt, baking powder, shortening, sugar, water, and lime juice in a medium-sized mixing bowl to form a doughy texture. If the mixture seems too runny, add more cornmeal. If it seems too dry, add more water.
3. Place 1 heaping tablespoon of the cornmeal mixture in the center of each corn husk and pat down until it is about ¼-inch thick.
4. Cut the dried peaches and apricots into ¼-inch pieces. Mix together the peaches, apricots, raisins, and almonds.
5. Add 1 tablespoon of the fruit mixture to the center of the dough on each corn husk. Roll up the husks so the mixture is centered in the husk.
6. Steam for 30 minutes.

How to Steam with No Steamer

If you don't have a steamer, add 1 inch of water to a large pot and place a stainless steel mixing bowl in the pot. Put the tamales in the mixing bowl and turn the heat on medium-high. Cover and check every 5 minutes to make sure the water doesn't boil away.

PEPPERY MANGO SALAD

Serves 12

This makes an excellent accompaniment to any beef dish.

10 ripe mangoes
2 large Vidalia onions
8 fresh jalapeño chili peppers
½ cup vegetable oil
1½ cups cider vinegar

½ teaspoon salt
½ teaspoon ground white pepper
½ teaspoon white granulated sugar

1. Peel the mangoes and slice the fruit into ½-inch-thick slices. Peel the onion and cut into ¼-inch rounds. Remove stem and seeds from jalapeño peppers and cut into ¼-inch rounds. Combine these ingredients in a large mixing bowl.
2. Stir together the oil, cider vinegar, salt, pepper, and sugar; pour over the fruit, onion, and pepper mixture. Toss gently until the mangoes, onions, and peppers are covered with the dressing.
3. Refrigerate at least 2 hours before serving.

SPICY PINEAPPLE SALAD

Serves 6

This makes an excellent counterpart to a heavy meat dish, such as Caldo de Rez (page 371).

1 pineapple
1 medium-sized red onion
2 garlic cloves
1 bunch fresh cilantro

1 jalapeño pepper
½ teaspoon dried oregano
½ teaspoon cayenne pepper

1. Remove the stem, rind, and core from the pineapple. Cut into 1-inch cubes. Reserve the juice. Peel the onion and cut into ¼-inch rings. Peel the garlic and chop into ¼-inch pieces. Remove the stems from the cilantro and roughly chop the leaves into ½-inch pieces. Remove the stem and seeds from the jalapeño pepper and cut into ¼-inch rings.
2. Combine all the ingredients in a medium-sized serving bowl; mix well.
3. Cover and chill in the refrigerator for at least 4 hours before serving.

FRUIT TACOS

2 ripe bananas
1 medium-sized sweet apple
½ cup raisins
1 teaspoon ground cinnamon

1 teaspoon ground nutmeg
½ teaspoon lemon juice
4 Flour Tortillas (see recipe on
  page 284)

1. Preheat oven to 350°.
2. Mash the banana. Peel the apple and remove the core and stem. Dice the fruit into ¼-inch pieces.
3. Mix together the banana, apple, raisins, cinnamon, nutmeg, and lemon juice.
4. Place ¼ of the mixture in the middle of each tortilla. Roll up and place on a baking sheet.
5. Bake for 5 minutes.

Serves 4

Try any mix of fruits in this delightful treat. However, be sure to drain juicy fruits so they don't turn the tortillas into mush while baking.

BANANA FRITADAS

6 ripe bananas
3 cups flour
1 teaspoon baking powder
½ cup granulated sugar

2 teaspoons ground cinnamon
2 eggs
2 teaspoons vanilla extract
2 tablespoons vegetable oil

1. Peel the bananas and mash well.
2. Combine the flour, baking powder, sugar, and cinnamon; mix well. Stir in the bananas.
3. Add the eggs and vanilla. Stir until all the ingredients are well blended.
4. In a medium-sized frying pan, heat the vegetable oil to medium-high heat. Make hand-sized patties about ½-inch thick out of the dough. Fry on both sides until light brown.

Serves 6

Serve these as a dessert to any meat dish, such as Beef or Pork Picadillo (pages 373 and 421).

FRUIT COMPOTE

1½ cups seedless green grapes
1½ cups fresh strawberries
2 medium oranges
4 medium kiwis
2 medium peaches

5 tablespoons confectioners' sugar
3 tablespoons Triple Sec or Cointreau liqueur
3 tablespoons tequila
1½ tablespoons lime juice

1. Cut the grapes in half. Remove the stems from the strawberries and cut the fruit in half. Peel the oranges and slice into ¼-inch rounds. Peel the kiwis and slice into ¼-inch rounds. Peel the peaches, remove the pits, and cut into ¼-inch-thick slices.
2. In a small jar, combine the sugar, liqueur, tequila, and lime juice. Cover and shake until well mixed. Combine all the fruit in a large serving bowl. Add the dressing and toss the fruit until well covered.
3. Cover and refrigerate for at least 4 hours before serving.

MEXICAN FRUITCAKE

2 eggs
2 cups white granulated sugar
2 cups self-rising flour
2 teaspoons baking soda

1 (20-ounce) can crushed pineapple, with juice
1 cup chopped walnuts
1 cup shredded coconut

1. Preheat oven to 350°.
2. Mix together all the ingredients thoroughly.
3. Grease and lightly flour a 9" × 13" baking pan. Pour the mixture into the pan.
4. Bake for 40 minutes.

MELON SALAD

1 cantaloupe
1 honeydew melon
2–3 jalapeño peppers
1 red bell pepper
1 yellow bell pepper
1 medium Vidalia onion
1 small jicama

4 scallions
1 bunch cilantro
3 tablespoons lime juice
3 tablespoons olive oil
3 tablespoons red cooking
  sherry

Serves 6

Surprise your breakfast guests by serving this with Huevos Rancheros, page 359.

1. Remove the rind and seeds from the cantaloupe and honeydew melons. Cut the fruit into 1-inch cubes. Remove the seeds and stems from the jalapeño and bell peppers. Cut into ¼-inch rounds. Peel the onion and cut into ¼-inch rounds. Peel the jicama and cut into ¼-inch-thick strips. Peel the scallions and cut into ¼-inch pieces. Remove the stems from the cilantro and roughly chop the leaves into ½-inch pieces.
2. Combine the melons, peppers, onion, jicama, scallions, and cilantro in a large mixing bowl; toss until well mixed.
3. In a small jar, combine the lime juice, olive oil, and cooking sherry. Cover and shake until well blended. Pour the dressing over the fruit and vegetables; toss lightly until evenly coated.
4. Cover and chill in the refrigerator for at least 3 hours before serving.

Choosing Ripe Melons
People say there is an art to finding a ripe melon, but it really is as simple as listening. Lightly thump the melon. It should sound hollow inside. An unripe melon is still dense and will make very little sound when thumped.

FLAMING FRUIT

Serves 6

This makes an elegant ending to a wonderful meal such as Grilled Shrimp in Prickly Pear Cactus Vinaigrette (page 515).

1 fresh mango
3 ripe bananas
1 cup fresh strawberries
1 cup orange juice
2 tablespoons granulated sugar

1 cup tequila
6 large scoops vanilla ice
   cream

1. Peel the mango and cut into 6 slices. Peel the bananas and slice lengthwise. Remove the stems from the strawberries and cut the berries in half.
2. Put the fruit in a chafing dish or large skillet on medium heat. Pour the orange juice over the fruit and sprinkle with the sugar. Heat to simmering, stirring gently to dissolve the sugar and coat the fruit.
3. Add the tequila. Flame the sauce by pouring a little tequila into a teaspoon and holding it over a flame until it catches on fire. Drop the flame into the fruit mixture. After five to 10 seconds, the flames will disappear or be very small. Gently blow them out if any remain. The alcohol has burned away but occasionally the sugar in the fruit burns slightly.
4. Serve over ice cream.

Pepitas
Pepitas are simply pumpkin seeds. They are a favorite snack food in Mexico but also a popular cooking ingredient. In many non-Mexican U.S. markets, when the green interior of the seed is sold separately, it is labeled as pepitas while the whole seed is labeled as pumpkin seeds. However, in a Mexican market, you will need to specify whether you want hulled or nonhulled. Note that pumpkin seeds can be eaten with the shell on for a less oily, fruity flavor.

FRUITY PICADILLO

3 bananas
3 nectarines
3 pears
1 cup strawberries
2 green apples
1 medium jicama
½ cup pistachio meats
1 medium-sized yellow onion
3 medium-sized red tomatoes

3 fresh jalapeño chilies
2 tablespoons olive oil
1 pound ground veal
1 pound ground chicken
½ teaspoon ground cinnamon
½ teaspoon ground cloves

Serves 8

Serve over white rice and garnish with fresh orange slices.

1. Peel the bananas and cut into ½-inch rounds. Peel the nectarines, remove the pits, and cut into 1-inch pieces. Peel the pears, remove the pits, and cut into 1-inch pieces. Remove the stems from the strawberries and slice in half. Peel the apples, remove the cores and stems, and cut into 1-inch pieces. Peel the jicama and cut into 1-inch pieces. Peel the onion and chop into ¼-inch pieces. Peel the tomatoes and chop into ¼-inch pieces. Remove the seeds and stems from the chilies and cut into ¼-inch pieces.

2. Heat the oil to medium temperature in a large frying pan. Add the veal and chicken. Fry on all sides until the meat is golden. Add the onion, tomatoes, chilies, cinnamon, and cloves; mix well. Lower heat and cover. Simmer, uncovered, for 30 minutes, stirring occasionally.

3. Add the bananas, nectarines, pears, strawberries, apples, jicama, and pistachios; stir gently to blend. Cover and simmer for 15 minutes.

Chapter 31
DESSERTS

BRIDE'S COOKIES

1 cup unsalted, roasted almonds
2 cups all-purpose flour
½ cup confectioners' sugar
¼ teaspoon salt
1 teaspoon ground cinnamon
1 cup softened butter
1 teaspoon vanilla extract

1. Preheat oven to 350°.
2. Use a food processor or nut grinder to grind the almonds into small pieces. (They should not be ground into a powder.)
3. Mix together the flour, sugar, salt, cinnamon, and almonds in a medium-sized mixing bowl. Add the softened butter and vanilla. Stir until the ingredients are well blended.
4. Make 24 balls about the size of golf balls and place on baking sheets.
5. Bake for 20 to 30 minutes or until lightly browned.

COFFEE CARAMEL

7 cups whole milk
3 cups granulated sugar
1 teaspoon soda
1 cup hot, strong coffee
½ teaspoon ground cinnamon
2 tablespoons butter

1. Combine the milk, sugar, and soda in a large pot on medium heat. Boil, stirring every few minutes, until the mixture turns thick and slightly brown.
2. Add the coffee and cinnamon; stir well. Turn the heat to low and continue cooking until the mixture is thick. When a small drop of the mixture is put in a glass of cold water, it should form a soft ball.
3. Spread the butter onto the bottom and sides of a 9" × 9" cake pan. Pour the mixture into the pan. Chill in the refrigerator at least 2 hours before serving.

MEXICAN TEA CAKES

¼ cup pistachio meats
1 cup butter
2½ cups flour
1¾ cups confectioners' sugar

2 teaspoons vanilla
½ teaspoon salt
1 teaspoon ground cinnamon

1. Grind the pistachio meats. Soften the butter in a medium-sized mixing bowl by stirring with a spoon.
2. Add the pistachio meats, flour, ¾ cup of the sugar, the vanilla, and salt to the butter; mix until a stiff dough is formed.
3. Cover and chill in the refrigerator for 2 to 4 hours.
4. Preheat oven to 350°.
5. Form the dough into balls about 1-inch in diameter. Place on a greased baking sheet and bake for 10 to 15 minutes. The cookies should be firm but not brown.
6. Remove the cookies from the oven and roll them in the remaining confectioners' sugar mixed with the cinnamon. When the cookies are cool, roll them in the sugar and cinnamon mixture again.

Mexican Chocolate

Mexican chocolate desserts often taste sour and not chocolatey enough to those in the United States. If you want a less traditional taste but one you're more familiar with, double the chocolate and sugar, and don't add the vinegar in the dessert recipes calling for chocolate.

MEXICAN CHOCOLATE CAKE

Serves 8

Serve this with Coconut Coffee (page 542) or Mexican Hot Chocolate (page 540).

1¼ cups flour
1 cup granulated sugar
¼ cup cornstarch
5 tablespoons powdered cocoa
1 teaspoon baking soda
2 teaspoons ground cinnamon
½ teaspoon salt

1 tablespoon white wine vinegar
1 teaspoon vanilla
1 tablespoon oil
1 tablespoon corn syrup
1 cup confectioners' sugar

1. Preheat oven to 350°.
2. Combine the flour, granulated sugar, cornstarch, 3 tablespoons of the powdered cocoa, the baking soda, 1 teaspoon of the cinnamon, and the salt; mix well. Add the white wine vinegar, vanilla, and 1 cup cold water; mix with a fork.
3. Pour the mixture into a 9-inch-square greased and floured cake pan. Bake for 30 to 35 minutes. Cool the cake to room temperature.
4. For the glaze, combine the remaining cocoa and cinnamon, the oil, corn syrup, and 2 tablespoons water in a small saucepan. Cook over low heat until all the ingredients are melded. Add the confectioners' sugar. Continue cooking, stirring constantly, until the sugar is dissolved.
5. Remove the glaze from the heat and beat until it is smooth and shiny. Spread over the top of the cake. Let cool before serving.

NATILLA

4 eggs
½ cup flour
1 quart milk
¾ cup granulated sugar

⅛ teaspoon salt
1 teaspoon ground nutmeg
1 teaspoon ground cinnamon

1. Separate the eggs.
2. Make a paste of the egg yolks, flour, and 1 cup of the milk.
3. In a medium-sized saucepan, add the sugar and salt to the remaining milk and scald at medium heat. Add the egg yolk mixture to the scalded milk and continue to cook, stirring constantly, at medium temperature until it reaches the consistency of soft custard. Remove from heat and cool to room temperature.
4. Beat the egg whites until stiff. Fold into the custard.
5. Cover and chill for at least 2 hours before serving.
6. Spoon into individual dishes and sprinkle with nutmeg and cinnamon right before serving.

Serves 8

This light custard is perfect after a spicy, heavy meal of chicken or beef.

Custards and Puddings

Mexicans enjoy custards and puddings after their meals, perhaps because they are an excellent way to get more milk into the diet. They also are a fun way to use the many spices available in this culture.

PISTACHIO-COCONUT FLAN

6 large eggs
1 (14-ounce) can sweetened
   condensed milk
2 teaspoons vanilla extract
2 cups whole milk

2 cups half-and-half
2 tablespoons grated coconut
1 tablespoon ground pistachio
   meats

1. Preheat the oven to 325°.
2. In a large mixing bowl, gently stir together the eggs, sweetened condensed milk, and vanilla extract.
3. Pour the milk and half-and-half into a medium saucepan and place on the stove on medium-high heat. Bring to a boil, then remove from heat. Gradually pour the egg mixture into the hot milk, stirring constantly. Make sure no clumps of egg remain.
4. Pass the mixture through a strainer, then pour into a greased 9-inch cake pan. Sprinkle the coconut and pistachio meats on top. Place the pan into a large roasting pan and fill the roasting pan with warm tap water until it is about halfway up the sides of the cake pan.
5. Bake for 60 minutes. The center should feel firm when pressed, but not be browned. The edges may be slightly browned. Remove from the oven and set aside to cool to room temperature. Cover and refrigerate for at least 4 hours before serving.

ALMOND CUSTARD

2 cups whole milk
6 egg yolks
¼ cup brown sugar
¼ teaspoon salt

1 teaspoon almond extract
½ cup slivered, toasted
   almonds

1. Heat milk in the top of a double boiler until too hot to touch.
2. Separate the eggs and discard the whites. Add the sugar and salt to the egg yolks and beat until light and fluffy.
3. Gradually add egg mixture to milk, stirring constantly. Heat while stirring until the mixture coats a spoon. Remove from heat and cool to room temperature. Add almond extract. Beat until the mixture is firm.
4. Line individual custard dishes with almonds. Pour mixture on top. Place a few almond slivers atop each custard. Refrigerate 2 hours before serving.

Serves 4

This makes an excellent holiday treat and complements poultry dishes very well.

PECAN PUDDING

½ cup roasted pecans
1 envelope unflavored gelatin
1 cup water

1 cup white granulated sugar
6 eggs
½ teaspoon vanilla extract

1. Use a food processor or nut grinder to break the pecans into small pieces. (They should not be ground into a powder.)
2. Put the water in a medium-sized pot on high heat. When boiling, add the gelatin. Stir until the gelatin is dissolved.
3. Add the sugar and stir until it is dissolved. Add the vanilla.
4. Remove from heat and let cool until the mixture begins to thicken.
5. Separate the eggs and discard the yolks. Beat the whites until they form stiff peaks. Fold the egg whites into the gelatin mixture until well blended. Gently stir in the pecans.
6. Pour into individual cups and chill until firm.

Serves 4

Pistachios and almonds can be substituted for the pecans to complement different dishes.

TROPICAL GELATIN

Serves 6

Use this as a special treat on a hot summer day. Serve with Jasmine and Rose Hips Tea (page 541).

1 cup papaya
1 cup guava
1 cup fresh pineapple
12 lady fingers
2 cups water

3 packages unsweetened gelatin
½ cup granulated sugar

1. Remove the rinds and cores from the pineapple, papaya, and guava. Cut the fruit into ½-inch pieces. Measure 1 cup of each fruit and mix together in a small mixing bowl. (Do not drain the juice from the fruit.)
2. Break the lady fingers into 1-inch pieces and line the bottom of 6 individual custard bowls with the pieces.
3. Bring the water to boil in a medium-sized pot. Add the gelatin and sugar; stir until both are dissolved. Remove from heat and stir in the fruit.
4. Let cool at room temperature until it begins to thicken.
5. Pour the mixture over the lady fingers. Cool in the refrigerator for at least 2 hours before serving.

Finding a Fresh Pineapple

Fresh, ripe pineapples have a distinctly yellow hue to their rind and smell only mildly sweet, while those beyond their freshness will have an almost sickly sweet smell and may even be oozing juice. A green pineapple will be just that—its rind will show very little deep yellow color.

RAISIN AND PISTACHIO PUDDING

½ cup roasted pistachio meats
½ cup raisins
1 cup dry white wine
1 key lime
1 cup water
½ cup rice
¼ teaspoon salt

4 cups whole milk
1 cup granulated sugar
1 teaspoon ground cinnamon
2 egg yolks

Serves 4

Many cultures have a rice pudding, but this is the ultimate recipe. Its subtle flavors instantly transport you to a coastal resort.

---

1. Grind the pistachios in a nut grinder or food processor until you have small pieces. (They should not be ground into a powder.) Put the raisins and white wine in a small mixing bowl and set aside. Remove the rind from the key lime and discard the fruit.
2. Bring the water to a boil in a medium-sized pan. Add the lime rind, rice, and salt. Cover and boil for 5 minutes, then reduce heat to low and simmer for 15 minutes.
3. Discard the lime rind. Add the milk, sugar, and cinnamon. Continue cooking, uncovered, on low heat until all the milk has been absorbed.
4. Separate the eggs and discard the whites. Drain off and discard the wine that has not soaked into the raisins. Mix the egg yolks, raisins, and pistachios into the rice mixture; cook for 5 minutes, uncovered.
5. Place the pudding in a serving dish, cover, and refrigerate for at least 2 hours before serving.

COCOA PECAN TREATS

½ cup pecans
½ cup whole milk
2 cups white granulated sugar
½ cup shortening
½ teaspoon salt

3 cups quick-cooking oats
½ cup shredded coconut
½ cup cocoa
2 teaspoons vanilla

1. Chop the pecans into ⅛-inch pieces.
2. Combine the whole milk, sugar, shortening, and salt in saucepan on medium-high heat; boil for 2 minutes.
3. Remove from heat. Stir in the oats, coconut, cocoa, vanilla, and pecans.
4. Drop by rounded teaspoonfuls onto waxed paper. Set in a cool place until the treats reach room temperature.

WINE COOKIES

1 cup margarine
1 cup white granulated sugar
1 egg

1 teaspoon salt
4 cups flour
¼ cup sweet sherry

1. Preheat oven to 350°.
2. Mix together the margarine and sugar until creamy. Add the egg and beat until the mixture is light and fluffy.
3. Blend in the salt and 2 cups of the flour. Stir in the sherry. Add the remaining 2 cups of flour and mix well.
4. Chill in the refrigerator for 1 hour or until firm.
5. Roll out the dough on a lightly floured surface until it's about ⅛-inch thick. Cut with cookie cutters.
6. Place on a lightly greased baking sheet and bake for 10 minutes.

BISCOCHITOS

6 cups flour
3 teaspoons baking powder
1 teaspoon salt
1 pound softened butter
1¾ cups white granulated sugar

2 teaspoons anise seeds
2 eggs
½ cup brandy
1 teaspoon ground cinnamon

Makes 5 dozen

The fleur-de-lis shape is traditional for these cookies.

1. Preheat oven to 350°.
2. Sift the flour with the baking powder and salt.
3. Cream the butter with 1½ cups of the sugar and the anise seeds using a mixer set on medium speed.
4. Beat the eggs until light and fluffy and add to the creamed mixture. Add the flour mixture and the brandy; mix until well blended. The dough should be stiff. If not, add more flour until it is.
5. Knead the dough and roll out to ¼- to ½-inch thick. Cut with cookie cutters.
6. Mix together the remaining ¼ cup sugar and the cinnamon. Use to dust the top of each cookie.
7. Place on baking sheet and bake for 10 to 12 minutes or until lightly browned.

MEXICAN CARROT CAKE

Serves 4

Serve with Mexican Coffee (page 545) or Mexican Hot Chocolate (page 540).

8 medium carrots
4 teaspoons lemon rind
4 teaspoons lemon juice
1 teaspoon vanilla extract
6 tablespoons granulated sugar

¼ cup vegetable oil
4 medium eggs
4 Flour Tortillas (see recipe on page 284)

1. Preheat oven to 350°.
2. Peel the carrots and finely grate. Grate the lemon rind.
3. In a small bowl, combine the carrots, lemon rind, lemon juice, and vanilla extract; set aside.
4. Combine the sugar with the vegetable oil. Beat the eggs, then stir them into the sugar and vegetable oil. Tear or cut the tortillas into ¼-inch pieces. Add the tortillas and carrot mixture to the sugar and egg mixture; mix well.
5. Pour the mixture into a 9-inch springform pan and bake for 1 hour or until the top is brown.

Carrots

When using carrots in a dessert dish, be sure to use medium or small carrots. They contain the most flavor and the most juice. Large carrots are fine with meat or vegetable dishes, but they are too acidic and flat tasting for desserts.

PECAN CANDY

2 cups white granulated sugar
½ cup margarine
1 cup canned condensed milk
2 tablespoons white corn syrup

1 teaspoon vanilla extract
¼ teaspoon cayenne pepper
½ teaspoon chili powder
3 cups pecans

Serves 8

If you're used to pralines from America's southeast, these will taste a little odd at first. However, this authentic candy complements a Mexican meal perfectly.

1. Combine the sugar, margarine, condensed milk, and corn syrup in a medium-sized pot. Heat on medium-high until the mixture forms a firm, soft ball when a small amount is dropped into cold water.
2. Remove from heat. Stir in the vanilla, cayenne pepper, chili powder, and pecans.
3. Using a tablespoon, drop into patties on waxed paper. Put in a cool place until the clusters reach room temperature.

MEXICAN ORANGE

Rind from 2 oranges
1 cup pistachio nuts
1½ cups condensed milk

3 cups white granulated sugar
½ cup butter

Serves 6

Vary the types of nuts used and add a mixture of lemon and orange rinds for a completely different treat.

1. Cut the orange rinds into ¼-inch pieces. Chop the nuts into small pieces.
2. Place the milk into the top of a double boiler and and heat until scalded—the milk will have a film on top.
3. Melt 1 cup of the sugar in a large kettle on medium-high heat until it is a rich yellow color. Add the hot milk to the sugar. Add the remaining sugar, stir, and cook until it reaches 238° on a candy thermometer.
4. Remove from heat. Stir in the rind, butter, and nuts.
5. Pour into a buttered 7" × 11" pan and place in a cool area until the candy reaches room temperature.

WINE CUSTARD

Serves 6

This makes a perfect ending to a romantic meal such as Grilled Shrimp in Prickly Pear Cactus Vinaigrette (page 515).

6 cups whole milk
2 cups sugar

¼ cup heavy red wine

1. Place the milk in the top of a double boiler and heat over boiling water. Stir in the sugar. Cook for 2 hours, stirring occasionally.
2. Remove from heat and let cool to room temperature.
3. Pour the milk mixture into a saucepan on medium-low heat. Stir in the wine until the wine is completely absorbed.
4. Transfer the mixture to a serving dish. Cover and chill in the refrigerator for 3 to 4 hours before serving.

SUGARED PUMPKIN

Serves 8

This is traditionally served as a dessert but makes an excellent vegetable course when served with a beef or pork dish.

1 medium pumpkin
½ cup butter

2 cups brown sugar
2 teaspoons ground cinnamon

1. Preheat oven to 350°.
2. Cut the pumpkin into pieces approximately 6 inches square, removing the seeds and interior fibers.
3. Poke holes in the pumpkin flesh with a fork. Spread a thin layer of butter on each pumpkin piece.
4. Mix together the cinnamon and brown sugar and spread on the pumpkin pieces.
5. Place in a baking dish and bake for 1 to 2 hours or until a fork slides easily into the flesh.

PINEAPPLE AND ALMOND PUDDING

1 fresh pineapple
4 eggs
½ cup blanched almonds
1 angel food cake
½ cup, plus 1 tablespoon,
 granulated sugar
½ cup dry sherry

¼ teaspoon ground cinnamon
½ cup orange marmalade
½ cup sour cream
½ cup toasted, slivered
 almonds

Serves 6

This is a perfect dessert for the rich flavors in Chicken Tablecloth Stainer (page 404).

1. Remove the skin, top, and core from the pineapple. Slice the fruit into ¼-inch cubes until you have 2 cups. Separate the eggs and discard the whites. Beat the egg yolks. Grind the blanched almonds into small pieces. (Do not grind into a powder.) Cut the angel food cake into twelve 4- by 1-inch slices.

2. Combine the pineapple, ½ cup of the sugar, ¼ cup sherry, egg yolks, and cinnamon in a medium-sized saucepan. Cook over low heat, stirring constantly, until thickened. Remove from heat and let cool.

3. Spread the cake slices with the marmalade. Arrange half the spread cake slices in the bottom of a 1-quart serving dish. Sprinkle with 2 tablespoons of the sherry. Spoon half of the pineapple mixture on top. Repeat layers of cake slices, sherry, and pineapple mixture.

4. Cover and refrigerate for 2 to 3 hours.

5. Mix the remaining 1 tablespoon sugar into the sour cream. Spread over the top of the chilled dessert. Decorate with the toasted slivered almonds.

The Secret to Good Rice

You can have too much water. You can cook it too long. But you can't peek at it. That's the secret to good rice. Even water-logged rice is salvageable by baking it in the oven for 30 minutes at 300°. But if you peek at it when you shouldn't, you will lose the value of the steaming process and could end up with a sticky, gooey mess.

PECAN CAKE

Serves 6

This is the perfect dessert for a traditional Mexican meal such as Beef Tamales (page 500).

3 eggs
½ cup pecans
½ cup butter
¾ cup cake flour
1 teaspoon baking powder
⅔ cup granulated sugar

1 tablespoon lemon juice
½ teaspoon salt
½ cup orange marmalade
¼ cup granulated sugar

1. Preheat oven to 350°.
2. Separate the eggs. Finely grate the pecans. Melt the butter in a small saucepan on low heat.
3. Blend together the flour and baking powder.
4. Beat the egg yolks in a large mixing bowl until they are thick and lemon-colored. Gradually beat in the ⅔ cup sugar. Beat in the lemon juice and grated pecans. Gradually beat in the flour mixture. Slowly beat in the melted butter.
5. Beat the egg whites with salt until stiff peaks form. Fold the beaten egg whites into the batter.
6. Pour the batter into a greased and floured 9-inch round cake pan.
7. Bake for 30 to 35 minutes or until a toothpick inserted in the center comes out clean. Let the cake cool for 10 minutes before removing from the pan.
8. Combine the orange marmalade and the ¼ cup sugar in a small saucepan over medium-low heat. Cook until the sugar is dissolved, stirring constantly. While still warm, use as a glaze for the cake.

Self-Rising Flour

Self-rising flour is simply flour that contains yeast. When water is added and the dish is placed in the oven, the yeast grows and begins to rise. If you don't have self-rising flour, add 1 tablespoon of yeast for every 2 cups of flour. Dissolve the yeast first in ¼ cup tepid water.

PEPITA BALLS

*1 pound unsalted hulled
    pepitas (pumpkin seeds)*

*1 cup sweetened condensed milk
3½ cups confectioners' sugar*

Makes 6 dozen
Mexicans love their sweets and will serve these equally as appetizers or dessert.

1. Grind the *pepitas* finely.
2. Mix the *pepitas* with the condensed milk and 3 cups of the confectioners' sugar.
3. Shape into 1-inch balls and roll in the remaining sugar. Place on wax paper on a baking sheet.
4. Refrigerate for 2 to 3 hours or until set.

MOLASSES CANDY

*1 cup light molasses
1 cup firmly packed brown sugar
2 tablespoons butter
1 teaspoon cider vinegar*

*¼ teaspoon almond extract
1½ cups toasted, slivered
    almonds*

Makes 1 pound
This makes an excellent holiday treat or a nice dessert to an informal meal.

1. Combine the molasses, brown sugar, butter, and vinegar into a heavy saucepan. Bring to a boil. Boil hard for 7 to 12 minutes or until the mixture reaches 260° on a candy thermometer. The mixture should form a firm ball when a small amount is dropped in cold water.
2. Remove from heat. Add the almond extract and almonds; stir well.
3. Pour onto a greased baking sheet. Spread out in as thin a layer as possible. Let cool.
4. Break into 2-inch pieces.

ORANGE LIQUEUR MOUSSE

1 (3-ounce) package orange-
  flavored gelatin
1 cup boiling water
¼ cup cold water
¼ cup orange liqueur

1 cup whipping cream
½ teaspoon ground cinnamon
½ cup shredded coconut

1. Dissolve the gelatin in the boiling water. Add the cold water and cool the mixture to room temperature. Stir in the orange liqueur. Chill in the refrigerator until the mixture starts to thicken, about 30 minutes.
2. Whip the cream until it piles softly. Gradually add the gelatin mixture and cinnamon, stirring gently until evenly blended. Pour into a mold. Chill until set, about 1 hour.
3. Turn the mold onto a serving plate and top with the shredded coconut.

Making It Nonalcoholic

If you want to make uncooked foods calling for liqueur nonalcoholic, simply substitute 1 tablespoon of the flavored extract mixed with half water and half corn syrup. You will get a very similar flavor without the alcohol.

Chapter 32

TRADITIONAL FAVORITES

GAZPACHO

4 large tomatoes
1 small yellow onion
1 green bell pepper
2 stalks celery
2 medium carrots
4 cups canned condensed
   tomato soup
2 tablespoons olive oil

2 tablespoons white wine
   vinegar
2 teaspoons salt
1 teaspoon ground black
   pepper
1 medium cucumber

1. Peel the tomatoes and cut into quarters. Remove the skin from the onion and cut into quarters. Remove the stem and seeds from the green pepper and cut into quarters. Peel the carrots and cut into quarters. Remove the leaves from the celery and cut the stalks into quarters.

2. Combine 2 cups of the tomato soup, the olive oil, wine vinegar, salt, pepper, and half of the vegetables in a blender. Blend until liquefied, about 1 minute. Pour into a bowl. Repeat with the remaining tomato soup and vegetables. Combine with the previous mixture.

3. Cover and chill in the refrigerator for at least 2 hours before serving.

4. Cut the cucumbers into thin slices and place on top right before serving.

Bell Peppers

Bell peppers have different flavors depending on their color. Green is the most acidic and sour tasting. Red has the most peppery flavor. Yellow and orange have a gentle flavor. Combine them to create unique flavors and a beautiful dish.

BLACK BEAN SOUP

2 cups dried black beans
2½ quarts water
2 garlic cloves
2 medium-sized yellow onions
½ cup vegetable oil
½ teaspoon salt
½ teaspoon ground black
   pepper
¼ teaspoon whole fennel seeds
¼ teaspoon dried basil
1 teaspoon granulated sugar
1 teaspoon dried mustard
1 teaspoon grated lemon rind
¼ teaspoon ground allspice
1 teaspoon dried cilantro
1 cup canned condensed
   tomato sauce
3 tablespoons lemon juice

> **Serves 4**
>
> Garnish with grated
> Cheddar cheese and
> sour cream.

1. Soak the beans overnight in ½ quart of the water.
2. Remove the skin from the garlic and mince. Remove skin from the onions and cut into ¼-inch pieces. Put oil, onions, and garlic in a medium frying pan on medium heat. Sauté until the onions are limp, not brown. Drain the oil.
3. Combine all the ingredients *except* the lemon juice in a large soup pot. Stir until well blended. Bring to a boil, then lower temperature to medium-low. Simmer, uncovered, for 2 hours or until the beans are soft.
4. Add the lemon juice and stir right before serving.

Beans Galore

Although we think of only a couple types of beans, there are many, many varieties that Mexicans routinely use. Traditional grocery stores are beginning to carry more of these varieties, but you also might try a local food co-op. Virtually any bean can be substituted in these recipes, depending on your taste.

CHURROS

Serves 12

These traditional treats also can be formed into small patties and served with jam.

3 cups vegetable oil
1 cup water
½ cup butter
1 cup flour
¼ teaspoon salt

3 eggs
1 cup powdered sugar
¼ cup ground cinnamon

1. Pour oil into a medium-sized frying pan (the oil should be 1 to 2 inches deep). Heat to 375°.
2. Heat the water to a rolling boil in medium-sized saucepan. Add the butter and continue to boil.
3. Quickly stir in the flour and salt. Reduce heat to low and stir vigorously until the mixture forms a ball,
4. Remove from heat and beat in the eggs 1 at a time, until the mixture is smooth and glossy.
5. Form the dough into round sticks about 10 inches long and 1-inch thick.
6. Fry the sticks 2 or 3 at a time until light brown.
7. Remove the sticks and cool on paper towels.
8. Mix together the powdered sugar and cinnamon on a large plate. As soon as the churros are cool, roll them in the mixture. Set aside until completely cool.

Frying Food
Although it seems easy, frying food is a great art. The oil must be hot enough to cook the food without soaking into the food. At the same time, if the oil is too hot, it will cook the outside of the food before the inside is completely cooked.

CHICKEN CHALUPAS

*12 Corn Tortillas (see recipe
    on page 283)*
*1¼ cups Chicken Stock (see
    recipe on page 286)*
1 pound Monterey jack cheese

1 cup sour cream
*2 cups Spicy Chicken (see
    recipe on page 289)*
1 teaspoon paprika

Serves 6
Serve with a fresh spinach salad and Fruit Compote (page 466).

1. Soak the tortillas in 1 cup of the stock. Grate the cheese.
2. Combine the remaining ¼ cup chicken stock with the sour cream.
3. Layer the ingredients in a casserole as follows: single layer of soaked tortillas, Spicy Chicken, sour cream mixture, cheese. Repeat until all the ingredients are used. Sprinkle with paprika.
4. Cover and refrigerate at least 8 hours.
5. Preheat oven to 350°. Bake the dish, uncovered, for 1 hour.

TRADITIONAL POLLO VERDE

1 medium-sized white onion
1 garlic clove
2 tomatillos
1 bunch fresh parsley
*1 cup Green Chili Sauce (see
    recipe on page 288)*

1 teaspoon salt
*1 teaspoon ground white
    pepper*
1 fryer chicken

Serves 4
Serve with Zesty Cheese Salad (page 351).

1. Peel the onion and cut into quarters. Peel the garlic. Remove the stems and peels from the tomatillos, then cut in half. Remove the stems from the parsley and roughly chop the leaves.
2. Combine the onion, garlic, tomatillos, parsley, chili sauce, salt, and white pepper in a blender or food processor; blend until liquefied.
3. Rinse the chicken and arrange in a large frying pan. Pour the sauce over the top. Cover and bring to boil. Reduce heat to low and simmer for about 1 hour or until chicken is tender.

TRADITIONAL FLAN

8 eggs
⅔ cup white granulated sugar
¼ teaspoon salt
3½ cups evaporated milk

2 teaspoons vanilla extract
½ cup light brown sugar

1. Preheat oven to 350°.
2. In a medium-sized mixing bowl, beat the eggs until the yolks and whites are well blended. Add the granulated sugar and salt. Beat in the evaporated milk and vanilla extract.
3. Sprinkle the brown sugar onto the bottom of a loaf pan. Gently pour the custard mixture over the brown sugar.
4. Place the loaf pan in a shallow baking pan containing hot water. Place in oven and bake for 1 hour or until a knife inserted into the center comes out clean.
5. Refrigerate for 8 to 12 hours. Before serving, turn the loaf onto a platter, then sprinkle the top with brown sugar. Place it under the broiler and lightly brown the top immediately before serving.

Different Sugars

Brown sugar is actually white sugar with molasses added. White sugar usually comes from either beets or sugarcane. Cane sugar actually tastes slightly sweeter. Confectioners' sugar is finely ground white sugar.

POLENTA

4½ cups cold water
1½ cups masa harina or
  yellow cornmeal
1 small yellow onion
1 garlic clove
2 pounds canned tomatoes
½ pound fontina cheese
½ pound Gorgonzola cheese
1 tablespoon olive oil

1 bay leaf
½ teaspoon dried basil
1 teaspoon salt
½ teaspoon ground black
  pepper
1 teaspoon white granulated
  sugar
1 bunch fresh parsley.

> **Serves 6**
>
> Serve with Spinach
> Salad (page 354).

1. Preheat oven to 400°.
2. Put the cold water into a medium saucepan over medium-high heat. Add the cornmeal or masa harina. Whisk the cornmeal or masa harina into the cold water. Continue whisking while bringing to a boil. Cook for 15 minutes, stirring frequently to prevent lumping.
3. Pour into a 9" × 12" pan and spread out evenly. Let sit until firm. Cut into 3" × 3" squares and remove from the pan.
4. Peel and mince the onion and garlic. Drain the tomatoes and chop coarsely. Grate the cheeses and mix together.
5. In a large frying pan heat the olive oil to medium temperature; sauté the onion and garlic for 3 to 5 minutes or until the onion is limp and clear. Set aside.
6. Combine the tomatoes, bay leaf, basil, salt, pepper, and sugar in a saucepan on medium heat. Bring to a boil, then reduce heat to low and simmer for 15 minutes.
7. Add the onion and garlic to the tomato mixture. Mash with a potato masher or blend in a food processor or blender.
8. Spread 1 cup sauce in the bottom of the 9" × 12" pan. Lean the squares at an angle in the pan. Between each square, add about ½ cup of grated cheeses. Pour the remaining sauce over the polenta and cheese.
9. Bake for 25 to 35 minutes. Roughly chop the parsley leaves and use as a garnish.

EMPANADITAS DE CARNE

1-pound beef roast
1-pound pork roast
3 cups flour
1 teaspoon baking powder
2 teaspoons salt
1 cup, plus 1 tablespoon, granulated sugar
3 tablespoons shortening
1 egg

1 cup water
1 cup raisins
2 cups applesauce
1 teaspoon ground cinnamon
½ teaspoon crushed cloves
½ cup chopped pecans
4 cups vegetable oil

1. Put the beef roast and pork roast in a pot and add just enough water to cover the meat. Cover the pot and turn heat to medium. Simmer until the meat is completely cooked, at least 1 hour. Do not discard the cooking liquid.
2. Combine the flour, baking powder, 1 teaspoon salt, and 1 tablespoon sugar. Blend in the shortening.
3. Beat the egg in a separate bowl and slowly add to the flour mixture. Add the water and mix to form a dough. Roll out the dough to about ⅛-inch thick and cut with a biscuit cutter.
4. Remove the meat from the bones. Discard the bones and grind the meat with a meat grinder or food processor. Place the meat in a large pot. Add the raisins, applesauce, 1 cup sugar, cinnamon, cloves, 1 teaspoon salt, and ½ cup chopped pecans. Mix to combine, adding enough of the cooking liquid from the meat to thoroughly moisten the mixture.
5. Simmer, uncovered, for 15 minutes, adding more water if the mixture seems dry. Make sure the mixture holds together, though; it should not be runny.
6. Put about 3 tablespoons of meat mixture in the center of each of the biscuits. Fold over and pinch the edges shut.
7. Heat the oil in a large frying pan until medium hot. Add several empanaditas. Fry on both sides until golden brown. Place on paper towels to cool.

ENCHILADAS

1 cup Tomato Salsa (see recipe on page 282)
12 Corn Tortillas (see recipe on page 283)
3 cups Shredded Beef or Refried Beans (see recipes on pages 287 and 284)

2 cups grated Monterey jack cheese
2 cups Red or Green Chili Sauce (see recipes on page 288)

Serves 4

Experiment until you find your own favorite ingredients. Try mixing beans and meat or adding Spicy Chicken (page 289). Or, for a cheesy enchilada, mix 3 different cheeses and don't include meat or beans.

1. Preheat oven to 375°.
2. Ladle ½ cup of the salsa into a 9" × 12" baking pan.
3. Put ¼ cup of the beef or beans in the center of each tortilla. Add 2 tablespoons shredded cheese. Roll up and place in baking pan.
4. When all the enchiladas are in the baking pan, cover with the remaining sauce and cheese. Bake for 15 to 20 minutes.

BURRITOS

1 cup Refried Beans (see recipe on page 284)
1 cup Red Rice (see recipe on page 286)
1 cup Shredded Beef (see recipe on page 287)
½ pound Cheddar cheese
1 cup Tomato Salsa (see recipe on page 282)

8 Flour Tortillas (see recipe on page 284)
½ cup Red Chili Sauce (see recipe on page 288)
½ cup sour cream
½ cup Guacamole (see recipe on page 287)

Serves 4

Burritos are the "Poor Boy" sandwich of Mexico. They literally contain whatever is left over from yesterday. Don't hesitate to add olives, lettuce, or even yesterday's ham.

1. Heat the beans, rice, and beef separately on low heat. Shred the cheese.
2. Add ¼ cup of the beans, ¼ cup beef, ¼ cup rice, and 1 tablespoon salsa to the middle of each tortilla. Drizzle 1 teaspoon of chili sauce on top. Roll up.
3. Top each burrito with a dollop of sour cream and a dollop of guacamole.

CHILI RELLENOS

6 large Anaheim chilies
½ pound Mozzarella cheese
1 small white onion
¼ cup canned jalapeño peppers, or 2 fresh jalapeños
2 cups canned tomatoes, with juice
½ tablespoon olive oil

2 cups Chicken Stock (see recipe on page 286)
2 tablespoons cornstarch
3 eggs
2 cups masa harina or cornmeal
1 teaspoon salt

1. Preheat oven to 350°.
2. Place the Anaheim peppers in the oven. Turn them when the tops are white. When both sides are white, remove the peppers and put them in a paper bag. Close the bag tightly, and let the peppers cool. (This makes it easier to peel off the skin.) Peel the skin from the peppers.
3. Cut the cheese into wedges about ½ inch wide. Stuff the wedges into the chilies.
4. Peel the onion and chop into ¼-inch pieces. Drain the jalapeño peppers and cut into ¼-inch pieces. Chop the tomatoes into ¼-inch pieces, reserving the juice.
5. In a medium-sized saucepan, heat the olive oil to medium temperature. Add the onions and sauté until the onions are brown. Add the chopped chilies and tomatoes with their juice. Add the stock and cornstarch; sauté on medium heat, stirring constantly until the sauce is the consistency of gravy.
6. Beat eggs, then combine with the cornmeal or masa harina; mix well. If the mixture is not sticky, add water until it is about the consistency of thick pancake batter.
7. Dip the peppers into the egg and cornmeal batter.
8. Put the peppers into a lightly greased frying pan on medium heat. Brown the peppers on all sides.
9. Cover with sauce before serving.

BEEF FLAUTAS

16 Corn Tortillas (see recipe on page 283)
3 cups Shredded Beef (see recipe on page 287)

1½ cups shredded Colby cheese
1 cup vegetable oil

Serves 4

Flautas can be made with spicy chicken meat, ground beef, or pork.

1. Place a tortilla on a flat surface; lay out another tortilla so that it overlaps the first tortilla about halfway. Spoon about ⅓ cup of the shredded beef down the center length, where the tortillas overlap. Sprinkle about 2 tablespoons of cheese on top of the meat. Roll up, starting with 1 long side and rolling toward the other. Pin closed with wooden picks or small skewers. Repeat with the remaining tortillas, beef, and cheese to make 8 flautas.
2. Heat the oil to medium-high in a large frying plan. Fry each flauta until golden brown on both sides.

When to Grease a Pan

Some recipes ask you to grease a pan before baking the ingredients. Others don't. The reason is that dishes with a fair amount of fat in them, such as that in cheeses, will create their own layer of grease on the bottom. Those that are primarily flour or have a lot of lean vegetables will have a tendency to stick to the baking dish if it isn't greased.

BEEF TAMALES

Serves 6

Serve with Mexican Coleslaw (page 352).

18 large, dry corn husks
½ cup lard
2 cups dehydrated masa harina
2 cups Chicken Stock (see recipe on page 286)

2 cups Shredded Beef (see recipe on page 287)

1. Wash the corn husks in warm water. Place in a saucepan and cover with boiling water. Let soak for at least 30 minutes before using.
2. Beat the lard until light and fluffy. Gradually beat in the masa harina and stock until the dough sticks together and has a paste-like consistency.
3. Shake excess water from each softened corn husk and pat dry on paper towels. Spread about 2 tablespoons of dough on the center portion of each husk. Spoon about 1½ tablespoons beef onto the dough. Wrap the tamale, overlapping the sides and then folding up the top and bottom.
4. Lay the tamales in the top section of a double boiler with the open husk flaps on the bottom. Steam over simmering water for about 1 hour or until the corn husk can easily be peeled from the dough.

Beef Myths

Many Americans believe that Mexicans spiced their ground beef with hot peppers to avoid tasting the decay that was obviously present given the hot weather and no refrigeration. The truth is that Mexicans rarely eat ground beef. Most of their beef, pork, and veal dishes use steak that traditionally was cut from freshly slaughtered animals.

CHAPTER 33
TEX-MEX

TEXAS CHILI

Serves 8

Serve with Jalapeño Corn Bread (page 330).

3 garlic cloves
2 large white onions
2 pounds lean ground beef
2 cups canned tomatoes, with juice
3 cups canned tomato sauce

4 cups canned kidney beans
1 tablespoon salt
½ teaspoon ground black pepper
3 teaspoons chili powder
1 teaspoon dried oregano
3 tablespoons granulated sugar

1. Peel and mince the garlic. Peel the onions and cut into ¼-inch pieces.
2. In a large skillet on medium heat, cook the ground beef until it is browned. Drain off the grease.
3. Combine all the ingredients in a large pot and simmer on medium heat until heated through.

WHITE CHILI

Serves 8

Top the chili with Monterey jack cheese, crushed tortilla chips, and a dollop of sour cream.

1 pound dry navy beans
12 cups Chicken Stock (see recipe on page 286)
2 garlic cloves
1 medium onion
4 cups cooked chicken, light and dark meat

2 (4-ounce) cans green chilies
2 teaspoons ground cumin
1½ teaspoons dried oregano
½ teaspoon ground cloves
¼ teaspoon cayenne pepper

1. Soak the beans in 4 cups water for 2 to 10 hours.
2. Place the stock in a large pot on low heat. Add the beans.
3. Remove the skin from the garlic and onions. Chop into ¼-inch pieces and add to the pot.
4. Remove the chicken skin and dice into ½-inch cubes. Add to the pot.
5. Add the remaining ingredients; stir well. Simmer for 3 hours.

PORK AND POTATOES

3-pound pork roast
3 large white onions
4 garlic cloves
10 assorted whole chili peppers
5 medium-sized new potatoes
10 whole cloves

1 cinnamon stick
10 black peppercorns
1 teaspoon whole cumin seeds
2 tablespoons white vinegar

Serves 6

Serve with Pineapple and Coconut Salad (page 462) for a blending of sweet and spicy.

1. Preheat oven to 350°.
2. Trim the fat from the pork roast. Peel the onions and cut into quarters. Peel and mince the garlic. Remove the stems from the chili peppers and cut in half lengthwise. (Do not remove the seeds.) Peel the potatoes and cut in half.
3. Place the pork in a large baking pan. Cover with the onions, garlic, chili peppers, cloves, cinnamon stick, peppercorns, and cumin. Add just enough water to cover the ingredients. Cover and cook for 1 hour.
4. Stir the mixture. Add the potatoes, cover, and cook for 1 hour or until the potatoes are soft. Ten minutes before serving, remove the spices and add the vinegar. Leave uncovered for the last 10 minutes.

Mushy Potatoes
Have your raw potatoes gone mushy? They're still good if you use them right away. Remove the peels and slice the potatoes thickly. Put them in a soup or stew and no one will know they were past their prime.

MEXICAN POPCORN

1 pound bacon
½ cup butter
1 teaspoon chili powder
¼ teaspoon garlic salt
¼ teaspoon onion salt
½ teaspoon paprika
4 quarts popped popcorn
1 cup canned french-fried onions

1. Preheat oven to 250°.
2. Cook the bacon in a large frying pan until very crisp. Drain off the grease and transfer the bacon to paper towels to cool. When cool, crumble the bacon into small pieces.
3. Melt the butter in a small saucepan. Add the chili powder, garlic salt, onion salt, and paprika; stir until well blended.
4. Pour the butter mixture over the popcorn and toss until well covered.
5. Add the bacon and onions to the popcorn and toss lightly.
6. Pour the mixture onto a baking sheet. Bake for 10 minutes.

LONCHES

6 slices bacon
6 large hard rolls
½ pound Monterey jack cheese
1½ cups Red Chili Sauce (see recipe on page 288)

1. Preheat oven to 350°.
2. Fry the bacon until crisp. Drain off the grease.
3. Thinly slice the cheese. Split the rolls in half horizontally. Fill generously with cheese and top with a bacon strip. Close the rolls to form sandwiches and place on a baking sheet.
4. Put in the oven for 5 to 10 minutes or until the rolls are hot and the cheese is melted.
5. While the rolls are baking, heat the sauce to bubbling.
6. Place each filled roll in a soup bowl and ladle ¼ cup of sauce over the top.

TACO SOUP

1 large white onion

1 green bell pepper

2 pounds lean ground beef

1 tablespoon paprika

1 tablespoon chili powder

1 tablespoon salt

1 tablespoon ground black pepper

3 15-ounce cans stewed tomatoes, with juice

2 cups canned pinto beans, undrained

1 cup canned kidney beans, undrained

1 cup canned golden hominy, undrained

1 cup canned whole-kernel corn, undrained

6 cups water

4 Tostadas (see recipe on page 285)

Serves 8

Serve with Mexican Hot Chocolate (page 540) on the next cool day.

1. Peel the onion and chop into ¼-inch pieces. Remove the stem and seeds from the green pepper and chop into ¼-inch pieces.
2. Combine the onion, green pepper, ground beef, paprika, chili powder, salt, and ground black pepper in a large frying pan on medium heat. Cook until the ground beef is browned.
3. Add the ground beef mixture to a large stockpot. Add the stewed tomatoes, pinto beans, kidney beans, hominy, and whole kernel corn, along with all their liquids.
4. Stir, add the water, and bring to a boil. Turn the temperature to medium-low, cover, and simmer for 2 hours.
5. Top with crumbled tostadas right before serving.

Hominy

Hominy is actually dried white field corn that has been cooked with powdered lime until its skin falls off. The kernels' eyes are taken out and the kernel opens up until it resembles a piece of wet popcorn.

LAYERED MEXICAN DIP

Serves 8

Serve with freshly
fried and salted Corn
Tortillas (page 283).

3 medium-sized ripe avocados
2 tablespoons lemon juice
1 teaspoon salt
1 teaspoon garlic powder
½ cup mayonnaise
1 teaspoon chili powder
1 teaspoon onion salt

1 bunch green onions
3 medium-sized red tomatoes
1 cup pitted black olives
½ pound Cheddar cheese
2 cups canned bean dip

1. Peel the avocados and remove the seeds. Mash together with the lemon juice, salt, and garlic powder. Set aside.
2. Mix together the mayonnaise, chili powder, and onion salt. Set aside.
3. Remove the roots from the green onions and chop into ½-inch pieces. Remove the stems from the tomatoes and cut into ½-inch pieces. Chop the black olives into ½-inch pieces. Grate the cheese.
4. Layer on a large plate or platter in the following order: bean dip, avocado mix, sour cream mix, onions, tomatoes, olives, cheese.
5. Cover and chill in the refrigerator for 4 hours before serving.

Cooking Beans
Any bean recipe gives you 2 options. Cook it longer and let the beans dissolve for a creamy texture. Serve it earlier in the cooking process, as soon as the beans are completely soft, for more distinct flavors in every bite.

ENCHILADAS RANCHEROS

2 garlic cloves
2 medium-sized yellow onions
2 fresh jalapeño peppers
4 large red tomatoes
2 tablespoons vegetable oil
1 teaspoon dried oregano
4 cups cooked chicken
1 pound Monterey jack cheese

¾ pound fresh button mushrooms
1 cup pitted black olives
4 cups sour cream
30 Flour Tortillas (see recipe
   on page 284)

Serves 8

Garnish with sour cream, guacamole, and chopped green onions.

1. Preheat oven to 350°.
2. Peel and mince the garlic and onions. Remove the stems and seeds from the jalapeños and cut into ¼-inch pieces. Peel the tomatoes and chop into ½-inch pieces.
3. Heat the vegetable oil to medium temperature in a medium-sized frying pan. Add the garlic, onion, and jalapeño peppers; sauté until the onion is transparent. Add the tomatoes and oregano; cook for about 5 minutes, stirring frequently.
4. Cut the cooked chicken into ½-inch cubes. Grate the cheese. Clean the mushrooms and slice thinly. Cut the black olives into ¼-inch rounds.
5. Mix together the chicken, cheese, mushrooms, and black olives. Stir in the sour cream.
6. Put 3 to 4 tablespoons of filling into each tortilla. Roll up and place into a 9" × 13" baking dish. Pour the sauce over the top.
7. Bake for 30 minutes or until heated through.

Mushrooms

Different mushrooms have very different tastes. Don't hesitate to substitute exotic dried mushrooms such as wood ear, enoki, and porcini even if the recipe calls for fresh mushrooms.

CHIMICHANGAS

1 medium-sized white onion
1 medium-sized red tomato
½ cup canned jalapeño pep-
 pers, or 4 fresh jalapeños
½ pound Colby cheese
1 pound lean ground beef
1½ teaspoons chili powder
½ teaspoon ground black
 pepper

1 teaspoon garlic salt
¼ teaspoon cayenne pepper
½ teaspoon dried oregano
8 Flour Tortillas (see recipe on
 page 284)
2 cups vegetable oil

1. Peel the onion and cut into ¼-inch pieces. Remove the stem from the
   tomato and cut into ¼-inch pieces. Chop the jalapeño peppers into
   ¼-inch pieces. Grate the cheese.
2. In a medium-sized frying pan, fry the ground beef and onions on
   medium heat until the meat is brown and the onions are translucent.
   Drain off the grease.
3. Add the tomatoes, jalapeños, chili powder, black pepper, garlic salt,
   chili powder, cayenne pepper, and oregano; simmer for 10 minutes.
4. Put 2 to 3 tablespoons of the mixture in the middle of each tortilla.
   Add 1 tablespoon of cheese on top. Fold the tortillas and secure with
   toothpicks.
5. Heat the vegetable oil to medium-high in a large skillet. Add 2 or 3
   tortillas at a time. Fry quickly until golden brown on each side.

A Word about Cheese

*Like virtually every culture in the world, the various regions of
Mexico have their own types of cheese. Unfortunately very few of
these are available outside of Mexico, even in authentic Mexican
restaurants. At the same time, because Mexican cuisine was influenced by Spanish cuisine centuries ago, the entire world of European
cheeses is used in their recipes.*

FAJITAS

1 pound beef, deboned and
  skinned chicken, and/or shrimp
1 garlic clove
1 medium-sized yellow onion
1 green or red bell pepper
1 tablespoon vegetable oil
¼ cup soy sauce
1 teaspoon ground black
  pepper

1 tablespoon Worscestershire
  sauce
½ tablespoon lemon juice
8 Flour Tortillas (see recipe on
  page 284)

> **Serves 2**
>
> Serve with Guacamole
> (page 287), Red Rice
> (page 286), and
> Tomato Salsa
> (page 282).

1. If using beef or chicken, cut the meat into ½-inch wide strips. If using shrimp, boil for 10 minutes, let cool, and remove the shells and veins. Peel and mince the garlic.

2. Combine the garlic, vegetable oil, soy sauce, black pepper, Worcestershire sauce, and lemon juice. Place the meat in a medium-sized mixing bowl. Pour the sauce on top. Cover and refrigerate for 4 to 8 hours.

3. Drain the meat. Peel the onion and cut into 1-inch pieces. Remove the seeds and stem from the bell pepper and cut into 1-inch pieces. Add the onion and bell pepper to the bowl with the meat; mix well.

4. Sauté the mixture on medium heat in a large frying pan until the meat is thoroughly cooked. Serve with flour tortillas.

How to Marinate Meat

Never marinate meat for longer than 24 hours. The meat begins to break down and the texture becomes mushy. The flavors should penetrate after about 2 hours. Always marinate in the refrigerator so that bacteria doesn't begin to grow.

SOUTHWESTERN FRIED CHICKEN

Serves 4

Serve with Calabacitas (page 435) for a well-balanced, slightly spicy meal.

3 pieces white bread
1 bunch fresh cilantro
2 garlic cloves
2 eggs
2 tablespoons masa harina or cornmeal
2 tablespoons pine nuts
½ teaspoon ground cumin
1½ teaspoons dried oregano
½ teaspoon salt

¼ teaspoon cayenne pepper
⅛ teaspoon ground cloves
2 tablespoons prepared yellow mustard
1 tablespoon water
2 teaspoons honey
4 chicken breasts
¼ teaspoon ground black pepper
2 tablespoons butter

1. Preheat oven to 400°.
2. Tear the bread into 1-inch pieces. Remove the stems from the cilantro. Peel the garlic. Separate the eggs and discard the yolks.
3. Blend the bread, cilantro, garlic, cornmeal, pine nuts, cumin, oregano, ¼ teaspoon of the salt, cayenne pepper, and cloves in a blender until you have fine crumbs. Add the egg whites and mix until the crumbs are moist. Spread out the crumb mixture on a large plate.
4. Mix together the mustard, water, and honey in a small bowl. Brush over the chicken with a pastry brush. Sprinkle the chicken with the pepper and remaining ¼ teaspoon salt. Dip the chicken 1 piece at a time in the bread mixture, pressing slightly so the mixture sticks.
5. Melt the butter in a 9" × 11" baking dish. Place the chicken breasts skin-side down in the butter; bake for 20 minutes. Flip the chicken and bake for an additional 20 minutes.

Masa Harina

Masa harina is flour made from dried corn dough that is then ground into a powder. Although similar to cornmeal, it does have a subtly different texture and taste because of the double-grinding process. You can usually substitute cornmeal in most recipes, although masa harina will give a more authentic flavor and texture.

TACO SKILLET CASSEROLE

1 small yellow onion
1 garlic clove
¼ head lettuce
8 Corn Tortillas (see recipe on page 283)
1½ pounds ground beef
1 teaspoon salt

½ teaspoon ground black pepper
1 teaspoon chili powder
2 cups canned tomato sauce
½ cup vegetable oil
½ cup grated Cheddar cheese

> **Serves 6**
>
> Add a side of Extra-special Frijoles Refritos (page 451).

1. Peel the onion and chop into ¼-inch pieces. Peel and mince the garlic. Shred the lettuce. Cut the tortillas into ½-inch-wide strips.
2. Crumble the ground beef into a large frying pan and brown on medium heat. Pour off excess fat.
3. Add the onion and garlic and cook for about 5 minutes longer, until the onion is soft; stir frequently.
4. Stir in the salt, pepper, chili powder, and tomato sauce, and continue cooking over low heat for about 15 minutes longer; stir frequently.
5. In a separate frying pan, heat the vegetable oil to medium-high. Fry the tortilla strips until crisp. Transfer to paper towels to absorb excess grease.
6. Stir the tortilla strips into the meat mixture and cook for about 5 minutes, stirring frequently.
7. Sprinkle with cheese. As soon as the cheese melts, remove from heat. Top with shredded lettuce and serve immediately.

Corn Husks as Spice

The Mexican culture is unique for using corn husks to spice food. Most often used in corn tamales, the husks are also used as a wrapper for other foods such as candy. Even when leaving the husk on for cooking the corn, you notice a distinctly earthy taste that is transferred to the food.

KEY LIME PIE

3 cups flour
1 teaspoon baking powder
1 tablespoon granulated sugar
3 tablespoons shortening
3 eggs
1 (14-ounce) can sweetened condensed milk

½ cup fresh squeezed key lime juice
3 teaspoons grated key lime peel
¾ cup whipping cream
2 tablespoons confectioners' sugar

1. Preheat oven to 350°.
2. Combine the flour, baking powder, sugar, and shortening; mix well. Spread on a floured surface and roll out to about ⅛-inch thick. Put into a 9-inch pie pan. Cut off and discard any extra dough. Place in the oven for 10 minutes.
3. Beat the eggs, milk, lime juice, and 2 teaspoons of the grated lime peel on medium speed in a medium-sized mixing bowl. Pour the mixture into the pie crust.
4. Bake for 30 to 35 minutes or until the center is set. Cool on a wire rack for 15 minutes. Cover and refrigerate for 2 to 8 hours before serving.
5. No more than 4 hours before serving, combine the whipping cream, remaining 1 teaspoon grated lime peel, and confectioners' sugar into a well-chilled bowl and whip until it doubles in size. Spread on top of the pie.

CHAPTER 34
CELEBRATIONS

MEXICAN WEDDING CAKE

2 cups flour
2 teaspoons baking soda
20 ounces canned crushed
  pineapple, with juice
1 cup chopped pecans, plus
  extra for garnish

2 cups granulated sugar
2 eggs
8 ounces cream cheese
2 cups powdered sugar
½ cup butter
1 teaspoon vanilla

1. Preheat oven to 350°. Grease and flour a 9" × 13" pan.
2. Combine the flour, soda, pineapple and juice, chopped pecans, granulated sugar, and eggs in a medium-sized mixing bowl; stir until well mixed. Pour into the prepared pan and bake, uncovered, for 30 to 35 minutes.
3. For the frosting, mix together the cream cheese, powdered sugar, butter, and vanilla until well blended. Let the cake cool thoroughly before frosting. Sprinkle with more chopped pecans.

CANDLEMAS DRINK

1 pound canned beats
½ cup pitted prunes
¼ head lettuce
1 green apple
¼ cup blanched almonds

1½ quarts water
½ cup sugar
¼ cup seedless raisins
¼ cup unsalted peanuts

1. Chop the beets and prunes into ¼-inch pieces. Shred the lettuce. Peel and remove the core from the apple; chop into ¼-inch pieces. Chop the almonds into small pieces.
2. Pour the water into a glass or ceramic container. Dissolve the sugar in the water. Add all the ingredients and stir gently. Refrigerate for 3 to 4 hours before serving.

GRILLED SHRIMP IN PRICKLY PEAR CACTUS VINAIGRETTE

28 large fresh shrimp
1 gallon water
2 prickly pear cactus fruits
1 bunch cilantro
½ cup red wine vinegar
1 tablespoon peanut oil
1 tablespoon olive oil

½ tablespoon balsamic vinegar
1 ounce hearts of palm
6 ounces arugula
1 teaspoon salt
1 teaspoon ground black pepper
2 tablespoons garlic paste

> **Serves 4**
>
> This is a favorite meal to celebrate a special event such as a wedding anniversary or birthday. Serve it with Pineapple and Coconut Salad (page 462).

1. Boil the shrimp in the water for 10 minutes. Drain, and run cold water over the shrimp. Peel the shrimp and use a fork tine to remove the back vein.
2. Peel the prickly pear cactus by cutting off both ends and slitting both sides. If ripe, the peel will easily come off. Cut into 1-inch pieces. Cut the stems off the cilantro.
3. In a blender, combine the prickly pear, cilantro, garlic paste, red wine vinegar, and peanut oil; blend at medium speed until smooth.
4. Place the shrimp in a glass or plastic container and pour the sauce over the top. Cover and refrigerate for 8 to 12 hours. Discard the sauce.
5. Preheat the grill to medium temperature. Grill the shrimp for 2 to 3 minutes on each side or until slightly browned.
6. While the shrimp are cooking, combine the olive oil and balsamic vinegar. Cut the hearts of palm into ½-inch pieces. Combine olive oil and balsamic vinegar mixture with the salt, pepper, hearts of palm, and arugula; toss gently.
7. Spread the hearts of palm and arugula onto a serving platter and top with the fresh-grilled shrimp.

What Is Arugula?

Arugula is a leaf that serves double-duty as both a spice and an eating green. It has a very peppery flavor that complements seafood and poultry very well. Discard the discolored leaves because they will be bitter. Its small leaves are usually added whole to salads.

CHILI RELLENOS EN CROUTE WITH TOMATO-CILANTRO SAUCE

Serves 4

This is often served for special events such as birthdays or anniversaries. Serve it with sides of Red Rice (page 286) and Fresh Cauliflower Salad (page 342).

4 fresh poblano chili peppers
¾ pound Monterey jack cheese
½ pound goat cheese
2 sticks butter
4 sheets whole-wheat phyllo pastry

1 large yellow onion
16 roma tomatoes
4 bunches fresh cilantro
1 tablespoon olive oil
1 teaspoon salt

1. Preheat oven to 350°.
2. Put the peppers on a baking sheet and roast for about 20 minutes or until well browned. (Leave the oven at 350°.) Remove the peppers from the oven and place them in a paper bag; close tightly and let the peppers cool. (This makes it easier to peel the peppers.) Remove the skin, stem, and seeds when cool. Do not cut the pepper open other than at the top.
3. Grate the Monterey jack cheese. Crumble the goat cheese. Combine the cheeses.
4. Fill each pepper with ¼ of the cheese mixture.
5. Melt the butter in a small saucepan on low heat. Remove the phyllo and lay it out flat on a work surface. Take 1 sheet of phyllo at a time and brush with butter, using a pastry brush. Put 1 chili in the corner of 1 sheet of phyllo dough and roll up, brushing all unbuttered surfaces with butter.
6. Place the chili rellenos on a baking sheet and bake for 20 to 25 minutes or until the dough is well browned.
7. Peel the onion and cut into ¼-inch pieces. Cut the tomatoes into ¼-inch pieces. Remove the stems from the cilantro and chop into ¼-inch pieces.
8. Sauté the onion in the olive oil at medium heat until the onions are clear and limp. Add the tomatoes and cook for 5 to 10 minutes or until the liquid is evaporated. Add the salt and chopped cilantro. Stir well.
9. To serve, pour the sauce on a plate and top with the chili rellenos.

CAPIROTADA

8 slices white bread
2 large tart apples
½ pound mild Cheddar cheese
2 cups water
1 cup white granulated sugar
1 cup firmly packed brown sugar
1 teaspoon ground cinnamon
½ teaspoon ground nutmeg

½ teaspoon ground cloves
½ teaspoon salt
2 tablespoons butter
2 cups raisins

> **Serves 8**
>
> This bread pudding is a Christmas tradition in most Mexican households.

1. Preheat oven to 350°.
2. Toast the bread and tear into 1-inch cubes. Peel the apples, remove the cores, and slice the apples into ½-inch pieces. Grate the cheese.
3. Combine the water, white sugar, brown sugar, cinnamon, nutmeg, cloves, and salt in a medium-sized saucepan and bring the mixture to a boil. Lower the heat and simmer for 10 minutes, until the mixture becomes syrupy.
4. Butter a rectangular baking pan on the bottom and sides. Place the bread cubes on the bottom. Sprinkle the apples and raisins on top. Then sprinkle the cheese on top of that. Pour the syrup over the top.
5. Bake for 30 minutes.

Cheese and Fruit

Many Mexican desserts feature milk and fruit products, taking advantage of the two sweetest, unprocessed items in their diet. When combined with their wide array of spices, the result is an unusual blending of flavors that at first seems odd but gradually grows to be a pleasant culinary treat.

MEXICAN CHRISTMAS SALAD

2–6 key limes
1 cup mayonnaise
3 tablespoons granulated sugar
2 tablespoons whole milk
1 small head iceberg lettuce
1 medium pineapple or 1 (20-ounce) can sliced pineapple

3 medium oranges
3 small bananas
2 large sweet apples
2 cups canned sliced beets
½ cup salted, skinless peanuts

1. Grate 1 tablespoon of peel from the key limes. Squeeze ¼ cup juice from the limes. In a small bowl, mix the lime juice, lime peel, mayonnaise, sugar, and milk.
2. Slice the lettuce into ½-inch-wide strips. If using a fresh pineapple, remove the stem, rind, and core; cut the fruit into ½-inch-thick pieces. If using canned pineapple, drain and discard the juice. Peel the oranges and slice thinly. Peel the bananas and slice into ¼-inch rounds. Core the apples and cut into ½-inch-thick wedges. Drain the beets.
3. Place the bowl of dressing in the middle of a large platter. Arrange the lettuce around the platter. On the lettuce, arrange separate piles of pineapple, oranges, bananas, apples, and beets. Sprinkle peanuts over the fruit.

Lettuce
Different lettuces have very different flavors. Iceberg lettuce tends to be the most mild. Leaf lettuces can be slightly more bitter. Experiment with different types of lettuce or the prepackaged lettuce mixes to find your favorites.

MEXICAN TRIFLE

¼ cup granulated sugar
1 tablespoon cornstarch
¼ teaspoon salt
2 cups whole milk
2 eggs
1 teaspoon vanilla
4 cups pound cake
4 tablespoons brandy
4 tablespoons apricot preserves

½ cup whipped cream
1 tablespoon confectioners'
sugar
4 ounces semisweet baker's
chocolate
½ cup toasted, slivered
almonds

Serves 6

This is often served as dessert for special holidays such as Cinco de Mayo or to celebrate an event such as a work promotion or getting a good report card.

1. Combine the sugar, cornstarch, and salt in a medium-sized saucepan. Stir in the milk until well blended. Cook over medium heat, stirring constantly, until the mixture boils.

2. Break the eggs into a medium-sized mixing bowl. Add about ¼ cup of the sugar mixture to the eggs and beat slightly. Add the egg mixture to the sugar mixture in the saucepan and cook on medium heat, stirring constantly, until the mixture starts to bubble. Stir in the vanilla. Remove from heat, cover with waxed paper, and let cool to room temperature.

3. Break the pound cake into 1-inch cubes. Place the cubes in a glass bowl. Sprinkle with 3 tablespoons brandy. Drizzle with preserves. Pour the sugar and egg mixture (which should be like a custard when cooled) over the pound cake.

4. Whip the cream with the confectioners' sugar until stiff. Fold in the remaining 1 tablespoon brandy. Top the cake and custard with whipped cream.

5. Grate the chocolate. Sprinkle the chocolate and almonds on top of the cake.

6. Cover and chill for at least 4 hours before serving.

CHRISTMAS CANDY BALLS

2 medium white potatoes
2 cups pecans
1 cup red candied cherries
1 cup confectioners' sugar

1 teaspoon ground cinnamon
1 cup granulated sugar
1 teaspoon vanilla extract

1. Scrub the potatoes but do not peel. Cut into 1-inch cubes. Chop the pecans into small pieces. Cut the candied cherries in half. Mix the confectioners' sugar and cinnamon in a small bowl.
2. Put the potatoes in a medium-sized pot. Add water to cover. Bring to a boil and continue boiling until the potatoes are soft. Drain off the water.
3. Press the potatoes through a ricer or put through a food mill. Mix in the granulated sugar, vanilla extract, and nuts.
4. Form balls about the size of marbles. Coat them with the confectioners' sugar and cinnamon mixture.
5. Store in the refrigerator until ready to serve. Put into small fluted paper cups and garnish with cherry halves.

Gingerroot
Ginger can come in many forms from jellied and crystallized to ground and pickled. Fresh gingerroot should have a silvery skin. It will have a slightly spicy flavor. To prepare it, first remove the tough outer skin with a heavy blade. It then can be chopped or grated.

STUFFED TURKEY

1 (12–16 pound) turkey
1 teaspoon salt
1 teaspoon ground black pepper
1 tablespoon fresh lemon juice
1 cup butter
1 medium-sized yellow onion
1 garlic clove
6 fresh jalapeño chilies
3 medium carrots
½ cup black olives

3 bananas
3 medium-sized red apples
¾ cup blanched almonds
5 slices bacon
3 pounds ground pork
½ cup tomato paste
¾ cup raisins
2 teaspoons granulated sugar
1 teaspoon ground cinnamon

Serves 12

Stuffed turkey is often made to celebrate events that bring large family groups together. It may be a wedding engagement party, a going away party, or a job promotion.

1. Preheat oven to 325°. Clean the turkey. Sprinkle with salt and pepper, then drizzle with lemon juice. Melt the butter on low heat, then soak about 1 yard of cheesecloth in the melted butter.
2. Peel the onion and chop into ¼-inch pieces. Peel and mince the garlic. Remove the stems and seeds from the jalapeños and chop into ¼-inch pieces. Peel the carrots and slice into ¼-inch rounds. Chop the olives into ¼-inch pieces. Peel the bananas and slice into ¼-inch rounds. Peel and core the apples; chop into ¼-inch pieces. Chop the almonds.
3. Fry the bacon until crisp at medium heat in a large frying pan. Remove the bacon and place on paper towels to cool. When cool, crumble into ¼-inch pieces. Brown the onion and garlic in the bacon fat in the skillet. Add the ground pork and fry until browned. Drain off excess fat.
4. Add the tomato paste, chilies, carrots, olives, bananas, apples, almonds, raisins, sugar, and cinnamon. Cook for several minutes on medium heat, stirring frequently. Mix in the bacon. Let cool before stuffing the turkey.
5. Spoon the stuffing into the cavities, pull the loose, hanging skin over the openings, and secure with skewers or twine. Put the turkey breast-side up on a rack in a shallow roasting pan. Cover with a double thickness of the cheesecloth soaked in butter. Roast for 4 to 5 hours or until the meat thermometer reaches 180° when inserted into the thickest part of the breast.

CHRISTMAS CODFISH

1-pound piece salted codfish
2 small yellow onions
2 garlic cloves
3 medium-sized red tomatoes
5 pickled jalapeño chili peppers
3 canned pimientos

1 teaspoon salt
1 teaspoon ground black pepper
3 tablespoons vegetable oil

1. Soak the codfish for 6 to 8 hours in cold water. Change the water several times.
2. Peel the onions and garlic cloves and chop into ¼-inch pieces. Peel the tomatoes and cut into quarters. Remove stems and seeds from the jalapeños and cut into ¼-inch pieces. Slice the pimientos into ¼-inch strips.
3. Drain the codfish and put into a saucepan. Add 1 onion and water to cover. Bring to a simmer. Cover and cook gently for about 15 minutes or until the fish flakes easily when tested with a fork. Drain. Sprinkle salt and pepper on top.
4. While the fish is cooking, put the tomatoes, remaining onion, and garlic in an electric blender or food processor; blend until puréed.
5. Heat the oil to medium temperature in a skillet. Add the tomato sauce. Cook until thickened, stirring occasionally. Mix in the chilies and pimiento strips.

Peppers or Peppercorns?

Chili peppers are not related at all to the plant that produces peppercorns. It's likely that they received the same name when the Spanish conquistadors arrived in Mexico during the 1500s and found that the chilies had a similar "bite" to the more familiar peppercorns.

CREAM-FILLED CHESTNUT CAKE

1¾ pounds fresh chestnuts in
   the shells
6 eggs
¾ cup butter
1 cup granulated sugar
1 teaspoon vanilla extract
1¼ cups flour

1 teaspoon baking powder
½ cup whole milk
1 cup whipping cream
⅔ cup confectioners' sugar

Serves 6

This is frequently used
as a birthday or
anniversary cake.

1. To prepare the chestnuts, rinse the chestnuts and make a slit on
   2 sides of each shell. Put into a saucepan. Cover with boiling water
   and boil about 20 minutes. Remove the shells and skins. Return the
   chestnuts to the saucepan and cover with boiling salted water. Cover
   and simmer until the chestnuts are tender, about 10 to 20 minutes.
   Drain and finely chop.
2. Preheat oven to 325°.
3. Separate the eggs. Cream the butter with the sugar and ½ teaspoon of
   the vanilla extract until fluffy. Add 1¼ cups of the chopped chestnuts,
   then the egg yolks 1 at a time. Mix well after each egg yolk is added.
4. Mix the flour with the baking powder and add to the chestnut mixture;
   mix well. Add the milk and mix well.
5. Beat the egg whites until stiff but not dry. Fold into the batter.
6. Divide the mixture among 2 greased and floured 9-inch round cake
   pans. Bake for 25 minutes.
7. Whip the whipping cream until thickened. Mix in the confectioners'
   sugar and the remaining ½ teaspoon vanilla extract. Blend in the
   remaining chopped chestnuts. Place a generous portion on the top of
   the bottom layer of the cake. Add the top layer of the cake and use
   the remaining frosting to frost the entire cake.

NONALCOHOLIC ROMPOPE
(MEXICAN EGGNOG)

Serves 4

Serve this as a bed-time treat or as an after-dinner drink.

4 cups whole milk
½ cup granulated sugar
12 egg yolks
1 teaspoon vanilla extract
2 tablespoons rum flavoring

¼ cup skinless sliced almonds
1 teaspoon ground cinnamon

1. Put the milk and sugar into a medium-sized pan on the stove and heat at medium-high temperature until it reaches boiling. Reduce heat and simmer for 10 minutes, stirring constantly. Remove from heat and cool to room temperature.
2. Separate the eggs and discard the whites. Beat the yolks with a fork until they are thick and frothy.
3. Add the yolks slowly to the milk and sugar mixture. Beat the mixture gently until the yolks are integrated into the milk and sugar. Add the remaining ingredients.
4. Put the mixture back on the stove and cook on medium heat, stirring constantly, until the mixture thickens enough to coat a spoon.
5. Store in a covered glass container in the refrigerator for at least 48 hours before serving.

CHAPTER 35
REGIONAL FAVORITES

YUCATAN TAMALE PIE

½ cup lard
3 cups masa harina or cornmeal
1 large white onion
2 garlic cloves
4 jalapeño chilies
4 medium-sized ripe tomatoes

1 (3- to 4-pound) whole chicken
4 cups Chicken Stock (see recipe on page 286)
1 teaspoon dried oregano
¼ teaspoon dried cilantro
½ teaspoon brown sugar

1. Preheat oven to 350°.
2. Combine the lard and cornmeal, adding small amounts of water until the dough is soft enough to work with. Grease an ovenproof casserole dish and line the bottom and sides with the dough.
3. Remove the skin from the onion and garlic cloves; chop into ¼-inch pieces. Remove the stem and seeds from chilies and chop into ¼-inch pieces. Cut the tomatoes into 1-inch pieces.
4. Place the chicken, onions, garlic, chilies, tomatoes, stock, oregano, cilantro, and brown sugar into a large stockpot. Bring to a boil. Reduce heat to medium and simmer, covered, for 1 hour.
5. Remove the chicken and let cool. Reserve the broth. Remove the bones and skin from the chicken and tear the meat into strips about 1 inch wide. Layer the chicken on the dough in the casserole.
6. Bake, covered, for 1 hour. Pour 1 cup of the broth over the pie before serving.

Try Turkey
For a lean alternative in your next chicken recipe, substitute turkey. It has much less fat and much more protein than chicken while often being a better per-pound buy at the grocery store.

PUMPKIN BLOSSOM SOUP FROM MORELOS

1 pound pumpkin blossoms
1 small white onion
3 sprigs fresh parsley (for a more authentic flavor, use epazote)
¼ cup butter

8 cups Chicken Stock (see recipe on page 286)
1 teaspoon salt
1 teaspoon ground white pepper

Serves 8

This is a wonderful first course for any chicken or red meat dish.

1. Remove the stems from the flowers and roughly chop into 2-inch pieces. Chop the onion into ¼-inch pieces. Chop the parsley. Melt the butter in a small frying pan at medium heat and sauté the onions until limp but not brown. Add the blossoms and sauté for 5 minutes.
2. Put the stock and parsley in a medium-sized stockpot. Bring to a boil and reduce heat to medium. Add the onions and blossoms, draining off and discarding any excess butter. Stir gently, add the salt and pepper, and simmer for 10 minutes.

NORTHERN BORDER CHILI CON CARNE

1 pound pork steak
1 pound veal steak
2 tablespoons olive oil
1 medium-sized yellow onion
2 garlic cloves

6 jalapeño chilies
1 teaspoon dried oregano
1 teaspoon salt
2 cups canned kidney beans

Serves 4

This is just as traditional if made with beef, but it never contains tomatoes.

1. Cut the pork and veal steaks into 1-inch cubes. Place the meat in a large frying pan along with the olive oil. Cook on medium heat until the meat is lightly browned.
2. Cut the onion into quarters. Remove the stems and seeds from the chilies and cut into ¼-inch pieces. Place the onion, garlic, chilies, oregano, and salt in blender and blend on medium setting until you have a purée. Add the purée to the meat. Stir and cook, uncovered, for 10 minutes.
3. Add the kidney beans to frying pan. Reduce heat, cover, and cook for 1 to 2 hours.

MAYAN LAMB

Serves 4

Serve with Red Rice
(page 286).

2 pounds boneless lamb
1 medium-sized yellow onion
1 garlic clove
1 cup canned red tomatoes
1 teaspoon salt
1/4 teaspoon ground black
   pepper

1 cup hulled pepitas (pumpkin
   seeds)
1 tablespoon annatto seeds
2 tablespoons vegetable oil
1 tablespoon lemon juice

1. Cut the lamb into 2-inch chunks. Peel the onion and chop into 1/4-inch pieces. Peel and mince the garlic. Drain the tomatoes and chop into 1/4-inch pieces.
2. Combine the lamb, onion, garlic, tomatoes, salt, and pepper in a heavy saucepot; stir well. Add water to cover. Bring to a boil. Reduce heat, cover, and simmer until the meat is tender, about 2 hours.
3. Combine the *pepitas* and annatto seeds in an electric blender or food processor; blend until pulverized.
4. In a small frying pan, heat the oil to medium temperature. Add the *pepitas* and annatto seeds and fry for 2 to 3 minutes, stirring constantly. Stir in the lemon juice.
5. Right before serving, stir the seed mixture into the meat sauce.

When to Use a Slow Cooker

Slow cookers are excellent appliances if you want to make a meal while you aren't at home or if you want to keep an appetizer warm for several hours. Soups and stews work well, as does any dish that doesn't require the food to brown and doesn't need to be quick-cooked, such as fried foods.

COLIFLOR ACAPULCO

1 large head fresh cauliflower
1½ cups vegetable oil
½ cup lemon juice
1½ teaspoons salt
1 teaspoon chili powder
¼ cup canned pimientos
2 cups canned pickled beets
1 large cucumber

2 cups canned garbanzos
8 red radishes
1 cup pimiento-stuffed olives
1 cup lettuce
1 bunch parsley sprigs
1 cup Guacamole (see recipe
  on page 287)

Serves 4

Serve on a buffet with traditional Mexican favorites.

1. Add water to a large saucepan to the depth of 1 inch. Bring to boil. Add the cauliflower, cover, and cook for about 20 minutes or until tender. Drain off the water.
2. Combine the vegetable oil, lemon juice, salt, and chili powder in a container with a lid. Cover and shake until well mixed to create a marinade.
3. Place the cauliflower head down in a deep bowl and pour the marinade over it. Cover and chill for at least 8 hours in the refrigerator.
4. Slice the pimientos into ¼-inch-wide lengthwise strips. Slice the pickled beets into ¼-inch-thick rounds. Slice the cucumber into ¼-inch rounds. Chill these vegetables separately for at least 2 hours, covered, in the refrigerator.
5. Drain off the water from the garbanzo beans. Cut the tops and bottoms off the radishes and slice slightly down the sides to create roses.
6. Thread the garbanzos, olives, and pimiento strips onto wooden picks to create decorative kabobs.
7. Drain the cauliflower. Line a chilled serving plate with the lettuce and place the cauliflower, head up, in the center. Arrange the pickled beets and cucumber slices around the base. Tuck in the parsley sprigs and radish roses.
8. Spread guacamole over the cauliflower. Decorate the cauliflower with kabobs. Serve cold.

TOSTADAS FROM GUADALAJARA

1 cup lettuce
1 tablespoon olive oil
2 tablespoons vinegar
1 teaspoon salt
½ teaspoon ground white pepper
4 spicy sausage patties
2 cups Refried Beans (see recipe on page 284)
1 medium-sized yellow onion
2 cups Guacamole (see recipe on page 287)
¼ pound mozzarella cheese
8 freshly made (still warm) Tostadas (see recipe on page 285)

1. Shred the lettuce and put in a small bowl. Combine the olive oil, vinegar, salt, and white pepper in a small container with a lid. Cover and shake until well mixed, then pour over the lettuce and set aside.
2. Crumble the sausage patties and heat on medium in a small frying pan. Sauté until browned. Heat the beans in a small saucepan.
3. Peel the onion and chop into ¼-inch pieces. Drain the lettuce. Grate the cheese.
4. Put the ingredients in layers on the tostadas in the following order: refried beans, sausage, onion, guacamole, lettuce, cheese.

PUERTO VALLARTA'S CATFISH SOUP

1 large white onion
3 garlic cloves
4 fresh jalapeño peppers
6 medium carrots
4 cups canned whole tomatoes
1 teaspoon dried oregano
1 teaspoon salt

½ teaspoon ground black pepper
½ teaspoon paprika
2 quarts water
2 pounds catfish fillets

Serves 8

For fishier flavor, cook the fish with the head and skin on. After 15 minutes of simmering, remove the head, skin, and bones and return the meat to the pot. Cook for another 5 minutes.

1. Peel the onion and chop into ¼-inch pieces. Peel and mince the garlic. Remove the stem and seeds from the jalapeños and chop into ¼-inch pieces. Peel the carrots and cut into ¼-inch rounds.

2. Fill a large pot with the water. Add the onion, garlic, jalapeños, carrots, tomatoes, oregano, salt, black pepper, and paprika to the pot; stir gently. Heat on high until boiling. Reduce heat to medium and simmer, uncovered, until the tomatoes have disintegrated and the carrots are tender (about 2 hours).

3. Cut the catfish fillets into 1-inch cubes. Add the cubes to the broth and simmer for 15 minutes.

4. Sprinkle with paprika before serving.

SEA BASS FROM VERACRUZ

If you can't find largo chilies, substitute 12 jalapeños. Serve with Spinach Salad (page 354) and baked sweet potatoes.

4 large sea bass fillets
½ cup flour
1 teaspoon salt
½ teaspoon ground white pepper
½ cup olive oil
1 medium-sized yellow onion
2 garlic cloves
3 fresh largo chilies

2 cups canned tomato paste
¼ teaspoon ground cinnamon
¼ teaspoon ground cloves
1 tablespoon lime juice
1 teaspoon granulated sugar
½ cup black olives
½ teaspoon ground black pepper

1. Coat the sea bass fillets with the flour. Sprinkle both sides with the salt and white pepper.
2. Heat ¼ cup of the olive oil in a large frying pan. Add the fish fillets and fry on each side until thoroughly cooked and golden brown. The flesh should be opaque and flake easily with a fork. Remove from heat and set aside.
3. Chop the black olives into ¼-inch pieces. Peel the onion and chop into ¼-inch pieces. Peel and mince the garlic. Remove the seeds and stems from the chilies and chop into ¼-inch pieces.
4. Add the remaining ¼ cup olive oil to the frying pan and heat to medium. Add the onion, garlic, and chilies; sauté until the onion is limp. Add the tomato paste, cinnamon, black olives, and ground cloves. Cook until heated through. Add the lemon juice, ground pepper, and sugar; gently stir in.
5. Reduce heat to low. Add the fish fillets. Cover and cook for 5 minutes.

Discovering Cilantro

Cilantro is a common weed that is used as a spice in Mexican cooking as well as in the dishes of other countries with warm climates. It has a rather strong and unusual taste that becomes stronger as it is cooked. If you're not sure about the taste, add just a little bit at the end of the cooking process.

COZUMEL CHICKEN

8 large boneless chicken
   breasts
8 key limes
2 lemons

1 cup orange juice
1 tablespoon butter
1 cup Red Chili Sauce (see
   recipe on page 288)

Serves 8

Serve with Grilled
Corn on the Cob
(page 430) and Fruit
Compote (page 466).

1. Preheat oven to 325°.
2. Melt the butter on medium heat in a large skillet. Add the chicken breasts and cook until brown on 1 side. Flip and brown the other side.
3. Wash the limes and lemons but do not peel. Slice as thinly as possible.
4. Transfer the chicken to an ovenproof baking dish. Top with the lime and lemon slices. Pour the orange juice over the top.
5. Cover with foil and bake for about 1 hour or until the chicken is tender.
6. Remove the lime and lemon slices and pour the chili sauce over the chicken. Heat for 5 more minutes.

GREEN MOUNTAIN STEW

1 pound mutton
1 pound chicken meat
6 tomatillos
2 large white onions
3 garlic cloves

2 chayote squash
12 fresh serrano chilies
1 tablespoon vegetable oil
1 teaspoon salt
1 teaspoon ground black pepper

Serves 6

Serve with Red Rice
(page 286) and
Refried Beans (page
284).

1. Cut the mutton into 1-inch cubes. Remove the skin and bones from the chicken and cut into 1-inch cubes. Remove the skin and stems from the tomatillos and quarter. Peel and mince the garlic. Peel and quarter the onions. Remove the rind and seed from the squash and cut into 1-inch pieces. Remove the stems from the chilies and split in half lengthwise.
2. Heat the vegetable oil to medium heat in a large frying pan. Add the mutton and chicken meat, and fry until golden. Add all the other ingredients and mix lightly. Fry for 5 minutes. Reduce heat to medium-low. Cover and simmer for 1½ hours.

MEXICO CITY'S CHICKEN WITH MUSHROOMS

Serves 8

Serve with Pineapple and Coconut Salad (page 462) and Refried Beans (page 284).

2 fryer chickens
1 pound fresh button mushrooms
1 medium-sized yellow onion
1 garlic clove
¼ cup olive oil
2 cups canned tomatoes,
   with juice

6 fresh jalapeños
1 cup Chicken Stock (see
   recipe on page 286)
1½ teaspoons salt
1 cup sour cream

1. Cut each of the chickens into 8 serving pieces (legs, wings, breasts, etc.). Wash the mushrooms and slice thinly. Peel the onion and chop into ¼-inch pieces. Peel the garlic and cut into quarters. Remove the stems and seeds from the chili peppers.
2. Heat the oil to medium temperature in a large frying pan. Fry the chicken pieces until golden brown. Transfer the chicken to a large saucepot.
3. Sauté the mushrooms in the oil remaining in the frying pan. Spoon the mushrooms over the chicken. Do not drain the oil from the pan.
4. Combine the tomatoes with their juice, the chili peppers, onion, and garlic in an electric blender or food processor; blend until puréed. Pour the purée into the skillet with the oil. Bring to a boil and cook for about 5 minutes. Stir in the stock and salt.
5. Pour the sauce over the chicken and mushrooms. Cover and cook over low heat until the chicken is tender, about 1 hour. Just before serving, stir in the sour cream and heat through, but do not boil.

Potatoes au Naturel

Potato skins contain many vitamins not found in the "meat" of the potato. Unless your recipe calls for a clean, "white" look, leave the skins on and savor the extra nutrition.

CARIBBEAN COAST PICKLED TUNA

1 pound fresh tuna steak
¼ cup lime juice
1 medium-sized yellow onion
1 garlic clove
2 canned jalapeño chilies
½ cup pimiento-stuffed olives

¼ cup vegetable oil
½ teaspoon dried oregano
½ teaspoon ground cumin
¾ cup white wine vinegar

Serves 6

This makes an excellent summer luncheon when served with Fruit Compote (page 466).

1. Put the tuna in a medium-sized stockpot. Add ½ inch of water. Cover and heat on low until the fish is cooked through. The fish should flake easily with a fork. When cool, flake the fish and put in a small bowl.
2. Pour the lime juice over the fish and let stand for about 10 minutes (while preparing the rest of the meal).
3. Peel the onion and slice into ⅛-inch rounds. Peel and mince the garlic. Cut the jalapeños into thin strips. Slice the olives into ¼-inch rounds.
4. Heat the oil to medium temperature in a medium-sized frying pan. Add the onion, garlic, and chilies. Cook for about 5 minutes, until the onion is limp but not brown. Stir in the oregano and cumin. Stir in the vinegar. Bring to boiling.
5. Pour the sauce over the fish and stir until well coated.
6. Cover and refrigerate for at least 8 hours before serving. Garnish with olive slices.

AZTEC POTATOES

Serves 8

Add onions, hot peppers, pimiento, minced garlic or even peas and carrots to the dough to create interesting alternatives.

1 cup masa harina or cornmeal
1/4 cup warm water
1 1/2 cups leftover mashed
   potatoes
1 egg

1/2 cup grated Monterey jack
   cheese
1 teaspoon salt
1 cup vegetable oil

1. Combine the masa harina with the warm water and mashed potatoes; mix well.
2. Beat the egg and add it to the potato mixture, along with the cheese and salt. Mix well and form into patties about 3/4-inch thick.
3. Heat the vegetable oil to medium temperature in a large frying pan. Fry the patties until golden brown on both sides.

FLOUNDER FROM IXTAPA

Serves 4

Serve with Red Rice (page 286) and Spinach Salad (page 354).

1 pound fresh flounder fillets
1/2 cup orange juice
1 small yellow onion
1 cup canned tomato paste

1 teaspoon chili powder
1 teaspoon salt
1/2 teaspoon ground pepper

1. Place the fish fillets in a medium-sized frying pan and add water to cover. Add 1/4 cup of the orange juice. Bring to a boil, reduce heat, and simmer for about 10 minutes or until the fish flakes when tested with a fork. Drain and skin, if necessary.
2. Cut the fish into finger-sized pieces and return to the frying pan. Peel the onion and chop into 1/4-inch pieces.
3. In a small saucepan, combine the remaining 1/4 cup orange juice, the onion, tomato paste, 1 cup water, and chili powder. Bring to a boil. Add the salt and pepper. Pour the sauce over the fish fingers. Simmer the fish, uncovered, until the sauce thickens and the fish is well coated.

BAJA-STYLE CRAB

1 cup dry white rice
1 pound crabmeat
1 medium-sized white onion
2 garlic cloves
2 fresh pimientos
2 medium tomatoes
2 medium carrots
¼ cup olive oil
1 teaspoon ground annatto seeds

2½ cups Chicken Stock (see recipe on page 286)
1 teaspoon salt
½ teaspoon ground white pepper
¼ cup dry sherry

> **Serves 4**
>
> Serve with Peppery Mango Salad (page 464).

1. Soak the rice in hot water for 30 minutes. Break the crabmeat into 1-inch pieces. Peel the onion and garlic, and chop into quarters. Chop the pimientos into quarters. Remove the stems and skin from the tomatoes; chop into quarters. Peel the carrots and slice into ¼-inch rounds.
2. Preheat oven to 350°.
3. Drain the rice and place on paper towels to dry. Heat the olive oil to medium temperature in a medium-sized frying pan; sauté the rice until it is golden brown.
4. Put the onion, garlic, tomatoes, annatto, and ½ cup of the chicken stock in a blender or food processor; blend on medium setting until smooth. Pour the mixture into a mixing bowl.
5. Add the remaining stock, salt, pepper, crabmeat, pimientos, and carrots. Mix well and pour into an ovenproof casserole. Cover and bake for 30 minutes. Gently stir in the sherry and heat covered in the oven for an additional 5 minutes.

STUFFED CHAYOTE SQUASH FROM MORELOS

Serves 6

While most Europeans tend to keep their fruit and vegetables separate, Mexicans make no distinction. This dessert offers a unique blend of flavors to complement any Mexican meal.

3 chayote squash
3 eggs
½ vanilla pound cake
1 cup golden raisins
1 cup dry white wine

1 cup granulated sugar
1 teaspoon ground nutmeg
1 teaspoon ground cinnamon
½ cup crushed saltine crackers
½ cup toasted whole almonds

1. Preheat oven to 350°.
2. Cut the chayotes in half and place in a large stockpot. Cover with water and bring to a boil. Reduce heat to medium and simmer for 15 to 20 minutes or until they are tender. Remove from water to cool.
3. When cool, remove the seeds and discard. Remove the pulp, leaving the shell intact. Mash the pulp.
4. Beat the eggs well. Combine with the pulp and mix well. Crumble the pound cake and add it to the mixture, along with the raisins, sugar, nutmeg, cinnamon, white wine, and crackers.
5. Stuff the chayote shells with the mixture. Press the almonds into the top. Place in a greased, ovenproof casserole dish. Bake for 15 minutes.

What's a Chayote?
Chayote is actually a fruit but is most often used as a vegetable. It is a member of the squash family that is very popular in warm climates. It has a single seed that is edible and considered a delicacy.

CHAPTER 36

NONALCOHOLIC DRINKS

MEXICAN HOT CHOCOLATE

Serves 6

Serve as an after-dinner drink with Capirotada (page 517).

3 ounces unsweetened chocolate
½ cup white granulated sugar
2 tablespoons instant coffee
2 teaspoons ground cinnamon
1 teaspoon ground nutmeg
¼ teaspoon salt
2 cups water
4 cups whole milk
Whipped cream

1. Place the chocolate, sugar, coffee, cinnamon, nutmeg, salt, and water in a large saucepan and heat over low heat until the chocolate melts and the mixture is smooth.
2. Bring to a boil. Turn heat to low and simmer for 5 minutes, stirring constantly. Stir in the milk. Beat with a hand beater until foamy.
3. Top with a dollop of whipped cream.

FRUIT SMOOTHIES

Serves 2

Substitute your favorite in-season fruits for a different treat each time.

⅔ cup milk
1 banana
⅓ cup fresh mango
⅓ cup fresh papaya
⅓ cup fresh strawberries
⅓ cup fresh peaches
1 teaspoon honey
¼ cup crushed ice

1. Remove the skins and seeds from the fruit and cut into 1-inch cubes.
2. Combine all the ingredients in a blender. Blend on high speed until smooth and frothy.

Substituting Frozen Fruits
The act of freezing fruit changes the natural sugars. As a result, many frozen fruits have sugar added. Those that don't often taste bitter. If you must use frozen fruit, especially berries, add extra sugar or honey to the drink.

PUMPKIN SEED TEA

2 cups pumpkin seeds   *8 cups water*
1 key lime   *½ cup honey*

1. Put the pumpkin seeds in a food processor or blender and grind until you have a coarse powder.
2. Cut the lime into ¼-inch rounds.
3. Put the water, lime, and pumpkin seeds in a covered glass jar and store in a warm place for 6 to 12 hours.
4. Strain the water and discard the pumpkin seed mash as well as the lime pieces. Stir in the honey.

> **Serves 8**
>
> Although it's tradition-ally served over ice, this tea also is excel-lent served warm with Bride's Cookies (page 472).

JASMINE AND ROSE HIPS TEA

8 cups cold water   *¼ pound rose hips*
¼ pound jasmine flowers   *½ cup granulated sugar*

1. Place all the ingredients in a glass container. Stir until the sugar is dissolved.
2. Cover and set in a warm place for 6 to 8 hours.
3. Remove the jasmine flowers and rose hips. Stir before serving.

> **Serves 8**
>
> Instead of using sugar, add a teaspoon of honey to each glass before serving.

Edible Flowers

Most flowers are edible, although it is best to consult a horticul-ture book before gorging on your garden. Pansies, for example, are a delightful addition to a salad. Rose petals give a soft, rosy taste to water, unlike rose hips, which provide a tangy almost bitter flavoring.

COCONUT COFFEE

Serves 8

Serve this coffee
with Capirotada
(page 517)

¼ cup shredded coconut
16 tablespoons ground coffee
½ cup coconut milk
8 cups water

1. Using a percolator or drip coffee maker, add the shredded coconut to the ground coffee.
2. Fill the coffee maker with 8 cups of water and brew as you normally would.
3. Stir in the coconut milk before serving. Top with a few strands of grated coconut.

Coffee Notes

As a general rule, the darker the color of the coffee, the stronger the flavor. Most of today's flavored coffees simply have a liquid flavoring poured over them, something you can do just as well at home. If you like full-bodied coffees, avoid commercial varieties that likely have fillers and are roasted to a lesser degree.

ANGELINA AND JOSE

6 ounces sparkling water
1 tablespoon grenadine

2 ounces orange juice
1 key lime

1. Combine the sparkling water, grenadine, and orange juice.
2. Cut the lime in half, squeeze the juice from half the key lime into the drink, and stir.
3. Use the other half of the lime as a garnish.
4. Serve over ice.

Serves 1

In the United States we have Shirley Temples. In Mexico, kids get these fruity drinks while their elders are drinking, well, fruity drinks mixed with other things.

MOCK SANGRIA

1 orange
1 lemon
4 key limes
6 cups purple grape juice

6 cups white grape juice
1 cup orange juice
½ cup lemon juice

1. Cut the orange, lemon, and limes into ¼-inch rounds, retaining the rinds.
2. Combine all the ingredients in a large pitcher. Refrigerate for at least 4 hours before serving.

Serves 8–12

Of course, there's no rule that you can't add some tequila to this drink to create a fruity masterpiece.

TAMARIND-ADE

2 cups frozen or fresh
  tamarind pulp

½ cup brown sugar
2 cups water

1. Combine all the ingredients. Stir until the sugar is dissolved.
2. Chill before serving.

Tamarind

Tamarind is more commonly known as the main ingredient in Worcestershire sauce. In its original form, however, it is a dried brown seed pod. It produces a distinctive sour taste and many herbologists believe it can help the body break down fatty acids.

RASPBERRY ATOLE

½ cup masa harina or cornmeal
4 cups water
3 cups skim milk

1 cup whipping cream
2 cups fresh raspberries
2 cups white granulated sugar

1. Place the cornmeal, water, milk, and whipping cream in a large saucepan. Heat at medium temperature, stirring constantly. Do not boil.
2. Crush the raspberries with a potato masher.
3. When the mixture thickens, add the sugar and raspberries, as well as the juice from the raspberries. Continue heating, stirring constantly. When the mixture produces small bubbles, it is ready to serve.

CHOCOLATE HORCHATA

½ cup uncooked white rice
4 cups water
4 cups whole milk

4 ounces unsweetened chocolate
2 cups brown sugar
1 teaspoon cayenne pepper

1. Grind the rice to a fine powder in a food processor or blender.
2. Place the rice, water, and milk in a large saucepan. Heat at medium temperature, stirring constantly. Do not boil.
3. Grate the chocolate with a vegetable grater.
4. When the mixture thickens, add the brown sugar, cayenne pepper, and chocolate. Continue heating, stirring constantly. When the mixture produces small bubbles, remove from the stove and whip with a hand mixer until it is frothy.

Serves 8

This hearty drink is a good start to a cold morning.

MEXICAN COFFEE

6 cups water
¼ cup packed brown sugar
3-inch stick cinnamon

6 whole cloves
¾ cup regular grind, roasted coffee

1. In a medium-sized saucepan, combine the water, brown sugar, cinnamon, and cloves. Heat at medium temperature, stirring periodically, until the sugar is dissolved.
2. Add the coffee. Bring to a boil. Reduce heat and simmer, uncovered, for 1 to 2 minutes. Remove from heat.
3. Cover and let stand for 15 minutes. Strain before serving.

Serves 6

Serve for breakfast with Mexican Sweet Rolls (page 332).

HIBISCUS AND LIME WATER

8 cups cold water
1 cup dried hibiscus flowers

½ cup white granulated sugar
4 key limes

1. Combine the water, hibiscus flowers, and sugar in a glass container. Stir until the sugar dissolves.
2. Cut 3 of the limes in half and squeeze the juice into the water. Discard the rinds.
3. Cut the remaining lime into ¼-inch rounds and put in the water.
4. Cover the container and store in a warm place for 6 to 12 hours.
5. Strain to remove the hibiscus flowers and lime rounds before serving.

SPARKLING FRUIT DRINK

4 cups watermelon meat
1 mango
1 papaya
1 pineapple
1 guava

2 cups fresh strawberries
1 cup white granulated sugar
2 gallons sparkling water
2 pounds ice cubes

1. Remove the rind, stems, seeds, and cores from the fruits. Cut the fruit into ½-inch pieces. Reserve all the juices.
2. Stir the sugar into the water until it dissolves.
3. Add the fruit and the juices to the water; stir well.
4. Add the ice cubes and serve immediately.

Appendix A

Glossary of Indian Cooking Terms

Appendix B

Suggested Indian Menus

Appendix C

Mexican Meals

Appendix D

Glossary of Mexican Food and Cooking Terms

Appendix A

Glossary of Indian Cooking Terms

anise seed *(sauf)*: These small, oval-shaped seeds have a strong licorice flavor and belong to the celery family. They are used to flavor curries, desserts, and drinks. They can be substituted for fennel.

asafetida *(hing)*: Also known as the stinking spice, this resin has a strong pungent smell. The smell totally disappears once the spice is cooked. It adds a garlic flavor to the recipe.

bay leaf *(tej patta)*: Leaves of the laurel tree, these add a delicate, sweet flavor to dishes. These are not a substitute for curry leaves. Remove from the final dish before serving.

black cardamom pods (*moti* or *bari eliachi*): These are about ½ inch in size and black in color. They have a woody smell and provide a strong and nutty flavor to the dish. Remove from the dish before serving.

black peppercorns *(kali mirch)*: Berries of the pepper plant, black peppercorns have a strong peppery taste. They can be used whole or crushed.

black salt *(kala namak)*: This grayish, light pink salt has a strong tangy flavor. It is often used to add zest to a recipe. It is not a substitute for regular table salt. It does have a characteristic aroma that disappears when it is added to a dish.

carom seeds *(ajwain)*: These tiny seeds are said to be very strong digestive aids. They are very similar to thyme in flavor. Gently

crush them (with a rolling pin) prior to use; this will help release their fragrance and flavor.

chana dal: Very similar in appearance to yellow split peas, *chana dal* are a bit larger in size. Since they are hard to digest, these lentils are generally cooked with asafetida, as it aids in digestion.

chickpea flour *(besan)*: This flour is made from chickpeas and is used as a thickener in curries or to prepare desserts. Also called gram flour.

cilantro *(hara dhaniya)*: Fresh cilantro, also known as Chinese parsley, has a lemony flavor and is a highly aromatic herb. It is used liberally as a garnish for most North Indian dishes. Dried coriander powder is not a substitute for fresh cilantro. Best when fresh, dried leaves are virtually flavorless.

cinnamon stick *(dalchini)*: Cinnamon comes from the inner bark of an evergreen tree. It is used in most dishes here in the whole stick form. It imparts a strong sweet flavor to the dish. Remove from the dish before serving.

cloves *(laung)*: These dried flower buds of an evergreen tree pack quite a punch. Bitter in taste, they are added to sweet and savory dishes.

coconut milk *(nariel ka doodh)*: Coconut milk is prepared by soaking the flesh of the coconut in hot water. Do not substitute coconut water.

coconut, desiccated *(sukha nariel)*: Dried coconut flakes used in many sweet and savory dishes. Make sure you do not select the sweetened variety unless specifically indicated in the recipe.

coriander seeds *(dhaniya)*: These lemony seeds are used whole or ground in Indian cooking.

cumin seeds *(jeera)*: One of the most versatile spices in the world, cumin adds a musk-like flavor to dishes. It can be used whole or ground. Buy the *safeed jeera*, or brown cumin seeds, for the recipes in this book. The black cumin seeds, *shahi jeera*, are more exotic and not used here.

curry leaves *(kari patta)*: These small pointed leaves are very fragrant and add a unique lemony flavor to dishes. Bay leaves are not a substitute.

fennel *(sauf)*: These small oval-shaped seeds are very similar to anise seeds. They are used whole or in powdered form to flavor curries. Similar in appearance to cumin seeds, they have a strong licorice-like taste.

fenugreek leaves, dried *(kasoori methi)*: Highly aromatic, these dried leaves are often used to flavor curries. Use sparingly, as too much will add a lot of bitterness to the dish.

fenugreek seeds *(methi dana)*: These small, flat brown seeds are very bitter tasting. The bitterness disappears during the cooking process. They are used in South Indian cooking. These seeds are also commonly used for pickling.

green cardamom pods *(choti eliachi)*: Cardamom is often called the Queen of Spices. These green pods are used in both sweet and savory dishes. Each green pod can contain up to 20 black, sticky seeds. Crush the pod before using it to help release the fragrance. Cardamoms are also chewed raw as breath fresheners.

jaggery *(gur)*: Thick boiled sugar cane juice, it has a unique sweet taste. Brown sugar can be used as a substitute.

kokum: There is no English name for this fruit and no substitute for its taste. This purple fruit is sold in its dried form in Indian grocery stores.

mango powder *(amchur)*: Made from dried green mangoes, it is used to add a tangy taste to dishes. In a pinch, you can use lemon juice.

mint *(pudina)*: A strong aromatic herb, it is used in preparation of chutneys, curries, and drinks.

mustard seeds *(rai)*: These tiny, round black seeds are generally sizzled in hot oil at the beginning of a dish preparation. They add a toasty flavor to the dish.

pigeon peas *(toor dal)*: These pale yellow *dals* are used extensively in South Indian cooking. Sold as oily or dry, pick the dry variety for the recipes in this book. Also called cajan peas or dahl.

pomegranate powder *(anardana)*: This powder is used to add sourness to a dish. Prepared from dried pomegranates, it is sold in a powdered form.

poppy seeds *(khus khus)*: Indian poppy seeds are white in color and are used to provide a rich nutty flavor to dishes.

pulses: Refer to any of a wide variety of dried beans, split peas, and lentils. Pulses are a staple in India.

red chilies, whole dried and powder (*sukhi lal mirch*): These dried whole red chilies are used to add heat to a dish. You can grind them to create the powder or buy prepared red chili powder. Cayenne pepper can be used as a substitute.

red lentils (*masoor dal*): These skinless red split lentils turn a creamy yellow when cooked. They are also sold with the skin on (brownish in color).

rose water (*gulabi jal*): Rose water is used sparingly to add a touch of elegant flavor. It is sold in bottles and should be refrigerated after opening.

saffron (*kesar*): This very expensive spice has a flavor so unique that it cannot be substituted. Use about 3 strands per person in a recipe, as a general rule. The world's best saffron comes from Spain and from India's Kashmir valley. It adds a beautiful amber hue to dishes.

sesame seeds (*til*): These small cream-colored seeds are used to add a nutty flavor to dishes. They turn rancid quickly, so make sure you taste them before using.

split black gram (*safeed urad dal*): Also called a split black lentil, this pulse is usually used to make fritters and curries. It has a sticky consistency when ground or cooked. When the black skin is removed, revealing the white interior, this lentil is referred to as a "white lentil" or "skinned and split black gram"; without the skin, it has a milder taste.

tamarind (*imli*): Sold as concentrate or in dried blocks, tamarind is used to add a sourness to dishes.

turmeric (*haldi*): Turmeric comes from a rhizome. It has a warm aroma and provides Indian dishes with the characteristic yellow color. In ancient India, turmeric was valued for its antiseptic properties.

whole black gram (*urad dal*): Small round and black, these lentils take a long time to cook and soften.

yellow fal (*peeli moong dal*): A tiny yellow lentil, it cooks quickly and has a very creamy texture when soft.

Appendix B

Suggested Indian Menus

Sunday Brunch

APPETIZER: Crunchy Bread Fritters (page 34)

BEVERAGE: Coconut and Tomato Soup (page 53)

ENTRÉE: Parsi-Style Eggs (page 114)

SIDE DISH: Indian-Style Coleslaw (page 56)

STARCH: Mint-Flavored Bread (page 209)

DESSERT: Creamy Milk Pudding (page 248)

Indian Chaat Party

APPETIZER: Potato Cutlets (page 37)

BEVERAGE: Mint-Ginger Cooler (page 43)

ENTRÉE: Chickpea Curry (page 189)

STARCH: Fried Indian Bread (page 206)

DESSERT: Instant Saffron Ice Cream (page 253)

Summer Cookout

APPETIZER: Corn Fritters (page 32)

BEVERAGE: Mango Yogurt Drink (page 44)

ENTRÉE: Ginger-Flavored Lamb Chops (page 129)

SIDE DISH: Green Beans with Coconut (page 90)

STARCH: Lemon Rice (page 167)

DESSERT: Mango Mousse (page 249)

An Elegant Dinner

APPETIZER: Chicken Tikka (page 26)

BEVERAGE: Fizzy Rose Drink (page 42)

ENTRÉE: Shrimp in Coconut Milk (page 135)

SIDE DISH: Fried Okra (page 81)

STARCH: Garlic Rice (page 174)

DESSERT: Mango Cheesecake (page 247)

Ladies' Luncheon

APPETIZER: Cucumber Cup Coolers (page 20)

BEVERAGE: Maharastrian Buttermilk (page 46)

ENTRÉE: Salmon in Saffron-Flavored Curry (page 156)

SIDE DISH: Potato and Yogurt Salad (page 61)

STARCH: Simple Basmati Rice (page 162)

DESSERT: Cheese Pudding (page 250)

High Tea

APPETIZER: Onion Rings (page 38)

BEVERAGE: Grandma's Chai (page 48)

ENTRÉE: Chicken Tikka (page 26)

SIDE DISH: Punjabi Onion Salad (page 68)

DESSERT: Honey Yogurt (page 258)

Quick Family Dinner

APPETIZER: Curried Mixed Nuts (page 40)

BEVERAGE: Rose-Flavored Yogurt Drink (page 42)

ENTRÉE: Sizzling Tandoori Chicken (page 95)

SIDE DISH: Carrot and Tomato Salad (page 64)

STARCH: Simple Basmati Rice (page 162)

DESSERT: Mango Cream (page 243)

Indian Chinese Night

APPETIZER: Indian Cheese Manchurian (page 23)

BEVERAGE: Fresh Lime Soda (page 43)

ENTRÉE: Lollipop Chicken (page 92)

SIDE DISH: Vegetable Fried Rice (page 176)

DESSERT: Rice Pudding (page 242)

Diwali Dinner
(Indian Festival Dinner)

APPETIZER: Indian Cheese Tikka (page 25)

BEVERAGE: Saffron Lemonade (page 45)

ENTRÉE: Indian Red Kidney Beans (page 190)

SIDE DISH: Cheese and Spinach Curry (page 73)

STARCH: Malabari Coconut Rice (page 179)

DESSERT: Mango Ice Cream (page 266)

An Autumn Dinner

APPETIZER: Sweet Potatoes with Tamarind (page 24)

BEVERAGE: Minty Yogurt Drink (page 47)

ENTRÉE: Butter Chicken (page 96)

SIDE DISH: Punjabi Mustard Greens (page 74)

STARCH: Indian Corn Flatbread (page 223)

DESSERT: Saffron Yogurt Pudding (page 244)

Appendix C
Mexican Meals

✹ SUMMER FIESTA ✹
Mexican Roll-Ups (page 310)

Jalapeño Rice (page 441)

Mixed Bean Salad (page 453)

Tostadas (page 285)

Pineapple, Mango, and Cucumber Salsa
(page 294)

Gazpacho (page 490)

Cactus Paddles (page 438)

Grilled Corn on the Cob (page 430)

Fruit Smoothies (page 540)

Jasmine and Rose Hips Tea (page 541)

Mexican Tea Cakes (page 473)

✹ ROMANTIC DINNER ✹
Sparkling Fruit Drink (page 546)

Mixed Vegetables with

Hot Pepper Dressing (page 348)

Cauliflower Tortas (page 311)

Bean-Stuffed Zucchini (page 457)

Grilled Shrimp in Prickly Pear

Cactus Vinaigrette (page 515)

Mexican Coffee (page 545)

Flaming Fruit (page 468)

✹ APPETIZER PARTY ✹
Mock Sangria (page 543)

Fried Plantains (page 309)

Cabbage Tamales (page 312)

Sweet Chili Rellenos (page 314)

Spinach Balls (page 312)

Mexican Roll-Ups (page 310)

Tomato Empanadas (page 311)

Bean-Stuffed Peppers (page 456)

Tostadas (page 285)

Dried Fruit Salsa (page 295)

Green Almond Salsa (page 296)

Chili Rellenos (page 498)

Natilla (page 475)

✹ BRUNCH ✹
Coconut Coffee (page 542)

Tomato Empanadas (page 311)

Sherried Raisin and Rice Pudding (page 449)

Mexican Frittata (page 357)

Easy Mexican Sweet Rolls (page 332)

Sugared Pumpkin (page 484)

Eggplant Casserole (page 435)

❂ HOLIDAY MEAL AND TREATS ❂

Candlemas Drink (page 514)

Mexican Christmas Salad (page 518)

Sweet Chili Rellenos (page 314)

Stuffed Turkey (page 521)

Creamed Rice with Chilies (page 450)

Cream-Filled Chestnut Cake (page 523)

Kings' Bread Ring (page 335)

Pepita Balls (page 487)

Mexican Orange (page 483)

❂ CELEBRATION MEAL ❂

Raspberry Atole (page 544)

Totopos (page 313)

Peppery Mango Salad (page 464)

Red Snapper with Pecan Sauce (page 383)

Mushroom-and-Nut-Stuffed Chayote
(page 432)

Mexican Chocolate Cake (page 474)

Mexican Hot Chocolate (page 540)

❂ MEXICAN BUFFET ❂

Chocolate Horchata (page 545)

Totopos (page 313)

Tomato Empanadas (page 311)

Mexican Roll-Ups (page 310)

Crab Salad (page 345)

Garbanzos with Sausage (page 460)

Lonches (page 504)

Pineapple Sopapillas (page 331)

Barbecued Pork Ribs (page 416)

Flour Tortillas (page 284)

Shredded Beef (page 287)

Spicy Chicken (page 289)

Green Tomato Salsa (page 282)

Refried Beans (page 284)

❂ MIDWEEK MEAL ❂

Hibiscus and Lime Water (page 546)

Queso Fundido (page 310)

Mexican Pork and Beans (page 459)

Beef Flautas (page 499)

Mango Corn Bread (page 333)

Pork Roast with Apples (page 414)

Almond Custard (page 477)

⊛ SPORTS SUNDAY ⊛

Spinach Balls (page 312)

Beer Beans (page 455)

Tostadas (page 285)

Roasted Red Pepper Salsa (page 293)

Crimson Prickly Pear Sauce (page 298)

Pumpkin Seed Salsa (page 300)

Eggs in Potato Shells (page 360)

Mexican Popcorn (page 504)

Churros (page 492)

Tropical Gelatin (page 478)

⊛ MEXICAN THEME MEAL ⊛

Tamarind-Ade (page 544)

Sweet Chili Rellenos (page 314)

Coliflor Acapulco (page 529)

Caribbean Coast Pickled Tuna (page 535)

Pumpkin Blossom Soup from Morelos
(page 527)

Rosquillas Fritas (page 334)

Chicken in Nutty Green Sauce (page 400)

Pistachio-Coconut Flan (page 476)

Mexican Coffee (page 545)

⊛ VEGETARIAN ⊛

Pumpkin Seed Tea (page 541)

Spicy Pineapple Salad (page 464)

Fried Plantains (page 309)

Mixed Vegetables with
Hot Pepper Dressing (page 348)

Jalapeño Corn Bread (page 330)

Scrambled Egg Tacos (page 362)

Black Bean and Avocado Burritos
(page 452)

Jalapeño Rice (page 441)

Scallops with Sesame Seed Sauce
(page 390)

Pineapple and Almond Pudding
(page 485)

Glossary of Mexican Food and Cooking Terms

A

achiote: a seasoning paste made from the seed of the annatto tree

adobado or adobo: mexican barbecue sauce

agua fresca: literally "fresh water"; refers to nonalcoholic teas and juices

ajo: garlic

ancho: a dried poblano chili

añejo: aged, as in cheese or liquor

arroz: rice

asada: roasted or grilled

B

blanco: white

brazo de reina: literally "queen's arm"; a type of large tamale

C

cajeta: caramel

caldo: broth

canela: cinnamon

carnitas: meat chunks

carne: meat, usually beef

cascabel: a small, red dried chili pepper

ceviche: a dish of small fish pieces marinated in lime juice

chayote: a small, green squash

chilaca: a long, thin, dark brown chili pepper

chili negro: a dried chilaca pepper

chipotle: a smoked and dried jalapeño chili pepper

comal: a round, flat cast-iron griddle (used for cooking tortillas)

comino: cumin

crema: Mexican sour cream

E

enchilada: stuffed and rolled tortillas with chili sauce

enfrijolada: stuffed and rolled tortillas in bean sauce

enmolada: stuffed and rolled tortillas in mole sauce

epazote: a wild herb used as a seasoning

escabèche: a sweet and sour marinade

F

fresca: fresh

frijoles: beans

frijoles refritos: refried beans

fuerte: a type of avocado

H

habanero: a type of chili pepper

huevos: eggs

J

jalapeño: a type of chili pepper

jicama: a white root vegetable usually eaten raw

L

limón: lemon

lima: lime

M

maiz: corn
manzanilla: a small green olive
masa: corn dough
mesa: table
molcajete y tejolete: a mortar and pestle; used to grind spices
mole: a traditional stew or sauce made with a variation of spices, nuts, chili peppers, and Mexican chocolate
morita: a small dried chili
naranja agria: a type of orange from the Yucatan

N

nopale: cactus paddle
nopalitos: "baby" cactus paddles

P

pasilla: a dried chilaca chili pepper
pepita: pumpkin seed
pescado: fish
picadillo: ground meat seasoned with spices, nuts, peppers, and sometimes fruit
picholines: large green olives
pico de gallo: a salsa made of fresh tomatoes
poblano: a type of green chili pepper
pollo: chicken
posole: a traditional stew with meat and hominy

R

raja: a roasted chili pepper strip
ranchero: ranch or country-style

S

salsa: sauce or dip
sandía: watermelon
seca: dry
serrano: a small, green chili
sopa: soup

T

tomatillo: a small green fruit that looks like a tomato
torta: sandwich

V

verde: green

Index